# BELIEFS

## THE HEART OF HEALING IN FAMILIES AND ILLNESS

LORRAINE M. WRIGHT

WENDY L. WATSON

JANICE M. BELL

BasicBooks
*A Division of* HarperCollins*Publishers*

Library of Congress Cataloging-in-Publication Data

Wright, Lorraine M., 1944–
    Beliefs : the heart of healing in families and illness /
Lorraine M. Wright, Wendy L. Watson, Janice M. Bell. —
1st ed.
        p.   cm.
    Includes bibliographical references and index.
    ISBN 0-465-02317-7
    1. Family psychotherapy.  2. Sick—Family relationships.
3. Cognitive therapy.  4. Family—Medical care—
Psychological aspects.  5. Sick—Attitudes.  6. Family nursing.
I. Watson, Wendy L., R.N.  II. Bell, Janice M.
RC488.5.W75     1996
616.89' 156—dc20                                          96-17805
                                                              CIP

96 97 98 99 ❖/HC 9 8 7 6 5 4 3 2 1

*To my friend extraordinaire, Fabie Duhamel, for her remarkable ability to accept the beliefs of others, while in a context of love and friendship, inviting me to challenge my own.*

LORRAINE M. WRIGHT

*To the loving memory of my mother, Laura Byrde McLean Watson, and to my father, Leonard David Watson, who cocreated a home filled with the passion for living together and who taught me, through example, to always believe.*

WENDY L. WATSON

*A Valentine's Day card from my seven-year-old daughter read "I like you as a Mom, I love you, and please finish your book!" So, to my husband Curtis and our three precious children: Brenden, Jordan, and Ashley, this book is dedicated to you with love and gratitude for your patience, encouragement, and for believing in me.*

JANICE M. BELL

What we believe is the most powerful option of all.
NORMAN COUSINS

# CONTENTS

# ACKNOWLEDGMENTS

THE CLINICAL AND RESEARCH odyssey that evolved into this book has been in process for over 15 years. The development and evolution of our clinical approach were initially made possible by Dr. Margaret Scott Wright, the former Dean of the Faculty of Nursing at the University of Calgary. She supported and assisted Lorraine Wright in realizing a dream in the establishment of the Family Nursing Unit in 1982. The dream expanded as first Wendy Watson and then Janice Bell became part of the faculty team of the Family Nursing Unit. The Faculty of Nursing has continued its support of the Family Nursing Unit through various stages since its inception.

The results of our research project, "Exploring the process of therapeutic change in family systems nursing practice: An analysis of five exemplary cases," funded by the Alberta Foundation for Nursing Research, form the backbone of the clinical research and practice described in this book. This research project illuminated, clarified, and offered new descriptions of our clinical practice. We are grateful to the five research families who participated in the project. We are also appreciative of our research assistants, Lori Limacher and Dianne Tapp, former and present graduate students, who listened, questioned, and laughed with us. We are particularly indebted to our colleague, Dr. Catherine (Kit) Chesla, Department of Family Health Nursing, University of California, San Francisco, who served as consultant to our research project for the past 3 years. Her extensive knowledge of hermeneutics was surpassed only by the manner in which she invited the three of us to open space to the possibilities of hermeneutic interpretation. We were truly captured by her knowledge, quiet strength, depth of character, spirituality, and passion for ideas. She remained ever enthusiastic, encouraging and affirming of our efforts and struggles to write about the interpretations of our practice, in the midst of her own personal struggle with illness and the short deadlines we imposed for her response. The best outcome of this professional consultation is that we gained a personal friend.

We are grateful to all the families we have assisted and learned from at the Family Nursing Unit over the past 15 years through the evolution of our clinical approach. We are also grateful to our graduate nursing students and externs at the University of Calgary and graduate marriage and family therapy students at Brigham Young University who, through their questions and comments, have helped us clarify our thinking.

The invitation to put our ideas into book form initially came in 1987 from Jo Ann Miller, former senior editor, Basic Books, New York. We appreciate immensely her patiently maintaining interest in our work until we believed we were ready to write about our clinical approach. Stephen Francoeur, former assistant editor, provided us with useful feedback on initial drafts of chapters. Eric Wright, acquisitions editor, has been ever patient and encouraging about our project as our academic lives and illnesses of our parents slowed down our writing. Michael Wilde, project editor, assisted us to refine the final manuscript through his masterful editing abilities.

The numerous changes to various drafts were competently and cheerfully achieved by Marlene Baier. She accommodated us on numerous evenings and weekends and even on New Year's Day, for which we are extremely grateful.

We also are grateful to our dear friends and colleagues, Dr. Fabie Duhamel and Anne Marie Levac, who have been strong supporters. Their encouragement and prodding with comments such as "we need this book; we're waiting for this book" have spurred us on.

Finally, we are grateful to one another: grateful for our different strengths and talents that were brought to this book; grateful for mutual patience and understanding when pressures of life took time away from the writing of the book; and grateful for those treasured times over popcorn, peppermint tea, chocolates, and Chinese food, when we were each fully present to develop, review, and refine this book, idea by idea, page by page, and line by line. We discussed, agreed, disagreed, and respected each other's ideas and beliefs until the wee hours of the morning and developed the working formula for decision making of "two out of three agree." In the end, the synergism of three women, friends and colleagues, has made this book more than any one of us could have written individually.

LMW, WLW, JMB

August 1996

For each of us there have been others to whom we would like to express special thanks and appreciation:

I would like to express my appreciation for the Killam Resident Fellowship, September to December 1994, which was awarded to me in support of this book project. I would also like to thank my friend and colleague, Dr. Maureen Leahey, who in 1988 after hearing my workshop presentation of some of these ideas said to me, "You've got a book there" and planted the idea. To my dear friend Sheldon Walker, who continually offered to critique chapters for us, thanks for always being there. To the best sister-in-law one could have, Carol Dodd Wright, I am grateful for your consistent and genuine interest, your encouragement, and all those muffins. And finally, I thank my mother, Hazel Schollar Wright, who has been an inspiration to me of how to live alongside chronic illness and still maintain enthusiasm for life and others. In the midst of all your illness experiences of these past 2 years, I experienced your interest in this book on numerous phone calls and visits through your consistent question: "How's the book coming?" Well, Mom, it's done.

LMW

I am grateful to my sisters, Virginia Watson and Kathryn Watson Card, who are also my friends, for their unwavering interest and encouragement. Thank you for your daily hugs (in person and through E-mail), your good humor, and your palpable prayers. I am also appreciative of the Marriage and Family Therapy faculty at Brigham Young University for the tangible support of laptop computers and time, which facilitated the completion of this project.

WLW

I am indebted to my parents, John and Violet Luchak Melenchuk, who have always been there for me. You provided me with opportunities to develop both roots and wings. Thank you for your godly example as you taught me about the strength of family and about courage and resilience through a lifetime of illness. I am also grateful to Blenda Arzadon, who joined my family when my children were babies. Your dedication to my children and capable management of my home over many years have strengthened and enabled me.

JMB

# INTRODUCTION

T HIS IS A BOOK ABOUT BELIEFS, families, and illness. It is also a book that describes our advanced clinical practice approach, complete with theoretical underpinnings and key therapeutic moves, for health professionals who encounter families experiencing chronic illness, life-threatening illness, or psychosocial problems. It is written to assist health professionals and families in understanding how beliefs are at the heart of health and healing. Practical ideas of how to help families with their emotional and physical suffering are offered on the basis of knowledge gained through clinical practice and research.

Health professionals are in the socially sanctioned and privileged position of offering ideas, advice, and information about the etiology, healing, treatment, prognosis, and management of various health problems. Unfortunately, the stories of families' experiences with illness are often undervalued, whereas professional stories about illness are too frequently privileged. Our book makes an effort to provide both kinds of stories by describing and analyzing conversations between families and clinicians that have occurred in our clinical interviews.

## A TOUR OF THE CHAPTERS

An assessment of a family's experience with illness is incomplete without a thorough understanding of each family member's beliefs. Likewise, an understanding of the clinical approach of any health professional is incomplete without a thorough knowledge of the clinician's beliefs about families, illness, change, and clinicians. In chapter 1 we

1

describe, define, and offer our preference for a biological–spiritual explanation of beliefs and consider ideas and notions that have been helpful from other disciplines, such as psychology, sociology, anthropology, family therapy, and religion. Chapters 2 and 3 offer our beliefs about families, illness, therapeutic change, and clinicians. We also address the beliefs that we have found essential to explore with family members about their illness experience: beliefs about etiology, treatment and healing, prognosis or outcome, the role of family members, the role of health professionals, and the role of spirituality–religion.

The most powerful clinical work that health professionals can do is to draw forth family members' beliefs about their illness. But clinicians need more than this injunction. A comprehensive clinical approach is needed, which includes specific ideas for assessment of and intervention with beliefs when families are experiencing difficulties with illness (chronic illness, life-threatening illness, or psychosocial problems). Because we intended this book to fill a void in the family health care literature, part II offers the key moves, or interventions, of our advanced clinical approach enriched by clinical examples. Specific ideas for how to create a context for changing beliefs are offered in chapter 4. Chapter 5 presents ideas about how to uncover and distinguish illness beliefs.

Once the important and often hard work of creating a context for change and distinguishing illness beliefs has occurred, family members are in a position to open space to altering, modifying, or challenging their constraining beliefs. Chapter 6 presents many practical ideas and specific micromoves for challenging constraining beliefs gleaned through several years of clinical research. Through the coevolution of a collaborative relationship, family members open space to ideas and notions of the clinician; of course, the clinician's own beliefs are also modified and challenged through therapeutic conversations with family members. The coevolution of the family–health professional relationship climaxes with the identifying, affirming, and solidifying of facilitative beliefs, discussed in chapter 7. Chapters 4 through 7 present the macromoves of our approach, and within each chapter, several micromoves are offered with clinical examples from our research demonstrating their effectiveness. Hermeneutic interpretation was completed on segments of text from clinical sessions with five families (see Appendixes A and B for description of families and research method). Our interpretations are offered in chapters 4 through 7.

The third section of the book includes a clinical exemplar that characterizes our work with patients and families. Chapter 8 describes a woman experiencing angina and anxiety attacks. Through our hermeneutic interpretation of the transcriptions of the sessions, the nuances of our approach are made clearer to the reader. This analysis demonstrates our particular relationship with families, the clinical moves that coevolved from our work with families, and our knowledge and beliefs. It also illustrates through verbatim transcripts the change moments that were most relevant and presents the clinical moves identified in those change moments. Finally, we end our book with some reflections on beliefs, families, and illness.

This is the first book to offer a specific clinical approach for examining family members' beliefs and intervening in that area. We believe that health professionals are in great need of an approach that recognizes the biopsychosocial–spiritual aspects of working with families experiencing illness. Our approach has an interactional and systemic focus. Specifically, it focuses on the interaction between the illness and the beliefs of family members and health professionals. The desired outcome is to create a healing environment for family members for the relief of suffering from their illness experiences. Remen (1993) eloquently offered the following notion:

> Healing is different from curing. Healing is a process we're all
> involved in all the time. . . . Sometimes people heal physically, and
> they don't heal emotionally, or mentally, or spiritually. And sometimes
> people heal emotionally, and they don't heal physically. (p. 244)

## WHERE IT ALL BEGAN

### The Professional Journey at the Family Nursing Unit

Our clinical approach has coevolved from our clinical practice and research over 15 years within the Family Nursing Unit (FNU) at the University of Calgary, Calgary, Alberta, Canada (Wright, Watson, & Bell, 1990). The FNU was established in 1982, under the direction of Lorraine M. Wright, for the interactional study and treatment of families experiencing health problems. The FNU offers assistance to families when one or more members are experiencing difficulties with a health problem (chronic illness, life-threatening illness, or psychosocial problems). Families seen at the FNU are either self-referred or referred by health care professionals such as family physicians or community health nurses. The FNU is a faculty practice unit. Each family benefits from a clinical nursing team approach. Each family is interviewed by a graduate nursing student (master's or doctoral level) or a faculty member. The interview is observed through a one-way mirror by the clinical nursing team, who participate in the therapeutic conversation using the telephone intercom (Wright et al., 1990) and through reflecting teams (see chapter 6). Each interview is videotaped, and an average of four sessions are provided to each family. Each session lasts 1 to 1½ hours.

The theoretical underpinnings of the clinical practice within the FNU include a foundation of "a biology of knowing," cybernetics, systems theory, communication theory, and narrative theory. We also introduce students to foundational models for assessment and intervention, namely, the Calgary Family Assessment Model (Wright & Leahey, 1994b) and the Calgary Family Intervention Model (Wright & Leahey, 1994a, 1994b). These models enhance trainees' appreciation and understanding of such basic notions as family genograms, family developmental life cycles, roles, and interactional communication patterns. Our previous writings and educational videotapes (Watson, 1988a, 1988b, 1988c, 1989a, 1989b) have included ideas for assessment and intervention to help in organizing and making sense out of massive amounts of data.

Highlighting the importance of beliefs in the context of an illness experience, as we do in this book, in no way diminishes the importance of adopting a comprehensive approach to working with families. To focus exclusively on one variable—beliefs—would constitute a deficient clinical approach. Throughout the book, we advocate that the identification of, assessment of, and intervention with constraining beliefs around illness have a powerful and sustaining influence on improving families' abilities to cope with the challenges of integrating illness into their lives. The program of research that accompanied our clinical work has provided this book with a rich description of research-based practice and practice-based research.

Within the FNU, our interest in, fascination with, and commitment to the important subject of beliefs coevolved and developed from our clinical practice and research with families experiencing physical and emotional suffering from illness. Over the years, we began to realize that it was the beliefs about a problem that were the problem when families experienced difficulties with an illness. This notion has become one of the most significant prevailing assumptions underlying our approach. It is similar to the idea expressed by the first-century philosopher Epictetus. He wrote that "men are disturbed not by things, but by the views which they take of those things" (Higginson, 1948). Through our conversations with families, the members experience a new or renewed appreciation of their strengths and resources and increased options to discover or uncover solutions to their suffering.

We attempted to capture the usefulness of focusing on beliefs in previous writings that portrayed our clinical work with families experiencing multiple sclerosis (Wright, in press); hypertension (Duhamel, Watson, & Wright, 1994); family violence (Robinson, Wright, & Watson, 1994); osteophytes and chronic pain (Watson, Bell, & Wright, 1992); cancer (Wright & Nagy, 1993); epilepsy (Wright & Simpson, 1991); angina (Wright & Watson, 1988); cardiac illness (Wright, Bell, & Rock, 1989; Wright, Bell, Watson, & Tapp, 1995); and the impact of loss by suicide (Watson & Lee, 1993). This book enables us to convey with greater depth and breadth our approach and the underlying theoretical assumptions.

Conceptually, we have been greatly influenced by Humberto Maturana and Francisco Varela's (1992) theory of the biology of knowing; Gregory Bateson's (1972, 1979) theory of mind; constructivist and narrative approaches; and the exemplary clinical work of Luigi Boscolo (Boscolo & Bertrando, 1993) and Gianfranco Cecchin (Cecchin, 1987) of Milan, Italy, and of Michael White and David Epston (1990) of Australia and New Zealand, respectively.

Our clinical approach can be useful to health professionals who work with families (e.g., nurses, social workers, family therapists, psychologists, physiotherapists, occupational therapists, and physicians) regardless of their working context and regardless of their opportunity, or lack of, to collaborate with other health professionals.

A guiding principle in our clinical work is the following statement by Norman Cousins (1979): "What we believe is the most powerful option of all."

Some beliefs are more useful than others in coping with illness. To uncover the beliefs that are useful and those that are not, we have conceived a simple dichotomy of beliefs: constraining beliefs versus facilitative beliefs. One of the fundamental premises of our approach is that family members hold beliefs about their problems that are constraining or facilitative. *Constraining beliefs* perpetuate problems and restrict options for alternative solutions to problems. *Facilitative beliefs* increase options for solutions to problems.

Beliefs are drawn forth through the medium of therapeutic conversations in which both the client and the health professional ask questions and provide answers. In our therapeutic conversations with families, we constantly make clinical judgments about the beliefs that are expressed by family members and in collaboration with the family. Are the beliefs expressed about illness facilitative or constraining?

We also constantly draw forth our own beliefs about families' illness experiences and offer those to families in as transparent a manner as possible. Our approach focuses on identifying and challenging, altering, or modifying families' constraining beliefs about illness and drawing forth, offering, coevolving, and solidifying more facilitative beliefs.

The outcome is that the family experiences a new or renewed appreciation of their strengths and resources and increased options to discover and uncover solutions to their suffering. In the process, our own beliefs as clinicians are continuously altered and modified from our involvement with families.

## THE WORK EXPANDS

The Family Nursing Unit, Faculty of Nursing, University of Calgary, continues to be the seedbed for the continuing refinement and advancement of our clinical approach. With the professional relocation in 1993 of Dr. Wendy L. Watson to the Marriage and Family Therapy Graduate Programs, Brigham Young University, Provo, Utah, a second location was established for theory courses, clinical practicums, and clinical research related to our approach. As well, we are aware of graduates and externs of our programs who are implementing these ideas in a variety of settings in Canada, Australia, Japan, Taiwan, and the United States.

## OUR PERSONAL JOURNEYS

*Lorraine M. Wright: Shaping Experiences with Illness: Child, Young Health Professional, Middle-Aged Daughter*

I grew up in a three-generational home with my maternal grandmother, mother, father, and younger brother. My English maternal grandmother suffered from chronic arthritis. She had tremendous status in our family because she was in the role of "mother" by day while my mother worked outside of the home with my father in our family business. I learned in my childhood years how chronic illness becomes a "family member." I observed the suffering that one can experience from chronic pain, whether it be firsthand, as my grandmother suffered, or secondhand, as I emotionally suffered with her. I also learned that this chronic pain controlled all of our lives, especially how well my brother and I would behave on any given day, how much my grandmother was able to "mother," and how we children were invited to be more compassionate because of having a pain sufferer in the family. My grandmother was the center of our family, but the chronic pain she suffered ruled her. The disease severely disfigured her hands, caused her knees to be swollen much of the time, resulted in her walking with a limp, and dictated how well she was able to live her life on any given day. But those disfigured hands made us apple pie, weeded our garden, and lifted numerous cups of tea while we exchanged stories of our lives with her.

Another significant shaping experience with illness occurred when I was a young adult. I was only 18 years old when I experienced my first death as a health professional. I was a first-year nursing student working in a hospital on Christmas Eve when a female patient for whom I was caring died in my arms. I do not remember her name or her illness, but the experience is frozen in time for me. The impact was profound and traumatic. One of the most significant results was that I began to experience my peers who were not health professionals as immature. I felt "out of sync" with them. I had been forced to deal with one of life's big events: witnessing the death of another for whom I was caring. No opportunity was provided to discuss this experience, my beliefs about it, or my sadness and fear.

Although there have been other illness experiences and deaths over the years with friends, friends' parents and children, and my own grandparents, the third most profound shaping experience has occurred over this past year and a half. I have been intensely involved in the illness experiences of my parents, predominantly those of my mother, who was diagnosed with multiple sclerosis (MS) at age 49. Until 1 year ago, she experienced only minor symptoms, such as occasional numbness in her legs and arms; consequently, she enjoyed an extended remission for 24 years. Now, at 73 years of age, my mother has experienced six major exacerbations in one year. She was hospitalized four times, with two of these hospitalizations extending longer than 2 months. With each exacerbation, she has been left more and more physically disabled after having led an active life. Throughout this time, I have witnessed my father becoming a caring "nurse" and husband while his own life became constrained; my sister-in-law has become a saint with her many caretaking kindnesses, and my brother has shown thoughtfulness and creativity in his ideas about health care for our parents. Many illness narratives are developing and redeveloping in my family as we have again opened the door to the "long haul" of chronic illness.

With each extreme MS exacerbation, my mother has had to crawl her way back to being able to feed herself with her unaffected arm, walk a few steps, and control bladder and bowel functioning. These extreme MS exacerbations have given my mother the additional burden of chronic fatigue. With each exacerbation, she never fully returns to the level of physical or cognitive functioning that she previously enjoyed. Currently, one of the most demoralizing aspects of this disease is the chronic pain my mother suffers in her left arm and hand.

Despite all these horror stories, there is good news to tell. My mother has now been out of the hospital for 6 months. We believe this is due in large part to the introduction of a new drug, interferon-beta 1b which seems to have controlled the exacerbations for the moment. We believe the improvement also is due to the incredible determination of my mother and my father to have her at home.

Unfortunately, in true interactional style, my mother's condition has had a profound impact on my father's health. For the past several months, my father has been suffering chronic pain from herpes zoster (shingles), which is generally believed to be triggered by stress. Although my mother's spirits are presently good and her physical condition has stabilized for the moment, the impact of the illness experience on my elderly father has been enormous.

One of the most painful aspects of this past year has been the incongruence and dissonance between my life as a professional and my life as a family member. My professional life is devoted to teaching, writing, presenting, researching, and doing clinical work with families experiencing illness. Yet in my personal life, I have not had one health professional ask me how I am experiencing my mother's chronic illness. Worse yet, no one has asked this question of either my mother or my father, nor have any other questions been asked of my parents about the impact of MS on their marriage of 54 years. The care by health professionals for the physical suffering of my mother from this disease has been adequate most of the time, but the emotional suffering has never been addressed by any health professional. I have been astounded and anguished at how I have been made to feel invisible during my hospital visits; most of the nurses and physicians do not even make eye contact with me, let alone speak to me. Being rendered invisible erases my existence in the illness experience, causes much dissonance, and leaves me suffering emotionally.

From my own clinical practice and research, I have come to believe that talking about the illness experience and being able to ask questions can often alleviate emotional and physical suffering. Consequently, I arranged for a family meeting during one of my mother's hospitalizations with a professional from the MS society. He gave us information about MS and the resources available. I do not know how much any of us absorbed or understood that day, but the visual impact of my mother, father, brother, nephew, and me sitting together talking about MS with a health professional made me believe, for a few precious minutes, that MS was smaller and had less strength than we had.

These profound shaping experiences with illness—as a child, as a novice health professional, and as a middle-aged daughter and experienced health professional—have left me more passionate and, I hope, more compassionate when collaborating and consulting with families suffering from illness.

*Wendy L. Watson: The Quest: The Connection Between Hearts and Healing*

When I was 5 years old, my younger sister was born. Although she was a well-anticipated baby, we did not anticipate that she would be born with all her organs on the reverse side from "normal." *Situs inversus, mirror image twin,* and *bronchiectasis* were the medical terms bestowed on her, almost before her name was given. The medical advice was just as powerful as the diagnoses: "Take her home and love her. She won't live very long." However, 40 years later she is completing her second master's degree and employed full-time as a university librarian.

My mother and father strongly believed that "children should be allowed their childhood" and operationalized that belief in many ways. My mother and father handled all the instrumental aspects of my sister's illness—medication, physician visits, chest percussion—and I was allowed the joy of being a big sister to her. The only time I was aware that something was a bit different was when I would hear her coughing or see my mother's tears as she would tell the story about "our miracle baby."

When I "put away my childish things," I became more aware of my mother's worries. Even in the midst of the remarkably good health of my sister, punctuated with episodic crises, my mother lived under the oppression of my sister's death sentence, which had been handed to her by a well-intended family friend, the physician. When does a mother believe she can stop worrying about the health of her miracle child? When does a mother know that her child has "thumbed her nose" at the medical system and is not proceeding down the predicted illness path?

At 17 years of age, I entered the nursing profession. It would be dramatic to say that this selection of career was motivated by my resolve, at the age of 5, to "find a cure" for my sister. I remember that resolve, but I have to admit that my choice of career was heavily influenced by the urging of my father to "learn a skill that allows you to give service." Nursing was good to me: It afforded me wonderful opportunities to "give service," opened my eyes to people's problems and suffering, and initiated my professional quest to understand and assist with people's emotional suffering whether induced by physical illness or psychosocial problems. One of the side advantages, but perhaps the best one, of being a nurse (even a nursing student) was the credibility my observations and opinions were given in my family. I was in my second year of nurses' training when my mother shared her "secret": She had been diagnosed with diabetes 8 years earlier. My mother, a closet diabetic! I have often wondered what beliefs prevented diabetes from being an openly acknowledged entity earlier on. My mother had been the quintessential buffer for the family, and her natural and insatiable enthusiasm for life had been her best cover.

The belief that it is possible to live alongside an illness and not let illness rule your life or the lives of other family members was taken to the extreme by my parents. Living alongside illness meant not even acknowledging illness. Was it their belief that when there is a child with a chronic, life-threatening illness, good parents do not burden family members with their own health problems? I saw additional evidence of this belief when my father, who had always been healthy, had a heart attack. At the time of the crushing pain, my mother could hardly get my father to go to the hospital, and after 2 weeks of hospitalization, my father commenced referring to his heart attack as "just a little problem" and forever after has not listed the episode on health history forms. My father—the optimistic ostrich in the presence of health problems!

I came to understand that illness narratives are more than stories of pain and suffering when I observed my mother's approach to life as her diabetes persisted and arthritis and hypertension were added. Even in her later years of increasingly frequent transient ischemic attacks, falls, and threatening blindness, my mother's illness narrative was one of courage and carrying on with life. Against all odds, she kept singing, literally and metaphorically. This belief in "carrying on" invited her and my father once again not to "make a big deal" about what some, including myself, would term *crises*. Living 3 hours away from them, I would learn several days after the event that my mother had fallen or had another stroke. When I would ask why they didn't tell me, they would say those notorious words, "We didn't want to worry you." Worry me? Worry . . . me? The irony was that the less they said, the more I worried. Now, no news could *not* be taken as good news. I consulted my two sisters, and we became the "disease detectives." We generated a list of questions to ask our mother and father on every phone call or visit, now believing that our parents would never initiate the telling of distress.

During my mother's chronic and increasingly life-threatening illnesses, I accompanied her to a myriad of medical appointments. These were intensely bonding times for us but also horrifying times for me when I would observe the medical staff talking to me rather than to my mother, who was now in a wheelchair. Did they not know who this was? This was my mother! Strong, funny, generous, brilliant, a great conversationalist, and wonderful singer! Yet they only saw me. When Mom became blind in the last few months of her life and could not see the health care professionals, it became even worse. I tried to counteract their view of her as a person without a life before hospitalization by posting pictures of her and my father in her "vital" years around her hospital bed. But none of this seemed to shift the view of the health care professionals, who were used to the protocol of the disease and who continued in their well-intended, although systemically insensitive, approach to focus only on the medical problems.

I remember one particularly painful day when my sister and I were invited to the geriatric assessment unit where my mother had been a patient for 6 weeks for a discharge planning meeting. I had just completed a full day of teaching family systems nursing concepts. Now here I was in a meeting with a variety of professionals making decisions about my mother's and father's (and our family's) lives without my mother, my father, or my older sister present. My younger sister and I were the "convenience sample." I believe what was operating that day was a belief about who should be involved in discharge planning. My mother was right across the hall in her room yet was not included.

I was clearly not a health professional in this context; I was a daughter—a daughter, in fact, who had been labeled by the female attending physician as the "overinvolved daughter." Overinvolved according to whose objective reality? Whose observer perspective was being privileged with such labeling? It was the daughter in me, therefore, responding to my mother's pleas not to "make waves"—not the context-sensitive professional in me—who sat with a pit in her stomach throughout the 2-hour meeting.

Six months following my mother's death, my father was diagnosed with colon cancer. Consistent with his view of life, Dad faced the prospect of a colon resection and gallbladder surgery with a heroic calm. A man at peace. Perhaps being at peace with oneself, with one's beliefs about life and death, health and sickness, can look like an ostrich approach to problems. In any case, my father rallied from the surgery aided by the nurturing of his three doting daughters. Two years later, when the cancer metastasized to the liver, accompanied by the total shutdown of his kidneys, this same peaceful approach and rallying sustained him through dialysis and a prognosis of a couple of weeks to live. According to my father, his 15 minutes of fame occurred on a September day, 5 months following the "2-week" prognostication, when I took him for an ultrasound-guided liver biopsy. My father's moment in the sun came when the doctor said he would not be able to do the biopsy because . . . there was no cancer present!

How does healing occur? Where did the cancer go? And how? Was it the 300 hugs on the day of his 75th birthday celebration 2 months earlier that strengthened Dad's immune system? Was it the faith and prayers and special blessings offered by my father's family members and large community of believers? Was it the breaking of his hip on the day he was to be discharged from the hospital in June that forced and allowed him to take time for his body to heal?

There is so much more to illness and families, to the healing connection between hearts and health, than we currently understand or have the language to articulate. But these experiences with my own family have heightened my curiosity to know. Here's to the continuing quest.

## Janice M. Bell: Arthritis—The Silent Family Member

I was 5, almost 6 years old, when the reality of illness entered my young life. My youngest sister and illness arrived together. My maternal grandmother was the temporary caretaker during my mother's postpartum confinement, and I recall she and I had very different ideas about the rules of my home. When my mother returned home after the customary 10-day hospitalization following childbirth, I expected life would finally return to normal. Unfortunately, my mother experienced her first disabling attack of rheumatoid arthritis, and her bedroom became a sickroom into which she disappeared for a long time. I remember a series of visitors and many home remedies undertaken to no avail. Thirty-nine years have gone by since the onset of my mother's illness and she continues to have active disease as evidenced by an elevated sedimentation rate, progressively deformed joints, and much chronic pain. Until recently, however, I have not been aware of the cost of this illness to my mother or to our family.

While I was growing up, I was not aware of my mother's suffering, apart from her "disappearance" at the time of diagnosis. Extended family members, particularly aunts, would frequently remark about my mother's courage, her unwillingness to complain about or even mention her illness, and her smiling, happy attitude in the face of great pain. I was always a little surprised at hearing this reality drawn forth; after all, my mother did have arthritis but she wasn't sick! She was like all my friends' mothers, although she was different in the domestic arena—she did not make Ukrainian food or sew. However, she outshone all other mothers in her creativity, intelligence, and sophistication.

When I became a nurse, I developed a new knowledge about her disease and the numerous medications she took to control the pain and inflammation. This new awareness allowed me to celebrate the times when she experienced a short-lived period of remission while taking a new drug and to sympathize during those times when nothing seemed to relieve her pain. The disease—symptom control and relief from pain—was the focus of my attention. About 15 years ago, as my interest in families and illness developed under the tutelage of Lorraine Wright, I asked my mother if I could accompany her to an office visit with a rheumatologist during a particularly disabling episode of acute inflammation. I recall initially feeling that I would make my mother look incompetent by accompanying her. Over time, I became more and more puzzled and angry by the way I was ignored in subsequent conversations that took place between my mother and the physician.

During my mother's subsequent hospitalizations for massive doses of intravenous cortisone or for joint surgery, I remained invisible to other members of the health care team as well: nurses, physical therapists, occupational therapists, and so on. I was seldom acknowledged as I sat beside her bed. My attempts to initiate conversations about my mother's illness were generally met with polite, perfunctory answers. I was never asked to participate in any conversation about her care or her progress, nor were other family members. My frustration drove me to become increasingly assertive in offering my ideas about my mother's care and in asking more questions. I even encouraged my mother to consult other health professionals who might be more interested in her experience of illness rather than focusing solely on her disease. My mother's response to my increasing anger at and assertiveness with health professionals was to placate me. She feared being labeled a "problem patient" or a "doctor shopper" and believed she would consequently receive less expert care.

I have only recently come to understand that one explanation for my early unawareness of my mother's illness experience is that she worked hard to protect me and the rest of my family from her illness. Carole Robinson's (1994a) dissertation research concerning families' responses to chronic illness documented that the mother plays a major role in buffering the family from the impact of illness. Whether it is the mother herself or another family member who suffers from the illness, it is the mother who assumes responsibility for the many instrumental and emotional demands of the illness in ways unknown to other family members. The work of protecting the family from the illness is demanding and often causes the mother to feel burdened, overwhelmed, and alone. I suspect my mother's devout spirituality enabled her to deal with the demands of illness and competently manage her roles of wife and mother.

In contrast to my family's later experience with the cardiac illness of my father and our enduring protectiveness and worry about him, my mother's protection of us from the impact of her illness rendered her illness silent. I can only wonder what the cost of her silence has been to her health and emotional well-being. What other costs or benefits have resulted from the ways she protected her husband and children from her illness? I can only wonder if her suffering could have been reduced if health professionals had invited her to voice her experience of illness rather than focusing solely on her symptoms. Finally, would her protectiveness have been necessary if all my family members had been invited by a competent health professional to talk about our understanding of and experience with this silent and insidious family member called arthritis?

## THEMES OF OUR PERSONAL JOURNEYS

When we read each other's personal journeys with illness experiences, we were struck by some common themes throughout each of our narratives. Each of us has had profound illness experiences with family members in childhood as well as in our adult lives. The illness experiences were far beyond the yearly flu or surgery for an acute illness. We all experienced the "long haul" of chronic illness as part of our lives as children. Our illness experiences had a tremendous impact on each of us individually and on our family dynamics.

Another fascinating theme was the major role each of us played and continues to play in illness care, illness burden, and illness resources within our families in adulthood. No doubt, this is due in large part to our professions as nurses and family therapists, but our taking these roles owes more, we believe, to the fact that we are women. The gender issues within our stories are profoundly evident.

We each have had many dealings with health professionals that have left us frustrated and disappointed by the "sins of omission" in the provision of family health care. One of the most striking aspects of our personal illness narratives is the lack of family health care in three different areas in Canada. We have each anguished because of the lack of invitation by health professionals to explore our own or other family members' experiences of the impact of illness on our lives and relationships. In adulthood, this deficiency of family health care collides with our strong core belief in the importance and necessity of involving families in health care. It also collides with a core belief that illness profoundly impacts family life and that, reciprocally, families profoundly influence the course, cure, and healing of illness. These beliefs have had and continue to have a profound influence on our approach of working with families experiencing physical and emotional suffering from illness. The result of this influence is more passion for our work with families, more passion for imparting this knowledge to our students, and powerful motivation to write this book, which we hope will encourage health professionals to involve families in health care.

Our beliefs about illness are truly embedded in the stories that we tell. But our illness narratives do not tell the whole story of our beliefs. Only by drawing forth our beliefs in a purposeful manner would one learn that each of us has strong spiritual–religious beliefs that influence our illness experiences, beliefs about the role of our family members in coping with and managing illness, and beliefs about control and mastery over illness, to name just a few. The important telling of illness narratives begins to open the door to the marvel of beliefs and believing and into the heart of healing in families and illness.

# PART I

# Beliefs: The Heart of the Matter

# CHAPTER 1

# Beliefs: Many Lenses, Many Explanations

BELIEFS ARE THE LENSES through which we view the world. Beliefs are the bedrock of our behavior and the essence of our affect. Beliefs are the blueprints from which we construct our lives and intermingle them with the lives of others. How can we learn and find out about our own and others' beliefs? In daily life, the best medium for hearing our own and others' beliefs is the stories we tell ourselves and others. Beliefs are embedded in the stories we exchange with one another in our conversations.

What influences one's belief lens? What causes one to believe what one does? How do beliefs arise? What one believes is determined by one's present biopsychosocial–spiritual makeup. Each person has her own unique makeup, or "structure," based on her genetic history and history of interactions with others and the environment. Through these interactions, the emerging, refining, solidifying, confirming, and challenging of beliefs occur. Beliefs are shaped and substantially shifted through one's interactions with others and oneself in concert with the context in which one is living. The answer to the question, "Do beliefs reside in cognition, in affect, or in behavior?" is a resounding *yes:* Beliefs reside in all three.

Beliefs distinguish one person from another, yet also join people together. Through our living and being together, we influence each other's beliefs. We develop our identities within our families, professions, and communities through the belief systems that we share and do not share with others. We live our lives only slightly aware, and sometimes not at all aware, of our beliefs and the effect they have on our own lives and the lives of others. We blithely sing songs that ask questions about beliefs—"Do you believe in magic?"—and others that proclaim firmly held beliefs: "I believe that somewhere in that great somewhere . . . ." The movie *Schindler's List* provided an extreme example of the influence of beliefs on the lives of people who assume life-or-death power over others.

The irony and challenge of life is that to survive and progress in the world, one needs both a commitment to strong beliefs and the ability to question those beliefs when they are no longer useful (Cecchin, Lane, & Ray, 1994). New ways of viewing ourselves, relationships, and experiences such as illness can be both exhilarating and frightening. Oskar Schindler was a man who was able to change his beliefs and consequently save many lives during World War II. The pronounced change in Schindler's beliefs about what is meaningful in life is represented in the following two conversations. The first occurred between Schindler and his wife at the beginning of the movie *Schindler's List:*

WIFE: They won't soon forget the name *Schindler* here.
SCHINDLER: Everybody remembers him. He did something extraordinary. He did something no one else did. He came here with nothing—a suitcase—and built a bankrupt company into a major manufacturing company and left with a steam truck—two steam trucks with money. All the riches of the world.

Compare this conversation to the one with his trusted Jewish accountant, Itzhak Stern, during one of the closing scenes of the movie. Schindler had just received a gold ring made by the Jewish people he saved from the gold in their teeth. The inscription on the ring was in Hebrew, from the Talmud, and translated as follows: "He whoever saves one life saves the entire world." Through tears of anguish, Schindler showed how his beliefs had changed:

I could have got more [people], I could have got more! If I made more money. I threw away so much money. You have no idea, if I just had more money. I didn't do enough. This car. Why did I keep the car? Ten people right there, 10 people, 10 more people. This pin, two people. This is gold, two more people. It would have given me two more people. It would have given me one more person. One more person. One more person; I could have gotten one more person. And I didn't.

The dramatic change in Schindler's belief and subsequent behavior is accompanied by the remarkable influence this change had on the lives of the Jews he helped and on the 6,000 today who are the descendants of the "Schindler Jews." Do our beliefs influence others? Definitely and infinitely.

What is equally fascinating is how we cling to some "truths" even when there is strong evidence to the contrary (Gilovich, 1991), a behavior that is particularly evident in the area of health beliefs and practices. One predominant example in our North American culture that Thomas Gilovich brings to our attention is the widely held belief that infertile couples who adopt a child are more likely to conceive later than are similar couples who do not adopt. Because clinical research has shown that this is not so (Lamb, 1979), Gilovich (1991) suggested that the remarkable phenomenon we need to understand is why so many hold this belief when it is not based on fact.

Similar beliefs invade our practices as health professionals. Nurses working on maternity wards often believe that more babies are born when the moon is full, and health professionals working on psychiatric wards believe that patients become more disturbed and upset under that same moon. Neither of these beliefs is supported by any clinical research evidence, yet the belief is handed down from one generation of health professionals to the next. What data do we choose to believe? From these examples, it appears that even research evidence does not convince most people to relinquish the beliefs they embrace.

## WHAT IS A BELIEF?

Man prefers to believe what he prefers to be true.
FRANCIS BACON

Many words have been used synonymously with the word *belief.* Michel Foucault (1978) used the term *discourse* to describe the constellation of assumptions that underlies ways of viewing the world at any given time. Other synonyms for *belief* include *attitude, explanation, construct, premise, assumption, preference, values, anticipation, meaning,* and *prejudice.* We prefer the term *belief* because we think it is more useful in capturing family members' efforts to make sense of illness and is used more commonly in conversational language than the other synonyms.

The sentence stem "I believe" can be completed by a statement of a religious belief: I believe in life after death; of a belief about the etiology of an illness: I believe that my rash is an allergic reaction; of a belief in a person or his words: I believe my doctor will find a treatment for my pain; or of a prediction of future events: I believe that my cancer will be cured. In addition to the wide range of meanings for the word, there are two other important aspects to understanding beliefs. First, the word *belief* contains the idea of a persisting set of premises about what is taken to be true; second, there exists a set of assertions with an emotional basis about what "should" be true (Dallos, 1991). For example, a person can express the belief, "I'm very healthy." This statement contains the premise that this statement is "true" and also the implication that this is a desirable state. If this belief were challenged by the discovery of a malignant tumor during an annual physical checkup, however, the person might become anxious or even angry.

Some beliefs are more useful than others; some allow more solution options; and some are more acceptable in particular cultures or contexts than in others. The usefulness or nonusefulness of a belief, however, is dependent on the judgment of an observer and the context in which the belief arises. We have chosen to distinguish useful from nonuseful beliefs through the dichotomy of *facilitative beliefs* versus *constraining beliefs*.

Gilovich (1991) devoted an entire book to examining what he refers to as "questionable and erroneous beliefs." He offered an in-depth discussion of how these beliefs are formed and maintained. Specifically, he discussed the cognitive determinants of questionable beliefs such as our tendency to see regularity and order when only chance is operating and our eagerness to interpret ambiguous and inconsistent data in light of our preferred theories and a priori expectations. Gilovich's use of the term *erroneous beliefs* implies that there are other beliefs that are "correct" or "true." We do not find this a useful way to think about beliefs; for us, the terms *erroneous beliefs* and *correct beliefs* are incompatible with our idea of the usefulness or nonusefulness of a belief.

## BELIEFS, STORIES, AND ILLNESS

Beliefs, stories, and illness are intricately intertwined. Consequently, if clinicians challenge constraining beliefs, new stories are drawn forth that may influence the illness experience. If a clinician assists persons and their families in reconstructing stories (revising or constructing new ones), old constraining beliefs are refuted. We do not concur, therefore, that "in mind-body problems, addressing beliefs instead of stories can be problematic" (Griffith & Griffith, 1994, p. 48). The preferred emphasis may be on reconstructing stories or on altering constraining beliefs; each approach has merit and influences the other. The approach to dealing with beliefs and stories is not an either–or one; it is a both–and, synergistic approach.

At no time are family and individual beliefs more affirmed, challenged, or threatened than when illness emerges. Consequently, how families adapt, manage, and cope with illness arises from their beliefs about the illness that is confronting them. These beliefs may be influenced by the stage in the life cycle of the individual, the family, and the illness (Rolland, 1994). Of course, there are circumstances when beliefs may have little or no influence over the reaction of the body. For example, if a person is given an injection of a thousand units of quick-acting insulin, no matter what she believes the chances are overwhelming that she will become unconscious as the blood sugar plunges (Dossey, 1993).

It is now well accepted among health professionals and supported with research documentation that illness has a significant impact on individual and family functioning (Covinsky et al., 1994; Deatrick, Faux, & Moore, 1993; Lewis, Hammon, & Woods, 1993) and that the family can influence the physical health of its members (Burman & Margolin, 1992; Campbell, 1986; Fisher, Ransom, & Terry, 1993; Ross, Mirowsky, & Goldsteen, 1990). However, the profound and overarching impact that beliefs have on how families experience illness has only begun to be addressed by health professionals (Dallos, 1991; Harkaway & Madsen, 1989; Kabat-Zinn, 1993; Ornish, 1993; Patterson & Garwick, 1994; Rolland, 1994; Wolpert & March, 1995; Wright & Leahey, 1994a).

Illness experiences occur in an interpersonal context affecting beliefs, behavior, and emotion. The beliefs derived from these experiences form the text, or narratives, of our lives. A mother who believes that her schizophrenic son's suicide was an act of love and thoughtful consideration grieves differently and recounts a different story from a mother who believes that her son's suicide was an act of rage and purposive cruelty.

When families present with emotional or physical suffering, the most pressing concern of therapists is assisting them with healing through the therapeutic process. We routinely ask ourselves, "Have we helped this family?" and if so, "How have we helped them?" According to our clinical and research experience, focusing on the beliefs of family members and of clinicians from a systemic perspective offers great promise for assisting families to decrease or eliminate emotional and physical suffering. In the process, our lives and relationships as clinicians are also profoundly affected.

## THREE SETS OF BELIEFS

Any healing transaction involves at least three sets of beliefs: those of the ill patient, those of other family members, and those of the health professional. Indeed, understanding the beliefs of the health professionals involved with a family is key to being able to help the family. Imagine all the health professionals involved with a family meeting in one room displaying placards stating their beliefs about fundamental issues: Families have problems because . . . ; the role of the clinician is to . . . ; change occurs when . . . . Imagine how different the process of that team meeting would be. Would it not be easier to understand the divergent ideas that the health professionals would offer about discharge, medication, and time of the next session? Would it not be interesting to have the family read the placards? What impact would such clinician transparency have on the healing of family members? Would their selection of a professional to assist them in their process of healing and change be altered?

It is becoming well recognized that health professionals have an impact on families' beliefs. One clinical example is the experience of a couple who presented with marital conflict about 8 months following the husband's second myocardial infarction. As the story of this couple's recovery experience unfolded, the constraining influence of the hospital nurses' beliefs on the wife's behavior throughout her husband's recovery became evident. The iatrogenically induced beliefs constrained the wife from voicing her concerns to her husband because she believed she could increase his stress and make him ill (Wright, Bell, Watson, & Tapp, 1995).

## BELIEFS ABOUT BELIEFS

> The outer conditions of a person's life will always reflect their inner beliefs.
>
> JAMES ALLEN

Just as clinicians have divergent beliefs about how problems emerge in families, how change occurs, and how a clinician can be helpful, they have divergent beliefs about beliefs themselves. There are many lenses that can be worn to explain, describe, and define the lens of "belief." We have looked through several lenses, tried them on for a time, and liked the fit of and view provided by some more than others. The lenses that we have looked through are those of sociology, philosophy, anthropology, psychology, spirituality–religion, family therapy, and biology. Extensive reading is available in all of these domains with differing explanations of beliefs and belief systems. Overall, the literature concerning beliefs is characterized by diverse individual opinions and interpretations that are based on personal reflection and empirical evidence; however, the literature is also characterized by many similarities, and the differences often involve subtle shades of meaning. By choosing to examine beliefs through a variety of lenses, we acknowledge a wide assortment of explanations about beliefs, believing, and belief systems.

In professional and personal lives, people unavoidably embrace particular lenses. From our extensive reading and clinical experiences, we have come to realize that beliefs occur not only in the domain of meaning, but also in the domain of emotion and behavior. We have also come to appreciate that beliefs influence even cellular functioning. To capture the many and varied explanations of beliefs, we offer a review of the existing diverse literature in the area. Following this overview, our preferred lens is offered as well as our definition and description of a *belief* and a *core belief.*

## THE LENS OF SOCIOLOGY

Key concepts gleaned from the well-respected and oft-quoted book *A Sociology of Belief* include the notion that a belief system is a set of related ideas (learned and shared) that persist over some period of time and to which people are committed (Borhek & Curtis, 1975). Three characteristics of all belief systems, whether secular or religious, are permanence, commitment, and connectedness (Borhek & Curtis, 1975). These notions are useful to consider when encountering beliefs that family members have about illness. If beliefs about an illness are characterized by permanence, commitment, or connectedness, they will influence the functioning of the family in coping with the illness. In addition, the social context in which beliefs arise influences the degree of permanence, commitment, or connectedness of a system of beliefs. For belief systems to persist, persons must remain committed to them; however, for commitment to persist, the belief system must be validated by a larger social structure.

Because beliefs have deep social and cultural roots, it is difficult to step outside one's social or cultural context to comment on one's beliefs. We *are* our beliefs. Health professionals do well to discover the shared or universal family belief system; however, with the assistance of the sociology lens, it is now conceptualized that families have correlated beliefs, not universal beliefs. These correlated beliefs arise through family members' interactions with each other. The shared orientations on which social and family life is based provide a meaningful context within which to understand one another. We understand one another by placing each other's statements within a particular social context. If the particular social context is one that includes illness, there will be a construction of core beliefs that evolve with and alongside the illness juxtaposed with a family's core beliefs from before the illness experience.

## THE LENS OF PHILOSOPHY

The field of philosophy offers a wide range of ideas concerning how individuals conceptualize reality. Sarah Taggart (1994) proposed that belief systems depend on the human imagination and reflect individual experiences of reality and that, therefore, our belief systems define reality. She suggested that our separate core beliefs, whether secular or religious, anchor us "in the dizzying vastness of the great unknown we call reality" (p. 20). Three structural elements, offered by Taggart as the distinguishing characteristics of all belief systems, are diversity, synergy, and boundary maintenance. Human belief systems are inevitably diverse, driven by synergistic energies, and defined by boundaries that do not succumb to reductionist analysis. Hymers (1995) offered the thought-provoking idea that "beliefs are not in the head . . . because then they're thought of as things. Rather we need to talk about believing—how believing affects one's certainty and behavior." But an ancient philosopher, Heraclitus, offered a slightly different idea about beliefs that we have also found useful: "Most men do not think things in the way they encounter them, nor do they recognize what they experience, but believe their own opinions."

Wolterstorff (1984), a contemporary American philosopher, has offered a "theory of theorizing" using the metaphor of a scholar practicing scholarship. He proposed that when the scholar enters the practice of scholarship and starts weighing the acceptability of a theory, he or she brings along a whole web or mantle of beliefs. First, the scholar has beliefs about the entities within the theory's range, which are taken as facts. These facts, or data, also have behind them background beliefs. Scholars bring a set of beliefs that function as constraints over the sorts of theories they regard as acceptable, which Wolterstorff refers to as *control beliefs*. To us, Wolterstorff's most useful idea is the notion that the beliefs that the scholar brings to the practice of scholarship cannot consist only of beliefs grounded in necessary facts. Rather, most of the beliefs stem from characteristics of the person; for example, she may be Canadian, female, Caucasian, and a health professional. Consequently, scholars and health professionals cannot *not* bring their particular beliefs into the practice of scholarship or caring for families. Beliefs are not just individuals' personal biases: They are the very heart of who we are and how we understand and make sense of our realities.

One philosophical belief frequently offered to those suffering with illness is that "life could be worse." This belief is offered to provide comfort and encouragement. One woman, suffering from endometriosis, did not find this belief useful, however. She responded: "I know life could be worse. I could have only one eye or leg, and I am very fortunate to have all I do have. . . . But those philosophies do not solve the disease, do not get rid of the pain, the tears, the frustrations, or the heartaches that come with the problems" (Donoghue & Siegel, 1992, p. 55). This example highlights the need for health professionals to recognize that each person's suffering with illness is unique and that attempting to have persons "count their blessings" can inadvertently trivialize suffering from illness.

## THE LENS OF ANTHROPOLOGY

One aspect of anthropology concerns the dynamics of how groups develop, maintain, and change belief systems. The study of witchcraft is one of the more illuminating explorations of beliefs in the anthropology literature (Evans-Pritchard, 1976). One of the many societies that practice witchcraft is that of the Azande of Sudan and Central Africa. The witch doctor holds a prestigious and highly respected position in the community. Witch doctors are expected to confirm that (a) a person is right in his or her observations of phenomena, (b) problems are not a person's fault, and (c) persons are not to blame when problems occur. In so doing, the witch doctor validates and affirms particular beliefs that enhance community cohesion.

One of the most fascinating aspects of witchcraft involves the *patterns of accusations or beliefs* about who is to blame for problems. Patterns of accusations provide a way of dealing with interpersonal tension or conflicts within a community and become a useful device for building social solidarity. Blame for things that go wrong inside the group is externalized. By accusing someone outside of the group, the patriotism of the group is strengthened. Similarities have been observed in Navaho and Pueblo witchcraft in North America; however, the Navaho direct their accusations outside their group, whereas the Pueblo direct accusations inside the group.

In our society, it is intriguing to consider the accusation patterns in families experiencing illness. Frequently, when disease arises in a family, interpersonal conflict within and between family members increases. To reduce the conflict, family members often accuse something or someone else outside of the family for their health problems. For example, families may blame their doctor for a misdiagnosis, the factory for an unhealthy environment, or a deceased relative for a genetic defect. On the other hand, we have found in our clinical practice that families who blame another family member for contributing to the health problem tend to have more interpersonal conflict and less solidarity than families who unite and direct accusations outside of the family.

White's (1988/1989) intervention of *externalization* can be seen as similar to the intervention used by witch doctors. Externalization of a problem separates the problem from the person and reduces blame or shame for having a particular health problem by giving the illness (or its symptoms) a life of its own, apart from the ill family member. Accusing or blaming the illness, rather than the ill family member, can serve the useful function of bringing family members together when illness strikes. A highly conflictual couple were invited to start working together, instead of against each other, when their polarized etiological beliefs concerning the husband's chronic back pain, which caused pain in their marriage, were labeled as something they had contracted through multiple exposures to the health care system (Watson, Bell, & Wright, 1992). See chapter 6 for an elaboration of the intervention of externalization.

## THE LENS OF PSYCHOLOGY

From the domain of psychology, Rokeach (1969) has offered the useful idea that the more a given belief is functionally connected with other beliefs—the more implications and consequences it has for other beliefs—the more central the belief. We refer to Rokeach's notion of central beliefs as *core beliefs*. We concur with Rokeach's further notion that the more central a belief, the more challenging it is to change. In addition, the more central the belief that is changed, the more widespread the repercussion in the rest of the belief system. One of the basic premises of cognitive psychology is the assumption that our thoughts play an essential role in our lives—that what we believe governs the way we feel, which governs the way we behave (Donoghue & Siegel, 1992).

Attribution theory, also in the domain of cognitive psychology, proposes that people construct beliefs about how things happen, especially significant personal events (Ajzen & Fishbein, 1980; Lazarus, 1991; Lazarus & Folkman, 1984). Albert Ellis (1962) and Aaron Beck (1988), operating from a positivist stance, both have identified irrational thinking or beliefs as the basis of human vulnerability. Beck asserted that three self-defeating cognitive distortions contribute to irrational thinking: (a) minimization (underestimating strengths), (b) magnification (exaggerating each mistake), and (c) catastrophizing (concluding total disaster). For example, an ill person who minimizes might downplay his ability to cope with an illness by saying, "I've never believed that I could cope with anything as serious as a heart attack." Magnification is observed when a woman experiencing chronic fatigue suggests, "I made a mistake today because of my illness. I think I'll have to quit my job." Catastrophizing is also seen in a young woman who has multiple sclerosis who concludes that her employer will "be furious with me if I'm not high energy all the time." Cognitive psychologists and nurses (Sideleau, 1987) have suggested that this type of "faulty" and "irrational" thinking can be challenged and changed through competent psychotherapy.

Psychology has also offered a distinction between a belief and a conviction (Buffington, 1990). Accordingly, beliefs can be fleeting, whereas convictions evolve from beliefs but have more stability and must meet stringent criteria. A conviction is resistant to persuasion, based on a depth of knowledge, stable over time, and passionate (i.e., there is an emotional commitment or certitude). It can be seen that these criteria are close to the criteria for belief systems set forth in the field of sociology. What psychologists have deemed *convictions,* we refer to as *core beliefs.*

The psychology lens also includes the significant contribution of George Kelley's (1955) personal construct theory. Kelley used the term *construct* as an alternative way of discussing beliefs. His definition of a *construct* included the useful idea of bipolar categorization: A belief always implies its opposite, what we do not believe in. This definition makes explicit what is often only implied. Kelley proposed that we see the world "out there" through our personal beliefs, or what he preferred to call *personal constructs.* How we construe the world around us, and even within our own skin, has consequences in terms of how we act; our beliefs have real consequences. We concur with Kelley's assertion that our beliefs and our actions are interdependent. This idea has a profound implication for relationships: Whatever choice of action we take on the basis of a construct or belief begins to inform and influence the interaction that will follow.

Kelley (1955) further expanded his ideas from an individual focus to an interpersonal focus. His contribution contains two main notions: commonality and sociality. *Commonality* refers to the extent to which one person applies a construction of experience that is similar to that applied by another. This notion emphasizes that people are not similar because they have experienced similar events but because they construe events and interpret the implications of events in the same way. *Sociality* refers to the extent to which one person construes the construction process of another. This implies that two people do not need to be similar to interact effectively but that they do require constructs about how the other sees things or a deep empathy with how the other might be seeing things. Kelley's (1955) commonality and sociality concepts offer the idea that people share some agreement about how they view their experiences and that they hold interpretations about each other's interpretations. Dallos (1991) offered a useful insight that Kelley and subsequent personal construct theorists have ignored: Constructs are constructed and constrained within a social reality. He believes that Kelley underestimated the power of groups; we would add the power of families, which create and enforce a social reality.

## THE LENS OF SPIRITUALITY–RELIGION

> Belief consists in accepting the affirmations of the soul; unbelief in denying them.
>
> RALPH WALDO EMERSON

> God made Truth with many doors to welcome every believer who knocks on them.
>
> KAHLIL GIBRAN

The terms *belief* and *belief system* often have seemed to be exclusively in the domain of religion, whereas in the more secular world, terms such as *premise, prejudice, bias, value,* and *assumption* have been used to capture the notion of beliefs. The domains of religion and spirituality provide many rich and useful ideas about beliefs. It is important and helpful to make a distinction between religion, which is extrinsic, and spirituality, which is intrinsic. *Spirituality* generally refers to a personal belief in and experience of a supreme being or an ultimate human condition, along with an internal set of values and active investment in those values, a sense of connection, a sense of meaning, and a sense of inner wholeness (Mackinnon, Helmeke, & Stander, 1994) within or outside formal religious structures. *Religion* includes shared, usually institutionalized, values and beliefs about God and implies involvement in a religious community. When a person's spirituality becomes embodied within a religious tradition, particular ideas and practices often are assumed to be right or true and, therefore, not necessarily questioned (Schultz Hall, 1995). However, spiritual experience is an expansion of awareness, and as awareness expands, so does a person's responsibility (Maturana, 1992, November).

It has been our clinical experience that persons and families with illness cope better if there is an absence of spiritual distress. Spiritual distress is the inability to invest life with meaning (Burnard, 1987). Marilyn

Mason (1995) offered the observation that the *Diagnostic and Statistical Manual of Mental Disorders* (DSM-IV; American Psychiatric Association, 1994) has no diagnosis for "spiritual flatness," which she claims is pervasive in our culture, but the DSM-IV does include the V code 62.61, religious or spiritual problem. (The V codes are restricted to conditions that are not considered psychiatric illness.) To find meaning in all events that arise in our lives seems to be a basic human need. Burnard (1987) proposed that such meaning can be framed within the context of religious beliefs or through adherence to a particular ideological viewpoint, be it philosophical, psychological, or political. By being clear about our view of life and possessing facilitative beliefs about life, we are less threatened by unexpected or unusual experiences.

The challenge of health professionals in working with family members who are experiencing spiritual distress is to avoid falling into the trap of offering ready answers but to listen, accept, and be curious. In so doing, one hopes that family members will discover their own meanings for illness and reasons for believing what they do about their illness. It is further hoped that the beliefs they adopt will assist them to alleviate or diminish their suffering.

Unfortunately, there are religious healers who attribute setbacks to the lack of spiritual purity of the patient or the impulses of God's will. This belief is often used as an explanation for failures to heal or respond to treatment (Gilovich, 1991). Some practitioners in the field of holistic health, with its emphasis on mental control over physical states and the importance of mind–body–spirit integration, have offered similar explanations for failures. Persons whose physical symptoms do not improve are sometimes labeled as not the right kind of patient.

Religious devotion in matters of illness and recovery has received increasing attention from health professionals. A study of African-American families explored the role of prayer and religious faith in the experience of life-threatening illness (Bernstein, 1994). In the initial findings, one of the investigators, Freida Hopkins-Outlaw, reported in her interview with Ann Bernstein (1994) that many of the patients in her study had an unshakable belief that they would be taken care of and that their prayers were answered. She also found that one of the main things that persons with cancer pray for is not to be a burden to their family. Hopkins-Outlaw admonishes systems thinkers to conceptualize a person as a biopsychosocial–spiritual being. She believes that health professionals have ignored the spiritual domain. We concur on both counts.

Larry Dossey (1993) reviewed numerous medical studies examining the efficacy of prayer in producing physical changes. In his text *Healing Words: The Power of Prayer and the Practice of Medicine* (1993), Dossey reported that the most effective prayers are not directly petitionary but rather "Thy will be done" prayers. Taking a stance other than that of divine intervention, Dossey offered a psychodynamic perspective of the connection between religious beliefs, religious rites, and health. For example, he suggested that the ritual of prayer may trigger emotions that, in turn, may lead to changes in health by positively impacting the immune and cardiovascular systems. Other religious rituals such as the laying on of hands may stimulate endocrine or immune responses that facilitate healing.

Dossey (1993) and Cousins (1989) invited health professionals to recognize that there are many nonphysiological reasons persons and families heal from illness. Over the past few years, we have adopted Dossey's (1993) practice of not only praying for our own family members and ourselves when ill but also, on occasion, praying for, although not with, the clients and families with whom we work. As Dossey (1993) suggested, if a health professional believes that prayer works, not to use it is analogous to withholding a potent medication or surgical procedure. "Both prayer and belief are nonlocal manifestations of consciousness, because both can operate at a distance, sometimes outside the patient's awareness. Both affirm that, 'it's not all physical,' and both can be used adjunctively with other forms of therapy" (Dossey, 1993, p. 141).

We concur with Taggart (1994) that religions are not vague philosophies. They are organized belief systems, with or without a supernatural component, and they provide a world in which to live. According to Taggart, traditional religion fulfills two functions: It provides consistent patterns for living out of core beliefs and organized ceremonies in which its adherents can participate, giving them a sense of collective self and a place in the chaos of reality. Perhaps one of the greatest differences between religious and other belief systems is that out of the definitions of reality by religious belief systems there evolves a moral awareness. This moral awareness sets religious belief systems apart; the "rules" of religious institutions grow out of this moral awareness and vary widely from culture to culture. Consequently, congruence between religious beliefs and one's behavior or operationalized beliefs results in a general sense of well-being and wholeness, whereas a lack of congruence frequently results in guilt or shame. One delightful exception to this correlation is seen in the story of a 90-year-old woman experiencing difficulty remembering past events, enjoying the game of bingo for the first time in her life. Her granddaughter relates that her grandmother does not remember that she does not believe in gambling!

Religious beliefs can be understood as having both a horizontal and a vertical axis. Hans Kung (1981) suggested that religious belief systems can be considered horizontally, with reference to our relationships with each other, and vertically, referring to our individual relationship with God.

Perhaps a synergistic interaction between the two axes would prevent some of the catastrophic consequences from the enforcement of the idea that there is only one "true religion," a proposition Kung (1981) has pointed out, that all major belief systems, both religious and secular, proffer. Even the field of psychotherapy is not immune from dogmatic propositions of truth. For many health professionals, their therapeutic approach *is* their "religion." Taggart (1994) offered an interesting comparison between religious and "therapeutic" wars. Both originate from arrogant and rigidly doctrinaire assumptions, with intolerance and dogmatism ever present; however, therapeutic wars use words, money, and reputation as their weapons.

It is important to note that it has not been religious beliefs that have brought about persecution and death; rather, it is the belief that others' religious beliefs are wrong and that they must change that has prompted the battles, both verbal and physical. Maturana (1992, May) offered a similar idea: that we kill each other for our explanations, not for our experiences.

To be able to hold strongly to one's own religious beliefs while allowing others to worship what, where, and in a manner that has meaning to them involves an inclusion of beliefs such as the following:

Freedom of religion is an inalienable right.

A difference in religious belief does not mean the other person is unworthy or unlovable.

It is important never to force the human mind.

Whoever I am relating with is my brother or sister.

A societal trend presently exists to trivialize religious devotion. *The Culture of Disbelief* by Stephen Carter (1993) offers a poignant discourse on how American law and politics have trivialized and denigrated religious devotion. In her text *Living as if: Belief Systems in Mental Health Practice*, Taggart (1994) argued that the exclusion of both religious and secular beliefs from mental health practice has diminished a crucial area of human experience and alienated a large clientele. Koltko (1990) concurred with these sentiments and suggested that even though religions include strong social and affective components in addition to beliefs, mental health practitioners do not seem to understand or take an interest in religious beliefs.

There is evidence, however, that mental health professionals are waking up to this neglected aspect of spirit in human experience, and family health care professionals may follow suit. Allen Bergin has been a pioneer in introducing to the mental health field the issues of values in psychotherapy and the relation of religion to mental health (Bergin, 1980, 1983, 1988a, 1988b). Increasing numbers of articles have appeared in professional journals, and entire issues of newsletters have been devoted to the theme of spirituality and couples and family therapy ("Spirituality," *Family Therapy News*, June 1994; "Spirituality: The Path and the Leap," *American Family Therapy Academy Newsletter*, spring 1995; "Soul Making," *The Calgary Participator*, winter 1995). There is also an expanding list of books—*Spirituality and Couples: Heart and Soul in the Therapy Process* (Brother, 1992); *Religion and the Family: When God Helps* (Burton, 1992); and *A Sourcebook for Helping People with Spiritual Problems* (Bragdon, 1994)—indicating a renewed appreciation of the influence of religious beliefs in coping with illness and interpersonal problems.

Carter (1993) emphasized the need to make clear distinctions between the act of believing and what is believed. He suggested that in our secular society, we need to be able to distinguish a critique of the content of a belief from a critique of its source. If not, the putative fanaticism of religions in which members do not seek (or refuse) medical assistance becomes indistinguishable from the "fanaticism" of other religious groups in which members pray and fast with great devotion in conjunction with responsibly seeking medical help for a family member.

Another area of great divergence in beliefs concerns the rituals adhered to by various cultures following a death. Table 1.1 contrasts the religious beliefs surrounding death and dying across the world's major religious traditions.

Finally, Koltko (1990) suggested that clinicians would benefit from thinking about metabeliefs in relation to religion. He suggested that the potency of religious beliefs depends on the importance of religion in a person's life. A *metabelief* is a belief about the belief itself. For example, the thought-provoking question by Kahoe (1987), "Does it matter if you believe that it doesn't matter what you believe?" would be answered with a resounding *yes* in the context of illness. Illness begs answers to the big questions in life, and frequently spiritual or religious beliefs offer meaningful and comforting answers as well as being an integral part of the healing process. Are health professionals prepared to aid family members in their search for the answers to the big questions? Or, as Goldberg (1994) questioned, "are religious or spiritual leaders best trained to help, for example, the suicidal Mormon, the anorexic Jew, the sexually abused Catholic, or the maritally troubled Protestant?" (p. 16). If health professionals are to be helpful, we must acknowledge that suffering and, often, the senselessness of it are ultimately spiritual issues (Patterson, 1994).

TABLE 1.1

**Death and Dying Issues Related to Religious Beliefs**

| Religion | Philosophy/Beliefs | Practices Related to Death |
|---|---|---|
| Buddhism | Seeks "truth" through middle way between extremes of asceticism and self-indulgence<br><br>"Right" living will enable people to attain nirvana<br><br>Reincarnation of soul<br><br>Emphasis on meditation to relax mind and body to see life in true perspective | Quietness and privacy for meditation important<br><br>Goal at death for mind to be calm, hopeful, and as clear as possible (may thus be reluctant to use medications)<br><br>No special rituals regarding body<br><br>Cremation common |
| Christianity (Catholic, Protestant, Eastern Orthodox, others) | Founded on teachings of Jesus Christ<br><br>World and everything that exists were created by and depend on God<br><br>Belief in afterlife and soul integral to faith | After death there is a 2- to 3-day visitation to home (funeral home) before funeral<br><br>Funeral/memorial service to celebrate life of deceased and departure of soul to afterlife<br><br>Burial or cremation occurs after funeral service |
| Hinduism | A wide variety of beliefs held together by an attitude of mutual tolerance—all approaches to God are valid<br><br>Goal is to break free of imperfect world and to reunite with Brahman (i.e., everything physical, spiritual, and conceptual)<br><br>Reincarnation and transmigration of soul until reunion with Brahman<br><br>Killing of living things outlawed (vegetarianism) | Married women wear a nuptial thread and red mark on the forehead; males may wear a sacred thread around the arm; dying patient wearing neck/arm thread may indicate special blessing—none of these symbols should be removed<br><br>Readings from Bhagavad Gita comfort patient<br><br>Important that last thoughts or words be of God to ensure rebirth to higher form<br><br>Prefer to die at home and as close to Mother Earth as possible<br><br>Important for family to wash body; eldest son arranges funeral<br><br>Cremation usual with ashes scattered on water (preferably the holy river Ganges)<br><br>Set pattern for mourning and final services 2 weeks after death |

TABLE 1.1 *(cont.)*

| Religion | Philosophy/Beliefs | Practices Related to Death |
|---|---|---|
| Islam (Moslem) | Complete way of life<br><br>Belief in God—all people created, live, die, and return to God by God's command<br><br>Death is part of life and a rebirth into another world<br><br>Pork and intoxicating substances prohibited | Friday is holy day; cleansing ritual prior to prayer; head must face toward Mecca<br><br>Reading from Koran to the dying; patient encouraged to recite verses<br><br>After death, a spouse or relative of same sex washes patient's body<br><br>Burial soon after death, simple with no coffin; 3 days mourning (spouse mourns 4 months, 10 days) |
| Judaism | God has a covenant relationship with humans; if one obeys God's laws, salvation may be achieved<br><br>Chosen to be examples to all<br><br>Messiah will come to bring world to perfection<br><br>Strong family focus | Practices at death seek to honor dignity of body, assist bereaved through process using laws of the whole mourning ritual, and affirm basic belief that life and death are part of God's plan<br><br>Burial takes place 24–48 hours after death; body must not be left unattended from death till burial<br><br>Family receives visitors and food gifts during 7-day shivah<br><br>Thirty days social withdrawal with 1 year official mourning<br><br>Specific services of remembrance after death and at unveiling of tombstone |
| Sikhism | Philosophy is combination of Islam (one God and the basic ethical beliefs) and Hinduism's world views<br><br>Common God for all mankind; preaches religious tolerance | Five traditional symbols—removal from dying person could cause distress:<br>  Kesh: long uncut hair of face and head<br>  Kanga: hair comb (symbol of discipline)<br>  Kara: steel bangle on wrist (strength and unity)<br>  Kirpan: sword, worn as broach (authority and justice)<br>  Kachha: special shorts (spiritual freedom)<br><br>Cremation with ashes scattered on water<br><br>Staff may prepare body<br><br>Mourning services last 10 days; final service marks end of official mourning |

## THE LENS OF FAMILY THERAPY

Family therapists have written about beliefs from a number of per-spectives. Some therapists have offered the notion that uncovering fam-ily myths and legends and the beliefs behind them is central to the ther-apeutic process (Byng-Hall, 1973, 1979, 1988; Ferreira, 1963). These approaches are positivist, however, and tend to assume that the family is wrong in their beliefs and that an inaccurate perception needs to be corrected (Dallos, 1991). This viewpoint is not congruent with our approach. Several writers on family therapy have suggested that beliefs are the essential element to the change process (Minuchin, 1974; Selvini Palazzoli, Boscolo, Cecchin, & Prata, 1980a; Watzlawick, Weakland, & Fisch, 1974); however, beliefs have not received prominence in many clinical models.

More recently, ideas from postmodernism, constructivism, and femi-nism have influenced various clinical models such as narrative and solution-focused approaches. One of the basic premises of these two approaches is that therapeutic change occurs when the therapist and family collaborate to obtain alternative meanings for problem-saturated stories or to invent new stories (Hoffman, 1990; White, 1988/1989). Little or no effort has been made, however, to explicate the beliefs of families coming to therapy or the beliefs of the therapists who work with families. Family therapists attempt to alter clients' perceptions so that the problem is seen as temporary, not anyone's fault, and arising out of circular patterns of causality (Stratton, Preston-Shoot, & Hanks, 1990). To date, only one study has attempted to compare the beliefs of therapists and families about the etiology of the presenting problem (Wolpert & March, 1995). This study obtained explanations of present-ing problems from 10 mothers of children referred for family therapy and their therapists. The authors found that therapists referred to envi-ronmental explanations (e.g., past events, present circumstances, rela-tionships, and possible future events) significantly more frequently than the mothers did. The mothers saw the problems as residing within their children, that is, as the children's character traits.

## THE LENS OF BIOLOGY

Beliefs or systems of meanings arise through our history of interactions across time. Individuals can experience changes in their biopsychoso-cial–spiritual structures through these interactions and vice versa (Maturana, 1992, November). Cousins (1989) simply but profoundly offered the notion that "beliefs become biology." Certain beliefs may con-serve or maintain an illness; others may exacerbate symptoms; others, alleviate suffering. If health professionals can invite persons to reflect on their beliefs, those persons are free to consider other possibilities.

Maturana and Varela (1992), both neurobiologists, offered the idea that there are two possible avenues for explaining our world: *objectivity* and *objectivity-in-parentheses*. To increase possibilities, clinicians need to help individuals drift toward objectivity-in-parentheses.

The view of objectivity assumes that there is one ultimate domain of reference for explaining the world. Within this domain, entities are assumed to exist independent of the observer. Such entities are as numerous and broad as imagination might allow and may be explicitly or implicitly identified as truth, mind, knowledge, and so on. Within this avenue of explanation, we come to believe we have access to an objective reality.

When objectivity is placed in parentheses, persons recognize that objects do exist but are not independent of the living system that brings them forth. The only truths that exist are those brought forth by observers, such as health professionals and family members. One's view is not a distortion of some presumably correct interpretation. Instead of one objective universe waiting to be discovered or correctly described, Maturana has proposed a "multiverse," where many observer "verses" coexist, each valid in its own right.

James Griffith and Melissa Griffith's (1994) concern that "therapies based on systems of beliefs evolve toward the clinician's holding an instructive, authoritative, or argumentative position in the relationship between clinician and patient (or family)" (p. 49) is moot when clinicians operate from an objectivity-in-parentheses stance. From this stance we emphasize a collaborative and consultative relationship between ourselves and the families with whom we work. Our approach of drawing forth family members' constraining beliefs and coevolving facilitative beliefs is based on a respect for the present biopsycho-social–spiritual structures of family members, which facilitates our efforts.

Reality does not reside "out there" to be absorbed; rather, persons exist in many domains of the realities that we bring forth to explain our experiences (Maturana & Varela, 1992). The ability to bring forth personal meaning and to respond and interact with the world and with each other but always with reference to a set of internal coherences can be seen as the essential quality of living. Maturana and Varela (1980) asserted that this statement applies to all organisms, with or without a nervous system. They further suggested that it is best to think of cognition as a continual interaction between what we expect to see (i.e., our unconscious premises or beliefs) and what we bring forth. In a telephone interview, Maturana (1988a) embellished this notion as follows:

> We exist in many domains of realities that we bring forth. . . . What I'm saying in the long run is that there is no possibility of saying absolutely anything about anything independent from us. So whatever we do is always our total responsibility in the sense that it depends completely on us and all domains of reality that we bring forth are equally legitimate although they are not equally desirable or pleasant to live in. But they are always brought forth by us in our coexistence with other human beings. So if we bring forth a community in which there is misery, well, this is it. If we bring forth a community in which there is well being, this is it. But it is us always in our coexistence with others that . . . are bringing forth reality. Reality is indeed an explanation of the world that we live [in] with others. . . . This at the same time means that one can live in hell or in heaven depending on what world [one is] bringing forth in coexistence with others. So the notion of living in, let's say in the kingdom of God, in spiritual life, which is harmonious with existence, is not denied. It is one of the realities that we bring forth, but it is validated in our living.

When an argument ensues between two persons, therefore, both make statements on the basis of their particular premises or beliefs. Each rational argument is constituted through the operation of preferences a priori; therefore, we have to look at each person's premises (Maturana, 1992, May). Maturana suggested that this is not a rational but an emotional domain; disagreements about politics, religion, or medication are examples. These differences can be resolved only in the domain of objectivity-in-parentheses, not in the domain of objectivity.

In the same telephone conversation, Maturana discussed and drew the distinction between two paths that can cloud our understanding and prevent a stance of objectivity-in-parentheses. He offered the idea that there are two temptations into which one can fall that obscure understanding: objectivism and solipsism. *Objectivism* is the idea that one can make claims about a reality that is valid independent of oneself. All one's cognitive statements then become demands to others for obedience.

In the other path that can screen understanding, *solipsism*, everything is an idea in the mind of an observer because the observer is the only source of validation. To avoid this trap, according to Maturana and Varela (1992), one must realize that understanding is a reflection of an observer who is a participant in what is being observed. This understanding can be obtained through comprehension of how we are involved in language and how we are involved through our language in what we know (Maturana, 1988a). If one adopts a particular view of reality, it follows that one inadvertently encompasses a particular view of persons, their functioning, relationships, and illness.

The idea that humans bring different perspectives to their understanding of events is not new, but Maturana's perspective on observation is much more radical: It is based on biology and physiology, not philosophy (Wright & Levac, 1992). This biological lens has had a tremendous influence on our clinical work. There are aspects of our work that we have increased because of the ideas of Humberto Maturana; there are parts of our work that we now understand and explain according to Maturana's theoretical framework of the biology of knowing.

## OUR PREFERRED LENS

From this review, we have come to appreciate the efforts of several disciplines to offer definitions, explanations, implications, and applications of beliefs. There are numerous beliefs about beliefs, and all of these explanations of beliefs have been useful to us in our clinical work with families. Despite the existence of these various lenses, there are few measuring instruments for examining individual and family beliefs. We refer readers to Appendix C for our review and discussion of instruments.

Many of the lenses discussed overlap; they are cleverly brought together in the following poem, which captures the dizzying circularity of beliefs, reality, and truth. One of the greatest movements across disciplines in the late twentieth century has been the reopening of questions about the nature of reality.

> Reality is what we take to be true.
> What we take to be true is what we believe.
> What we believe is based upon our perceptions.
> What we perceive depends on what we look for.
> What we look for depends on what we think.
> What we think determines what we take to be true.
> What we take to be true is our reality. (Zukav, 1979, p. 328)

All of the lenses we have reviewed have illuminated and deepened our understanding of this neglected aspect in clinical work with families. After studying and peering through the variety of lenses, however, the explanation of beliefs that we have found most useful and a fit for us is a biological–spiritual explanation. The explanations that have become the most important for us in clinical work are the biology and spirituality lenses. Biology is a concern for how living takes place (Maturana, 1992, May). We wonder if our attraction to a biological explanation of beliefs is related to the biological foundation of one of our "home" disciplines, nursing. Our attraction to the spiritual lens has been clearly influenced by experiences with our own and clinical families who are suffering; we increasingly appreciate that suffering invites one into the spiritual domain.

To understand our own and others' beliefs, we must understand the contexts in which we all live: the interactional, social, and cultural contexts. If the basic cognitive operation is the distinction (Maturana & Varela, 1992), beliefs arise out of distinctions that evolve through our history of interactions (ontogeny) with those we encounter in our lives as well as out of our own structure or genetic makeup (phylogeny) all within the contexts of our lives.

To alter existing beliefs, health professionals need to invite family members to a reflection about their constraining beliefs. Through these reflections, a person begins to entertain different, or alternative, beliefs in order to get out of a state of confusion, struggle, or suffering. Explanations of our experiences can be based in the past or the future. One can invite distinctions in a variety of ways, such as through a particular line of inquiry or through the offering of ideas that invite persons to consider alternative views to their difficulties with illness. Because we are not just cells but also souls, the heart of our approach is a biological–spiritual lens.

## OUR DEFINITION OF A BELIEF

The definition of belief that we most favor is as follows: A *belief* is the "truth" of a subjective reality that influences biopsychosocial–spiritual structure and functioning. In our conversations, we speak and listen to one another from these domains of "truths"—explanations, values, and obligations based on our beliefs—that have arisen from the social, interactional, and cultural domains in which we live.

## CORE BELIEFS: THE HEART OF THE MATTER

As a man thinketh in his heart, so is he.

PROVERBS 23:7

There are numerous beliefs operating and emerging within every person every day, about every situation and every person encountered. But not all beliefs matter; not all beliefs invite an emotional or physiological response. The beliefs that do matter are our *core beliefs*. We all possess core beliefs, which are personal and often unconscious. Core beliefs are fundamental to how we approach the world; they are the basic concepts by which we live. Our core beliefs are our identity. Core beliefs are generally about the nature of reality, and thus we live as if certain absolutes were true.

All beliefs are not equally important to an individual, whereas core beliefs are the beliefs that are at the heart of the matter. These beliefs are accompanied by intense affective and physiological responses. Core beliefs powerfully and profoundly influence the family system and its functioning. Core beliefs are the beliefs that matter and are most relevant to how family members cope with illness. They involve a certitude about the issue at hand and are central to our individual lives and relationships.

Core beliefs differ from perceptions and thoughts. A perception varies more easily and is based on observation. For example the perception "My father is very ill" is based on the observations of a daughter that her father's skin is pale and breathing is slow. A thought concerning this situation might be, "I think my father needs help." This is the offering of an opinion or idea. Core beliefs are based more strongly on the believing of the truth of some statement and are laden with affective and physiological responses. In this example, a core belief may be "Responsible daughters care for their ill parents." Rules for behaving follow. The daughter may ask for time off from work to care for her ill father.

Core beliefs can be good or bad for one's health; they can be constraining or facilitative. On the positive side, a belief that one is loved and cared for is more likely to motivate individuals to take care of their health. Jim Henson, the creator of the Muppet characters, provides a sad example of how core beliefs can be detrimental to one's health. Henson was a brilliant but shy and retiring man who died of a massive infection that could have been successfully treated; however, he hated to bother anybody (McKay & Fanning, 1991). Henson's belief—a good person doesn't bother others when he doesn't feel well—constrained him from seeking and securing the help that might have saved his life.

## CONSTRAINING VERSUS FACILITATIVE BELIEFS

McKay and Fanning (1991) contended that core beliefs can group experiences into positive or negative categories and are dichotomous by nature. We prefer to call this dichotomy *constraining* versus *facilitative beliefs*. By the term *constraining beliefs*, we refer to beliefs that decrease solution options to problems; *facilitative beliefs* increase solution options. We tend to accept only information that confirms our existing views and to ignore information, ideas, or opinions that contradict established beliefs; therefore, constraining and facilitative beliefs are confirmed. Core beliefs are also sustained by what McKay and Fanning refer to as "mental grooving." They suggest that these grooves are the psychological ruts that everyone returns to in situations of stress or uncertainty. Certainly, when persons experience illness and stress, uncertainty follows. When illness enters a person's life, core beliefs are brought to the fore. To understand people's experience with an illness, therefore, we need to focus on their core beliefs.

## CONCLUSION

This chapter has offered a look at a variety of explanations of beliefs using various lenses. Our clinical practice has been influenced over the years by all of these lenses. In both our personal and our professional lives, we unavoidably embrace particular beliefs that guide us in living. The belief lens that is the best fit for us professionally is a biological–spiritual lens. We currently define a *belief* as the "truth" of a subjective reality that influences a person's biopsychosocial–spiritual structure and functioning. Core beliefs are the "beliefs that matter" within our relationships and within significant events in our lives, such as illness. Our beliefs and our believing inevitably influence the way we interact, and differences of beliefs are unavoidable because our lives and experiences differ. Beliefs arise out of the life one is living. Although beliefs of clients and health professionals may be similar, they are more likely to be different. Our assistance to persons and families experiencing physical and emotional suffering from illness is effective only if we first listen curiously to and then understand sensitively the core beliefs of the persons with whom we are privileged to work. As health professionals, we believe that change and healing intersect family members' and health professionals' beliefs.

# CHAPTER 2

# Beliefs About Families
# and Illness

**"I** DON'T THINK I've been a bad person all my life. Why should this happen to me?" These words of a man, age 62, speaking about the chronic illness of his son, express specific beliefs about the cause of illness.

Everyone has beliefs about families and about illness. Some families view illness as a sign that they are sinful and disease as a punishment for ungodly living. Other families believe that being ill is a natural physical sign that the ill member should slow down and take care of himself, that he can no longer go on neglecting his health. Everyone also has beliefs about how family members should behave if illness enters the family. Families who believe that an illness can be intensified by upsetting the ill family member may withhold information or over-protect. Repetitive encouragement (also known as nagging) about taking medication or following a diabetic diet is believed by some families to be a way of showing concern. Some families believe the ill person needs more nurturing and attention; others believe the ill one should be allowed more solitude.

Health care professionals bring their strong personal and professional beliefs about families and illness to the clinical domain. Their beliefs influence how they view, assess, and most important, care for and intervene with families. For example, health care professionals' beliefs about etiology may influence how a family is received, perceived, and treated. A health care professional who believes alcoholism is a consequence of irresponsibility and personal weakness will likely respond differently to a family experiencing alcoholism than to a family experiencing the effects of a congenital heart defect, an illness over which she believes the individual or family has no control.

## BELIEFS ABOUT FAMILIES

Our beliefs as health professionals determine whether we view families as "dysfunctional" or "healthy"; see them as pathological or resourceful; put them on the "Board of Directors" by involving them in their health care or foster dependency; and empower or disempower families with our clinical interventions. Our ideas of who and what constitutes a family are among the beliefs that impact clinical practice, affecting how we offer assistance to families experiencing illness. Table 2.1 illustrates five beliefs about families that influence our clinical practice.

TABLE 2.1

**Beliefs About Families**

| |
| --- |
| A family is a group of individuals who are bound by strong emotional ties, a sense of belonging, and a passion for being involved in one another's lives |
| Individuals are structurally determined |
| Problems do not reside within individuals but between persons in language |
| All families have strengths, often unappreciated or unrealized |
| Individuals are best understood in their relational contexts |

*A family is a group of individuals who are bound by strong emotional ties, a sense of belonging, and a passion for being involved in one another's lives.*

Families are individuals who "give a damn" about one another. Families can be portrayed as long-term committed relationships in which persons organize themselves in relationship to each other (Tomm, 1994). Family health professionals need to find a definition of family that moves beyond the traditional boundaries of limiting membership using the criteria of blood, adoption, and marriage. One useful definition proposes that the family is whoever they say they are (Wright

& Leahey, 1994a). With this view, the clinician can honor individual family members' ideas about which relationships are significant to them and their experience of health and illness. Research has shown that a powerful and reciprocal connection exists between health and the nature of a person's long-term relationships (Radley & Green, 1986; Ross & Cobb, 1990). Inviting the individual to define who constitutes "the family" provides access to important beliefs. Through the construction of a genogram, the clinician may learn that the individual believes support and affection received from a neighbor, coworker, or even a family pet is more significant than that received from a spouse or sibling.

The idea of the family unit as a system composed of individual family members and having characteristics of its own that transcend those of the individual members is a fundamental assumption of systems theory. However, the distinction between family and individual family members is an important one to consider. We do not concur with the well-accepted conceptualization that certain behaviors and beliefs of the individual are transformed through interaction and history with others to take on family meanings and become family constructs or paradigms (Dallos, 1991; Patterson & Leonard, 1994; Reiss, 1982). Despite our interest in working with the entity called the *family*—a word used to symbolize a focus on relationships, interaction, and reciprocity—we believe the clinician cannot know "a family." Humberto Maturana (1992, May) persuasively argued that "family" is an idea brought forth in our minds through language to account for the special relationship that occurs over time among individuals who call themselves and think of themselves as part of a family; however, a family can be known only through its individual members. This belief has implications for family research as well as for clinical work with families.

Maturana and Varela (1992) proposed that an independent reality does not exist but is brought forth by the observer. The act of bringing forth an entity, that is, the describing and distinguishing of anything, is accomplished by the individual through language. "Without the observer nothing exists. . . . The event itself has no existence separate from our distinguishing it through words and symbols" (Efran & Lukens, 1985, pp. 24–25). One of the authors (WLW) recalls her new cleaning woman returning for a second appointment and commenting on the "new tree in the living room." The tree, complete with its bright red apples, had been there for several years, according to WLW's reality, yet the cleaning woman had not interacted with it on her initial visit in such a way to bring it forth into her reality.

If reality is observer-dependent, there are as many families as there are family members, because each family member has his distinct view of "the family." In a family of five, therefore, there are not five different views of one family; there are five different families. Even when meanings, beliefs, and experiences are consensually shared through language by several individuals within a family and evolved through interaction among the individuals, there can be no such thing as a family belief, a family construct, family meaning, or family health. Instead, there are many individual descriptions of family beliefs, family meanings, or family health, each one equally valid.

Jay Efran and Michael Lukens (1985) have stated the following warning:

> It is crucial to notice that the description of the family that a therapist creates is not any more objective or real than the families that exist in the language patterns of each of the family members. Further, the words and symbols they each use for describing families (and other occurrences) are not just abstractions, but tools used to coordinate complex action patterns in social domains. But unless we are careful, we tend to fall prey to a common illusion: as social consensus in a domain is achieved—i.e., people in the same "club" begin to talk similarly—we think that something objective has been discovered. (p. 25)

*Individuals are structurally determined.*

One of Maturana's ideas that has greatly influenced our clinical practice is the concept of structural determinism (Maturana & Varela, 1992). This concept states that each individual's biopsychosocial–spiritual structure is unique and is a product of the individual's genetic history (phylogeny) as well as her history of interactions over time (ontogeny).

Central to the notion of structural determinism is that an individual's present structure specifies what environmental influences will be experienced as "perturbations," that is, interactions that yield structural changes. We cannot say a priori which health care interventions will be useful in promoting change for *this* particular family member at *this* time and which will not. Individuals are selectively "perturbed" by the interventions that are offered according to what "fits" or does not fit their current structure. Changes in family members are thus determined by their own biopsychosocial–spiritual structures, not predetermined by others. We cannot predict which interventions will fit for a particular person and which, therefore, will perturb that person's structure and which will not.

The initially static-sounding notion of structural determinism is heard differently when one considers it in conjunction with Maturana's concepts of "plasticity" and "structural coupling." Living systems are highly plastic, that is, able to make changes through interactions and through structurally coupling with other systems (Maturana & Varela, 1992). There is a hopefulness for change and tenacity for therapeutic competence that is generated through the integration of the concepts of structural determinism, plasticity, and structural coupling. Chapter 3 contains a further description of these concepts and their influence on beliefs about therapeutic change.

We experience that a deep respect for and curiosity about family members develops in clinicians who are cognizant of the notion of structural determinism. Application of Maturana's concept of structural determinism has led us to believe that the description of families as noncompliant, resistant, or unmotivated is not only "an epistemological error but a biological impossibility" (Wright & Levac, 1992, p. 913). This concept has revolutionized the way we think about families and, more important, the way we interact with families.

One way we have applied the idea of structural determinism in our practice has been through the use of a particular question, "What stood out for you?" For example, when families come to a session, we routinely ask, "What stood out for you from the last session?" In so doing, we are acknowledging the uniqueness of each family member and that what is experienced as significant, meaningful, and perturbing at each session varies among family members. We are curious about which of all the ideas and opinions offered during a session stood out and were selected as meaningful perturbations for particular family members. We have found this to be a respectful way to work with families, realizing that not everything we offer families will fit or be helpful.

During a clinical interview, we frequently use the clinical intervention form of the *reflecting team* (Andersen, 1987). Families have the opportunity to listen to and observe, from behind a one-way mirror, the team discussing their situation. Following the team's discussion, we encourage family members to reflect on the team's reflections by asking, "What stood out for you?" In this way, the idea that each individual's structure is unique is honored. It is not what the clinician says or does that effects change; rather, it is the fit between the individual's present structure and what the clinician says or does that effects change.

*Problems do not reside within individuals but between persons in language.*

Health professionals struggle to define what is "healthy" family functioning (Smith & Stevens, 1992). Does the word *healthy* refer to characteristics of the family system or of individual family members? It is not unusual, given the strong biomedical influence of health professional education, to distinguish and draw forth pathology and dysfunction and thus to become blind to family member's health, resources, and strengths. The influence of this prevailing deficit model on health professionals is sometimes subtle and yet dangerously pervasive. Professionals in various health fields often pride themselves on being the first one on the block to identify what is "really wrong" with a family. Frequently, problems are seen to reside within individuals: the depressed cancer patient, the acting-out adolescent, the abusive father. Health professionals often believe that it is necessary to find the cause of a problem before a cure can be suggested. That belief generates a clinical approach that focuses on etiology—the endless search for "why"—and invites blame and accusation of the individual and other family members.

An alternative viewpoint is offered by Harlene Anderson, Harry Goolishian, and Lee Winderman (1986), who have conceptualized problems as being distinguished in language rather than residing within individuals. A "problem-determined system" is not an individual or family but a language system with boundaries marked by whoever communicates about a shared problem. We agree and therefore believe there is no such thing as a "dysfunctional" individual or family! This is not to say that there are not individuals who inflict horror and pain on others. However, our experience is that once the beliefs behind behavior are understood, each individual's behavior makes sense, especially to the individual. For example, one physically abusing husband's beliefs included the idea that he was supposed to control his wife and was responsible for her behavior. If behavior makes sense, it is not clinically useful to label family members or families as "dysfunctional."

To label a family as dysfunctional suggests that the clinician is, in Maturana's words, operating in the domain of "objectivity-without-parentheses" (Maturana & Varela, 1992). When one operates from a stance of objectivity-without-parentheses, one believes that there is one correct view and "I have it!" We need to ask whose point of view is being privileged in the labeling of behavior as dysfunctional. The objectivity-without-parentheses stance in the health care setting frequently honors the clinician's observations and judgments as the "truth" about a family. It implicitly and hierarchically values the clinician's observations over other observations and descriptions. It also limits both the clinician and those being labeled "dysfunctional" from proposing other distinctions. The term *dysfunctional* also serves to trivialize and minimize problems, offering only one label to capture a wide range of difficulties and travesties ranging from behavioral problems to incest. We find the term *dysfunctional* itself to be dysfunctional, serving no useful purpose and prohibiting wider views of situations.

We have found it useful to think about difficulties as problems that are drawn forth in language and occur between rather than within persons. This conceptualization removes the temptation to engage in linear thinking through conversations of causation (i.e., asking and answering "why" questions) or of accusation (blaming particular individuals). Different conversations unfold when a depressed cancer patient is not asked why he is depressed but rather how family members respond to his depressed behavior, who is most or least supportive of his depressed behavior, whether there was ever a time he felt more optimistic and hopeful about his illness, and if so, what was different then. A systemic description of interactions between people that maintain or perpetuate problems or that are focused toward solutions (i.e., "how" questions) provides many possibilities for intervention.

We wish to emphasize that, although we hold to the view that problems reside between persons in language, we would not want readers to conclude that concerns about genetic structure have no place in our approach. Of course, our professional backgrounds and common sense compel us to adopt a both–and view (i.e., a view embracing both interactions and genetics) to understand and make sense of the difficulties that families often experience when dealing with health problems. The focus and emphasis of our work, however, is on altering the types of conversations family members experience by challenging the constraining beliefs that exist. In so doing, we believe that healing from physical and emotional suffering can occur.

*All families have strengths, often unappreciated or unrealized.*

As clinicians abandon the lens that pathologizes families, they adopt a view of families as resourceful. All families possess the strengths and abilities necessary to solve their own problems. David Reiss (1982) has supported the idea that families have the capacity for self-healing and are able to foster their own recovery. Although all families possess these strengths and abilities, their solution capabilities may be hidden, inaccessible, and forgotten. When families get stuck in their problem-solving efforts, they may benefit from being reminded about forgotten strengths and abilities or from having current strengths, to which they are blind, brought into their awareness. John DeFrain and Nick Stinnett

(1992) suggested that a strength-oriented perspective can provide a strong foundation for family renewal.

In our experience, families generally seek help for problems once their own efforts at problem solving have been exhausted or they have reached an impasse. They come seeking professional help feeling inadequate, exhausted, fearful, frustrated, or incompetent. Through an understanding of the family's experience with illness, the clinician looks for opportunities to invite the members to a new view of their strengths or to help them regain a view of their competence that has been lost. One way we attempt to accomplish this is by offering commendations at each family interview.

In the early evolution of our clinical approach, we were influenced by the work of the Milan team (Selvini Palazzoli, Boscolo, Cecchin, & Prata, 1978) concerning *positive connotation:* a systemic opinion that connects the symptomatic behavior to other behaviors in the system and conceptualizes the presenting symptom as a solution to some other hypothetical or implied problem that would or could occur should the symptom not be present (Tomm, 1984a). We began to experiment with offering families ideas about how a symptom might be useful to them and how they might be maintaining the symptom. For example, a 66-year-old woman presented with angina and angst concerning a trip that her 39-year-old married daughter had taken to visit her father, the mother's divorced husband. Both believed that their persistent mother–daughter conflict was life threatening to the mother. As part of a split-opinion therapeutic letter, we positively connoted the conflictual distancing as a solution to their previous experience of being too close. Both were included in the perpetuation of the problem, which was couched as a system-sensitive solution, and the door was opened for them to enter now into a search for the right balance in their relationship. Following receipt of the letter, the mother and daughter spontaneously went for lunch together, something they had not done in years, and the mother made an appointment to see a physician about her heart condition. This was a major change from the mother's previous stance that she was just going to die and would never seek medical attention (Wright & Watson, 1988).

We agree with others that positive connotations must be sensitively and selectively offered so that a positive connotation does not unwittingly blame a family. We no longer look for the functionality of symptoms but continue to be interested in possible beneficial outcomes of symptoms. An illness may draw family members together, even giving them opportunity and permission to say and do tender, heart-nurturing things heretofore unexpressed. The wife of a man being treated for colon cancer expressed that it was during the initially intense, critical phase of the illness that she and her husband reached out to each other in words and actions. Six months later, she nostalgically wondered out loud, "Why can't my husband and I keep talking and doing those things that brought us so close? We are now just back to normal."

Positively connoting symptoms and looking for beneficial outcomes provide opportunities to experiment with distinguishing other family strengths and resources. Drawing forth family strengths through commendations has become a characteristic of our practice. (For more information on commendations, see chapter 6.) For example, in Research Family 4, we worked with a woman (identified as Linda in the transcript that follows) who was a single parent to four children. She had numerous concerns about her children ranging from fear that they might be experiencing long-term effects of early abuse from her brain-injured, ex-husband to concern about their schoolwork and friends. At each session, we provided commendations related to her concern for her children, her mothering skills, and her astute observations of her family. Following is the excerpt of the therapeutic conversation during the final session, in which the clinician (WLW) inquired about the impact of the clinical sessions at the Family Nursing Unit:

WLW: What difference did coming to the Family Nursing Unit make to you? Did it make a difference?

LINDA: It helped me realize we're really not so bad. I figured that we were the worst bunch on the face of the earth. I thought that we were really a problem family because we have been labeled as such by the schools, by the church, by just various places and various people that I've dealt with. We've been stigmatized and labeled as a "problem family" possibly because we were a single-parent family.

WLW: So by coming here, what do you now believe?

LINDA: I'm not so bad. I'm doing okay, and these kids are alright, and I'm not bad either, and it's okay for me to be human. It's okay for me to once in a while have a bad day.

WLW: Alright!

LINDA: As long as I handle it properly, which I try to do. I'm not always successful.

WLW: From your point of view today, what was helpful? You're saying one new idea that you got was, "We're a normal family. We're an okay family. I'm doing some good things." What did we do that helped you come to that idea, that we should remember to do again with other people?

LINDA: I think what you did was you voiced that, "Hey we've worked with other families. We think you're exceptional. We think you're okay." And it was nice for me to hear from someone who has dealt with other families, who is professional, who deals with it as a profession. It was really nice to hear that. You know, it was verbalized. Also there is a lot of really positive reinforcement, you know, "I've noticed that you do this or do that with your kids, or we've noticed that there's a lot of affection in your family." That sort of thing.

WLW: So, pointing those out to you, you liked that?

LINDA: That helped a lot, as opposed to, "Your kids are driving us crazy, they're running all over the place." Instead, you said, "Oh they're such curious, lovely children," and I'm going, "Okay."

WLW: That had some impact on you?

LINDA: Yes, because we'd been labeled, first of all, and stigmatized for so long.

This mother developed an entirely new perspective of herself and her children as a result of the commendations offered to her and was able to highlight those comments that had the most effect on her.

*Individuals are best understood in their relational contexts.*

Individuals are powerfully connected, emotionally and biologically, in their relationships with others. Maturana contends that through their history of interactions with each other across time, individuals experience changes in their structures; we would say the changes are in their biopsychosocial–spiritual structures. Studies have documented numerous structural changes in individuals connected to family relationships, such as the striking similarity between family members in smoking behavior (Doherty & Whitehead, 1986) or decreased immune system functioning in grieving widows (Reichlin, 1993; Schmidt, 1983). A clinician can gain a richer understanding of an individual's experience and behavior by inquiring about the interconnections between family members and the health problem. Anderson (1993), a physician concerned with implementing principles of mind–body medicine, offered the following poignant comment about individuals and their relational contexts:

I think it's [the mind–body connection] the art of understanding the whole person and not just the physiological system. In medical schools we deal with diseases and tissues and organs and body systems. But when you put the art in medicine, you deal with persons and

with their families and communities. You have to have that connectedness. You deal with the spirit. (p. 29)

This mind–body–spirit reconnection that appears to be emerging in
some health professions and reemerging in others is a welcome concept. Some professions, such as medicine and nursing, have paid significant attention to physiological systems but not to "mind" or healing
systems (Cousins, 1989). Other professions, such as family therapy and
psychology, have given devoted attention to "mind," language, and
narratives but not necessarily to physiological systems.

Although the idea of systems being interrelated and interconnected
is attributed to systems theory, which postulates that there are connections between wholes and parts of any system, it has been our clinical
experience with families that has convinced us of the importance of this
interconnection. Families have taught us this systems concept. For
example, a man who was experiencing difficulties with chronic back
pain (Watson, Bell, & Wright, 1992) believed that the spurs in his back
(osteophytes) had been caused by a variety of inept and unknowledge-
able health care professionals. This belief about the etiology of his illness made him angry and bitter. The impact on the marriage relationship of this man's response to his illness was explored with him and his
wife. His wife eloquently and systemically noted the connection
between how she and the marital relationship were affected by the husband's beliefs about his illness: "He's not just bitter and angry and mad
about his arthritis; he's bitter and angry and mad all the time about
everything, and I think it affects our whole relationship. When he acts
that way, I act that way, and so we're just always bitter and angry and
mad." The clinician (WLW) then asked, "So what would happen if John
never gave up this belief?" The wife responded, "Then I would leave
him, I'm sure. I don't think I could live with him the way he is now."
The beliefs about the etiology of the osteophytes changed the personality of the husband, invited the wife to withdraw, exacerbated problematic marital and parental issues, and had the potential of motivating the
wife to leave the marriage. Not only was the clinical understanding of
the client enhanced through an examination of the relational context
and reciprocity, but also many more options for intervention were subsequently available.

Family members are frequently overlooked or unacknowledged, by
health professionals, as powerful resources for persons coping with illness. One study provides significant evidence for the necessity of
involving family members in supporting their ill family member.
Lynam (1995) conducted a qualitative study with young adults experiencing cancer to determine the processes of providing support that are

most useful for family members. The processes of offering and receiving support revealed that family members' responses to the young adults in the study were inextricably linked to how the illness was experienced and managed. Most revealing in the analysis of the data were the implicit assumptions inherent in the relationships between the young adults and their family members and how such assumptions are drawn on and confirmed as illness-related issues were addressed. One assumption of the young adults was that when they felt supported, they believed they were important and that their family members wanted to alleviate their discomfort. In addition, there was an important reciprocal nature to the support.

## BELIEFS ABOUT ILLNESS

What one believes about illness contributes dramatically to how one experiences an illness. No two people have the same experience with the same disease, whether it be the common cold or Crohn's disease. It is this uniqueness that opens up possibilities for the Terry Foxes of the world: individuals who do not let their illnesses limit their world, but rather use their illnesses to connect with and inspire the world. Beliefs shape our experience with illness far more than the disease itself. McGuire and Kantor (1987) maintained that two people with the same chronic condition could have totally different experiences of that condition because their beliefs shape their perceptions and interpretations differently. For this reason, we prefer to use the language of "experiencing an illness" rather than "having an illness."

How persons experience an illness depends on the beliefs that they have embraced prior to the illness experience as well as the beliefs that evolve through the experience of the illness. The beliefs that family members hold are often reconstructed after the experience of an illness; conversely, family member beliefs influence and shape the processes and outcomes of illness. For example, how persons treat a cold depends on their beliefs concerning how they "caught" the cold in the first place. If one believes that colds are related to experiences of loss, one will probably treat one's cold differently than if one believes a cold is due to inadequate rest and working long hours. If a person believes that the best remedy for a cold is to rest, drink plenty of fluid, and take vitamin C, he will probably follow that regime on experiencing a cold. If the treatment remedy does not work, will he maintain his belief about the etiology? Will he be more open to other treatment remedies? Many factors influence what people consider treatment options when their original beliefs about the etiology and the cure of an illness have been challenged.

Health professionals' beliefs about their ability to influence an illness are also an important factor in how people experience illness. If we believe that the mind–body–spirit has a powerful influence on health and healing for better or worse, our inquiry of ideas, opinions, and advice offered to persons experiencing illness will differ significantly from those of health professionals who do not hold that belief. Table 2.2 illustrates five beliefs about illness that influence our clinical practice.

TABLE 2.2

**Beliefs About Illness**

Health and illness are subjective judgments made by observers

Illness and families are linked in recursive, reciprocal relationships

Illness narratives include stories of sickness and suffering that need to be told

Options for managing illness increase options for healing

Illness arises and is influenced by interference with fundamental emotional dynamics

*Health and illness are subjective judgments made by observers.*

> Because you are diagnosed as ill, it is not a requirement that you feel sick.
>
> RONNA FAY JEVNE

Who decides when someone is well or ill? Health and illness are subjective judgments made by observers. Observers may include family members, friends, health professionals, and the ill person. The decision about health or illness is too often a unilateral decision made by health professionals, primarily physicians or nurses. A diagnosis is made on the basis of the combination of clinical expertise, medical science, and intuition; however, it becomes meaningful only when placed in an interactional context (Wright & Leahey, 1987). It is also important to consider the professional context in which diagnoses are made. Health professionals may be exquisitely sensitive to selecting a diagnosis that is billable to third-party payers. The context in which health care providers work, as well as their professional lens, may invite some to pronounce a particular diagnosis repeatedly. How is it that attention deficit hyperactivity disorder (ADHD) has become the diagnosis of choice for troubled children in certain areas of the country at certain times?

A diagnosis is a social contract that occurs when one person—the medical or nursing expert—affixes a classification to another—the identified patient (Glenn, 1984). At this point, the person pronounced with a diagnosis, other family members, and the health care professionals enter into a "contract" regarding the diagnosis. The diagnosis implies that a cluster of signs and symptoms exists, places those manifestations in context, gives them meaning, and suggests a treatment.

As all health professionals know, however, it is difficult to have all parties in the contract agree on all aspects of the diagnosis. All diagnoses are subject, therefore, to negotiation. Initially, family members may accept a diagnosis of a myocardial infarction, but the patient may not. In other cases, family members may accept the label of the disease but disagree with the proposed treatment. Part of the social contract of the diagnosis requires family members to think of themselves in relationship to the illness. What does it mean that this diagnosis is part of the family? One family with whom we worked whose adolescent had been diagnosed with a life-threatening illness explained their ability to cope by saying, "God knew that our family could handle it. Other families would have fallen apart." The meaning of the diagnosis to family members is important to determine. Some families perceive certain illnesses as a challenge, whereas other families consider the same illness a punishment or perceive it as a threat. Some diagnoses unite families (everyone in our family has weak joints), whereas other diagnoses initially estrange family members (e.g., HIV and AIDS). The diversity of responses to and beliefs about diagnoses extends to health professionals, who rarely present a united front regarding the management of an illness.

There is increasing difficulty between health professionals and family members in coming to agreement on medical diagnoses because of the phenomenal impact of alternative health practices. Health care providers in Western culture are frequently critical of alternative or complementary treatments that do not fall within accepted beliefs about what is helpful. However, both family members and health professionals are adopting more complementary health practices for illness prevention. Conventional medicine still gets top marks for dealing with trauma and crises such as bacterial invasion. But for many other health problems, alternative health practices are gaining an overwhelming acceptance based on the belief that these practices take a more holistic approach to health problems and healing. Alternative health practices frequently offer hope when the limits of more conservative medical treatment are exhausted. Beliefs about diagnosis and treatment vary, therefore. Many individuals use home remedies that they do not readily reveal to health professionals. Some remedies are probably no different from Francis Bacon's belief that warts could be cured by rubbing them with pork rinds or George Washington's belief that various bodily ills could be cured by passing two 3-inch metal rods over the afflicted area (Gilovich, 1991). What is deemed erroneous for one person may truly be a lifesaver for another.

Health and illness are distinctions that are brought forth through our relationships and languaging with each other. Distinctions such as health and illness are subjective judgments made by observers (i.e., individuals experiencing illness, family members, and health professionals) about adaptation. Family and individual systems are in continuous effective adaptation to their unique and changing environment (Maturana & Varela, 1992). The most powerful components of adaptation are the family members' beliefs about the illness.

The following verbatim transcript is from a telephone interview of Humberto Maturana (1988a), conducted by LMW, which illuminates Maturana's ideas about health and illness as distinctions of observers:

> LMW: Another question that we have been struggling with is that as nurses we encounter persons experiencing illness and we have been wondering if you perceive illness as a perturbation and also do you, when you say that nothing is an accident, do you also feel the same way about illness?
>
> MATURANA: In illness there are several aspects. One is of course the assessment that there is illness. The assessment is made by someone, it could be a physician, or it could be the person him- or herself, it could be a nurse, someone must make the assessment for the illness to occur. That means that there is a situation which one considers an inadequate variance with respect to what one considers to be a normal or healthy flow. That of course puts the responsibility of the assessment on the person that makes it and the person that accepts it. Now if the person who is considered to be ill accepts such assessment, then a conversation for treatment or whatever takes place about illness. Now in the instant in which one makes the assessment of illness one is claiming that the flow of structural coupling of this person within the domain in which one is assessing is inadequate, this person is flowing in a different domain of structural coupling. What one indeed does, is to claim that the person considered ill is flowing in a domain of structural coupling different from that which one considers should be the case.
>
> For example, let us suppose a tumor. I have a tumor and I live with it in perfect harmony; I am not ill. Somebody else can say "do something about this tumor. This is going to kill you." And I say, "Oh, no. Forget it. I mean it doesn't bother me. I'm quite all right with it. I do not even notice it." From my perspective there is no illness and from the perspective of the other person there is illness, but in the instant in which you make the assessment, you don't make

the assessment in a vacuum. You make the assessment in a distinction of the structural dynamics of the person and so the assessment reveals you and the person assessed to the extent that you have adequately grasped the structure of the person and the domain of structural coupling in which you look at him or her. As one makes the distinction of an entity in a particular domain of existence, one brings forth implicitly its whole history of the person if one knows how to look at it. It's telling you how the structure of this entity is now and hence what kind of history this entity may have lived if it is an entity of this particular kind. Now in human beings, it has particular significance because the flow of our body structure is not independent of how we live both materially and spiritually.

We human beings exist in cultures as networks of coordinations of languaging and emotions, so it is the manner we live in a culture that has certain consequences in the manner our bodyhood flows as it modulates or interlaces with its own internal structural dynamics. So at any moment, one is an expression or revelation of how one has lived and how one feels in one's living. This is why a good clinical eye allows one to see much more than a particular symptom in a person. If one knows how to look one can see almost in a glance the psychological and physiological history of a person, and that knowing must be learned.

LMW: One of the things that we experience in nursing, once a particular illness has been assessed or diagnosed, is then trying to have patients comply to certain things that we think will make their life better in terms of their health. Patients aren't always willing to do the kinds of things that we ask them to do. This brings us to the notion of instructive interaction and we have been very curious about this as we have studied your ideas. How can we impart knowledge to patients about their health without getting into the trap of instructive interaction?

MATURANA: You cannot do instructive interactions. The most that you can do is to talk to the patient and seduce him or her to a reflection that will allow that person to accept or realize the validity of your assessment of illness, and see that there are certain things that can be done. At the same time there is a responsibility that the doctor or nurse must accept, since she or he will never convince another person to take a particular medicine if she or he is not convinced or appears convinced of its value. Understanding cannot be forced.

*Illness and families are linked in recursive, reciprocal relationships.*

Families spend much time thinking about the origins and implications of illnesses. The responses by family members to a diagnosis vary widely from anger to sadness to relief. However, some family clinicians (M. Selvini Palazzoli, personal communication, 1985) propose that patients respond more to their family's responses to the illness than to the condition itself. This idea has been powerfully demonstrated in the research of Reiss, Gonzalez, and Kramer (1986), who suggested that affected families who are too emotionally close may inadvertently precipitate death in the sick member. Death may represent an "arrangement" between the family and the patient: The patient dies so that the family may live. This is often an extreme but perhaps the only "reasonable" response of the patient to the family's feelings of grief and burden. John Rolland (1984) concurred that "some families' hope to resume a 'normal' life might only come through the death of their ill member" (p. 255).

Families adapt better when they possess facilitative beliefs about the perceived benefits of the illness experience. For example, in a study by Patterson and Leonard (1994) of families with a medically fragile child, it was found that parents coping well were able to report positive aspects of having a child with profound medical needs, such as emphasizing the closeness felt in the family unit and positive aspects of the child's personality.

In our clinical work with families, therefore, we are concerned with understanding the recursive interactions between illness and the family and between family members and health professionals. Family members' beliefs and subsequent reactions to illness can significantly influence the decision to initiate or delay treatment, the perceptions of seriousness of symptoms or the disease, treatment compliance, and satisfaction with the treatment outcome (Weakland & Fisch, 1984). In extreme cases, the family may even influence the patient's will to live. Consequently, we are always curious about what subjective judgments family members have made about their health and illness and how they match with our judgments as health professionals. In our clinical work with a frustrated couple—the man suffered with chronic back pain and had been diagnosed and treated for a multitude of illnesses—a turning point occurred when we attempted to access the diagnostic and statistical manual of the family: the "DSM-FAM," as we term it, as opposed to the DSM-IV. By listening to the language of the family and the predominance of bitterness, anger, and madness, we coevolved the diagnosis: They were suffering from the BAM syndrome: a condition of being chronically bitter, angry, and mad (Watson et al., 1992). As the family's and our subjective judgments are drawn forth, we coevolve new distinctions about health and illness. A health professional's judgment or assessment of any family is not the "truth" about that family, but rather one subjective judgment from an observer perspective influenced by the clinician's core beliefs about illness and families.

*Illness narratives include stories of sickness and suffering that need to be told.*

We spend our years as a tale that is told.

PSALMS 90:9 (AV)

Illness invites a wake-up call about life. It arouses the need to be known, to be heard, and to be validated—the need to know that one's life matters in the life of someone else and that the life one is living and has lived is and has been worthwhile (Frank, 1994). These needs fuel the telling of one's illness narrative. Illness narratives include stories of sickness and suffering that need to be told. We believe that all too often family members are encouraged to tell the narrative of the disease or condition (i.e., the medical narrative, complete with medication, dosages, and tests) rather than the narrative of the illness (i.e., personal experiences of illness).

Arthur Kleinman (1988) created a useful distinction between the terms *disease, illness,* and *sickness.* He defined *disease* as a biomedical description or interpretation of a family member's condition. Dealing with disease is dealing in the domain of diagnosis, treatment, and cures. Other authors (Robinson, 1993; Thomas, 1984) favor the term *condition* rather than disease. Robin Thomas (1984), most notably, has offered a compelling definition of *condition* as any anatomic or physiological impairment that interferes with an individual's ability to function in the environment. Chronic conditions are characterized by relatively stable periods that may be interrupted by acute episodes requiring hospitalization or medical attention. The individual's prognosis varies between a normal life span and unpredictable death. Chronic conditions are rarely cured, but they are managed through individual and family effort and diligence.

When someone is newly diagnosed with diabetes, a chronic condition, much of the conversation between patient and physician focuses on symptoms such as excessive thirst and frequency and urgency of urination. The hypothesis of diabetes is then confirmed by medical science through such tests as the fasting blood sugar. Following diagnosis, the conversation broadens to include other health professionals and switches to topics of diet, oral medication, and perhaps even insulin. These conversations are reasonable and necessary; however, following the diagnosis, patients and their families live predominantly within the domain of *illness* rather than disease or condition. To continue to limit the therapeutic conversation to the aforementioned topics is to limit healing.

Kleinman (1988) offered a useful definition to describe a person's experience within the illness domain, in contrast to the domain of disease:

> By invoking the term illness, I mean to conjure up the innately human experience of symptoms and suffering. Illness refers to how the sick person and the members of the family or wider social network perceive, live with, and respond to symptoms and disability. (p. 3)

Operating from a family systems perspective, Rolland (1994) offered a rewording of Kleinman's descriptions. Instead of *disease*, Rolland used the term *biological*; instead of *illness*, he referred to "human experience of individuals and families"; and instead of *sickness*, he spoke of "societal levels of meaning." We prefer the term *chronic condition* to *disease*, and we prefer Kleinman's (1988) term *illness experience* to Rolland's (1994) "human experience of individuals and families," believing human experience is implicit within the term *illness experience*.

The illness experience is distinguished and drawn forth within the family and between the family and health professionals through conversations, both social and therapeutic. In the situation of a man with diabetes, the conversation would shift to how he and other family members experience his illness: How much does diabetes affect his sexual relationship with his wife? What response of his wife to the diabetes has been the most helpful? A focus on such issues broadens the conversation within the family and between the family and health professional from the medical narrative to the illness narratives.

In our clinical work, we try to create a trusting environment for therapeutic conversations that invites open expression of family members' fears, anger, and sadness about their illness experiences. Robinson's (1994a) study, examining the process and outcomes of interventions within our clinical practice in the Family Nursing Unit, revealed that "the two major components of therapeutic change from the families' perspective are: creating the circumstances for change and moving beyond/overcoming problems" (p. 99). The clinicians' acts of bringing the family together and creating a sense of comfort and trust were the fundamental moves that enabled family members to convey their illness experiences. Providing the opportunity for each family member to express the impact of the illness on the family and, reciprocally, the influence of the family on the illness gives validation and voice to their experiences. This method is different from limiting or constraining family stories to topics of symptoms, medication, and physical treatment, that is, to stories of the chronic condition.

By providing a context for the sharing among family members of their illness experiences, intense emotions are legitimized. Kleinman (1988) proffered the idea that an inquiry into the meanings (beliefs) of illness is a journey into relationships. By inviting family members to share their illness narratives, which include stories of sickness and suffering, one allows them, as Arthur Frank (1994) has suggested, to reclaim their right to tell what are their own experiences and to reclaim a voice over and against the medical voice and a life beyond illness.

In our clinical work with families, our goal is to alleviate or heal emotional and physical suffering. One beginning effort to alleviate suffering is to acknowledge that suffering exists. Our aim is consistent with that of Janice Morse and Joy Johnson (1991), who suggested that the "goal of those involved in the illness experience is to decrease the suffering of the ill person or the shared suffering, thereby increasing well-being" (p. 315). We have found that a discourse of suffering frequently opens up a discourse of spirituality. During an initial interview with a family that included an adult daughter, her father who had been diagnosed with Alzheimer's disease, and his wife, the clinician (WLW) asked the daughter about her own family of procreation. A story regarding the death of her 16-year-old son in a snowmobiling accident quickly unfolded. When asked what helped her during that particularly difficult time of intense grieving, her ready response was "my faith." The shift to and emphasis on spirituality is frequently the most profound response to illness and suffering.

Positive responses and reduction in emotional and physical suffering have convinced us of the necessity to invite family members to tell their illness narratives. In our professional encounters with families, we move beyond social conversations about the illness to purposeful therapeutic conversations. We direct the conversation in a manner that we hope will give voice to the human experiences of suffering and symptoms as well as to the experiences of courage, hope, growth, and love.

Physicians are most interested in hearing the disease being spoken through the patient's words (Armstrong, 1984). Both medical narratives about the chronic condition and illness narratives, including stories of suffering, sickness, strength, spirituality, tenacity, and tenderness, are important. In our clinical experience, however, we are astounded that families seem conditioned primarily to relate stories of medications, diets, and symptoms when speaking within the health professional culture. Their inability or hesitancy to speak about their illness experiences powerfully attests to the need to provide opportunities to invite the illness narratives to be told in clinical work. The conceptualization of the illness experiences as focusing predominantly on symptoms has been extensively described in the literature as the "medical model"; a second conceptualization focuses on the person and considers illness behavior the challenge of the ill person to cope with or respond to the disease process (Morse & Johnson, 1991).

Listening to, witnessing, and documenting illness stories provide a powerful validation of an important human experience. Through the telling of the story, "the patient can interpret her own suffering [and we would add, strength]; the role of witness is to provide moral affirmation of the struggle to find that interpretation. Thus the patient's voice must be cultivated, not cut off" (Frank, 1994, p. 14).

Written accounts of illness narratives also give a legitimate voice to the possibility of including illness in one's life. These accounts not only affirm the writer but also validate countless others' experiences with illness. Significant contributions to the growing illness-narrative literature include Marvyl Loree Patton's (1994) *Guide-Lines and God-Lines for Facing Cancer*; Art Frank's (1991) *At the Will of the Body: Reflections on Illness*; Cheri Register's (1987) *Living with Chronic Illness: Days of Patience and Passion*; Norman Cousins's (1979) *Anatomy of an Illness as Perceived by the Patient*; and Michael Ignatieff's (1994) *Scar Tissue*.

As a way of bringing the two dominant narratives—medical and illness—together, an "illness constellation model" has been developed (Morse & Johnson, 1991). This model views illness as an experience that affects the sick person and his family and friends. The core variable in this model is the minimization of suffering for both the patient and his family and friends. Suffering *is* the illness experience, whether it is short and intense or prolonged and pervasive.

Health professionals are in a privileged position to hear and affirm illness narratives. By acknowledging illness narratives, we engage in the essential, ethical practice of recognizing the ill person as the "suffering other" (Frank, 1994). In our clinical practice, we also want to open possibilities, through our therapeutic conversations, for recognizing the ill person and other family members as the heroic other, the joyful other, the giving other, the receiving other, the compassionate other, the passionate other, and the strengthened other. We want to open space for a breadth of human experiences with illness to be spoken by each family member.

*Options for managing illness increase options for healing.*

Cultural beliefs that have arisen through interaction and eventual consensus between persons may influence how people manage illness. One striking example of the influence of a belief about the management of illness in our culture is the paradigm of control. When illness is experienced, there is frequently an accompanying North American cultural belief that it's bad to be out of control and good to be in control. Frequently, we attribute catching a cold to a belief that our lives are "out of control" and therefore we are susceptible to illness. Commonly heard phrases about illness are "my diabetes is out of control" or "I'm going to get my cholesterol levels under control." Individuals describe how they are going to "fight and conquer the cancer," which is another way of languaging the belief about gaining control over disease.

What if someone is not able to endure the experience of illness and loses control? In a fascinating qualitative study, Dewar and Morse (1995) examined the phenomenon of bearing a catastrophic health event related to illness or injury and described aspects of the health event that were considered by the respondents to be "unbearable." Examples of such characteristics attributed to interpersonal sources were not being believed, not being listened to, being treated as an object, and being made to feel a burden by the caregivers. Other examples of unbearable aspects were insensitive comments, disregard from significant others, burdening significant others, and unexpected and unanticipated problems.

When the experience of illness became unbearable, behavioral manifestations of losing control included verbal and physical aggression. "Losing it" was considered unacceptable behavior; family and institutional sanctions were frequently brought against these individuals. Unfortunately, the issue of losing control is problematic for ill persons and their families because of the emphasis and demand placed on being in control, even during times of extreme suffering.

This predominant cultural belief—that one must be in control—ignores the spiritual and subjective sides of the illness experience and limits options for healing. We have found it useful to offer the additional options of "living alongside illness" or "putting illness in its place" as other possible ways of dealing with illness, as opposed to the "control or eliminate" options. (See chapter 5 for clinical exemplars of these options.) Palliative care is a good example of an area of health care that helps people learn to "live alongside illness" rather than try to "fight" or "control" it.

Rolland (1994), in his discussion of family beliefs about control of illness, distinguishes three possibilities: internal control, external control by powerful others, and external control by change. He further suggests that it is not uncommon for a family to cling to a different set of beliefs about control when dealing with biological problems of the body than when dealing with "day-to-day" problems. A family member who would approach financial problems from a stance of internal control (I can begin to spend less and get control of things again) may shift to a stance of external control by powerful others when illness arises (I wonder why God chose me for this illness right now?).

Research supports the cultural norm of control. Taylor (1989) found that exaggerated beliefs about control were correlated with positive health outcomes, whereas lack of beliefs about control adversely affected health. A similar correlation was reported by investigators in the California Health Project (Ransom, Fisher, & Terry, 1992): a negative association between emotional health and a locus of control emphasizing chance or powerful others. Emotional health was positively associated with family religiousness and optimism. These authors also found that a belief in chance may result in loose connections with the health care system, whereas a strong belief in health care professionals may lead to either searches for cures or passivity in managing a disease. Patterson and Leonard (1994) found that high internal control led to more active management.

As clinicians, it is important to examine our own beliefs about the place of power and control in illness. Some health professionals (Ornish, 1993; Rolland, 1994) are strong proponents of assisting individuals and families to gain control, or mastery, over their illness. Dean Ornish (1993) has gone even further by suggesting that if one believes one has some control over one's life, one behaves differently by making choices instead of being the passive recipient of medical care or considering oneself the victim of bad luck or bad genes. He claimed that the outcome of such a belief about control is that one is more likely to make changes that will enhance the direct effects of mind on body and positively influence health.

Gilovich (1991) has taken a slightly different tack on the issue of control, suggesting that most people do not appreciate how much healing is done by our bodies themselves rather than by external controls such as doctors, drugs, or surgery. He suggested that this is why a worthless treatment can appear effective: When an intervention is followed by an improvement, the intervention's effectiveness stands out as an irresistible product of the person's experience, resulting in misplaced faith in treatments with no substantiation in terms of medical evidence of healing. Gilovich's stance comes from a positivist explanation of the world: that professionals' beliefs about healing are more accurate and reliable than patients' beliefs.

Another powerful example of health professionals' beliefs about the need for control is offered by David Felten (1993), who has identified nerve fibers that physically link the nervous system and the immune system. Using the example of terminal cancer patients who manage their own morphine injections versus those who receive them from a nurse or doctor, Felten observed that those who managed their medication generally had better pain control yet self-administered less medication. Less narcotic, better pain control? What makes the difference? Felten offered one hypothesis: that feeling in control results in an increased production of endorphins, which lessens the pain.

Because we are aware of all these professional and personal beliefs about being in control, being out of control, external control, and internal control, we have found it useful in our clinical work to ask persons what their preferred goal is. Would they like to control, submit to, overcome, or live alongside their illness? Simply asking this question invites a reflection on the issue of control and perhaps an awareness of greater options for control. We have found that asking these types of questions often increases a person's options about the issue of control and frequently provides a way to escape the predominant belief in our culture that the only way to manage an illness is to control it.

The notion of controlling an illness is intertwined with the belief about what needs to be healed. Proponents of both conventional and complementary healing approaches have strong ideas about how healing occurs. One dominant belief is that the treatment of illness involves the restoring of the balance of power, either by weakening the power of the disease or by strengthening the victim's power (McGuire & Kantor, 1987). An example of strengthening the victim's power is provided by the case of a woman receiving chemotherapy for treatment of colon cancer. When she was asked what her beliefs were about her healing, she stated that she believed that 50% of her healing was due to the medication (chemotherapy), 30% to what she and her friends and family were doing for her, 10% to interventions by nurses, and 10% to assistance by physicians. We have experienced that the very act of asking a question about beliefs about healing draws into the awareness of the person her own individual resources. One thing this woman purposely did to assist her healing was to diminish external negative influences. She stopped watching or listening to the news on television or radio. Her belief was, "I cannot worry about global things because I have to put my energies into healing myself. I only have so much energy, and it has to go into getting well." She was focused on strengthening her own power.

The option of living alongside illness seems to be a more "collaborative" and manageable option than controlling illness. With many illnesses, living alongside takes less energy and is probably more effective than trying to overcome or completely control an illness. The crucial issue here, we believe, is to present options to family members to help them decide how they would like to manage their illness. Perhaps the very act of presenting options about how to manage illness is itself one way of increasing an individual's control.

*Illness arises and is influenced by interference with fundamental emotional dynamics.*

Dossey (1993), Frank (1991), and Kushner (1981) all remind us that bad things can happen to good people and vice versa. Larry Dossey pointed out that in medical practice, physicians encounter "health reprobates" all the time: people who breach every rule of good health but do not become seriously ill. Frequently, clinicians explain this by saying, "It will catch up with them one day," "they must have good genes," or "they're just lucky." Another, interesting explanation that challenges the cause-and-effect belief is that a "time-displaced" event may be occurring (Dossey, 1993). So-called health reprobates may continually be reshaping their present condition before illness can result from their destructive behavior. The particular structure of such an individual may be offset by other variables such as loving conversations, prayer, a sense of well-being, and genuine satisfaction and contentment with one's life. Furthermore, some individuals experience horrible conversations, dissatisfaction with their lives, and poor health habits, but nothing happens to them. These situations invite health professionals to maintain their curiosity about what triggers illness and what makes symptoms and disease disappear, that is, what triggers healing.

According to Frank (1991), some diseases are hard-wired; they just happen. We concur with Frank that at times our bodies act up, break down, refuse to function, and get sick without ever consulting us. Our bodies are susceptible to genetic diseases and prone to infection. We also believe that many diseases arise from or are influenced by particular kinds of interactions in which families engage over the course of numerous years that interfere with fundamental emotional dynamics (Maturana, 1988a). Family members respond to such interference based on their own biopsychosocial–spiritual structures, which consist of their own unique genetic makeup (phylogenetic history) and history of interactions or past structural changes (ontogenetic history). If someone with a genetic predisposition to a particular disease has been involved for numerous years with conversations containing criticisms and accusations (see chapter 3), this combination may trigger a particular disease to occur. We emphasize, however, that we do not concur with representatives of health movements who purport that thinking more positively or being more hopeful can prevent or relieve illness. These ideas put undue pressure on ill people and draw forth immense guilt when things go wrong despite efforts to be positive.

Larry Dossey (1993) has suggested that we need to treat each other more as we treat animals or plants when they get sick. He reminds us that it is not a dog's "fault" that it develops hip dysplasia, and a cat is not innately defective because it is stricken with leukemia. The emergence of disease is not a sign of ethical, moral, or spiritual weakness. But it could be a sign that there has been interference with fundamental emotional dynamics.

Humberto Maturana (1988a) offered the idea that the basic emotion for health and healing is love: "The only thing that I know is that love is a fundamental emotion in human beings" (p. 9). Maturana (1988a) further proposed that "most human diseases, most human suffering arises from interference with these fundamental emotions" (p. 9). *Love* is defined as the ability to open space for the existence of another or acceptance of the other beside us in daily living (Maturana & Varela, 1992). Love is a biological dynamic with deep roots.

The sixteenth-century physician Paracelsus said that "the main reason for healing is love"; it has been said further that "the only reason for healing is love" (Dossey, 1993, p. 115). The importance of love in the healing process is a complex notion that need not be trivialized by health professionals. Neither should sick people feel guilty in the name of love for not being well. It is instead important to appreciate the profound connection between emotions (particularly love) and biology and their influence on each other.

The power of the presence or absence of love to change biology is legendary; it is built into folklore, country and western songs, everyday experience, and even research. Medalie and Goldbourt (1976) surveyed 10,000 men with heart disease and found a 50% reduction in the frequency of chest pain (angina) in men who perceived their wives as supportive and loving. John Gottman (1994a), who is renowned for his marital interaction research, found that women in ailing marriages experienced physiological arousal and subsequent illness when their husbands showed a pattern of stonewalling and withdrawal from marital conflict. Gottman also found that as marital interaction became aversive, the cascade of distance, isolation, and loneliness had a negative effect on the husbands' health.

In our own clinical work with families, we have been amazed at how physical and emotional symptoms diminish or disappear when familial conflict is reduced and when powerful loving emotions return. We believe that illness often appears simply to "strike" because we cannot see or know all that may have led up to its appearance. If we were able to peer into one another's organs or cells throughout our lifetimes, we could monitor the effects of our relationships and life experiences on the functioning of our organs and cells. Although we agree that disease can "just happen," we wonder if we would notice organs or cells malfunctioning when the emotional dynamics in our relationships were disturbed. Could a change in our biology be observed if we were able to open space to the existence of another, that is, if we were able to love? And what changes would be noted if we reciprocally experienced love from another?

One clinical family sought help to resolve long-standing marital conflict and resentment. The couple reported trying a marital separation and having several previous, unsatisfactory experiences with marital counseling in their attempts to resolve their conflict. The wife was suffering with terminal cancer and wanted to resolve these marital issues with her husband before she died. We wondered if she would be free to die following resolution of the emotional conflict and, therefore, wondered about the pace of therapy. If the couple resolved things quickly, would she die quickly? The wife's question to the clinician summarized her dilemma well: "Why did a relationship that started out so precious become so very destructive?" We saw this couple three times over 3 weeks. By the third session, the couple were reporting less conflict and increased ability to show caring to each other. The wife commented, "I feel like it's been very special. . . . He's made a much bigger effort to listen." The wife died shortly after the third session. Did her husband's healing words "heal" her and set her free? The husband was seen alone a month later and reported that his wife had died peacefully. He reported they had been able to forgive each other and had begun to write a new story for their relationship.

Another example of a significant change in the physical and emotional suffering of a family occurred with Research Family 1. The family consisted of elderly parents and their 34-year-old son experiencing multiple sclerosis (MS). The parents had moved from eastern to western Canada to help care for their son in his home. The parents described much tension in the home, which they attributed to their own caregiver burden and lack of respite. They believed they needed their son's permission and initiation to take a break.

In her efforts to be helpful to the family, the clinician (LMW) encouraged all family members to tell their illness narratives. Specifically, she invited each family member to describe his or her story of sickness and suffering. Their narratives unfolded as the clinician conducted a purposeful inquiry through the asking of interventive questions such as the following: What has been the biggest surprise about your illness? Has any good come out of this illness? Do you have more influence over your illness, or does your illness have more influence over you? The clinician also highlighted the interactional relationship between the illness and the family, that is, the effect of the illness on the family and the influence of the family on the illness. During the conversation, the son drew an important distinction between doing things "in spite of" the illness and "having influence over" the illness.

The clinician's purposeful drawing forth and distinguishing of the illness narratives in this family paved the way for a heart-to-heart conversation about the son's emotional suffering with MS. He had never spoken of his suffering to his parents. By acknowledging and thereby diminishing the emotional suffering of both parents and son, a context was created wherein all family members were able to talk openly about their need for family members to have a vacation from each other. The outcome was positive: respite for the parents *and* the son and reduced tensions and improved health for all family members. The MS was positively influenced by the occurrence of more loving interactions in the family members' conversations. Our primary goal as clinicians, therefore, is to bring forth conversations—conversations of affirmation and affection as well as conversations of growth and change—that invite new or renewed beliefs about problems, persons, and relationships.

## CONCLUSION

This chapter has presented our beliefs about families and illness. We believe family members are the experts on their illness experiences, whereas we clinicians have expertise to offer for the managing of illness. The intertwining of these areas of expertise enables change to occur. We view families as strength-laden even in the face of horrendous illness experiences. We strongly believe that how families experience illness depends on the beliefs they embrace more than the disease itself. In the same way, the beliefs of health professionals about families and illness profoundly affect how we approach, engage, and assist families in the healing process.

# CHAPTER 3

# Beliefs About Therapeutic Change and Clinicians

The world will be different only if we live differently.
HUMBERTO MATURANA AND FRANCISCO VARELA

OUR BELIEFS ABOUT therapeutic change and clinicians are fundamental to what we do in our clinical work with families, as well
as when we do it, how we do it, and perhaps even where we do
it. To have clinicians complete the sentence stem "change occurs . . ."
opens a window into their clinical practices. In this chapter, we present
our worldview, which influences how we view therapeutic change and
clinicians; theoretical underpinnings for therapeutic change, which
have implications for the therapeutic stance of clinicians; and guiding
principles concerning therapeutic change and clinicians. In this chapter,
therefore, we open the windows and doors on our clinical practice.

Our beliefs about change influence our day-to-day experiences and
vice versa. Our lives are filled with experiences that invite, encourage,
request, and often require that we change our names, addresses,
weight, clothes, minds, outlook, and sometimes our hearts. Just like
beauty, change is in the eye of the beholder. We not only observe each
other's and our own change, we judge and critique it. If there is too
much change, too frequently, one is judged as fickle; if there is too little
change, too infrequently, one is "rigid." But always we need to ask—too
much or too little, too frequently or too infrequently, according to
whose objective reality?

Beliefs about change abound and, therefore, naturally differ. Some observe that change is not desired or is a hopeless pursuit: "Only a wet baby likes change," teases the bumper sticker. "The more things change, the more they stay the same" is a French proverb. A cartoon shows a husband on the doorstep while his wife says, "The tie is different, the pants are different, the shirt is different. Just because everything's different doesn't mean anything's changed."

When we report the same complaint to a friend year after year; when we have the same resolutions every New Year's Eve; when the bathroom scales obnoxiously declare we are still 15 pounds overweight; when the waiting rooms of outpatient mental health clinics are filled with the same patients week in and week out—we may wonder if there is such a thing as *change*. Yet our clinical experience tells us that people desire change, they do change, and more important, change is always occurring.

In almost all professions, change is measured, named, invited, and constrained. From archaeologists to dermatologists, from spelunkers to seismologists, from geologists to golfers, change is part of professional pursuits. As family clinicians, we desire and are in awe of change. It is not ironic that we are amazed at something that is always occurring, that is inevitable. Sunrises, sunsets, births, deaths, and change are things that are spectacular yet inevitable. We know they happen. Yet the inevitability does not dilute the sense of freshness with each occurrence.

Family clinicians are fascinated by change, devoted to uncovering and discovering change, and committed to facilitating family members' efforts to uncover and discover the changes they are seeking to decrease their suffering and increase their passion for living together. Our beliefs about change influence our beliefs about the behavior of clinicians and vice versa. Both categories of beliefs influence our clinical efforts and offerings to families experiencing difficulties with health problems. To understand our beliefs about therapeutic change and about the therapeutic stance of clinicians more fully, however, one needs to understand the worldview that facilitates our clinical practice.

## WORLDVIEW: OBJECTIVITY-IN-PARENTHESES

The world everyone sees is not *the* world but *a* world which
we bring forth with others.
HUMBERTO MATURANA AND FRANCISCO VARELA

We believe that people bring forth their realities through interacting with the world and with others. Our views are dependent on our current biopsychosocial–spiritual structures, which arise from the life we are living, that is, from the social, cultural, and interpersonal contexts within which we find ourselves. We believe that because of this process, there are multiple realities in and of "the world."

For those aware of postmodern culture or immersed in constructivism, it seems a natural stance and almost axiomatic to make statements such as the following: The observer is part of what is observed; the world is constructed through language; and communication is the ongoing construction of realities by social interaction among people (Gergen, 1985; Reiss, 1981). The notion of multiple realities was explicated by Ludwig Wittgenstein (von Wright & Abscombe, 1979) and the impossibility of directly contacting reality was preferred by Kant in 1855 (Jahn & Dunne, 1987). Gregory Bateson (1972) also struggled with the issue of reality in a conversation with his daughter, Catherine:

> F: There are scientists who try to talk that way, and it's becoming quite fashionable. They say it is more objective. . . .
> D: What does "objective" mean?
> F: Well. It means that you look very hard at those things which you choose to look at.
> D: That sounds right. But how do the objective people choose which things they will be objective about?
> F: Well. They choose those things about which it is easy to be objective.
> D: You mean easy for them?
> F: Yes.
> D: But how do they *know* that those are the easy things?
> F: I suppose they try different things and find out by experience.
> D: So it's a subjective choice?
> F: Oh yes. All experience is subjective. (p. 47)

Von Glaserfeld offered a view of radical constructivism, saying that it was "less imaginative and more pragmatic. It does not deny an ontological 'reality'—it merely denies the human experiencer the possibility of acquiring a true representation of it" (Segal, 1986, p. 86). It was the "new biologists," however, sometimes called "epistemological biologists" Maturana and Varela (Maturana, 1970; Maturana & Varela, 1992; Varela, 1979), who offered the stance that the nervous system is a closed system and therefore cannot know about "external reality in any direct manner" (Mince, 1992, p. 327). Maturana proclaimed, "I explicitly acknowledge the biological impossibility of making any statement about an objective reality" (Simon, 1985, p. 37). That statement, along with the following observation, is fundamental to his biological explanation of explanations: "Everything said is said by an observer to another observer that could be him- or herself" (Maturana, 1988b, p. 27).

As we discussed in chapter 1, our views have been influenced by Maturana's (1988b) distinction between two explanatory paths of listening for explanations: (a) the path of objectivity-without-parentheses and (b) the path of objectivity-in-parentheses. According to Maturana (1992, November), "explanations are matters of human relations. Experience is not the problem in human relations. The explanation of the experience is the problem." The path of objectivity-without-parentheses leads one to make claims about *one* objective reality that is valid independent of oneself as the observer. The path of objectivity-in-parentheses leads one to include oneself as observer and participant in what is being observed and continually to ask oneself, "What do I do to claim that such and such is the case?" Although others have classified Maturana as a constructivist (Efran, Lukens, & Lukens, 1988), on one occasion he termed himself "something much more terrible: 'a bring-forthist'" (Maturana, 1988a). Later, however (Maturana, 1992, May), his explanation about why he was neither a constructivist nor a bring-forthist revealed his passion about responsibility: "I want to remain aware that existence depends on what the observer does."

These two paths of explanation have implications for personal responsibility. Within the path of objectivity-without-parentheses, one's actions are "always acts of irresponsibility because one attributes actions to someone else" (Maturana, 1992, November). Within the path of objectivity-in-parentheses, one's actions are intrinsically one's own responsibility. Operating from a position of objectivity-in-parentheses "always contributes to acts of responsibility" (Maturana, 1992, November).

We have found in working with families experiencing difficulties with health problems that it is less than therapeutic to operate from a stance of "objectivity," or objectivity-without-parentheses. The beliefs undergirding an "objective" stance include "what I see is reality" and "there is one correct view and I have it!" These beliefs do not invite change. They invite blame and "emotional violence" according to Maturana's (1992, November) definition that "violence is holding an idea to be true such that another's idea is untrue and must change." From the "objectivist" view, "a system and its components have a constancy and a stability that is independent of the observer that brings them forth" (Mendez, Coddou, & Maturana, 1988, p. 154). The DSM-IV (American Psychiatric Association, 1994), nursing diagnoses, emotional conflict, and pride are some of the products of an "objective" view of reality. Lynn Hoffman-Hennessy has strongly denounced the harm done by normative models of psychotherapy with their all-too-ready diagnoses and treatment plans (Hoffman-Hennessy & Davis, 1993). When clinicians adopt an "objectivist" view, they bring forth pathology and suppress healing. We concur with Salamon, Grevelius, and Andersson (1993) that "iatrogenic injury," the exacerbation of disabling psychiatric symptoms, springs from the many guilt-inducing explanations "and insulting suggestions advanced in the course of mental health practice. Under the weight of such explanations and suggestions, innate healing powers are stifled or paralysed" (p. 330).

We believe that possibilities are opened up for change when a positivist–objectivist stance is given up. A stance of objectivity-in-parentheses, hereafter written as (objectivity), is a therapeutic stance because it allows an appreciation of both "paths of explanations": the path of "objectivity" and the path of (objectivity). From (objectivity), other individuals are experienced as having legitimate views; respect and responsibility follow.

The beliefs fitting with a stance of (objectivity) include "I and the other person with whom I am interacting bring forth the world in our interaction with it" and "there are many equally legitimate views, although they are not equally desirable or pleasant to live in." Maturana (1988a) has stated that "one can live in hell or in heaven depending on what world one is bringing forth in coexistence with others." Just as therapeutic curiosity about and respect for others and their views are among the products of (objectivity), so is love! According to Maturana (1992, November), love is a fundamental emotion in human beings. Love is the domain of actions that bring forth another as a legitimate other in coexistence with oneself. Love is "opening space for the existence of another" (Maturana, 1992, November). Maturana and Varela (1992) stated the following:

> If we know that our world is necessarily the world we bring forth with others, every time we are in conflict with another human being with whom we want to remain in coexistence, we cannot affirm what for us is certain (an absolute truth) because that would negate the other person. If we want to coexist with the other person, we must see that his certainty—however undesirable it may seem to us—is as legitimate and valid as our own because, like our own, that certainty expresses his conservation of structural coupling in a domain of existence—however undesirable it may seem to us. (p. 245)

When clinicians are able to maintain an (objectivity) stance, they are increasingly able to invite family members to resist the sin of certainty.

An example of how clinicians can draw forth experiences for family members in order to resist the temptation of certainty is the following: A couple presented with marital conflict around mother-in-law issues. The husband–son was so affected by the conflict that he became physically ill before and after his mother's visits to the couple's home. During the therapy session each spouse clung to his and her "objectivist" view of the situation. The clinician (WLW) invited the husband to sit behind the mirror with the team while she had a conversation with the wife. After offering the wife Maturana's definitions of love and emotional violence, the conversation continued:

WLW: You've said that you love this man. You've said several times to us behind the mirror, "If you're not married, find a man like this!" haven't you?

WIFE: Yes.

WLW: If you say love is opening space for Fred's ideas, what idea of Fred's do you want to open your heart to? Which one of Fred's ideas, that he has either said out loud or that he has said through his suffering? You've said, "Before his Mom and I have to be together, this man that I love, this man that loves me and that loves his mother—talk about divided loyalties—this man gets sick hours before and is sick after. If you say, "I want to open space for Fred and for his ideas . . . "

WIFE: I guess I would just [*pause*] try and see his family and his mother in that situation from his point of view.

WLW: Wow!

WIFE: And try to understand the loyalty he feels.

WLW: I love the way you say that. What do you think you might come to appreciate or discover about his family that would be newsworthy news for Fred to hear?

WIFE: I know through Fred's eyes—and this could be *true* too—that the things his mother says are motivated through love.

WLW: So Fred would say, "Whatever my Mom does, put a great big heart around it and you've got it." Is that it?

WIFE: Yes, that's it!

WLW: If you were able to experiment with this for 2 weeks and hear everything that his mother says in that way, what would it do for yours and Fred's relationship?

WIFE: Improve it.

WLW: And for Fred's suffering?

WIFE: I don't think he'll feel as bad. I think it would relieve a lot of stress.

WLW: Did you notice your breathing right then? You let out a big sigh.

WIFE: Of relief.

WLW: What can Fred do that will allow you to keep this perspective of "okay, everything my mother-in-law says is motivated by love"? I love your words.

WIFE: Perhaps he could say something other than "I don't know."

WLW: I don't know how to tell you . . . ?

The phone rang at that moment, and the husband called in to say to the wife, "I *do* know that I love you." The wife's openness to her husband's legitimate, even "true," view allowed him to open his mouth and say the words she had been waiting and needing to hear. As each reflected on the circumstances of the other, love arose. The mutual negation, or conflict, was over. Maturana's definition of love had opened space for this husband and wife to move to an (objectivity) view of their worlds and to commence cocreating "new worlds."

Having offered the reader our worldview of (objectivity), we next present two theoretical underpinnings for change. These underpinnings are derived from Maturana and Varela's (1992) biology of knowing and have implications for the therapeutic stance of clinicians.

## THEORETICAL UNDERPINNINGS FOR THERAPEUTIC CHANGE

### UNDERPINNING 1: CHANGE IS DETERMINED BY STRUCTURE

We believe that the changes that occur in a living system are governed by the present structure of that system. However, we have found that when clinicians initially encounter the concept of "structural determinism"—that the structure of an organism determines every change it will undergo (Maturana & Varela, 1992)—the reactions vary from frustration to re-cognition. These varied reactions beautifully demonstrate the concept of structural determinism, because if change were not determined by structure, all clinicians would respond in exactly the same way to the same "stimulus." It is not the information that specifies how a system will "respond" but rather the system itself.

In their seminal paper, "What the Frog's Eye Tells the Frog's Brain," Lettvin, Maturana, McCulloch, and Pitts (McCulloch, 1988) showed that the retina transforms, rather than transmits, the external image. Thus, perception is not a picture of the world coming in and recording on the frog's brain; rather, it is the frog's structure that determines what it sees.

Perhaps we should amend the words of one of Simon and Garfunkel's songs: "A man hears what he wants to hear and disregards the rest." We believe instead that "a man hears what he is currently structurally able to hear and doesn't know (is not able to regard) that he is disregarding the rest." Although less lyrical, it fits our view of perception influenced by Maturana and Varela's (1992) ideas that "we do not see *that* we do not see" (p. 19) and "we do not see *what* we do not see, and what we do not see does not exist" (p. 242).

These ideas are illustrated by the experience of one of our graduate students, who brought into class the storybook of "Little Red Riding Hood" to use as an introduction to his presentation on White and Epston's (1990) narrative therapy. He read the story aloud from the book. Each time he came to the words *Little Red Riding Hood*, he saw and read them as *Little Red Rodding Hood*. When he finished reading the story, his classmates asked him why he had said the words *Rodding Hood* instead of *Riding Hood*. When they told him the name of the story was "Little Red Riding Hood," he did not believe them until he looked and saw—*that* he had not seen before and *what* he had not seen before.

The idea of structural determinism needs to be connected with Maturana's concepts of *plasticity* and *structural coupling*. The static-sounding notion of structural determinism can even sound like "predeterminism" if one is operating from an "objective" stance; however, it is heard differently when one considers the structural coupling (discussed in a later section) and the plasticity of the systems involved. *Plasticity* refers to the ability of an organism to make constant changes through its interactions with itself, its environment, and other structurally plastic systems (Leyland, 1988). This is no dismal, static view of change. It is vibrant, ever changing, and highly respectful, based on the view that "although the structure of the system determines how it will 'react' to a particular disturbance at a given instant, that interaction, in turn, leads to structural change which will alter the future behavior of the system" (Leyland, 1988, p. 362).

Although we believe that changes that occur in a living system are governed by the structure of that system, we also believe that the systems with which we interact as clinicians are highly complex and, therefore, highly structurally plastic, or malleable, and richly coupled with other highly complex, structurally plastic systems. We believe that changes in a living system arise from the system's "internal structural dynamics and from the structural changes triggered in it through its interactions, or from the interplay of both" (Mendez et al., 1988, p. 155). Maturana distinguishes between a one-celled organism that "doesn't care and doesn't exist in language" and human interaction. He said, "Never compare a human organization with an organism, because people care and exist in language" (Maturana, 1992, November).

We concur with his admonition and would add one of our own that has arisen through our recurrent interactions with families experiencing difficulties with health problems: Do not neglect the spiritual structure. Change within families is dependent on the biological *and* spiritual structures of family members. We would amend the opening paragraph of this section to read: We believe that the changes that occur in a family are governed by the present biological, psychosocial, and spiritual structures of family members, the very structures that have been triggered to change through previous perturbing interactions and structural coupling with their environment.

## UNDERPINNING 2: CHANGE INVOLVES STRUCTURAL COUPLING AND CHANGES IN STRUCTURES

We believe that change involves changes in the biopsychosocial–spiritual structures of the individual family members and the clinician. Change occurs as the structures of the clinician and the family members are triggered to change through the mutual perturbations arising from their recurrent interactions with each other, that is, through structural coupling. When family members and the clinician encounter each other, the possibility for structural coupling exists (Maturana, 1988a).

*Structural coupling* is a term that describes the process through which the structural changes in living systems occur. Structural coupling involves two unities coming together in a medium. Through structural coupling, two distinct entities become less different from each other. "We speak of structural coupling whenever there is a history of recurrent interactions leading to the structural congruence between two (or more) systems" (Maturana & Varela, 1992, p. 75).

When two distinct entities interact, each interaction triggers structural changes in both, and of course, the changes triggered are structurally dependent. Mutual triggering of structural changes (mutual perturbations) lead to increasing structural congruence. They "fit" together. They are structurally coupled, like feet and shoes, or like two stones rubbed together, which increasingly "fit," changing congruently, changing in concert with the other (Maturana, 1988b). These structural changes can occur in the domain of positive or negative interactions (Maturana, 1988a).

Are parents' cautions of "I don't want you hanging out with that gang" expressions of fear of structural coupling and structural changes? Are fears that "you'll become just like them" based on this biological principle? Do congruent changes arising from recurrent interactions explain why friends begin dressing alike and talking alike? Could structural coupling and structural changes explain why couples over time often look alike? Do we grow to look like those we love? Is structural coupling the way we become more and more like those we admire and honor? Do we, through our recurrent interactions with someone, not only start *looking like* them, but start *seeing like* them? Our structure determines what we see. And what has influenced that structure? Our interaction with others and the environment.

Families talk about these structural changes in terms such as, "I'm seeing things differently these days" or "his heart has softened toward our son." Structural changes involve actual biopsychosocial–spiritual changes. Eyes change, hearts change, and cells change through structural coupling. Change involves transformation: structural change, change at the cellular level, and change at the "soulular" level.

We need to be mindful of our structural coupling and structural changes in our clinical work with families. Are we able to acknowledge how family members are influencing us in the process of our work with them? How are family members triggering perturbations in us in the process of our triggering of perturbations in them? With the worldview of (objectivity) in mind and an understanding of the two theoretical underpinnings that greatly influence our beliefs about change and thus have implications for our beliefs about clinicians, we set forth in the following section our beliefs about therapeutic change.

## BELIEFS ABOUT THERAPEUTIC CHANGE

Our beliefs about change have changed. How did this change occur? Through years of clinical practice and clinical research (most recently, the hermeneutic analysis of our clinical practice), we have coevolved our current beliefs about change. What we offer at this point are four core beliefs that presently guide our approach to change. These beliefs that serve as guiding principles for therapeutic change are illustrated in table 3.1.

*Therapeutic change occurs as the belief that is at the heart of the matter is distinguished, challenged, or solidified.*

> As a man thinketh in his heart, so is he.
> PROVERBS 23:7 (AV)

Ancient Hebrew tradition held that the heart could think. It is the heart-generated and heartfelt thoughts, those affectively saturated cognitions, those beliefs of the heart—even those beliefs in one's deepest

TABLE 3.1

**Beliefs About Therapeutic Change**

Therapeutic change occurs as the belief that is at the heart of the matter is distinguished, challenged, or solidified

Therapeutic change occurs through a fit between the therapeutic offerings of the clinician and the biopsychosocial–spiritual structures of family members

Change is inevitable, but the direction and pace of therapeutic change are unpredictable

Therapeutic change needs to be distinguished and languaged

---

heart of hearts—that we are interested in distinguishing, challenging, or solidifying. These are the beliefs that matter: the beliefs of the heart that are at the heart of the problem. These are the beliefs that provide the greatest leverage for change.

Families have taught us that *it is the belief about the problem that is the problem*. If a family is experiencing cancer, it is their beliefs about the cancer—where it came from, implications for the family's future, what treatment will be best—that invite difficulties, *not* the cancer itself. In our clinical research, we have learned from families that beliefs have a pivotal, profound, and palpable influence on families' experiences with illness and other problems.

Families have beliefs about many things, but our clinical exploration is a purposeful inquiry about their beliefs about their health problem. Within this exploration, we are seeking the belief that is at the heart of the matter: the belief at the core of the problem with which family members are suffering.

The belief that is at the heart of the matter is the belief that perpetuates and exacerbates the problem or solution: the belief that constrains or facilitates solutions. Just as there are questions that clinicians can ask family members to begin to distinguish a belief at the heart of the matter, WLW formulated the following questions for clinicians to ask themselves to begin hypothesizing about the core belief:

• How are the belief and the problem or solution connected?
• How does the belief perpetuate the problem or solution?
• How does the problem or solution perpetuate the belief?
• What does the belief invite the system (family members) to do?
• What does the belief constrain the system from doing?
• How does the system invite the belief?
• What belief do all or several family members hold?
• How do family members believe differently?

- What belief invites the problematic interaction between family members?
- What belief underlies that belief?

To introduce students to the idea of beliefs that matter, we ask them to think of a family-of-origin motto, slogan, or saying. We ask them to identify the belief in that motto and to write about how that belief still influences their life today, personally or professionally. One favorite family-of-origin saying was "the work of the world is done by people who don't feel well." The belief is that good people who don't feel well still get their work done. How may that belief influence the person's life? He may not be exquisitely attuned to his body and may work right through serious, even life-threatening, illness. Or he may rarely get ill because illness is not an excuse for not working. A problem may arise when that person becomes so ill that he cannot work. Now what happens to the belief that "good people who don't feel well still get their work done"? In the face of a life-threatening illness, when work is impossible, does this mean "I am not a good person because I cannot get my work done"? Is the view of oneself undermined rather than sustained at this point? Does this belief about work and illness stop working *for* the person and start working *against* him at this point? Does it shift from being facilitative to being constraining, even generating a problem?

How do we bring forth core beliefs, those beliefs at the heart of the matter? How do we distinguish them in order to challenge or solidify them, depending on whether they constrain or facilitate solutions to the problem? We agree with Peggy Papp (1983), who proposed that beliefs can be deduced by listening to the family members' "metaphorical language, tracking behavioral sequences, and picking up key attitudinal statements such as, 'I knew all these things about him when I married him, but I thought the love of a good woman would cure him'" (p. 15). Generally we agree that beliefs "cannot be arrived at through direct questioning but must be deduced" (p. 15). However, family members' answers to the "one question question" (Wright, 1989) may give a beginning hint of what the belief at the heart of the matter may be or may be related to. Our experience is also that family members are sometimes more ready to think about and reflect on their beliefs than we have heretofore given them credit for. Questions such as the following may invite reflections on beliefs:

- What have you come to believe about your son through our session today?
- What belief about yourself, your spouse, or your marriage will allow you to make the necessary changes you so desire?

- Are you the kind of man who believes . . . ?
- Some people in your situation would believe . . . . Does that fit for you?

We use a both–and approach when distinguishing the belief at the heart of the matter. Sometimes we need to begin to deduce information from statements made in a session. For example, a husband says to his wife in an emotionally explosive tone, "If she doesn't get off her fat butt, she is going to have problems with her diabetes and die." The belief at the heart of the matter may be, "If I shame her, she will change," or it may be, "I worry she will die and I will be left alone." Further exploration and embellishing of the core belief at the heart of the matter—the core of the marital conflict—needs to follow this palpable invitation from the husband (see chapter 5).

At other times we find that people initiate the offering of a core belief. A husband and wife were talking about the problems in their recent marriage. The husband had been previously widowed, and the wife, divorced. Recently the wife had experienced severe depression and had attempted suicide. As a graduate student of WLW was exploring the impact of grief and loss on this couple, he used a metaphor related to grief and then spontaneously shared a core belief of his own, which shored up the belief at the heart of the matter for the wife:

WIFE: [*speaking about efforts with stepchildren*] I've tried as hard as I would like someone to try with my own children.

GRADUATE STUDENT: You've been under the influence of depression recently. How does that make you feel when you say, "I've tried as hard as I would like someone to try"?

WIFE: It makes me feel really good.

GRADUATE STUDENT: Forty years down the road, could your epitaph be, "Here lies a woman who tried as hard as she would like other people to try"?

HUSBAND: Yes, and that would apply to how she tries with our marriage too.

GRADUATE STUDENT: I have a belief about people who try. Would you like to know what it is?

WIFE: Yes.

GRADUATE STUDENT: I have a really hard time—I'm getting emotional [*long pause*]—when I try and things don't work out. That's, for me, unfair. But I've come to believe that things work out for people when you don't stop trying. I take hope in that. I cling to that belief.

Spontaneous affection from the husband toward the wife occurred as the student offered his belief at the heart of the matter, which was connected to the suffering of the wife. This was a turning point in the session. A heart-to-heart conversation between the husband and wife followed.

Perpetual hypothesizing about the core belief transpires throughout a session as the clinician listens for cues and clues. This is a time of insatiable curiosity, which seeks specifics and brings forth the core belief. The therapeutic move of "bringing the belief to life" came to life for us through hermeneutic interpretation of a first session with Research Family 5. The clinician (LMW) was creating the context for change with a couple in which the husband had experienced two coronaries. The presenting problem had not yet been distinguished. LMW was exploring the beliefs about the prognosis and about how family members could influence the illness:

LMW: Well, speaking about your life—if I can be so blunt—what have they told you about the future for yourself in terms of future heart attacks?

Through the conversation, LMW catches hold of the husband's belief that he can prevent further attacks. She brings the belief to life and deepens it:

LMW: Are you a man that believes this? You are doing a lot of things to prevent another attack. So do you believe . . . ?

When the husband confirmed that he did believe his efforts could prevent a future coronary, instead of just rejoicing by saying "it's a wonderful belief," LMW shored up the husband's belief by offering a contrasting view:

LMW: I've met some people that have had a coronary and they don't believe that if they exercise and do these things that it will make a difference.

This counterposition invited the husband to elaborate the story of his former lifestyle, pointing out why he now believed as he did. His belief in his belief was deepened through this process. The husband's belief came to life, opening the door to his wife's belief, which was similar. She also believed she could influence her husband's future attacks. But her belief at the heart of the matter was that she could trigger an attack by bringing up stressful topics:

JULIE: If we would fight or if I would create a stressful situation, he would get stress pain and then I would feel guilty as all get out.

Her belief originated from being told by nurses not to visit her husband in the hospital if she could not keep her composure. When LMW asked her if she believed that keeping all that stress to herself could trigger a coronary for herself, the wife replied as follows:

JULIE: Yes. My dad died of a coronary. I sat at my mother's bedside when she had two heart attacks; she had one in our home. And my brother had a heart attack this summer. So I believe it a lot!

The wife believed that the behavior that was lifesaving for her husband—not talking about stressful things—was life threatening for herself: that keeping the stress inside could trigger a coronary for herself. The belief at the heart of the heart attacks, past and potential, was the belief at the heart of the marital conflict. The core belief had been distinguished and brought to life, and it could now be challenged, modified, or altered (Wright, Bell, Watson, & Tapp, 1995).

When we are able to distinguish the belief at the heart of the matter, opportunities for change are opened up. How do you know when you are getting close to the belief at the heart of the matter? How can you tell when you are on the core belief? Experience has taught us that affective and physiological arousal are indicators that we are getting close. The affective–physiological arousal can be on the part of family members, the clinician, or both. Affective leakage—analogic and paralinguistic showings of emotion such as tears, raised voice, or long silences—can point to the proximity of a bedrock belief. It would be an interesting research project to check heart rates, breathing rates, and hormonal secretions when asking questions or offering ideas that distinguish the core belief. As constraining beliefs are challenged and more facilitative beliefs are solidified, how do you measure change at the cellular and "soulular" level? How do you measure a change of heart?

When we identify a core belief with family members, we want to make it real; we want to distinguish it. When LMW met with Research Family 1, the family in which the son was experiencing MS, she held the family members' attention when the belief at the heart of the matter was distinguished, before moving on: "No, wait. This is important. Do you believe him?" This, of course, is a judgment call by the clinician. The father and mother were then able to explore further their belief that they needed to have their son give them permission to take a holiday from caregiving.

A core belief at the heart of the matter may include divergent beliefs about the etiology of the illness. This was the case with the couple described in our article "Osteophytes and Marital Fights" (Watson, Bell, & Wright, 1992). The husband's belief that his back pain was iatrogenically induced was vigorously countered by his wife's belief that the cause of the osteophytes was irrelevant. The spiraling symmetry in beliefs about the etiology of the illness was key to the exacerbation in the chronic pain both in the husband's back and in the couple's marriage.

Accessing the core belief (or beliefs) at the heart of the matter provides a glimpse of the internal structures of the family members. Beliefs are reflections of a person's structure; therefore, we believe a change in belief corresponds with a change in structure. Our clinical efforts are focused on challenging core beliefs at the heart of the matter once they are distinguished.

Maturana and Varela (1992) ended their book *The Tree of Knowledge* with a story of island people who do not know how to swim and sail. When a student on the island approaches someone saying that he wants to learn to swim to another land but must take his ton of cabbages with him, he is told that the cabbages will prevent him from swimming.

> (STUDENT): Then I can't learn how to swim. You call my cabbages weight. I call them my basic food.
> (ISLANDER WHO KNOWS HOW TO SWIM): Suppose this were an allegory and, instead of talking about cabbages we talked about fixed ideas, presuppositions, or certainties? (p. 250)

We believe that people's constraining beliefs are the cabbages they want to take with them as they learn to swim to a new land. The challenge of the clinician is to distinguish which beliefs are cabbages and which may be floats or buoys: beliefs that would assist with the swimming rather than constrain it. Chapter 5 offers further ideas on how to distinguish constraining beliefs; chapter 6 offers ideas on how to challenge or alter those beliefs; and chapter 7 provides our ideas on how to solidify facilitative beliefs: how to buoy up the buoys.

*Therapeutic change occurs through a fit between the therapeutic offerings of the clinician and the biopsychosocial–spiritual structures of family members.*

The concept of "fit" arises from the theoretical underpinnings that change is structurally determined and that change involves structural coupling and a change in structure. It is the family member's structure, not the clinician's therapeutic offering, that determines whether the clinical move is experienced as a perturbation that triggers change or not. Structural coupling between the clinician and the client can increase the possibility that the offering will be selected. However, what the structural changes will be are unknown (see Belief in the next section concerning change).

The concept of fit also meshes with the guiding principle that the clinician is not a change agent (see p. 96) but rather is one who, among other things, creates a context for change (see chapter 4). Our clinical experience is that family members who *do* respond to particular therapeutic offerings do so because of the fit between their current biopsychosocial–spiritual structures and the therapeutic intervention. In this instance, there is a fit and the intervention becomes a perturbation.

An awareness of fit moves the clinician in the direction of therapeutic love and therapeutic uncertainty (Tomm, 1990). Karl Tomm's terms *therapeutic love* and *therapeutic violence* are derived from Maturana's definitions of love and violence (Maturana, 1992, November): *Love* is opening space for the existence of another; *violence* is holding an idea to be true such that another's idea is wrong and must change. There seems to be a generative reciprocity between therapeutic love and fit. Each drifts toward or enhances the other.

The concept of fit allows us to be nonblaming of clients and ourselves when "nonfit" and, therefore, "nonadherence" and non-follow-through occur. Clinicians, operating from a therapeutic stance appreciative of fit, are able to be highly curious about ways to increase the fit for *these* family members at *this* time. We also can scrutinize our therapeutic offerings for languaging, timing, and contextualizing to increase the likelihood that fit will occur. The need to be exquisitely sensitive to our clients' responses to our therapeutic moves is heightened. This nonblaming, non–guilt-inducing stance, along with increased and persistent sensitivity, engenders therapeutic loving.

When the concept of fit is neglected, overlooked, or not appreciated, what happens between the clinician and family members? Therapeutic violence and therapeutic decisiveness (Tomm, 1990) reign, reducing options and closing space for therapeutic conversations, curiosity, and collaboration. Prescriptions abound, as does the discouragement of the clinician with herself and her clients, and vice versa, when nonadherence to the therapeutic interventions occurs. Without the lens of fit, clients are labeled as noncompliant, not ready for change, or as challenging the professional system.

Matthew Selekman (1993) pointed out that a theoretical assumption of solution-oriented therapy is that resistance is not a useful concept. Having been influenced by Maturana's notions discussed previously, we say that resistance not only is *not* a useful concept, it is a biological impossibility. Lorraine Wright and Anne Marie Levac (1992) previously elaborated on our belief that noncompliant families are nonexistent! Sometimes there simply is not a fit between what we offer family members and their current biopsychosocial–spiritual structures.

When clinicians are mindful of "fit," we open space for conversations about what family members want from therapy and what they are experiencing in our work with them. We have called these "goodness-of-fit" conversations. These conversations explore questions such as the following: How did you experience our work together today? What do you wish we had spent more or less time discussing? Are we moving faster or slower than you anticipated? Is this a fit for you? (There is an example of a goodness-of-fit conversation in chapter 4.)

Our responsibility as clinicians is not only to assess whether there is an overall fit in our work with family members but also to be aware of the fit or nonfit of particular offerings or perturbations for particular family members. Often it takes time to learn whether a therapeutic offering fit or did not. Other times the evidence of fit is present in a single session. For example, in Research Family 4, a single-parent mother was concerned about her 13-year-old son, whom she believed was depressed. While the mother was placed in a reflecting position— remaining in the room, listening, but not commenting—WLW co-evolved a therapeutic conversation with the son. Through a variety of therapeutic moves, a nondepressed, socially well-adjusted 13-year-old son was brought forth for and by the mother. There was a fit between the therapeutic interventions and the biopsychosocial–spiritual structure of the son and the mother. And the "fit" made a difference! At the end of the therapy session the mother, who had been the problem proclaimer, the one to distinguish the problem, now made new distinctions and a final proclamation: "Okay [son], you're normal!"

Duncan, Hubble, and Rusk (1994) offered the poignant case example of 10-year-old Molly, who, even in the midst of "compliance" to multiple treatment tasks, was not making any improvement in her life. The ideas did not fit and did not make a difference. These authors pointed out that "what we learned here is that when Molly tried to be a good patient and comply with her therapists' goals, the therapy stalled" (p. 25). Information, instruction, and interventions cannot be imported onto someone. They can only be offered as part of an interaction. How an individual responds is determined by his structure at that point in time. If living systems were able to be instructed, we would all respond in the same way to any given perturbation, from how to cook pasta to how to cope with an illness.

In light of the preceding concepts and consequences, it is more consistent with our view of change to phrase the heading for this section as follows: The possibility for therapeutic change is increased through an increased fit between a therapeutic offering and the biopsychosocial–spiritual structures of family members. Phrased this way, the belief not only sounds less linear and less imposing, it also opens space for clinicians to put their energies and abilities into accessing the current fit and into trying to increase the fit between their ideas, opinions, and questions and the biopsychosocial–spiritual structures of family members.

*Change is inevitable, but the direction and pace of therapeutic change are unpredictable.*

What could be more compelling and challenging for a family clinician than these two beliefs about therapeutic change: (a) Change is always happening and inevitable and (b) the direction and pace of change are unpredictable. The juxtaposing of the *certainty* that change will happen with the *uncertainty* about what that change will be and when it will happen is the kind of conundrum that is liberating, not constraining.

When we are under the influence of the "temptation of certainty" (Maturana & Varela, 1992, p. 18), it is the "not-knowing" that invites worry, fear, and anxiety. "If I only knew . . ." commences many internal and external conversations ranging from "if I only knew when my pain would stop" to "if I only knew what's going to happen next."

In our personal lives, prognostications and predictions are sought and paid for, from those of the weather predictor to those of the stockbroker. We want to know how things will turn out. Shall we plan that picnic for Wednesday? Shall we invest in that newest stock? In the professional sphere, many clinicians want to insert Intervention A and receive Outcome B. However, family members experiencing difficulties with health problems are not tabula rasae. They are thinking, feeling, behaving, experiencing beings with histories and stories of those histories. Family members' biopsychosocial–spiritual structures have been changed through those histories, and these changed structures determine how future interactions will influence family members.

Because it is the current, unique structure of a person that determines what will be selected from the environmental perturbation, we cannot say a priori what a particular interaction with self, others, or the environment will "cause" a person to do. Clinicians do not know and cannot predict how family members will respond to an interaction because their response is determined by their present structures, not the clinician's ideas, plans, and interventions. We cannot assume to know another person's structure. The question is always, "How will family members respond?" There is no family-outcome template we can lay on family members beforehand that will indicate how the family will "be" following a therapeutic interaction.

Where does that leave family clinicians, who are in the business of change? What is our "purpose"? We hope that leaves us in a more respectful place with family members: nonoppressively passionate about change, nonimpositional about "the next step" and "the right outcome." We want to be insatiably curious about what is selected by family members from our therapeutic offerings and what the outcome of those perturbations will be. Lynn Hoffman's (1985) article title "Beyond Power and Control" is fitting for the therapeutic work with families that is brought forth when objectivity is put in parentheses and the principles of structural determinism and structural coupling are appreciated. The family clinician is moved beyond power and control into a domain of respectfulness, wonder, and curiosity. There is respect for the uniqueness of the family members, their current biopsychosocial–spiritual structures, and their coevolved relationships; wonder at change; and curiosity about what family members will select from the therapeutic interactions. Clinical energy and ideas are put into efforts to understand family members' current structures; into the generation of creative, tenacious clinical moves to offer family members and their relationships; and into a heightened sensitivity in observing clients' responses to the therapeutic moves. Clinical energy and ideas are focused on increasing the structural coupling with and between family members and on increasing the likelihood that a move will be selected as a perturbation. Therapeutic moves are offered with therapeutic intent but without therapeutic predictions.

Our work with Maria, a 65-year-old never-married daughter of an 85-year-old mother, provides an example in which therapeutic intent did not equal therapeutic outcome and through which the unpredictable nature of the direction and pace of change came to our attention. Maria contacted the FNU on the advice of the Alzheimer's society. The society believed that Maria needed assistance "in coping with her mother, diagnosed with Alzheimer's disease." However, in our first session it became apparent that Maria did not believe that her mother had Alzheimer's. Rather, she believed that her mother's symptoms were "caused" by her mother's anger toward her son, Maria's brother, for spending some of the family's money. The influence of this belief invited the following: (a) Maria experienced her mother's profanity toward her as intentional personal verbal abuse, not as the response of an impaired brain; (b) Maria believed that *she* had caused her mother's suffering by telling her mother about her brother spending the family money (her core constraining belief was that a daughter who has caused her mother's suffering must suffer until the last day); (c) Maria withdrew from her brother, who lived out of the country, and therefore received no emotional support from him for their mother's care; and (d) Maria was not willing to consider a nursing home or alternative living arrangements for her mother.

Part of our therapeutic intervention involved offering Maria another perspective of her mother's anger—that perhaps her mother was more anguished than angry. The anguish could have evolved from not being able to forgive her son for his wrongdoing. Maria was invited by our clinical team to sacrifice for her mother yet again, as suffering daughters do, and serve as a scribe for her mother, who would dictate a letter to the son. Perhaps this would assist her mother to forgive her son. Our therapeutic intent included helping Maria with her own feelings of anguish and soliciting assistance from the brother; however, the therapeutic outcome was totally unexpected. Maria returned to the next session declaring that she now believed that her mother *had* Alzheimer's disease and she was willing to consider a nursing home placement for her mother now out of a desire for her mother's well-being, not as an escape for herself—which intent had only induced guilt in the past. What had happened? Three attempts to scribe a letter for her mother had taken place. With each attempt, her mother's cognitive impairment became more and more obvious to Maria. The letter finally did get written, but with Maria now writing to tell her brother not of their mother's anger but of their mother's Alzheimer's disease. The brother responded not only with a letter but with an international visit.

Maria, her mother, and brother showed us once again that what the changes in structure will be, or the pace with which they will occur, are unknown. We have found that as we persist in resisting the "temptation of certainty," our attraction to typologies and trajectories of illness has diminished. In speaking about the inability to control an entity from the outside, Hoffman (1985) declared, "Give it a bump and watch it jump" (p. 388). We believe that the uniqueness of the biopsychosocial–spiritual structure of each family member from moment to moment prevents us from predicting that it will "jump." Perhaps it will fly. Perhaps it will fall over. Perhaps it will do nothing. We do not know what it will do. We also do not know whether what we as observers distinguish to be a bump will be selected by the system as a perturbation that will change its structure or whether it will be experienced as a destructive interaction.

*Therapeutic change needs to be distinguished and languaged.*

Change needs to be distinguished and languaged to become real. Like other "realities," change is brought forth through the distinguishing of it. "The act of indicating any being, object, thing or unity involves making an act of distinction which distinguishes what has been indicated as separate from its background" (Maturana & Varela, 1992, p. 40).

Change has occurred when the observer who distinguished the problem no longer distinguishes the problem; that is, the person who was saying there was a problem no longer says there is a problem. Maturana (1992, May) explained that "an explanation is not an explanation until it meets the criterion of the observer." The same is true for change: A change is not a change until it meets the criterion of the observer. When we say or hear that "something has changed" or "something is different," we need to ask questions such as the following: Who noticed it? Who distinguished it? Who is the observer of the change that has been distinguished? Who has distinguished a difference?

Because different observers have different criteria, change has been given many different names in the therapeutic world: first-order change, second-order change, continuous change, discontinuous change, paradoxical change, spontaneous change, and so on. We agree with Salamon et al. (1993), who state that "an experience of change is . . . personal, and depends on the expectations of the observer" (p. 334). They define change as "a course of events in the being of a phenomenon that is not embraced within the frame of the observers' expectations as belonging to that phenomenon" (p. 334). Thus it is that change, like beauty, is in the eye (the biopsychosocial–spiritual structure) of the beholder.

We also agree with Insoo Berg and Steve de Shazer (1993) that "the therapist's job is to . . . help the client notice differences so that these noticed differences can be put to work. Then these noticed differences can make a difference" (p. 19). That change is always occurring is a theoretical underpinning for the work at the Brief Family Therapy Center (Nunnally, de Shazer, Lipchik, & Berg, 1986). Their "formula first session task" developed from their observations of change, and they "began to see that the therapeutic task had shifted from promoting change to 1) eliciting news of difference, 2) amplifying the differences, and 3) helping the changes to continue" (p. 83).

We believe that without distinguishing and languaging change, change is not "real." Change that is not distinguished is diminished. The importance of distinguishing change through describing it and languaging it is reinforced through Maturana and Varela's (1992) words: "The experience of anything out there is validated in a special way by the human structure, which makes possible 'the thing' that arises in the description" (pp. 25–26). We want change to arise as a real thing. As we draw forth descriptions of change from the observers, change is brought forth. We also believe that the ability of clients to language the effects of perturbations can be evidence of a change in their biopsychosocial–spiritual structure.

We are passionate about our efforts to distinguish and language change. (Chapter 7 describes in detail beliefs that undergird a clinician's tenacity in distinguishing change. See in particular the section entitled Passionate Persistence in Pursuing Change.)

In the following dialogue with Research Family 4, the single-parent mother (Linda) has just told the clinician (WLW) that physical violence between her children and her is no longer a concern. The importance in distinguishing this change is obvious. In this case the change becomes more and more real through the clinician's pursuit of how the change has come about. The languaging of the explanation for the change reifies the change and verifies the mother's words that things are different. There is reciprocity between languaging the change to make change real and making change real so that the languaging is real. Change in the following case is reified through the mother's words, and reciprocally, the mother's words are verified through the reality of the change.

WLW: Let me ask you some very direct questions. Are you less physically violent with the children?

LINDA: Yes.

WLW: You are?

LINDA: Mmhm. Much less.

WLW: Okay. Much less. And are they less physically violent with you?

LINDA: Yes, and with each other. It's diminishing. It's not as much of a problem as it was when we first came in.

WLW: And what's the difference there? How has this come about?

LINDA: How did it happen?

WLW: So you say to yourself, "Gee, I'd like to continue this happening. What do I need to still keep doing?" What are you doing differently? Or thinking differently? Or. . . ?

LINDA: Um . . .

WLW: What is different?

LINDA: [*pause*] I'm just trying real hard to get in touch with my family's feelings before I explode.

WLW: And what helps you do that? What helps you get in touch? This is very good, I mean, these are the very things that we need to know to help other families. To say, "How I get in touch with my feelings."

LINDA: How do I accomplish that?

WLW: How do you do that?

LINDA: Um, it's just—you have to really develop a habit of, "Okay, I feel angry about this. What is it exactly that I'm angry about?" And then I've got to remove myself physically even and sit down and think about it. "Why am I angry? What's making me angry? Is this important? Do I really need to feel angry about this?"

WLW: That's what you're doing?

LINDA: Yes.

WLW: Good for you.

LINDA: You know, "How important is it to this child that I go to him and say, 'Look I feel angry because you've done such and such'?"

The mother has provided a useful explanation of the change, but the clinician pursues the explanation that underpins that explanation. With this move, more of the explanation of the story of the mother coevolving change with her children unfolds. Change is further distinguished.

WLW: And what helps you get into that really useful pattern of stopping yourself, asking yourself, "What am I feeling? What am I thinking?" What helps you do that?

LINDA: It's hard for me to answer that. Um [*pause*] I really don't know how I got into that.

WLW: When did it start? When did you start doing that, because that's very useful—that thought stopping, action stopping, holding yourself back.

LINDA: Probably about 6 months ago when I just thought, "I just am not as kind to my kids as I could be. I'd like to be kinder." I just developed it more or less myself. I just sat down and I thought about it, "Okay, why am I not kind to these kids? Okay, I'm overwhelmed. Okay, how can I deal with being overwhelmed?"

WLW: Good for you.

LINDA: "And what is it that's making me overwhelmed?" So I just sat down and I analyzed the whole thing.

The explanation for the change in violence has added strength and staying power to the change. This example distinguished change that occurred outside the session. We can also distinguish change that occurs in the session. Change is always happening and is there for the distinguishing and languaging of it. We believe that as we bring forth change—all aspects of change—and distinguish it, language it, and give it an identity, family members will reflect on the change. This reflection will magnify and sustain the changes. We also believe that to distinguish and celebrate change is not to obliterate or deny suffering.

## BELIEFS ABOUT CLINICIANS

Our beliefs about clinicians flow from our worldview of (objectivity) and the two theoretical underpinnings for change: first, that change is determined by structure, and second, that change involves structural coupling and a change of structure. What do clinicians do? They assess change, uncover change, facilitate change, solidify change, monitor change, and undergo change. Following are six beliefs that serve as guiding principles that influence what family clinicians do and how we do what we do (see table 3.2).

Table 3.2

**Beliefs About Clinicians**

| |
| --- |
| The clinician is not a change agent |
| The clinician's preferred stance is nonhierarchical |
| The clinician coevolves therapeutic conversations |
| The clinician offers invitations to reflection |
| The clinician and family members change through their interaction |
| The clinician is not invested in a particular outcome |

*The clinician is not a change agent.*

The term *change agent* implies a linear–positivist view of change and a pejorative view of clients. We believe that we cannot and do not "change" anyone. Lest third-party billers turn away from us, we explore here what a clinician is and is not and what he or she can and cannot do.

Some may say, "What's in a name?" Just as different terms about therapy open or close space for change (Wright & Watson, 1982), what we call ourselves as family clinicians also impacts change. In a name are embedded assumptions, expectations, and permission to behave in certain ways. The term *change agent* can imply that the therapist is the only one in charge of change. It implies a linear relationship with change—"I change others"—inviting one to forget or dismiss that clinicians are also changed through therapeutic conversations with family members. Thinking of oneself as a change agent can invite a clinician to focus on the word *agent* and grow into the permission embodied in that term, which the Oxford dictionary defines as "one who exerts power or produces effect." This stance totally negates the ability of a family member to be a "free agent," that is, according to the dictionary, "one whose actions are not subject to another's control." We often find that novice clinicians, enchanted by the title of change agent, spend their time taking on the problems of the clients rather than drawing forth the clients' abilities to solve their own problems. Anderson, Goolishian, and Winderman (1986) tell their trainees that "the only person they can change in the therapy room is themselves. What changes within the therapist is the therapist's map (theory) of the client" (p. 115).

The term *change agent* can imply a one-up position: a stance of superiority and hierarchy. Predetermined hypotheses about how families should function, the laying on of goals, too frequent sessions, and a display of expertness distance the clinician from family members. To invite and entice someone to a reflection, to offer someone a new view of a situation, and to open space for solutions involve a humble and curious stance. We agree with Kierkegaard (1859/1939) that "the helper must first humble himself under him he would help, and therewith must understand that to help does not mean to be a sovereign but to be a servant" (pp. 27–28). We believe that the family clinician's strength is ironically increased through humility.

If clinicians do not change anyone, what do they do? "Rather than saying that the therapist enables change to occur, our view is that change is constantly occurring, stability is an illusion, and change cannot be prevented" (Berg & de Shazer, 1993, p. 19). We see that part of our work is to clear away the obstacles that have been inhibiting solutions; uncover and distinguish constraining beliefs; alter, modify, and challenge constraining beliefs; and affirm and solidify facilitative beliefs. (Chapters 4 through 7 elaborate on the four major therapeutic moves that constitute our advanced clinical practice.)

Through these moves the clinician invites, entices, and as Maturana (1988b) said, "seduces" the family members to a reflection. A reflection facilitates family members in seeing and softening their internal structure and beliefs. Another part of our work as clinicians, therefore, is to offer interventions and interactions that invite reflections. These have an increased likelihood of being selected as perturbations. According to John Mince (1992), the work of the family clinician involves "generating linguistic perturbations in the hope of eliciting compensations to change a family's customary transactional patterns and the co-constructed beliefs about those transactions" (p. 333). Although we do not believe that clinicians are change agents, we do believe that they bring expertise to the therapy room, which allows them to resist the passion to change the other (which involves imposing one's will on the other; Maturana, 1992, November) while allowing them to enact the passion to "invite the other to an exchange" (Salamon et al., 1993) and to a reflection.

To say we are not change agents does not mean we do not possess expertise. Graduate students studying nonhierarchy have sometimes assumed that this means they have no expertise. This belief fits with their frustrating experience as neophytes, as strangers in the strange land of therapy. The clinician possesses much expertise gained through clinical work with other families, life experience, research, and professional literature. Tomm (1993), in commenting on Michael White's tendency to downplay his own professional contribution to the construction of the new stories of his clients, stated that this underemphasizing

> obscures and devalues the importance of a therapist's active contributions to the change process. In my opinion, deliberate therapeutic initiatives are indispensable in clinical work. Hermeneutic listening, circular questioning, empathic reflection, and systemic understanding are not enough, especially when problematic patterns of injustice are entrenched. (p. 66)

To say that we are not change agents does not mean we are not passionate about change. We are. We expect change. We embrace change. We are in the business of change. We believe that change is always occurring; therefore, if we do not find change in one place, we look in another. We tenaciously pursue avenues to invite change, but we are not passionate about change bringing about one particular outcome. We have a passion *for* change but not a passion *to* change others. We are passionate about helping, but not passionate about how family members will "be" after that help is offered. Maturana's (1988a) definition of a family is that "a family . . . has a passion for living together." Perhaps the role of the family clinician is therefore *not* to change the family members but to draw forth their passion for living together.

Considering the preceding, what names reflect the preferred stance of family clinicians and the preferred way of being with clients? Cynthia Mittelmeier and Steven Friedman (1993) say that "we act as facilitators or 'resource catalysts' who work 'unremittingly under positive auspices' (cited in Friedman & Fanger, 1991) to generate conversations that offer the client new possibilities and options for the future" (p. 159). Salamon et al. (1993) found that the characteristics they wanted to develop were supported best by the term *commissioner*. They find this word assists them in their efforts to keep themselves in a serving position and to be loyal to the commission giver (client), who is the one who authorizes them and defines the goals, termination, and satisfaction of the commission. Perhaps we could call ourselves passion seekers, possibility seekers, cocreators of change, persuaders and seducers of change, proscriptors of prescriptions, detectives for change, noticers of difference, or facilitators of change. What *is* in a name? What would these different names draw forth from us as clinicians and allow us to coevolve with family members?

The experience of one graduate student therapist who wrestled with

initially wanting to be a change agent and slipped into being a "dictator of change" is highlighted in the following letter. Through the
process of supervision with WLW, this courageous student opened
space for some new beliefs about himself as a family clinician. In this
letter, coauthored with his supervisor, he shares those new facilitative
beliefs with a family with whom he was losing engagement and who
had stopped coming to therapy.

Dear Brian and Barbara,
  I recently have had a few experiences that have challenged some
of my constraining beliefs about therapy, families, and therapists. I
thought it might be helpful for both of you and for me if I were to
put them down on paper. Would you be interested in hearing and
thinking about these ideas?
  One of the beliefs that I brought with me to therapy, almost like
extra baggage, is that therapists know everything about relationships
and therefore it is their right and responsibility to tell others what to
do. This belief invited me to be overly confrontational and rigid with
any clients who courageously dared to present an opposing view.
This constraining belief also invited me to continually draw forth
problems from couples and families, no matter how much they
wanted to focus on solutions and exceptions to problems, just so I
could show my extensive knowledge. And finally, this belief invited
me to treat families as if they were incapable of change without me. I
do not want to believe these things about families, therapy or therapists anymore. In a way, this letter is an emancipation proclamation
for me, and a letter of intent to you.
  Starting today in our work I would like to make the following
changes:
  1) See you as you really are: a hard working, goal oriented couple
with passion and energy.
  2) Alter my therapeutic stance from one of sergeant to a coach;
from a dictator of change to a facilitator of change.
  3) Leave the issue of initiating or ending therapy to you, the couple who knows what is going well and how to deal with the details
of daily living.
  4) Invite instead of demand; open doors instead of push you
through.
  5) Remain neutral (or equally curious about other possibilities) to
both of you, your problems and your solutions.
  I sincerely hope these changes will open space for you as a couple
and for me as your therapist. I want to apologize for taking responsibility for your problems and solutions in the past and for trying to
force you to change like I thought you should. Please feel free to be
in charge of your therapy, and to change as you see best. I think I can
see more clearly now, that you have already faced courageously and

dealt with many of your issues. Thank you for teaching me that families are their own best therapists and for allowing me the privilege of working with you.

> Sincerely,
> Jonathan Sandberg,
> Marriage and Family Therapy Graduate Student,
> Wendy L. Watson, Ph.D.,
> Marriage and Family Therapy Clinical
> Supervisor & Professor

The outcome? The couple phoned the student and commenced therapy again, this time taking a different direction, one *they* chose. They made significant progress and terminated therapy because of a relocation to another state, which represented another positive change in their lives as a couple.

The outcome for the student therapist? His reflections 18 months later about coauthoring this letter and two others were as follows:

> I think those letters helped me more than the families. By writing them I solidified in my own mind what I believed about the role of the therapist. I learned that therapists are facilitators of change. I know this because I tried for 6 months to be a dictator of change. It does not work because it disempowers and subjugates clients instead of freeing them up to live and change and grow. I became a better therapist because I knew what my role was and I no longer took over their role. . . . I also learned that it is easier to just tell people what to do, but much less effective.

*The clinician's preferred stance is nonhierarchical.*

The relationship between the family and clinician invites a traditional hierarchy to exist. The clinician is frequently perceived to be the only expert, a one-up position; the family comes to the relationship needing help, a one-down position. The clinician often possesses power and control through knowledge, professional position, and skill; the family usually has exhausted its resources, and the members are looking for new ideas and solutions to their problems. Clinicians are offered money for their ideas, whereas clients most often have to pay.

Frequently, specific rules, albeit unspoken and implicit, govern a hierarchical relationship. Rules that perpetuate hierarchy include the following: "If you are in a one-down position, never comment directly about the relationship—especially the rules that govern the relationship" and "never express dissatisfaction with the relationship nor raise problematic interactions of tension or mistrust." Family members frequently have a constraining belief that if they express their concerns, dissatisfactions, or frustrations directly, they might not receive adequate care or will be punished for challenging the health professional's knowledge or authority. One rule of many health professionals who prefer the one-up position in relation to their clients is as follows: "Label families as resistant and noncompliant if they do not follow your ideas and advice or are dissatisfied or distrustful." In doing so, health professionals do not have to share the responsibility of creating a context for change. Duncan et al. (1994) embellished these implicit rules in their tongue-in-cheek formula for therapeutic failure as follows:

> Treat clients as though they are incapable of helping themselves, expect the clients to give over to the expert the power to define their personal reality, then go one-up and tell them exactly what they need to do to get better. Expect compliance regardless of whether or not the client agrees with the expert's prescriptions. Then ignore the client's wishes and abilities. When all else fails, argue the rightness of the theory adhered to and tell the client of all the successes achieved with other clients diagnosed with their particular diagnosis. Do this before you fire them from therapy. (p. 27)

Nonhierarchy occurs when the beliefs and actions of the clinician turn these implicit rules and behaviors upside down. When the clinician's fundamental beliefs about reality challenge the traditional notions of hierarchy and status, nonhierarchy is possible. Constructivist perspectives of reality assert that knowledge is subjectively created and that therefore there are many perspectives or explanations of reality that can fit any situation. The ideas of Maturana and Varela (1992) concerning objectivity and objectivity-in-parentheses, while similar to those of the constructivists, assert that reality is not constructed but rather is brought forth in coexistence with others through language. These worldviews provide the clinician with a new lens: a new way of viewing families.

Beliefs about families such as "all families have strengths" and "problems do not reside within individuals; rather, problems reside between persons in language" open up new possibilities for a different kind of relationship to exist. (See chapter 2 for our beliefs about families.) However, White (1995) cautioned that "there is always an unequal distribution of power in the therapeutic context, regardless of the steps that are taken by therapists to render the context of therapy more egalitarian" (p. 187).

An invitation to clinicians to behave in nonhierarchical and collaborative ways with families was offered by the Milan team in the early 1980s. They proposed three guidelines for the systemic clinician to use in conducting a therapeutic conversation: hypothesizing, circularity, and neutrality (Selvini Palazzoli, Boscolo, Cecchin, & Prata, 1980a). *Hypothesizing* refers to the clinician's perpetual effort to evolve different conceptualizations of the presenting problem and develop alternative explanations for family behavior. The clinician continually looks for new ways to understand the problem without getting stuck trying to find the one correct view. *Circularity* refers to the reciprocal influence between clinician and client and to the clinician's use of particular questions to understand family patterns of behavior and confirm or discard hypotheses (Fleuridas, Nelson, & Rosenthal, 1986; Loos & Bell, 1990; Tomm, 1987a, 1987b, 1988; Wright, 1989; Wright & Leahey, 1994a). *Neutrality* describes the clinician's attitude toward the family system, which constrains the clinician from taking sides or blaming family members. Neutrality with respect to change and therapeutic outcome is another level of neutrality shown by the clinician (Tomm, 1984b). Cecchin (1987) later refined the ideas about neutrality by suggesting that the essence of neutrality is curiosity. *Curiosity,* he argued, "is the key element of therapeutic neutrality which invites the clinician to be constantly interested in alternative views and in inventing multiple punctuations of a behavior, interpretation, event, relationship, etc." (p. 407).

In seeking to understand a multiplicity of perspectives, the clinician avoids becoming trapped by one idea or one point of view about family members, about the problem, or about solutions. The clinician's views are not more correct or more privileged than the family's views. In the process, clinicians become more respecting and more in awe of families' abilities and become more humble about their own ideas, however well conceptualized and informed they may be.

It is in this spirit of wonderment with a new lens and a new way of being with families that collaborative and nonhierarchical relationships with families are born. Greater equality and status are given to the family's expertness, which is drawn forth in the therapeutic conversation. The therapeutic relationship becomes more transparent. Family members are invited to comment on the therapeutic relationship in terms of what is useful to *them* and what is not useful. The family's ideas for the focus and direction of the session are invited and used. Hoffman-Hennessy asserted that in "non-hierarchy, we are talking about a shift that changes the nature of the professional relationship toward a more equitable one, if only symbolically, not a technique that works better with some people than others" (Hoffman-Hennessy & Davis, 1993, p. 370).

Are clinicians to remain neutral and nonhierarchical when confronted with illegal or dangerous behaviors? We respect that each family functions in the way that they desire and in a way that they determine is most effective; however, being part of a larger system, clinicians are bound by moral, legal, cultural, and societal norms that require them to act in accordance with those norms regarding illegal or dangerous behavior. Cecchin (1987) asserted that in these situations "clinicians may need to take a different position—one which is distinct from a non-hierarchical, collaborative stance. Confronted by illegal behavior, a clinician may have to abandon a curious, therapeutic manner and become a social controller" (p. 409) in order to conform to the moral or legal rules and their consequences. In other words, there are situations in which the clinician is required to behave within the domain of objectivity.

Our practice of offering family members a choice about how they would like to use the session is one way we operationalize the concept of nonhierarchical, collaborative relationships with the families with whom we work. We frequently ask the following question at the beginning of a session—"How would you like to spend our time together?"—rather than commencing with a preconceived idea about what *this* family should be talking about at *this* time. Although our graduate students are required to develop a presession presentation before commencing a session, we advise them to go to the session so well prepared that they can respond spontaneously to the surprises that family members may bring that day. Presession hypothesizing is viewed as a way to start focusing on the family, churning up the gray matter, making connections, and generating questions that the team would like to ask, rather than preparing an agenda for the session that is imposed on the family regardless of what the family members desire and despite changes that may have occurred since the last session. A nonhierarchical stance does not prohibit the clinician from bringing her own wonderings and unsettledness from a previous session to the present session, however. She can inquire of the family members what stood out for them from the last session, and she can offer what stood out for her.

Nonhierarchy is demonstrated in our practice through our use of closing letters. In the past, we followed the traditional format of providing a closing letter to the referring professional, which summarized our impressions of the family and the assistance provided them. Over the past few years, we have experimented with a different format for the closing letter: The closing letter is still a summary of the clinical work, but it is written in a language that both family members and referring professionals can understand. Instead of addressing the letter to the referring professional, we address the letter to the family and send a copy to the referring professional. In the letter we summarize what the clinical team learned from the family and what we believe we offered the family. The following closing letter was sent to Research Family 5:

Dear Julie & Robert:

Greetings from the Family Nursing Unit. Our clinical nursing team was happy to meet with you for four sessions from January 26 to March 16, 1993. You initially consulted the Family Nursing Unit with concerns about sharing family responsibilities. In this letter summarizing our work with you, we will share our impressions of your family, what we learned from you, and some key ideas we offered.

Our Impressions and What We Learned from You:

You taught us how a deeply caring couple, willing to work together as a team, can find ways to get their marriage back on track.

Julie, the team was impressed by your devotion as a caring and responsible mother and wife, and by your efforts to find ways to manage your exhaustion, both for the sake of yourself and that of your family. You helped us understand how your entire family is affected by Robert's heart attacks and chest pain. This knowledge will assist us in our work with other families.

Robert, you taught us that a person can overcome difficulties in his past and make challenging lifestyle changes. We were touched by your ability to express your love for Julie and your children, especially since you have said that it is difficult for you to talk about your feelings. We have also learned how parents cope with the stress of living with a child who is hyperactive.

The Clinical Nursing Team's Opinions/Ideas:

The clinical nursing team agreed that your marriage was off track, and we offered ideas of how to help you get back on track, and to perhaps lessen the frequency of future derailments. We were impressed that even though the third session was difficult and painful for each of you, that you were both willing to open space to our ideas and some new ideas of your own of how to get back on track.

Some of the ideas included:

1. Try to spend time enjoying each other as a couple on a regular basis.

2. Plan regular consultation time as a way of supporting each other's efforts in managing areas of personal responsibility. We offered the idea of Julie being a Cardiac Consultant to Robert, and of Robert being a Tiredness Management Consultant to Julie.

We also offered ideas to each of you individually that may or may not have proven helpful. We look forward to our check-up session with you on June 1 at 2 p.m.

Approximately six months after our last session, a Research Assistant from the Family Nursing Unit will contact you to complete

an outcome survey. Your assistance in participating in this study will allow us to evaluate the effectiveness our service offers to families.
    We send you our best wishes.

> Sincerely,
> Lorraine M. Wright, R.N., Ph.D., and other
> members of the clinical nursing team

Another method we have used to flatten the family–clinician hierarchy is to invite families to coauthor articles that describe our clinical work with them. More and more, clinicians are involving clients in their presentations and writing (Hoffman-Hennessy & Davis, 1993; Roberts, "Alexandra," & "Julius," 1988). In work with a couple who were experiencing grief following the death of their adolescent son, the members of our clinical team and the couple shared and documented their reflections of the therapeutic process (Levac, McLean, Wright, & Bell, in press).

Therapeutic transparency is often cited as yet another way that clinicians operationalize the preferred stance of nonhierarchy. *Therapeutic transparency* involves talking out loud about the therapeutic process. David Epston is quoted in a chapter by Freeman and Lobovits (1993) as saying that "therapeutic transparency involves making the choices and dilemmas of the therapist available for communication and reflection by clients" (p. 195). For example, in Research Family 5, the clinician (LMW) talks out loud about her dilemma in finding a focus for the first session. At this point in the session, she has been speaking with the couple, Robert and Julie, for 1 hour and 10 minutes. The couple has described in great detail the difficulties they were experiencing. Listen to the clinician voicing her dilemma:

LMW: Let me tell you what I'm feeling right now. I'm feeling like you've been very open with me and I've gotten a lot of information. But I feel like I should start on another whole session just to know about your stress—how have you dealt with stress, what have you tried in the past. I'm wondering if it would be premature for me to offer any ideas about stress until I know all the different things you've tried on your own before now.

JULIE: I've tried lots of things and meditated for a while.

LMW: Yes? You see and that part, I don't know yet, do I? And so I need to be careful that I'm not plunging in and offering you ideas and then disappointing you because you've already tried that. And I'm sure you wouldn't be here if you hadn't tried and hadn't exhausted a lot of your own ideas already. So, let me take a break with the team. You know what I'm saying? It's been useful. I really needed to get all this part, but I'm wondering if maybe my assessment should really continue for another session, to be sure that I understand. I understand stress is a major problem. I understand some of the issues that are causing you stress. I don't think I have an assessment yet of the different things you've tried to reduce stress on your own, so that we don't just, simply say, "Try this and that," when you've already done it yourselves. So, that part I'll probably have to follow up on next time. But let me just take a little break with the team and see what ideas they have.

Therapeutic transparency also includes admitting a mistake. An example of this occurred with Research Family 5 in Session 3. In this session, the family were invited to listen to the presession team meeting in a reflecting position from behind the one-way mirror. The presession hypotheses, developed by the clinical team on the basis of therapeutic conversations of Session 2, focused on enhancing the couple's relationship by encouraging them to "date" and to plan more activities for themselves. After listening to the presession meeting of the team's ideas, the wife, Julie, was upset and expressed concern that perhaps the clinician and the clinical team did not seem to understand the seriousness of the marital issues. The clinician's (LMW) therapeutically transparent response followed:

LMW: The other thing that we were struck with is wondering if maybe this [the expression of their concern about the seriousness of their situation] was your way of telling us that some of the things that we were suggesting last week were a bit premature. You have told us today, you're not quite ready. We were getting concerned about introducing more fun into your marriage. You're doing a bit more dating, but maybe we were a bit premature with that, going too fast with that, I don't know. It was too quick or something. I'm wondering if we need to slow down a little bit and appreciate that things are more complex than we had originally thought.

The transparent processing of a therapeutic error with the family members in this instance was a necessary and highly significant segue to uncovering spousal abuse in the marriage.

*The clinician coevolves therapeutic conversations.*

The Latin *conversa* translates as "turning around together." To discuss the human phenomenon of conversations, it is useful to ask the question, "Why do we talk?" Because we frequently complain to one another—we're just not communicating, I don't feel heard, you're interrupting me, you're not listening, or we just don't talk anymore—one might infer it would be better if we just did not talk to one another. Certain groups and individuals have chosen to do just that. Members of some religious orders take an oath of silence and do not talk, and some individuals choose to live in the woods or the mountains far away from friends and family members to avoid talking. Individuals who remain among their family and friends yet choose not to speak are given the diagnosis of mutism. Frequently, clinicians working with adolescents and their families become caught in the challenge of trying to get "mute" teenagers to talk.

It becomes readily evident that we value and even demand talk from one another, which brings us back to ponder the question, "Why do we talk?" Our answer to that question is that we talk to exchange ourselves and to render ourselves human. Our conversations are the stories that we tell of our lives and experiences. Our conversations make us human and enable us to love. In fact, the nineteenth-century German philosopher Nietzsche said that love is a long conversation. The influence of our conversations is also set forth boldly by Maturana's (1992, May) statement that "if we are not well in our conversations with others, we are in disease."

All human life takes place in conversations. To be human consists of being part of a network of conversations. In fact, the family may be best characterized as a network of conversations with an interweave of several different kinds of conversations. Genograms and ecomaps are assessment tools that are useful for defining with whom we have conversations.

Conversations are a medium for story telling and story listening in which all participants are speakers and listeners at the same time. A conversation is a verbal exchange of beliefs, opinions, ideas, observations, and sentiments that are embodied in our stories and myths within our social and cultural domains.

The stories people live, as well as the stories about those stories, are all that a clinician has to work with. Therapy is a conversation, or an exchange of stories. Bateson (1979) noted that "a story is a little knot or complex of that species of connectedness which we call relevance . . . [and there is a] connectedness between people in that all think in terms of stories" (p. 13). The world is known through our storying of it. Although conversations, stories, narratives, and discourse are currently popular metaphors in therapy circles, we prefer the term *conversation* to describe the medium in which clinicians and families encounter each other.

## Social Versus Therapeutic Conversations

It is useful to draw a distinction between social and therapeutic conversations. Social and therapeutic conversations involve both internal and external conversations, but the similarity ends there. Social conversations are those that occur as we move about in our daily life and interact with those we encounter. Therapeutic conversations, on the other hand, are purposeful and time-limited, as are the relationships. Persons and clinicians engaged in therapeutic conversations come together for a particular purpose, generally because the clinician, a family member, or both, have identified some emotional or physical suffering that needs to be alleviated or reduced. Although the clinician's job is to invite the client–family to an alternative, facilitative belief of what is needed to get past a problem, the client–family's job is to invite the clinician to an appreciation of the problem. Between the two, a therapeutic conversation coevolves.

Both client and clinician bring expert knowledge to the therapeutic conversation. We concur with de Shazer's (1993) respectful definition of a therapeutic conversation, which acknowledges the expertness of both family members and clinicians: a "talking together between or among experts sharing and exchanging ideas and information in language" (p. 88). As the expertise of both families and clinicians is acknowledged, appreciated, and expressed, both clinicians and families change together through their conversations.

Clinicians are socially empowered and privileged to bring forth either health or pathology in the conversations in which they engage with families. The conversations that we want to bring forth with families are those that draw forth a "passion for living together in physical or emotional proximity" (Mendez et al., 1988, p. 157). We believe with other "fourth wave" clinicians* that therapeutic conversations are the medium for change, that is, the medium for changing hearts, minds, cells, and souls.

Descriptions and verbatim clinical examples of therapeutic conversations have gained substantial recognition and emphasis in the family therapy field as evidenced by entire books being devoted to the discussion of therapeutic conversations, such as the following: *Solution Talk: Hosting Therapeutic Conversations* (Furman & Ahola, 1992), *Therapeutic Conversations* (Gilligan & Price, 1993), and *The New Language of Change* (Friedman, 1993). Authors who prefer the term *narrative* to *conversation* have also made worthwhile contributions by writing texts devoted to

---

* According to Ahola as quoted in O'Hanlon (1993), the first wave in psychotherapy was pathology-based, the second wave was problem-focused (problem-solving therapy), and the third wave was solution-focused or solution-oriented.

descriptions and clinical examples of narrative, for example, Alan Parry and Robert E. Doan's (1994) *Story Re-Visions* and Michael White and David Epston's (1990) *Narrative Means to Therapeutic Ends*.

### RULES AND NORMS OF CONVERSATIONS

The rules and norms of both social and therapeutic conversations are influenced by context, gender, ethnicity–culture, beliefs, and previous history of interactions; however, the rules and norms for a therapeutic conversation are not the same as those for a social conversation. One example of a difference in rules is the rule of interrupting. In social conversations, there are implicit rules of not interrupting while another is speaking. To do otherwise is considered impolite or controlling. In therapy, however, there exists an implicit rule that permits interrupting in situations such as when family members are not being given an opportunity to offer their ideas and opinions—when their voices are not being acknowledged.

Another predominant difference between social and therapeutic conversations is the rule, or norm, about asking questions. In social conversations with family and friends, it is expected that there will be a mutual exchange of asking questions, telling stories, and taking an interest in one another. When reciprocal questioning is absent in social conversations, one may believe that the other person does not care or is not interested. In therapeutic conversations, however, there is no expectation that clients and family members will ask questions or take an interest in the clinician.

The persistence with which questions are asked may also be different in social versus therapeutic conversations. Because we know the world through our explanations and because an explanation is not an explanation until it meets the criterion of the observer (Maturana, 1992, May), clinicians continue to ask questions concerning problems or solutions if explanations are not satisfying. Clinicians must be free, or at least believe they are free, to ask any and all questions about a family member's experience with illness. If clinicians are constrained to ask only certain questions, it is because of their own constraining beliefs about problems, change, their "role," and so on.

In both social and therapeutic conversations, the art of listening is paramount. The need to communicate what it is like to live in our individual, separate worlds of experience is a powerful need in human relationships (Nichols, 1995). Consequently, nothing can be more painful than the sense that those with whom we are close are not really listening to what we have to say. No conversation is ever trivial. Each conversation in which we participate influences changes in our biopsychosocial–spiritual structures.

## LANGUAGING PLUS EMOTIONING EQUALS CONVERSATION

Human beings exist in language. It is not possible to refer to ourselves or to anything else without language. But language does not take place in the brain. Languaging is a social phenomenon rather than a phenomenon of the nervous system (Maturana, 1992, November). Every reflection takes place in language, which is our unique way of being human and humanly active (Maturana & Varela, 1992). Every human act takes place in language, and therefore all of our social acts have ethical implications (Maturana & Varela, 1992).

Languaging interaction is as powerful as physical interaction. A loving conversation can be experienced as a caress; an angry conversation, as a hit. Such interactions trigger structural changes of many different types, including changes in blood pressure and respiration. We do not believe the childhood saying "sticks and stones will break my bones but words will never hurt me." Words influence our biopsychosocial–spiritual structures.

The braiding of languaging plus emotioning equals conversation (Maturana, 1992, May). Emotioning is interconnected with the notion of languaging. In our conversations, we may observe a range of emotions from anger to joy. Emotions arise from structural changes caused by the mutual perturbations between individuals that have occurred through their languaging. Recursively, emotions may give rise to structural changes that may trigger an "illness" response or an interactional dilemma.

It is important to emphasize and clarify that emotions do not require language (Maturana, 1992, May). As humans, we experience emotions but language feelings. There is a difference between emotions and feelings. For example, if a person says, "I feel angry about my diagnosis," this is an expression of feelings about how that person is experiencing emotion, but it is not the emotion itself. Our description in language of our emotions constitutes our feelings.

## TYPES OF CONVERSATIONS

There are numerous types of conversations. People usually participate in many different conversations, simultaneously or successively. Drawing forth facilitative beliefs in therapeutic conversations is one way to help create new conversations in and out of the therapy room. Clinicians distinguish themselves from other conversationalists by the way they enter and create novel conversations with clients–families. Clinicians want to trigger reflections for family members. As family members contemplate their behaviors and subsequently their beliefs about themselves, their relationships, and their illnesses, they are able to begin to open space for new patterns of relating. By inviting family members to distinguish their distinctions—to think about their thinking—the clinician is inviting family members to participate in the process of self-reflection. The process of self-reflection is foundational to the coevolution of new, more facilitative beliefs.

Different kinds of conversations give rise to different emotions based on one's view of reality. (See the earlier description of "objectivity" and objectivity-in-parentheses in this chapter.) Some conversations are simply obscured by actions and emotionally inert, whereas others are emotionally saturated. Conversations can range from emotionally violent to emotionally loving. Conversations that can be distinguished as emotionally violent are generated by the belief that one has access to a true, right, or correct reality. We have found the definition of emotional violence offered by Maturana (1992, November) to be a useful one in our clinical practice: holding an idea or opinion to be true, such that another person's opinion is not only untrue, but must change. The first part of his definition is characteristic of any good argument: People try to convince others of the correctness of their point of view. But the conversation becomes violent when one person insists that another person's opinion must change and be in accordance with the first person's. This behavior of emotional violence, if predominant over a number of years, may lead to emotional suffering, physical violence, physical illness, or all three. Whatever the manifestation, the biopsychosocial–spiritual structure is changed.

The belief that we are right and others are wrong and must change generates conversations of accusations, recriminations, and negative characterizations (Mendez et al., 1988). On the other hand, loving interactions or conversations are based on a belief that there are many views and realities and, therefore, many ideas and opinions: a "multi versa," according to Maturana. As we discussed in chapter 1, there are many equally legitimate views, but all are not equally desirable or pleasant to live in.

We call conversations that draw forth love "conversations of affirmation and affection" and "conversations of growth and change." We have embraced Maturana's (1992, November) definition of *love:* the opening of space for the existence of the other person beside us in daily living. Furthermore, Maturana has suggested that love is the domain of those actions that constitute another as a legitimate other in coexistence with one's self. Consequently, even the admonition "love your enemies" can be an acknowledgment that your enemy is a legitimate other. If we believe that our enemies are mistaken and must change, however, we are operating in the domain of objectivity-without-parentheses.

Clinicians are socially empowered to bring forth either health or pathology in our therapeutic conversations. Clinicians are most interested, therefore, in altering, modifying, or stopping conversations of negative characterizations and conversations of accusations and recriminations, which are types of conversations that we believe bring forth pathology. Our primary goal as clinicians is to bring forth conversations that invite new or renewed beliefs about problems, persons, and relationships: conversations of affirmation and affection and conversations of growth and change.

We propose that the most powerful way to change the network of conversations is to change the beliefs. Beliefs can be altered or modified by inviting clients–families to a reflection; the clinician operates from a worldview of objectivity-in-parentheses and invites family members into that world. Here is where the passion and the commitment of the clinician should appear, not as a passion or commitment to change others in the manipulation of their existence, but as the passion for bringing forth a type of conversation that allows family members to put objectivity into parentheses (Mendez et al., 1988). One of the tasks of health professionals, therefore, is to help families put objectivity into parentheses. By putting objectivity into parentheses, the validation and worth of all our fellow humans is possible (Maturana, 1988a); in this way, we recognize that we generate and validate all reality through living together in language, deriving consensus, and drawing distinctions.

## CONVERSATIONS THAT CONSTRAIN AND CONVERSATIONS THAT FACILITATE

We have identified, through relevant literature and our own clinical experiences, several types of conversations that constrain solutions, relationships, and lives, and several types of conversations that facilitate solutions, relationships, and life itself. These types of conversations include conversations of agreement, conversations of characterizations, conversations of accusations and recriminations, conversations of command and obedience, conversations inviting growth and change, and conversations of affirmation and affection. These types of conversations are briefly described in the following sections, with accompanying examples. They are not inclusive of, but only introductory to, the full range of conversations that we have found useful in our clinical work.

### Conversations of Agreement

*Conversations of agreement* are conversations that consist of agreements for action in a domain in which requests and promises either are or are not accepted (Maturana, 1988b). These types of conversations are indifferent to truth and do not strain or challenge the basic identity of participants. Two examples follow:

Would you like to go to the movies tonight?
Yes, in fact there's one I've been wanting to see. Whose turn is it to chose?
You can. I just want to go to a movie.

Could you review this paper that I wrote? I need your input.
Yes, I'd be honored.

### Conversations of Characterizations

The reciprocal assigning of positive or negative characteristics of the participants is typical of conversations of characterizations (Maturana, 1988b). An example of a conversation including a positive characterization is as follows:

I appreciate your visiting my ill husband. You're such a thoughtful person.
Well, thanks for the nice compliment.

John Gottman and his research team set out to discover what distinguishes stable marriages from unstable ones (Gottman, 1991, 1994b, 1994c; Gottman & Silver, 1994). They discovered several behaviors that differentiated marriages that ended in divorce from those that did not. Gottman found that marriages that did not last resembled each other in one overriding way: They followed the same, specific downward spiral before coming to a sad end. One behavior distinguishing unstable marriages was criticism. By criticizing, one is attacking and usually blaming another's personality or character rather than a specific behavior. Following is an example of this type of conversation:

Where have you been? I thought you were someone I could count on to be on time.
This is one of the few times that I've been late.
No, you're self-centered and disrespectful of others' time.

### Conversations of Accusations and Recriminations

Complaints of unfulfilled expectations occur within conversations of accusations and recriminations (Maturana, 1988b). These types of conversations give rise to emotional contradiction because they make claim to a knowledge of an objective reality and thus there exists a mutual negation. With these conversations, opinions and descriptions take place in a domain of rejection and frustration. These conversations may lead to emotional and physical suffering, deny the existence of others, and interfere with structural coupling between members, leading to possible disintegration of a relationship. Following is one example:

I had so much hope that you were going to finally stop drinking.
Well, you know that I've been trying, and if you had more confidence in me, I'd be farther along now.
Oh, so it's all my fault, is it? Well you're the one with the problem.
Yes, well, my problem is you.

### Conversations of Command and Obedience

Conversations of command and obedience occur against an emotional background of mutual negation and self-negation in which some of the participants obey (Maturana, 1988b). This behavior results in the negating of self by the one who obeys and, simultaneously and ironically, negates the one who commands. The negation of the "commander" occurs because he negates those who obey by accepting their self-negation as legitimate. For example, in a nursing home, a health professional may command an elderly person to get out of bed, negating the elderly person (and herself):

Mr. Valquez, get out of bed; you've been sleeping too long.
Not yet, I'm tired.
You're tired because you sleep all the time and don't move around enough, now get up.
Okay. You're the nurse.

### Conversations Inviting Growth and Change

Conversations inviting growth and change work through disagreements, differences, and conflict. One of the most interesting findings by Gottman and Silver (1994) was that hot marital conflict by itself is not destructive; in fact, the discussion of conflictual issues is useful for a marriage. Even in spicy marriages in which there was a lot of fighting and bickering, stable couples were able to find a way to balance their frequent arguments. The difference between deteriorating and stable couples was that stable couples used certain phrases and actions during arguments that prevented negativity from spiraling out of control. In effect, the guarding of one's tongue through the choice of conciliatory words and gestures acts as a glue that holds the marriage together during tense times.

Coevolving conversations that facilitate the resolving of disagreements involves the following: letting go of certainty or the need to be right, validating the other person's experience, listening with one's heart and drawing forth the other's heart, giving up being defensive, letting the other know one understands or is trying to, and staying calm. An example follows:

I know we haven't been getting along well these last few weeks. What do you think is wrong?

Well, I can only speak for myself, but I've been really stressed with our son being ill and you don't seem to want to talk about it.

I do want to talk about it; perhaps I don't because I don't know how to stop you worrying.

I don't need you to stop me worrying; I just need to be able to say that I'm worried.

Okay, let's sit down right now. I'd like to learn what you're worried about . . . and then I've got a couple of things to say.

Great, thanks for bringing this up, it's been a really hard time.

### Conversations of Affirmation and Affection

Conversations of affirmation and affection consist of reciprocal confirmations of another's worth and value as a human being. This type of conversation opens space for the existence of another. It is these conversations that assist in emotional healing by triggering structural changes that restore the dynamic biological equilibrium. "Heart-to-heart conversations," an example of conversations of affirmation and affection, can be observed between the clinician and family members and between family members in our hermeneutic interpretations of our research families.

Couples in Gottman's research who were sliding into criticism or contemptuousness corrected their interactions with an abundance of positive comments. The balance is critical: Gottman found that the magic ratio of this balance is 5:1. As long as there is at least five times as much positive as negative communication—five times as much affection, humor, smiling, complimenting, agreement, empathy, and active nondefensive listening as there is negative communication—the marriage is on a pathway to improvement and increased happiness. Detailed examples of this type of conversation are offered in chapter 6. We believe that clinicians need to make an effort toward drawing forth and coevolving conversations of affirmation and affection, because these are conversations that promote healing.

In summary, we become our conversations and we generate the conversations that we become (Mendez et al., 1988). Therapeutic conversations constitute deliberate and purposeful actions on the part of the clinician. It is hoped that these actions will trigger in family members structural changes such that they will no longer participate in conversations of negative characterizations, accusations, and recriminations: conversations that characterize a family in which individuals suffer. Clinicians and families "remain human only as long as our operation in love and ethics is the operation basis of our coexistence" (Maturana, 1988b, p. 82).

The privilege of working with families invites clinicians to consider that our participation in therapeutic conversations influences emotional and structural changes in ourselves as we witness the healing in others. But how do we coevolve and draw forth conversations that invite change? Through our intensive hermeneutic interpretation of our clinical practice (see Appendix B), we have uncovered interactions in our therapeutic conversations with families that have triggered dramatic changes. These interactions, major and minor moves, and interventions are described in chapters 4 through 8.

*The clinician offers invitations to reflection.*

"The moment of reflection . . . is the moment when we become aware of that part of ourselves which we cannot see in any other way" (Maturana & Varela, 1992, p. 23). Maturana and Varela speak of this reflection as being a phenomenon that occurs when one looks in the mirror. They say it is the moment when we are aware of ourselves in a new way. We believe that people also become aware of others in a new way (and of others' views of others and of others' views of themselves) through the process of reflection. A reflection can be about the past, present, or future. It does not just mean looking back. Reflections on the present and future can be powerful influences as well.

> Reflection is a process of knowing how we know. It is an act of turning back upon ourselves. It is the only chance we have to discover our blindness and to recognize that the certainties and knowledge of others are, respectively, as overwhelming and tenuous as our own. (Maturana & Varela, 1992, p. 24)

It seems that in some manner the dizzying circularity increases the clarity of what is "seen." Comments of family members after or on reflection sound like the following: I've never seen it like that before; I have a new view; I saw my son again for the first time; I've never heard my husband say those things before—it was wonderful; I felt so freed up to listen; I had time to think.

The importance of having time to think was emphasized by

Andersen (1991a), who was the innovator of the formal concept of the reflecting team. Talking about "inner talk" and "outer talk," he stated, "When we take part in the 'talking cure' we should probably ask ourselves all the time: is the talk I have with this person slow enough so that the other person and I have time enough for our 'inner' talks?" (p. 29). Invitations to reflection allow time for "inner talks" and time to reflect on the inner talk.

We believe that an important part of our work as family clinicians is to invite, entice, and as Maturana (1988a) has said, "seduce" the family members to a reflection: "You will never be able to do instructive interaction. The most that you can do is to talk to the patient and invite this person to a reflection that will allow the realization that there is an illness. . . . Understanding cannot be forced" (Maturana, 1988a).

Andersen (1991a) noted that when someone believes he can instruct another, the other defends himself and is actually less open. For Andersen there is an important distinction between change that is imposed from the outside and change that occurs when "premises, namely the knowing and the sensing aspects, are widened" (p. 30). We would say when facilitative beliefs are drawn forth. It is the kind of change described by Andersen that we want to encourage and in which we want to participate. We are continually attracted to various ways to invite family members to a reflection.

Questions invite reflection. Reflexive questions have been developed and described by Tomm (1987b, 1988). White's (1988) self-description question—"What do you think that says about you?"—is a simple yet elegant example of the doubling back on oneself with an invitation to reflect that is extended through therapeutic questions. Invitations to reflect come to us in day-to-day conversations through questions as well. We are invited to a reflection when a previous lover returns and asks, "How do you explain that it never worked for the two of us before?" We are invited to reflect when a friend asks, "Why do you think I'm so terrific?" Reflexive questions can be quite elaborate but may appear simple. In the following example, a quite homely, even linear, question is asked: "Do you know who I am?"

A wife visited her severely cognitively and physically impaired husband in the nursing home. She asked him as she sat to visit: "James, do you know who I am?" Her husband studied her face for what seemed to be several minutes and then said, "No, but I know you're someone who loves me." Was something seen that had not been seen before? Did reflection occur? Although this man could not identify the person of his wife, he was able to reflect on other times and experiences of a loving face.

Following the offerings to a family by a reflecting team, Andersen

(1991a) invites himself to a reflection about all the "available but not used questions. . . . What would be seen then? And which explanations could be constructed based on all these other not-seen descriptions? I find myself more and more curious by thinking of the content of all the alternative conversations we could have had" (p. 41).

In addition to questions, we can invite others to a reflection by "creating a context for change; creating an environment in which persons change themselves; offering ideas, advice and suggestions that can serve as useful perturbations" (Wright & Levac, 1992, p. 916). The ideas, advice, and suggestions that may serve as perturbations are offered in a manner that appreciates objectivity-in-parentheses. Invitations to reflect are offered in a spirit of wonderment and tenacity. These invitations are not of the "you're invited but not expected" variety. The invitations to reflect are laden with the clinician's belief that new ways of seeing may be awaiting family members as they participate in a reflection. The invitation to reflect may be extended by the clinician to family members through the reflecting team, the reflecting position, stories of other families, sermonettes, split opinions, research findings, and therapeutic letters. (See chapter 6 for further elaboration of these therapeutic offerings.) We are tenacious in discovering or uncovering ways to invite family members to a reflection because of our belief that interventions that involve reflection have an increased likelihood of being selected as perturbations and of triggering changes in the biopsychosocial–spiritual structures of family members.

With invitations to a reflection, the challenging of constraining beliefs commences. Family members are moved from "seeing through a glass darkly" to seeing through a glass magnified. Through inviting family members to a reflection, the "truth" of their stance, which has constrained solutions, is gently challenged. It is now possible to offer, entice, and invite them to consider that what they believed was *true* was only an illusion—that it "appeared to be" that way because of their original constraining beliefs about themselves, others, and life. We cannot *make* people believe something. We cannot *give* them a new facilitative belief. It happens through the process of structural coupling and invitations to a reflection.

A highly volatile, polarized, conflictual couple were sequentially offered the reflecting position during a therapy session. Alternately, one spouse came behind the mirror to observe with the clinical team while the other spouse continued in the therapeutic conversation with the therapist. Dramatic shifts in stances occurred. It was as though they had their eyes rotated, so different was the view each had of the other following their reflections. Maturana said that "you discover that disagreements can only be solved by entering a domain of co-inspiration" (Simon, 1985, p. 43). Perhaps inviting family members to a reflection allows the domain of co-inspiration to be more accessible to all.

*The clinician and family members change through their interaction.*

Health care professionals have tended to behave as though their influence on the client is unidirectional: The clinician does to or for the client. The ideas of structural determinism and structural coupling help us appreciate the bidirectional, coevolving nature of the therapeutic conversation and of change. All interventions are interactional: The responses of the clinician are invited by the responses of the client–family, which in turn are invited by the responses of the clinician. The direction and focus of the therapeutic conversation are coevolved. The clinician may experience structural changes in response to family members' ideas, just as family members may experience changes in their biopsychosocial–spiritual structures in response to the clinician's ideas.

Therapeutic conversations are brought forth when clinicians take a cooperative and collaborative stance with families that is based on mutual respect. When clinicians demand obedience (e.g., to have a client follow a particular diabetic diet, take medication at a prescribed time, or stop nagging a spouse about his lack of exercise for his heart condition), they are coevolving a conversation in which the beliefs of the health professional are esteemed as more correct than the clients' concerning how to manage an illness. Health professionals who engage in these efforts at instructive interaction, rather than inviting individuals to a reflection and engaging in collaborative interaction, typically operate from a worldview of objectivity-without-parentheses. The outcome of these efforts to interact instructively with family members often invites clinicians to distinguish certain family members as "noncompliant." By incorporating Maturana's notion of the impossibility of instructive interaction, however, it becomes clear that the distinction, or label, of "noncompliance" not only is not useful, but also is a biological impossibility (Wright & Levac, 1992).

The word *intervention* has recently come under scrutiny (Duncan et al., 1994). Do we intervene or do we collaborate with families? Is intervention a discrete act or the therapeutic conversational process itself? Are there distinctions between assessment and intervention, or does assessment become intervention? Our working definition of the term *intervention* follows:

An *intervention* is any action or response of the clinician, which includes the clinician's overt therapeutic actions and internal cognitive–affective responses, that occurs in the context of a clinician–client relationship offered to effect individual, family, or community functioning for which the clinician is accountable.

We believe that clinical interventions are actualized only in a relationship between the clinician and the family members. For this reason, we prefer the term *move* to the term *intervention* to account for the seamless flow of conversation between the clinician and family—all of which is intended to be interventional.

The term *move* includes all of the conversational processes that occur between clinician and family members, as opposed to the singling out of a specific aspect of a therapeutic offering, such as a question, advice, suggestion, or homework, or the singling out of a temporal aspect, such as what is offered at the end of an interview versus what is done at the beginning. In chapter 5, the terms *move, macromove, micromove,* and *intervention* are defined, and in chapters 4 through 7, the former three terms are distinguished from the term *intervention*.

Interventions are offered to the family with the intent of effecting change (Wright & Leahey, 1994a). Not all interventions accomplish this goal. We consider effective interventions to be those for which a fit exists between the intervention offered by the clinician and the biopsychosocial–spiritual structure of the client–family member (Wright & Levac, 1992). The client's structure may be perturbed by the ideas (interventions) offered by the clinician and vice versa. The central issue is again one of fit.

*The clinician is not invested in a particular outcome.*

We are in the business of change yet we are not invested in a particular outcome. When we appreciate the uncertainty that arises when people select what fits for them on the basis of their own present structures, it becomes impossible to be invested in a particular outcome. Maturana's passion about his ideas has been contrasted with his statement that he is not passionate about changing others (Colapinto, 1985). To us, Maturana's passion about his ideas is not inconsistent with, but rather evidence of, what he believes. People will select out what fits for them. A person's selection of an idea is dependent on her current biopsychosocial–spiritual structure, not on another's passionate presentation.

The respect we have for others' structures leads us to put our energy into areas other than pushing a particular outcome. Our approach to therapy is not a hopeless *que sera sera* stance, but rather an exciting, optimistic stance that invites continual curiosity and increasing humility as we approach family members and stand in amazement at their ability to change and the direction and pace of those changes.

Our wonder and amazement about particular outcomes influence even the language we use when writing academic course outlines. We do not state, "Students will learn/understand . . . "; we write, "Students will be provided with opportunities to learn/understand. . . ." We cannot say a priori what the student will learn. Any professor knows that any one seminar is experienced in as many ways as there are students in the class, plus one—the professor's!

Mince (1992) pointed out one of the pitfalls of being invested in a particular outcome: "[The] therapist's need to watch change occur can tempt the therapist to act too instrumentally. If the therapist must always know the outcomes, she may not be able to make the context changes which can help change occur" (p. 337). Being invested in a particular outcome is an occupational hazard for those in the healing arts. As Rossman (1989) pointed out, clinicians need to be aware that "their healing ability consists mainly of influencing, stimulating and inspiring clients to move along the course of their own healing path" (p. 81).

The danger of being invested in a particular outcome is illustrated in a therapeutic letter of apology to a family coauthored by a graduate student following a supervision session with WLW. Part of the letter follows:

Dear Claude and Madeline,
    Following our session, we discussed your family and my role in therapy and frankly, I have been extremely excited to tell you about some of the insight I gained through the experience. I am beginning to think that maybe I have been the one that is stuck in the problems, maybe even at times holding you back a bit. Would it be alright if I shared with you some of the things we talked about that have led me to see your family and our work together in a new way?
    Third, and probably most impactful for me, one of my long held beliefs was challenged—that families are not finished with therapy until the presenting problem has totally disappeared. I am not sure where I picked up this belief, but I now know it is constraining for both the family and me as a therapist. Dr. Watson asked me, "How do you know when therapy is over? Here we have a wonderful family that has been coming to therapy for over 50 sessions. They have successfully dealt with a divorce, school difficulties, teenage troubles and a minor surgery. What else do they need to do before we will let them go home? Maybe therapy is over when their resources are freed up so they can successfully live with their problems" . . . So, I ask

you the question Dr. Watson asked me, "How will you know when you no longer need to come to therapy?"

I am excited to hear from you and look forward to hearing your voice and seeing your strength.

Sincerely,
Jonathan Sandberg, MFT Graduate Student,
Wendy L. Watson, Ph.D., MFT Professor &
Clinical Supervisor

We agree with Hoffman-Hennessy (Hoffman-Hennessy & Davis, 1993) that setting goals for a normative outcome "often hides a therapeutic or social bias; second, getting too attached to it can seriously get in the way—the more you push, the less likely it is that it will happen. That is a principle of zen, but it is a principle of therapy as well" (p. 371). Again, when clinicians are too passionate about change occurring in one direction, we become imposing in our ideas and we close space for change. It is options and requests that facilitate the coevolution of change, not demands. We have come to believe that in the domain of clinical work with families, passion for a particular outcome promulgates prescriptions, and prescriptions preclude progress!

Noninvestment in a particular outcome does not mean we are not interested in what the outcome is for *these particular* family members at *this particular* time. We are extremely interested in the outcome with each family and want to know what has happened. We are curious about the continuing changes that are occurring. This interest in outcome is what prompted LMW, in her final session with Research Family 1, to take as much interest in the outcome of the respite trip for the parents of the son with MS as she previously had taken in the catastrophically demoralizing events that initially prompted the family to seek help. Details of the vacation buffet and bus ride were explored with as much therapeutic curiosity as the dilemmas of the devoted caregiving parents and debilitated son had been, in the earlier sessions. Our interest in each family's particular outcome and our investment in outcome as a genuine issue are also evidenced by our conducting of outcome follow-up interviews with families. Six months after the last session, families are invited to provide an evaluation of the services they received and to comment on the changes they have experienced.

"We are not attached to any particular outcome, only to one that would remove or diminish the reason people come to talk to us" (Hoffman-Hennessy & Davis, 1993, p. 371). What is the outcome the family wants? A frequent experience for clinical supervisors is to hear supervisees describe frustrating, fruitless, and protracted work with a family. However, when the supervisee is asked about what the family wants out of therapy, the clinician is unable to say. The "one question question" focuses the clinician's therapeutic efforts on the desired outcomes of family members: "If you could have just one question answered during our work together, what would that one question be?"

Clinicians have desired outcomes, in a general way, for each session and for our overall therapeutic work with families. For us, a "good" family session may include creating the context for change, clearing away obstacles, opening space for conversations that may decrease suffering and increase healing, and other macro- and micromoves described in chapters 4 through 7. Our therapeutic goal is to uncover, discover, and challenge constraining beliefs: beliefs that prohibit, impede, constrain, restrain, restrict, and diminish family members' lives. We want to identify, offer, and solidify facilitative beliefs that bring forth the passion of family members living together.

We have offered six beliefs about clinicians that influence the manner in which we approach and assist families experiencing difficulties. The following description of a session by one of WLW's graduate students portrays the student's ability to use the six beliefs to guide her therapeutic work. The description of the case was written in the student's (EmRee Pugmire's) own words. The analysis of the beliefs that influenced the student's therapeutic moves has been added:

A client presented to therapy wanting to help herself; however, the help she sought was for me to teach her how to get her boyfriend into therapy as "he" was the one that needed help. As she described this man that she loved so much, I couldn't help thinking "why would any woman (or man for that matter) subject herself to the misery she was currently in?" She described her relationship as one where she was the martyr and caretaker for this boyfriend. It appeared that he was giving her signals that he wanted the relationship to be over; yet, she "knew" that he needed her and that eventually he would start to love her again. I truly felt she should get out of the relationship but did not want to give this as a directive in the first session.

This client was very passionate about her story, and try as I or the team might, she was very invested in retelling the same story over and over. Her story was one of how horrible he was to her and how she stood by and took it just because she believed the relationship would eventually work. Even when the team asked about the boyfriend's good points, my client would quickly jump back into her story of how rotten this guy was to her. She gave evidence of this over and over again. Not only was she telling the team and myself this story, but it appeared that she had enlisted a very active audience in her boyfriend's family and her own family of origin. She was very close to his sisters and spent hours a day on the phone talking to them or to her boyfriend's mother telling them how horrible he was to her. They had originally said that she was the "only one for him" as well as the "best thing that ever happened to him," but by this point they as well as her parents had suggested that she get out of the relationship because she "deserved more" than what she was getting from and in him.

At the start of the second session, she began to give me her latest evidence which included the many rotten things that he had done to her in the past week. As I listened I was absolutely confused about why she would continue to let this happen to herself. It became obvious to me that she was not going to listen to me tell her to get out of the relationship [*The clinician is not a change agent*] because everyone else had told her to do so and she had chosen not. It was at this point I took a break from the session. [*The clinician offers invitations to reflection*. In this case the clinician invited herself to a reflection.] It was during this time I realized that I needed to understand where she was coming from in order to be helpful to her. As I thought about what she was seeing, I realized that she truly believed that she was the "only one" that could help this guy. The more I thought about how she saw this, the more I began to believe that she was right. It made perfect sense from her view, and I found myself totally believing that she was the only one that could help this boyfriend.

As I returned to the session, I told her that the way I saw it we had two directions that we could work with. These came from my personal beliefs about her problem. I then presented my two options as (A) I would help her get out of the relationship (which any good feminist therapist would do), or (B) I would help her help the boyfriend be a better person. With this I offered ideas of what I thought would be helpful to the boyfriend. I also noted that if option B were chosen that it would not be consistent with this goal to spend time tearing him down by telling about his horrible actions to her.

I'm not sure how to explain this, but I feel that my heart was truly changed so that in some way I experienced her boyfriend in the way that she was able to see him. Because of this change I found that I could believe, along with her, that she was the one to help him. I was totally comfortable with either the A or B choice and felt I would be able to help her on either decision. [*The clinician is not invested in a particular outcome*.] The important thing was that she needed to make the choice of which way or direction she wanted to seek therapy for. [*The clinician's preferred stance is nonhierarchical*.]

BELIEFS OF MINE THAT WERE CHALLENGED AND HOW: [*The clinician and family members change through their interaction*.]

> 1: "This is a horrible guy and you're crazy to stay in this relationship." This belief was challenged by my client's insistence on telling her story over and over. I became interested in what she felt I had not yet heard. I assumed that if I had heard what she had wanted me to hear she would have told a new story.

2: "This guy is never going to change and you will have no influence on him." As I heard her stories I realized how impressionable he really was. He seemed to be most influenced by the word "not." When he was told he was "not" good at something, he truly became "not" good at it. I was curious if this was a cycle and thought that if it was, she probably was the only one that would have the patience with him to break through it.

3: "There is one solution to this problem." I could see benefits for working with both plan A and plan B.

4: "I have to have a direction for therapy by session number 3." After giving her plan A and plan B options, I cautioned her that I did not think she was quite ready to make that decision but that she should think about the changes she should make that would help her be successful in following either plan. This helped me not feel pressured as well.

HOW THERAPY CHANGED:

1: My client became the active force in therapy. [*The clinician is not a change agent.*] I attribute this to someone believing her story [*The clinician coevolves therapeutic conversations*] and to clarifying her concerns by saying there are two plans [*The clinician offers invitations to reflection*] and when you choose one we disregard the other. [*The clinician's preferred stance is nonhierarchical.*]

2: I did not feel "unfruitful" while she was deciding which plan to go with. [*The clinician is not invested in a particular outcome.*] This began by my cautioning her not to make the decision right away.

3: She actually did choose to leave him.

4: I was a bit remorseful that she made this choice but would have felt the same if she would have chosen to stay. [*The clinician is not invested in a particular outcome.*]

This summary by the student of the process of therapy, the changes in beliefs of the clinician, and evidence of change in the client highlights our six beliefs that serve as principles about clinicians and demonstrates that when clinicians use the six beliefs, the therapeutic process unfolds and therapeutic progress occurs.

## CONCLUSION

This chapter has provided an in-depth discussion of our beliefs about therapeutic change and clinicians, influenced by the worldview of objectivity-in-parentheses. We believe that change is determined by structure, involves structural coupling, and is evidenced by changes in structure. Four beliefs serve as guiding principles for therapeutic change: (a) Therapeutic change occurs as the belief that is at the heart of the matter is distinguished, challenged, or solidified; (b) therapeutic change occurs through a fit between the therapeutic offerings of the clinician and the biopsychosocial–spiritual structures of family members; (c) change is inevitable, but the direction and pace of therapeutic change are unpredictable; and (d) therapeutic change needs to be distinguished and languaged.

Six beliefs about clinicians guide therapeutic conversations: (a) The clinician is not a change agent; (b) the clinician's preferred stance is non-hierarchical, (c) the clinician coevolves therapeutic conversations; (d) the clinician offers invitations to reflection; (e) the clinician and family members change through their interaction; and (f) the clinician is not invested in a particular outcome. These beliefs about therapeutic changes and clinicians are the bedrock of our clinical work with families.

# PART II

# Key Macromoves of Our Advanced Clinical Approach

CHAPTER 4

# Creating a Context
# for Changing Beliefs

A MONG THE MOVES we have identified in our research, the macromove we have come to call "creating a context for changing beliefs" constitutes the central and enduring foundation of the therapeutic process. It is key to the relationship between the clinician and the family. It is not just a necessary prerequisite to the process of therapeutic change, it *is* therapeutic change in and of itself. The clinician is like a gardener, carefully preparing the ground and clearing away the obstacles to ensure that, as the seeds are planted, they will have the greatest possibility of growing and flourishing. Without the careful preparation and caretaking of the ground, there is no growth, no change, no garden.

Through our research and clinical practice, we have come to the conclusion that a context for changing beliefs must be created and maintained if healing is to occur. In the clinical domain, interventions such as creating a collaborative relationship or offering questions, ideas, advice, and opinions are the clinician's seeds. The "relationship" interventions are no less important than the "opinion" interventions. One hopes that all the clinician's seeds will be received by the ground in a manner that will result in growth. It is hoped that the interventions offered by the clinician will be experienced as perturbations that will have an impact because they fit with the individual's biopsychosocial–spiritual structure. Within that fit, change is possible. Not all of the interventions offered by the clinician will fit with the individual's structure. There appears to be an increased likelihood of fit, however, when the context for change has been created. More seeds seem to fall on receptive, fertile ground when the ground has been carefully prepared and continuously maintained through the process of creating a context for changing beliefs. It is important to note that the term *intervention* is not limited to the therapeutic conversations that happen after a context for change has been created. Interventions include all of the ways the clinician coevolves a relationship, and therefore a context for change, with the client.

The therapeutic relationship is not a one-way street. In the process of preparing and maintaining the ground, not only does the ground undergo change, but the gardener changes as well. Maturana and Varela (1992) referred to this phenomenon as "structural coupling." (See chapter 3 for elaboration of this concept.) Because the gardener also changes through the process of preparing and maintaining the ground, the gardener is more likely to select the seeds (interventions) from among a large selection of those that may flourish in that particular ground (for that particular client–family at that time). Beginning at the first interview, the clinician and the family coevolve together, with both the family and the clinician changing in response to the other and according to their individual biopsychosocial–spiritual structures, which have been influenced by their history of interactions and by their genetic makeup.

The dance of structural coupling is illustrated in a conversation that took place between the clinician (WLW) and the 13-year-old son of Research Family 4. The mother was concerned that her son was depressed and withdrawn. The therapeutic conversation between clinician and son begins with the topic of hockey; the son oriented the clinician to his collection of hockey cards. This hockey talk is more than social chitchat; it is an important part of preparing the ground. Even more important, it becomes the vehicle through which, not only do the clinician and the son structurally couple, but also the son, the mother, and the clinician all coevolve to view the son in a new way. This example provides evidence that creating a context for change does not precede therapeutic change; rather, relationships between family members and the clinician unfold together with therapeutic change.

WLW: So what about this hockey player—Pavel Buré? What about this guy do you really admire? What would you love to have as your characteristic or quality?

SON: I like him because he won the Calder trophy last year.

WLW: So he's a good player.
SON: Yeah.
WLW: And what makes him a good player? I want to write this down.
SON: He's a real good shooter and he can pass and he can score.
WLW: And how do you think, I'm asking your Mom this, how do you think that your son in some ways is like Pavel Buré, in ways perhaps that he doesn't even know?

In this excerpt the son gets to be a teacher and guide to the clinician, who is naive about the world of hockey—even though she is Canadian! The clinician uses the hockey conversation to engage the son and expands hockey into a metaphor for the game of life. The mother is invited to distinguish her son as a good sportsman and exclaims how she loves watching him play: "He plays his heart out on his team." The story of "son as hero" begins to emerge. Later, the mother offers that her son is similar to herself in that he has "had some pretty tough obstacles stuck in his way over the years and he has just more or less bounced around them and gone on," thus praising her son for his persistence and tenacity in the game of life. The son's expertise is drawn forth in the hockey conversation, making him feel not only "engaged" with the clinician, but also more aware of his strengths and competencies. The more the clinician draws forth the hockey conversation, the more a 13-year-old with passions rather than problems emerges. Most important, however, is the deliberate way the clinician invites the mother to comment on her son's strengths, thus providing opportunities for the mother to challenge her own belief that her son is problem-saturated and full of pathology. The clinician uses this opportunity to affirm, commend, and elevate this family's abilities and beliefs about themselves. All who take part in the therapeutic conversation, including the clinician, change in response to the other and in response to their own internal dynamics.

Through our research, we have identified that the macromove of creating a context for change has three major components, or micromoves: preparing and maintaining the ground, distinguishing the problem, and removing obstacles to change. An in-depth description of each micromove follows.

## PREPARING AND MAINTAINING THE GROUND

There is a special but taken-for-granted process of preparing the ground that occurs in the first meeting between the clinician and the family. Subsequently, each session provides further opportunities to maintain the ground. The process of developing and maintaining a relationship is not immediately tangible but is embedded invisibly in the conversation that occurs between the clinician and the family. It becomes obvious only through its absence. Clinical authors have referred to this process using a variety of terms such as *engagement* (Tomm & Wright, 1979; Wright & Leahey, 1994a); *joining* (Minuchin, 1974); and *therapeutic alliance* (Marmar, Horowitz, Weiss, & Marziali, 1986). So important is the process of developing and maintaining a relationship between the clinician and the family that the research literature unequivocally champions the presence of a therapeutic relationship as one of the best predictors of success in therapy (Duncan, Hubble, & Rusk, 1994).

The literature on health professionals as healers also supports the importance of preparing and maintaining the ground. Richard Carlson and Benjamin Shield (1989) encourage health professionals to think of themselves as healers; however, "the role of the healer is *not* to do the healing. Instead, the healers empower and enable the individual to achieve healing" (p. 112). How is this empowerment accomplished? "Healers create an environment for healing to occur; an environment that generates possibilities for healing" (p. 117). We argue that an important aspect of the environment is the creation of a collaborative relationship between the clinician and the family members.

In a deliberate first step, the clinician begins preparing the ground in the first session by providing structure: introducing himself, explaining the setting and nature of the work (e.g., We are interested in learning about families experiencing difficulties with illness), offering an agenda for the session, and offering parameters about the duration and scope of the therapeutic relationship. The provision of structure seems to reduce the unknown, making people who are strangers feel more comfortable, and is a first, concrete step in preparing the ground. Bordin (1979) suggested that the following three conditions must be present for a therapeutic alliance to occur: (a) agreement on the goals; (b) agreement on the tasks of therapy: specific techniques, topics of conversation, interview procedures, frequency of meetings; and (c) development of an ongoing relationship bond between the clinician and client.

One useful tool in preparing the ground during the first session is the use of the genogram as a vehicle to begin a purposeful therapeutic conversation and elicit information about the family's experience in a nonthreatening manner. Through the seemingly simple and highly structured process of asking about names, ages, and occupations of family members, information about everything from drug abuse to sexual abuse of family members can be identified. For example, a question such as the following can be included: "These days a question we routinely ask all families is 'Has anyone in your family had difficulties with alcohol or drugs?'" These questions, when asked as a matter of course within the safety of the genogram, prepare the ground for later elaboration and exploration of other difficult topics.

The clinician tries to use the family's language to make the explanations and questions increasingly palatable to all family members. For example, the clinician might use humor if it fits with the family, or she may use more casual, less formal language when talking with adolescents and children. Even within the first few minutes of conversation, the clinician looks for opportunities to make connections among the pieces of data elicited through the genogram in a manner that may be new information to the family. These observations are offered as "trial balloons" and passing comments, without any need on the part of the clinician to persuade the family or for the family to agree. In the following example with Research Family 2, the clinician (LMW), through the process of collecting genogram data, noted the possible connection between the numerous challenges the family was dealing with and the health problem:

LMW: Okay, let's just go back and finish up [referring to the genogram, which elicited information about marital tension that existed around stepfamily parenting and concern about the health of another family member]. That was very helpful to me because it is an important aspect of your family life and other challenges you have in addition to your health problems. Sometimes these issues can affect your health problems, sometimes not. Would you guess that these issues affect your health problems?

CONNIE: It's hard to say because it's been like that for so long, I don't know.

LMW: It's like the old chicken and the egg, we don't know which comes first. Your family problems get exacerbated or become worse because of health problems, or do the health problems become worse because of family problems?

The clinician senses she may have stumbled onto something here: the client's beliefs about the etiology of her health problems. By offering the possible connection between the stresses in the family and the mother's cardiac illness and anxiety attacks, the clinician brings into awareness an issue that may be new information for this client. The connection is deliberately offered in a tenuous manner. Without needing to convince the client of the correctness of this idea, the clinician watches to see how the mother responds to the idea that health problems and family stress may be connected in a recursive manner.

From the beginning of the first interview, the clinician chooses to make a clear distinction between a social conversation and a therapeutic conversation (see chapter 3). Although there is initially an element of social conversation in the meeting and greeting, the ground is carefully prepared for a therapeutic conversation to occur. This includes deliberately breaking the strongly sanctioned, unwritten rules of social conversation. Being insatiably curious, which is enacted through the asking of questions (particularly tough questions such as those concerning violence, alcohol, or substance abuse), breaks the rules of social conversation. Speaking the unspeakable, such as commenting on strong affect in the room as soon as it is noticed (e.g., You look really unhappy about being here), invites conversations that are outside the social domain.

A powerful belief that is challenged throughout the process of preparing and maintaining the ground is that related to the hierarchical stance of traditional health care relationships: that the clinician is the only expert and maintains a one-up position, and the client–family, persistently in a one-down position, must do all the expert clinician says or be labeled noncompliant. (Refer to Beliefs About Families in chapter 2 and Beliefs About Therapeutic Change and Beliefs About Clinicians in chapter 3.) In a hierarchical relationship, there is an unspoken rule that the person in a one-down position must never speak aloud about the relationship or about the process. One question offered by the clinician that encourages families to break that relationship rule and enter into a nonhierarchical relationship is, "I have asked you a number of questions today; is there anything you would like to ask me?" (Wright, 1989, p. 15).

The belief that a good clinician–client relationship is a hierarchical relationship is also challenged when the clinician models and invites transparency in speaking about the relationship between clinician and family. Questions such as, "Have you had a chance to tell your story?" or "How did you experience our session today? Was it useful?" invite commentary about the relationship and the therapeutic process. The invitation for commentary on the therapeutic relationship clearly gives the message that the client's experience matters. It is as though the clinician, in concert with the clinical team, declares, "Here is who we are; this is how we work; and here is what you can expect from us." More important, the clinician is asking, "Does this way of working fit for you? Are we meeting your expectations and needs? What do you need us to do differently?" In short, the clinician ascertains whether he has prepared and maintained the ground.

However important it is for the family to feel comfortable or "engaged" with the clinician, engagement is not all the skilled clinician offers. The second major component of creating a context for changing beliefs is the process of identifying the specific problem with which the family desires assistance.

## DISTINGUISHING THE PROBLEM

Clarifying the problem, exploring the problem, naming the problem, and defining the problem all constitute distinguishing the problem: the second major component in creating a context for change. Papp (1983) suggested that a "battle" for definition of the problem occurs between family members and clinician: "Whoever controls the definition of the problem controls the therapy" (p. 27). We prefer that the definition of the problem be jointly distinguished by clinicians and family members. Although we concur with Kenneth Stewart, LaNae Valentine, and Jon Amundson (1991), who suggested that the battle for definition might be defined as a battle to loosen and widen perceptions and beliefs of both family members and the clinician, we prefer that the problem-defining process be referred to as "coevolving the definition" rather than a "battle for definition," which sounds too adversarial, implying it is "us against them." Cecchin (1987) warned clinicians to accept neither their own nor the client's definition too quickly, and Maturana and Varela (1992) cautioned clinicians to adopt an attitude of permanent vigilance against the temptation of certainty. By remaining curious (Cecchin, 1987), a clinician has a greater chance of escaping the sin of certainty: the sin of being too invested in one's own opinion.

Once a definition of the problem has been coconstructed by family members and clinician, the therapeutic process can proceed to the next phase. In so doing, definitions of the problem will widen and expand as beliefs that support, maintain, and sustain a problem are brought to the fore. We are concerned with two levels of conceptualization: the problem (definition and other aspects of it) and beliefs about the problem. Although both are important, we believe that family members' beliefs about the problem are more illuminating and central to treatment and healing.

The following transcript segment offers a rich description of the clinician's persistence in distinguishing the problem. In a first session with a single mother (Linda) and her four children (Research Family 4), the mother expressed concern that her children had been abused by their biological father and believed the children continued to be affected by this past abuse. She viewed herself and her family as very troubled and problem-saturated. The clinician (WLW) invites the perceptions of the children by asking them two questions that attempt to distinguish the problem. The clinician's first question is intended to define the source or origin of the beliefs about the problem:

WLW: You know, sometimes we remember things because other people have told us stories, or sometimes we remember because it's in our mind, or sometimes we remember things because of pictures. How do you remember?

The answer the child provides is tangential, so the clinician persists in discovering who is distinguishing the problem as a problem. Who concurs with mother's problem-saturated view of the family? To do this, the clinician offers another set of distinctions: good family memories and bad family memories.

WLW: There are good memories that we have and then there are some not so good memories. Would you say in this family that you are a family that have more good memories or more not good memories? What would you, David [eldest son], say? Because, again, you could have a different idea than somebody else. Would you say, "Yes, I have more good memories about my family" or more not good memories?

DAVID: More good ones.

WLW: More good ones? Okay, alright, so let me ask my question again. What's the problem that brought you here today? What's the thing that's on your mind the most, that we could help you with today?

The child responds with an answer that does not seem to support the mother's concern. One could hypothesize other possibilities, for example, that there has been abuse but the children are fearful or reluctant to talk about it. Notice the clinician's message to all family members that each person's perception is unique and valued. Next, the clinician draws a temporal distinction between behavior now and behavior in the future, which is of most concern to the mother:

WLW: Now tell me this, from your reading in psychology, like you say, you look at something and then sometimes think how that might be down the road. Is it more the children's behavior that you're seeing now, I'm trying to understand this, or is it your fear of what this behavior might turn into, that is more of a concern for you?

LINDA: Ah . . . both.

WLW: Both? Okay, is it a little bit more one than the other?

LINDA: Um, it's a little bit more the potential.

WLW: More the potential.

This temporal distinction implicitly opens space for the mother to have some influence on the future. A further distinction is offered by the clinician: "Is the concern the family experience of violence or the children not talking about the problem?" The clinician probes for more specifics about the children's behavior that is concerning the mother by asking a question that uncovers the mother's beliefs about the problem.

The question externalizes the mother's beliefs about the problem by giving the problem a voice and life of its own:

WLW: When you say, "What does this behavior mean?" If the behavior could talk, what do you guess, or what do you fear, what would you worry it might be saying? You have thought about this a lot, I'm sure.

LINDA: Well I guess it's saying, "I'm hurting, Mommy, I need attention."

WLW: So, "I'm hurting. I need attention. Love me?"

LINDA: It could be saying, "I worry and am concerned about something." It usually happens after his dad's been around. When I was going to school, I was going to school in this full-time program. I wasn't in just part-time. With four kids, my husband was supposed to do the looking after. I didn't realize at the time that he was sick and that he was abusing him [referring to Timothy, child 4]. The other kids were in school, he wasn't. I think there was some abuse at the preverbal stage. He [Timothy] was acting out and trying to tell me, but I just don't know how to cue into it.

WLW: Okay, so again, "I'm angry about . . . ?" What do you think it might be about his father?

LINDA: "I'm angry about Daddy having done this, and I'm angry at you for having allowed Daddy to do it," because, you see I was gone.

WLW: When you ask yourself some of those questions—"How come Timothy is showing these behaviors?"—is your best guess that he might be saying, "I'm hurting, I need attention, love me, I'm angry about my dad hurting me, I'm angry at you for having allowed it"? Is there any other explanation that fits for you, that he's doing these hurtful behaviors?

There is a continual effort to draw forth distinctions and coevolve new distinctions. This is essential for understanding the problem and creating a context for change. Notice the clinician summarizing the mother's responses and pursuing other explanations for the child's behavior.

One of the most effective questions to distinguish the problem is the "one question question": "If you could have just one question answered in our work together, what would that one question be?" (Wright, 1989). The "one question question" uncovers the family's most pressing concern. We have experienced the focusing power of this question, such as when the family's answer to the question is different, sometimes dramatically so, from "the problem" that has unfolded to that point in the therapeutic conversation. The response to this novel question always refines "the problem," as illustrated in the following example from the end of the first session with Research Family 4:

WLW: Let me just ask you this one last question. If you could have just one question answered in our work together, what one question would you most like answered?

LINDA: Ooh [*laughs*], are you talking about with me or with the family?

WLW: I'm talking about, in our work together, so that can be either.

LINDA: The question I would most like answered? Um . . . how can we overcome what's happened to us and where do we go from here?

WLW: How can we, meaning the family, how can we as a family, and when you say "we, as a family," you mean you and . . .

LINDA: You know, my sweethearts.

WLW: Okay. "How can we as a family, me and my four sweethearts, okay, how can we . . . "

LINDA: How can we overcome the things that have happened to us? Where do we go from here?

WLW: Overcome the things that have happened to us and where do we go from here?

LINDA: Like, how do we "be normal," if you can figure out what "normal" is? Like how can we go on and just live a functional life?

WLW: Okay, and again, we talked about some things, maybe we talked about the most important things, maybe we didn't. But if there was something that you'd hoped that we might talk about today that we didn't get to, I could just make a little note of it and we could go for it next time. What did you hope we would have talked about that we didn't get to today?

LINDA: I think we covered it.

WLW: Did we?

LINDA: I think we covered it pretty well.

WLW: Okay, so do you think you're starting to be able to tell your story that you need to tell?

LINDA: I am. Yes. I've held a lot in for a long time . . .

There is evidence that the process of distinguishing both the problem and what was not the problem was useful to the mother. Notice that the mother's answer focuses on the future and how to have a normal functional life, in contrast to her original presentation of herself and her children as dysfunctional and problem-saturated. After asking the "one question question," the clinician puts the mother on the Board of Directors by asking her to comment on her experience of the session. This move is collaborative and nonhierarchical. By inviting commentary on the relationship, mismatched expectations can be discussed, and ultimately, engagement is strengthened. The mother confirms that she is telling the story she needs to tell, confirming that the work of distinguishing the problem was useful.

In another example, the use of the "one question question" with Connie, who was experiencing angina and panic attacks (Research Family 2), illustrates the way this question is used not only to clarify the beliefs about the problem but also to clarify the client's beliefs about the solution.

LMW: Well, I guess that brings me to a question that we always like to ask in our first meetings with people we see here at the FNU: If there were just one question that you could have answered during our work together, what would that one question be? What is the question that you would most like to try to get some help with or to get answered?

CONNIE: Ah.

LMW: What is the question that you would have for myself or the team to try and help answer for you in our work together?

CONNIE: How I can either get over this or how can you help me deal with it [panic attacks]? Like put it in perspective or something.

LMW: Well now, that's a very important distinction, isn't it? Is your question, "how can I get over it," which means getting total control of it, or "how can I deal with it?"

CONNIE: Well . . .

LMW: Which do you want? Do you want to be totally over it or do you want . . .

CONNIE: I want to be totally over it.

LMW: You want to be totally over it. So you don't want to just learn how to live with it like you do with your arthritis?

CONNIE: No.

LMW: No, you don't want that. For this, you want to be rid of it?

CONNIE: Yes.

The "one question question" is an example of asking a question that is more than a question. It invites the client to narrow the field and uncover the most serious concern at the heart of the matter. In this process, the clinician is invited to a deeper level of understanding about the suffering of the family. Note the persistence and the tracking involved in making the distinction between living alongside a problem versus getting past a problem. The client is invited to reflect on her beliefs about the problem and the solution: What is the main concern and what does she most want from therapy? Knowing the client's preferences has implications for treatment; the question provides a deliberate opportunity for the client to be clear about the focus of therapy that would be most useful to her.

## REMOVING OBSTACLES TO CHANGE

The action-packed movie *Indiana Jones and the Last Crusade* portrays the undaunted, tenacious hero, Indiana Jones, in his arduous quest for the Holy Grail. The similarity between the experiences of Indiana Jones and the work of the clinician in creating a context for change is humorous yet striking. When Indiana Jones finally, after many adventures, locates the cave and proceeds toward the Holy Grail, numerous obstacles constrain his progress: crisscrossing knives, uncertain stepping-stones, unexpected chasms. He is required to discover the clue to defusing each new obstacle to continue his progress toward his goal. The clinician's role is similar. While preparing and maintaining the ground and distinguishing the problem, a variety of obstacles may constrain change, from a dissatisfied, angry family member to conflictual involvement of multiple health care professionals. No further perturbations can be offered until these obstacles are cleared away. No ideas or questions chosen to alter, challenge, or modify constraining beliefs are useful until the context for changing beliefs has been fully prepared.

Although many clinicians have the ability to engage the family, identify the problem, and generate ideas for solutions, a high level of expertise is necessary for removing obstacles to change. Examples of obstacles to change that we have seen in clinical work include a family member who does not want to be present or attends the session under duress, a family member who is dissatisfied about progress in therapy, unclear expectations of therapy, previous negative experiences with health care professionals or therapy, simultaneous involvement with multiple health care professionals, and unrealistic or unknown expectations of the referring person about treatment. Clinical examples are provided in the next section to demonstrate how the skilled clinician deals with these obstacles in the process of creating a context for change.

### OBSTACLE: A FAMILY MEMBER WHO DOES NOT WANT TO BE PRESENT OR ATTENDS THE SESSION UNDER DURESS

One of the hallmarks of our clinical approach is the ability of the skilled clinician to "speak the unspeakable": to raise issues that are implicit and outside the norms of social conversation. One such issue is the family member who shows, usually nonverbally, a disinterest in the session or resentment or even anger at having been coerced to attend. In a social conversation, particularly in the early stages, one would normally feel constrained from commenting on nonverbal communication or inquiring about affect that is impeding a relationship. In a therapeutic conversation, if a clinician feels socially constrained, it is usually a sign that she needs to act contrary to social graces by acknowledging the socially nonsanctioned issue and raising it for discussion.

In a clinical family referred to the Family Nursing Unit by a homecare nurse, the intake information indicated the mother suffered from several chronic illnesses and was living with a male partner and her 13-year-old son. In the process of obtaining the genogram information, the graduate student clinician learned that the male partner was not the mother's common-law husband but a roommate. His resentment at being present for the session was evident as he relayed, with an irritated tone of voice, the story of the referral: "I have no idea what kind of information you were given. The only information we were given is that we had no choice but to come here. We had no choice. We were told we had to show up, otherwise all of Jane's [the mother's] rights and privileges would be taken away by homecare. . . . None of us are here willingly. We were forced to come by homecare."

Having learned this information, the graduate student clinician had several options. It was tempting to try to define the problem by exploring the family's perception of why the homecare nurse had coerced the family into seeking help. It was more important, however, to deal first with the obstacles of coercion, disinterest, and resentment. The clinical supervisor (LMW), observing behind a one-way mirror, phoned into the session and quickly instructed the student to redirect the therapeutic conversation: "Before we deal with this, we must deal with the larger issue of them being here under duress and . . . validate that this is not a fun way to be here. We don't see people under duress, so we're wondering if we should even proceed at this point. Would they be willing to stay if we could change the idea that they're here because they have to be, or should we end the session right now and talk to the homecare nurse? I would just like to get their opinion on that, because I would like to tell them we have a very strong belief that we do not see people here who are required to be here. We don't believe in that."

A further supervisory suggestion was phoned into the graduate student clinician to put her notepad down and clearly say to the family that "we are [not going] to proceed as if this is a clinical session because we need to talk about what we should do with a situation of a homecare nurse who wants you to be here more than you want to be here. So what should we do about this?"

The focus of the conversation was purposefully redirected from talking with the family about their illness experience to helping them deal with the homecare nurse who had made the requisite referral. The dilemma of what to do about the homecare nurse invited a humorous, playful element into the formerly oppressive, tense conversation.

Should the family come for "pretend therapy" or should they tell the homecare nurse they did not need therapy? Several possibilities were explored. Note that the therapeutic conversation centered on how to deal with the coercion experienced by the family members from the directive of the homecare nurse. This is in contrast to distinguishing the problem or assessing the need for the family to be in therapy. To do otherwise would fail to clear away a major obstacle to facilitating change, that of the family being at the FNU under duress.

The end-of-session intervention offered by the clinical team consisted of suggesting four options in response to the family's and clinician's dilemma: (a) pretend therapy (the clinical team could have social tea parties with the family, exchanging cookies and engaging in social chitchat); (b) homecare therapy (the clinical team could send a letter to the homecare nurse about the problems of a coercive referral); (c) archaeology therapy (the clinical team could "dig" for problems and assess whether there were any problems or challenges the family was confronted with in managing the mother's chronic illness); and (d) research therapy (the clinical team could learn from this family what was working well for them in managing a chronic illness and use the clinical videotapes as teaching tapes for other families). The family were asked their opinion of which option would be most helpful and whether they had other ideas that might work even better.

The adolescent son chose a combination of talking about problems and talking about what was going well, as long as cookies accompanied the discussion! Both the mother and the roommate agreed that an integration of the four options would be useful, with the family bringing the cookies the first time. The whole mood changed from one of antagonism toward the clinician and the therapeutic process to one of collaboration on how the therapeutic process would be defined. Defining the kind of therapy (Wright & Watson, 1982), rather than defining the presenting problem, cleared away the obstacle of coercion in a respectful and focused manner. A context for change was cocreated without which the dramatic positive outcomes would not have occurred. These outcomes included less conflict between the mother and son and greater control for the mother over her illness.

OBSTACLE: A FAMILY MEMBER WHO IS DISSATISFIED ABOUT PROGRESS IN THERAPY

A form of speaking the unspeakable has to do with acknowledging and talking about strong affect in the session, be it anger, sadness, or other strong emotions. Any strong affect is a priority that demands immediate attention. This guideline is especially relevant when the affect is around dissatisfaction with the progress of therapy. Research Family 5 was seen for five sessions over a period of 8 weeks. The couple initially presented with concerns about their ability to cope with stress related to the husband's cardiac illness. In the first few minutes of the third session with the couple, the wife (Julie) showed sadness and began crying. She said, "The only reason we are here is because I'm screwed up. . . . We're not getting anywhere, nothing is changing." This statement was surprising, definitely news of a difference, because the couple had responded positively to the first two sessions. Notice the clinician's (LMW) immediate exploration and insatiable curiosity about Julie's affect:

LMW: I'd be interested in knowing what's troubling you today?

JULIE: [*sighs*] I don't know where to begin or how to talk about it. I just feel like he's [husband] trying, but things aren't getting better. [*crying*] I basically feel like just giving up. Like things just keep happening . . .

She describes a variety of stressful situations she has been dealing with in between sessions as an explanation for her discouragement. However, the clinician does not get caught in the explanations. She persists.

LMW: Okay. But I'm still trying to understand how come you're so troubled today?

Julie suggests that her husband (Robert) looks like the "good guy." She provides examples of his behavior that show he was trying to be supportive of her but contends that these are not the complete story of what has been going on at home.

LMW: You feel that through the story he [the husband] presented here that somehow I'm getting the idea that he's a good guy and you're the bad guy? So when you said the comment to me right when we started this session that "we're here because of me," and you said it in a certain tone, that somehow you're worried that I'm getting the perception that you're at fault, that you're to blame?

JULIE: Yes!

LMW: Really! Is there anything that I've been doing to give you that impression?

This question shows the importance of inviting and facilitating the client's ability to speak the unspeakable about the clinician's behavior. What is the origin of the wife's belief that she is the "bad guy" and to blame? The clinician shows curiosity and an openness to facilitate speaking the unspeakable—that perhaps the clinician's behavior has contributed to the wife's belief. The clinician flattens the hierarchy by transparently talking out loud about the therapeutic relationship in a nonthreatened and nonthreatening manner.

JULIE: No, it's just, I don't see a lot of positive coming out of it [therapy].

LMW: And if there were more. . . ?

JULIE: The first time [first session] I did. And I went home last time, and I felt really good because I felt we were being really honest and open. But I felt really angry because I remember Robert saying things, like the one I just brought up, where he took all that time off [*crying*] so that I could get away, and he gets to be the hero. And I get to be the unappreciative bitch. [*laughs*] And I don't think, maybe that's right, maybe that's the way it is. I don't know, but that's not certainly the way I want it to be.

LMW: Well, I've got a lot of things I want to say to you, but first of all I want to tell you, I in no way perceive him as the "good guy" and you as the "bad guy." I want to be real clear about that. I see my job here to be an advocate for your relationship. I'm not trying to be more on one side than on another person's side. If I do that, then I don't feel I'm doing my job. Because if I'm starting to take sides— you can do that—you're on your side and he's on his side.

JULIE: I don't feel that you're doing that, but I was really afraid to say what I just said because I know it's going to make him angry. And yet that's what I see happening. I didn't come in here to say he's a "bad guy" and he did this and he did that, but unless I do some of that, I'm not giving you a clear picture of how I feel either.

LMW: Well, I'm trying to understand what would constrain you from getting your anger out.

JULIE: Well, first, I don't want to make him mad. I don't want to hurt him. [*crying*]

LMW: So what would be wrong with getting him mad? So what? So he gets mad.

JULIE: It's really unpleasant when he's mad.

LMW: Oh, it's unpleasant. Well, that's different then. So, you're saying if you come in here and tell me some not nice stories about your husband, that you don't want him to get mad. But now you're saying, it's not just that you don't want him to get mad—he's not nice when he's mad. Is that right? So what's the worst thing he does when he's mad? [*long pause*]

JULIE: He loses his, loses control.

The persistence to understand the wife's suffering uncovers the belief that the wife thinks the clinician is allied more closely with the husband. Through the explicit discussion of the therapeutic alliance, the clinician shows a willingness to speak the unspeakable and process strong affect. Her declaration of neutrality to persons and advocacy for the marital relationship draws forth the significant news of a difference: the news of violence in this couple's relationship. The wife is caught in a bind. Her catastrophic fear is that if she makes her husband mad or upset, he will lose control and possibly have another heart attack. However, if she constrains her feelings, she becomes stressed and angry. Could it be that the open, frank discussion of the therapeutic relationship between the clinician and wife allowed the wife to speak the unspeakable about violence? We believe this is what enabled the wife to be so open.

OBSTACLE: UNCLEAR EXPECTATIONS ABOUT THERAPY

How can the clinician move toward challenging constraining beliefs and affirming facilitative beliefs when the client's beliefs and expectations about therapy are unclear? One way the clinician can inquire about expectations of therapy is by asking the family about prior "best and worst advice" they have received from health professionals: "What is the best and what is the worst advice you've been given in terms of trying to get a handle on these panic attacks?" This allows the clinician to know what has fit for the family in the past and what has not fit or not been palatable for them. It prevents the clinician from falling into the trap of offering ideas similar in content or process to past offerings or advice the family has previously experienced as not helpful.

Another move that lends clarity to expectations about therapy is "distinguishing the solution." For example, the clinician might ask, "If you saw something positive happening, what would you be seeing that would be different?" de Shazer (1991) offered the "miracle question" as another useful way of distinguishing the solution: "Suppose that one night there is a miracle and while you are sleeping the problem . . . is solved. How would you know? What would be different?" (p. 113). These questions allow for opportunities to explore the specifics about what the family members would like to see changed in the future and how they might be helped to achieve the future vision.

The clinician can also inquire about what the family has already tried in their attempts to solve the problem. The question may be phrased, "What have you been doing to try to deal with this problem?" Again, this information is critical for the clinician in learning about the family's expectations of therapy. By learning what the family has tried in the past, the family's resourcefulness is drawn forth and may be admired by the clinician and the family. Knowledge about past efforts also guides the clinician's efforts to offer perturbations that may be "news of a difference" rather than more of the same.

The clinician needs to assess the family's goals for the therapeutic relationship. In the first session with Research Family 2, Connie described her experience of angina and panic attacks. The client's beliefs about therapy were explored:

LMW: Is that important to you to find out why it's [the panic attacks] happening?
CONNIE: No, I just want to get rid of it.
LMW: You just want to get rid of it? Okay . . .
CONNIE: I just want to get back to normal.
LMW: Okay, that's helpful for me to know because some people I meet, they want to know why they have a problem. It's like a search, and they're not going to be happy until they know why. And then there are other people, like you, that don't care why they have it, they just want to get rid of it.
CONNIE: I just want to get rid of it.
LMW: So that helps me to know.

An important distinction is made about the client's expectations of therapy. Is it more important for this client to understand why she has a problem (the etiology of the panic attacks) or more important to get rid of the problem (the cure)? This is an extremely important distinction because it will direct the treatment focus the clinician offers. Because the clinician has clarified the client's beliefs about therapy, the clinician and client can work together on the same agenda and goals. Through the invitation to reflect on the treatment goals, the client may also develop a new understanding of the problem or the solution.

OBSTACLE: PREVIOUS NEGATIVE EXPERIENCES WITH HEALTH CARE PROFESSIONALS OR THERAPY

It is important to learn about the family's previous experiences with the health care system or therapy. This knowledge allows the clinician to learn more about what kind of relationships have worked for the family in the past, what their beliefs about health professionals are, and where the pitfalls lie. Research Family 3 presented in the first session with concerns about chronic fatigue syndrome in the youngest daughter, who also experienced diabetes. Thirty minutes into the first session, during the completion of the genogram, the clinician explored the origin of the belief about the diagnosis of chronic fatigue syndrome. This initiated a discussion about the family physician, in which the family indicated that they were changing doctors. Notice the clinician's (LMW) immediate curiosity about the reason for the change and the way she inquires about all of the family members' experiences with the physician. (C1 = eldest daughter, C2 = youngest daughter.)

LMW: Okay, and who made the diagnosis of chronic fatigue syndrome, do you know?

C2 AND FATHER: Dr. D.

LMW: But you said you're changing [doctors] right now?

MOTHER: We're changing our family doctor.

LMW: You're changing your family doctor. And the reason for changing?

C1: Whenever we're sick, she doesn't really buy it. She thinks we're just wasting her time and that we're hypochondriacs, me and my sister.

LMW: How did you get that idea that she thinks these things?

C1: Well, every time I go in, she goes, "What seems to be the problem this time?" [*mimicking a sarcastic tone of voice and elongating the emphasis on "seems"*] . . . And she was really rude.

LMW: Does she say it in that tone to you?

C1: Yes, and whenever I'm sick, she always does tests, and if there's nothing major wrong, she thinks I'm faking it, even though I'll be coughing, I sound like I have a cold, or I feel lousy, she . . .

LMW: But does she ever say to you, "I think you're faking," or is this sort of something you're picking up?

C1: No, it's something I pick up because she'll say, "Okay I'll give you a prescription for this, but I don't really think you need it," and stuff like this, and she thinks I should go to school even if I'm feeling really sick and stuff like that.

LMW: Does she doubt anybody else in the family besides you?

C1: Yes, Sarah [C2] too. Because with this [the chronic fatigue syndrome], she thought my sister was faking. The only reason she didn't quite believe she was faking was because she was going to the doctor.

LMW: [*to C2*] What do you think? How does she treat you?

C2: Well, I don't think she really acts like I'm faking it, but she's just kind of, she's really a textbook doctor, everything has to be black or white, you know, and she just seems like you can't talk to her. She's not a very good listener but that's my impression.

LMW: Okay, so you came to a decision to stop going to her. [*to parents*] Have you been going to her as well?

MOTHER: Yes.

LMW: Do you ever get this impression that she doesn't believe *you*? That she thinks that you're faking things?

MOTHER: My impression was that I felt that whenever I asked a lot of questions, because I want to know the answer, I felt that she was very defensive whenever I would do that. [*Mother relates several other examples of instances when she was dissatisfied with the physician.*] We were definitely not on the same wavelength at all.

LMW: No, it doesn't sound like it's a fit for you. I mean we all have to figure out what fits for us, and I'd like you to think the same way about us. That if you feel after today or another session that this is a fit, that's great, we should continue working together. But if you go home and say, "You know, this isn't a fit for us, those things they're telling us don't fit," then I'd really like you to tell us that and let's talk it through, because I don't want you to feel you have to stay with us if it's not fitting. I admire you, because you know, we give doctors a lot of status in our society, and I admire you for being able to say, "Gee, if it doesn't fit for us, we'd rather go some-where else."

MOTHER: That's for sure.

LMW: I'm really glad you've taken responsibility for that . . .

The clinician responds to the family's disparaging language of the physician by calling it a "lack of fit." She uses this information about fit in a therapeutic manner to legitimize the family's assessment of the present relationship with her and the clinical team regardless of whether the family's assessment is positive or negative. She commends the family for their ability to know what fits for them in spite of society's beliefs about appropriate conduct with doctors, which would normally silence the family. The clinician confirms the family's ability to know and recognize a fit or nonfit with professionals; that is, the family members are "one-up" to professionals who usually put them "one-down." The clinician voices not only that she expects the family to be evaluating the goodness of fit with the present clinical team, but also her belief that the decision to continue or discontinue with therapy necessarily falls to the family. A spirit of collaboration and nonhierarchy is modeled, with the clinician again speaking the unspeakable: that the family may not wish to continue therapy and are invited, even expected, to say so, because *they* are experts on their experiences with "experts."

## OBSTACLE: SIMULTANEOUS INVOLVEMENT WITH MULTIPLE HEALTH CARE PROFESSIONALS

When many health professionals are involved with a family concurrently, it may be difficult to distinguish the problem that should be addressed in the present therapeutic relationship or determine the boundaries of concerns dealt with by the different clinicians. Until these issues are sorted out, the clinical work cannot proceed.

In one clinical family, both the single-parent mother and her adolescent daughter reported multiple, chronic health problems. In the process of understanding who was involved in the family's health care, the clinical team learned that there were physiotherapists, a chronic fatigue specialist, and an immunologist currently providing health care. In addition, both the mother and daughter were receiving individual counseling and the daughter was also taking antidepressant medication under the supervision of a psychiatrist. The question immediately raised by the clinician was, "How can we be helpful to you in a manner that is different than the other health care providers?" An opportunity to hear ideas of the reflecting team (see chapter 6) was offered to the family, during which two issues were raised: (a) the pros and cons of having so many health care providers in the family members' lives and (b) ideas for how the family might deal with conflicting advice. Family members were encouraged to remember the importance of their own voices and ideas by deciding which opinions offered by health professionals fit best for them.

Several authors have concurred that understanding the other, larger systems with which the family is involved and the nature of those relationships is an important issue to be assessed early in the therapeutic relationship (Colapinto, 1995; Connell & Connell, 1995; Glenn, 1987; Imber-Black, 1988, 1991; Thorne & Robinson, 1989). A context for change is difficult to create if larger system issues have not been acknowledged and discussed with the family.

OBSTACLE: UNREALISTIC OR UNKNOWN EXPECTATIONS OF THE REFERRING PERSON ABOUT TREATMENT

The challenges posed by the expectations of the referring person have been addressed by other authors (Selvini Palazzoli, Boscolo, Cecchin, & Prata, 1980b). Our response to the referral of a family by a health professional is to have the referring professional request that the family contact our unit directly for an initial appointment. Using this model of referral by health professionals serves two purposes. First, it requires that health professionals explain to families *their* reasons and expected benefits of a referral. This removes the confusion or anger families can experience when referred to another health professional or agency. Second, it provides an opportunity for the family, rather than the referring professional, to respond to our questions regarding initial intake information (genogram of the nuclear family and description of the presenting concern). In this way, information about the family, from the

family's perspective, is privileged over that of the referring professional. The following example illustrates how the clinical team dealt
with the unrealistic expectations of a referring professional for a clinical
family.

The family consisted of a single-parent mother and her four children,
ranging in age from 9 to 24 years. The mother indicated that she wished
help with the stress of her chronic degenerative disc disease, which
made her wheelchair-bound; she was also concerned about her daughter's school truancy. The family were referred to the Family Nursing
Unit by the welfare caseworker and the family physician. The letter of
referral from the family physician described many health and social
concerns including chronic illness, codependency, alcoholism, school
truancy, depression, mild mental retardation, sexual assault, economic
difficulties, and chronic pain. The physician requested help from the
FNU to "get us out of what seems to be a treadmill of disasters in this
family and their treatment." The family was "the worst and most
chronic" the physician had seen in his practice. The physician and the
caseworker were discouraged in their attempts to assist this family: "In
summary there exists a variety of maladaptive dynamics that will delay
or sabotage any progress." The physician's letter concluded by saying,
"Considering the severe noncompliance of this family . . . , I am hoping
that your service can provide at least an overview of the family dynamics in order that we can plan some 'damage control' over the next few
years and maximize their potential."

One of the obstacles to creating a context for change was the temptation of the clinician and clinical team to join isomorphically in the discouraging, problem-saturated view of the referring physician about the
family. The family was seen for four sessions over 6 weeks. After meeting with the family for two sessions to understand their concerns, the
following letter was sent to the physician:

Dear Dr. Smith:
   Greetings from the Family Nursing Unit! Thank you very much
for your referral letter regarding this family. As you know, we have
now seen them on two occasions, and found it very helpful to have
your impressions. Our team was struck by your obvious interest and
concern for this family, as reflected in the care and time you took to
write to us.
   We appreciate your perspective of this family's numerous problems, and acknowledge that it can often be quite challenging to avoid
the trap of becoming discouraged and overwhelmed by the magni-
tude of their problems, and the degree of suffering experienced by
them. In our work with families, we also find we have to resist the
temptation of becoming disheartened about families who face multi-

ple challenges/problems. It is our belief that [in] focusing on the family's strengths and resources, rather than only their problems, [we can help them to] open space to new solutions, and a new view for family members of themselves as competent, capable individuals, who are able to survive despite the many adversities they face.

In our conversations with the family, the mother described a sense of feeling overwhelmed by their situation, and felt she could only manage to survive by living day to day. We have found the mother's belief an extremely facilitative one for her. We invited the family to continue working on one issue at a time, in order to punctuate their strengths and abilities, and gain a sense of mastery over their lives.

As you know, the Family Nursing Unit has a collaborative relationship with families, in which mutuality and reciprocity are integral components of our approach. In keeping with this philosophy, we have offered the family a copy of this letter.

Sincerely,
L. M. Wright, R.N., Ph.D., and members of the
Family Nursing Unit clinical nursing team

The letter to the referring physician helped create a context for changing beliefs on several levels. First, it was an opportunity for the clinical team to declare their beliefs about the resourcefulness of the family (which had been drawn forth and coevolved with the family) rather than get trapped into seeing pathology. By providing a copy of the letter to the family, a further opportunity was provided to write about their strengths. The clinician read the letter to the family members prior to mailing a copy to the referring physician and asked if they would like to change or add anything. They did not, but they seemed pleased as well as surprised that this opportunity was provided for them to comment. In sending the letter to the referring professional, it expanded the audience and made the commendations of the family even more public, thereby solidifying them. Finally, the letter may have been a useful perturbation to the physician. The letter both communicated respect and understanding for his view and offered an alternative view of the family and their problems. Perhaps it opened space for a different family–physician relationship to coevolve.

## CONCLUSION

How does the clinician know that a context for change has been created? Expert clinicians talk about "knowing the moment has been created," just as they talk about "sensing that a context has not yet been created." Some of the signposts that a context for change has been created are that the family is engaged, structural coupling has occurred, the problem has been clearly defined, and the customers for change have been identified. A family may move from feeling resentful about being coerced into therapy to wanting a chance to talk about their illness experience; a wife may disclose the existence of violence in her marriage because she feels safe in the therapeutic relationship and that her voice has credibility. There is a sense that the hard work of clearing away the obstacles is over and that an openness to new ideas exists. Therapeutic change is not about to happen; it has already begun. The micromoves of creating a context for changing beliefs have now provided the foundation for the macromoves of uncovering and distinguishing illness beliefs; altering, challenging, modifying, or constraining beliefs; and distinguishing change by affirming and solidifying facilitative beliefs. The skilled clinician moves back and forth between these interventions in a fluid rather than stepwise fashion and continues to create and maintain a context for changing beliefs throughout the duration of the clinical work.

# CHAPTER 5

# Uncovering and Distinguishing Illness Beliefs

The secret of the care of the patient is in caring for the patient.

FRANCIS PEABODY

"**W**HAT'S THE TOUGHEST part about managing multiple sclerosis every day and coping with it?" This question commenced an extremely useful therapeutic conversation with a 34-year-old man (Research Family 1) about his experience with multiple sclerosis (MS). The therapeutic conversation was not about symptoms, nor medication, nor treatment, but rather about the young man's illness experience—in particular, what he found the most difficult to manage. This question invites both the client and the clinician to move away from medical narratives to illness narratives by inviting a reflection about what is the most difficult part of managing MS on a daily basis. The young man (Mark) answered as follows:

MARK: I don't know, just that things that seemed so trivial, I can't really do anymore.
LMW: Yes?
MARK: They're not really important things, but everyone does them.
MOTHER: Like you would be stampeding now, right? [Mother is referring to attending the Calgary Stampede.]

This client helped us, as clinicians, to learn and remember that many of the daily tasks and routines that are normally out of our awareness and taken for granted are now *out* of his capabilities yet very much *in* his awareness in the context of illness. More important, it helps us to begin to uncover his beliefs about coping with and managing MS.

To be able to distinguish and uncover illness beliefs we (a) articulate and operationalize our own beliefs about families and illness through a biological–spiritual lens (see chapters 1 and 2), (b) adopt the notion that emotioning and languaging involve the braiding of the physiological and interactional domains, (c) think of languaging as an interactive phenomenon that involves more than words (see chapter 3), (d) observe for patterns of languaging and emotions between family members, (e) observe our own patterns of relating to the family, and (f) choose language with care and precision. We uncover and distinguish illness beliefs that we have found most useful in our clinical practice.

Through the process of our hermeneutic research, we have expanded our view of therapeutic behaviors beyond interventions. The term *intervention* usually implies a onetime act with clear boundaries, frequently offering something or doing something to someone else (see chapter 3). Interventions are the overt therapeutic actions initiated with an intent to change, actualized in the relationship between client and clinician. An intervention is an encapsulated moment with a beginning and an end (Wright & Leahey, 1994a). Interventions are normally purposeful, conscious, and usually involve observable behaviors of the clinician.

We have come to favor the term *move* to describe the process and flow that are coevolved between the clinician and family members.* The word *move* has less of a boundary and weaves as a seamless whole, implying intertwining between persons and ideas. A move is an ongoing process, flowing over time, bringing together a series of interventions. The process of uncovering and distinguishing illness beliefs, the subject of this chapter, is one example of a macromove. An example of a micromove within this macromove is drawing forth beliefs about prognosis; a specific intervention within this micromove is offering a commendation of a family's courage in the face of a life-shortening illness.

## DRAWING FORTH ILLNESS BELIEFS

The illness beliefs that we are most interested in uncovering and distinguishing are beliefs about etiology; diagnosis; healing and treatment;

---

* We are grateful to Dr. Catherine Chesla for introducing us to the word *move* as a useful description of aspects of our clinical practice.

prognosis; the role of family members; the role of health professionals; religion–spirituality; and the place of illness in lives and relationships. How does a clinician uncover these beliefs, and what meaning or interpretation does one give to those beliefs once they are uncovered? This chapter offers specific ideas, clinical examples, and interpretations related to the uncovering and distinguishing of some of these important illness beliefs.

## INVITING FAMILY MEMBERS INTO THE ROLE OF EXPERT

One useful way to distinguish illness beliefs, to make them real, is to invite family members into the role of expert about their illness experience. In the session with Research Family 1 (son Mark and his elderly parents), the clinician (LMW) invited questions from the son about his MS. What questions would he like answered? When he did not have further questions, the clinician invited Mark into the expert role by suggesting that there might be things that she could learn from him.

LMW: Can I shift a bit and ask if there is anything else you want to ask me, Mark?

MARK: No, I don't think so.

LMW: Okay, is there anything else about experiencing MS that you think would help me to understand better? Anything else you want to tell me about your experience that you think would . . .

MARK: Well, it's just very frustrating to deal with.

LMW: Yes. Do you feel like it rules your life at this point, or do you feel like you are able to rule MS sometimes?

MARK: Well, a lot of things I don't do because of it.

LMW: Yes. Are there any ways that you think you influence MS, that you have an influence over it?

MARK: Yes.

LMW: Yes? Terrific, can you tell me what those are? What ways do you think you influence the MS?

MARK: Well, not really influence, things that I do in spite of it.

The dominant theme in this therapeutic conversation with the son, in the presence of his parents, was distinguishing his illness experience as a real entity. Various distinctions were drawn through questions exploring such things as the toughest part of the illness and relative influence over the illness. These types of questions are asked on the basis of our belief that beliefs arise out of distinctions that are drawn. This manner of questioning embeds the clinician's beliefs into the therapeutic conversation and clarifies the young man's beliefs. Many different paths of questioning could have been taken. For example, the son responded to the question, "anything else you want to tell me about your experience . . . ?" with "well, it's just very frustrating to deal with." Although exploration could have been attempted to further understanding of his frustration, the clinician instead confirmed his experience with a simple *yes* and then moved on to ask a relative influence question (White, 1988/1989): "Do you feel like it rules your life at this point, or do you feel you are able to rule MS sometimes?" This type of inquiry moves away from examining more of Mark's suffering to drawing forth his beliefs about his competence in managing MS.

This compression of the therapeutic work, or leapfrogging ahead in a session, is consistent with advanced clinical practice. This is not to imply that advanced-practice clinicians should leapfrog over suffering. It was simply a useful move in the moment to focus on Mark's capabilities rather than his hurt. This leapfrog micromove facilitated the clinician's uncovering of beliefs about Mark's suffering later in the session.

Emphasizing this young man's competence enables a story of determination and courage to be expressed as he tells of doing things "in spite of" MS. It was this response of the client that helped the clinician better understand the experience of MS for Mark and introduced the clinician to a new illness paradigm. Mark's admission that he did not consider that he influences his illness but rather does things "in spite of it" lifts the illness experience out of the control paradigm, which the line of inquiry about relative influence is based on, and moves it into the "in spite of illness" paradigm. (See chapter 2 for further elaboration of the "control paradigm" concept.) An extremely useful facilitative belief had been distinguished: "I can do things in spite of MS." The "in spite of illness" paradigm versus the control paradigm has continued to be a useful distinction and has influenced our clinical work with other families. Drawing forth this distinction is not used as a therapeutic technique but rather as a powerful alternative way to conceptualize living with illness.

The questions asked by the clinician were based on a belief about the importance of exploring the illness experience from every direction to obtain a richer understanding of the expertness of this young man in his experience of illness. The clinician's view of the clients' expertise was embedded in the shift from asking questions to inviting questions and further explanations from the client. In so doing, the clinician stepped out of the expert role of "I know what to ask," opening space for the client to step into the expert role.

What stood out for the clinician from the therapeutic conversation was learning that the toughest part for Mark was dealing with everyday "trivial" things and that the notion of influence over illness was not a fit for him because he preferred to think of "doing things in spite of" the MS. Following the intense affective sharing by Mark, the relationship between the clinician and him became much less hierarchical. Both clinician and client had their expertise acknowledged: the clinician's expertise about ideas and possibilities for alleviating emotional and physical suffering and the client's expertise of experiencing illness.

## BELIEFS ABOUT DIAGNOSIS

A specific way to recognize the expertise of clients related to their illness experiences is to encourage them to express their beliefs about the diagnosis of the illness. It is an effort to learn whose voice is the privileged voice of authority. Family members' beliefs about diagnosis influence how open they will be to various ideas about healing and treatment. Part of exploring the beliefs about the diagnosis is to learn whose ears are privileged to hear the diagnosis. In some cultures, such as the Japanese, the belief that knowledge of a life-threatening diagnosis will cause a patient to lose hope and the illness to become worse often leads to collusion between health professionals and family members to avoid informing a patient of the diagnosis.

In our clinical work with a woman who was suffering from panic attacks related to the fear of another heart attack (Research Family 2), the clinician (LMW) drew forth the client's (Connie's) experience of the illness and what she believed about the diagnosis by accessing the questions that the client had been asking herself. Beliefs are often embedded in the questions we ask ourselves; therefore, it can be useful to learn more about clients' internal conversations.

LMW: You know when you have fears like this, or anxiety, you have a lot of conversations with yourself. We also have conversations like you and I are having with each other right now, but we have a lot of internal conversations with ourselves. What kinds of conversations have you been having with yourself? Like what kinds of questions do you ask yourself in a day?

CONNIE: Well, I get up in the morning and I think to myself, "Now, am I going to be able to get through today?" Or, "Is this [anxiety] going to start?" And sure enough, 15 minutes after I'm up [*crying*], I get that gut feeling in my stomach and I'm trembling inside and I'm trembling outside. I'm past the stage of feeling like I might be having a stroke because the physical symptoms are so strange . . .

LMW: Mmhm.

CONNIE: . . . that you just wonder what's going to happen, eh? I've been to the doctor and that's what he thinks it is.

LMW: So you ask yourself the question, "Am I going to get through the day?"

CONNIE: Like "Am I normal today . . . ?"

LMW: Or, "Am I going to be normal today?" Okay, and then I'm sorry I didn't catch the last part of what you said. When you went to the doctor . . .

CONNIE: Well, he said he thinks it's anxiety too.

LMW: Yes? And you thought that's what it was? Did you believe that before you went to see him?

CONNIE: No, I didn't know what it was.

LMW: You didn't know what it was. Okay, so he gave you this idea.

In this segment, the clinician explores the belief about the diagnosis and the origin of this belief by drawing a distinction: Was the diagnosis her idea or was it "given" to her? It is also an effort to determine whose voice is being privileged.

In Research Family 3, a teenager of 13 years (C2 = youngest daughter) was experiencing chronic fatigue syndrome (CFS). Beliefs about the diagnosis of CFS were explored, and in the process another diagnosis, "chronic uncertainty syndrome," was uncovered.

LMW: And what do you think about your doctor's diagnosis of chronic fatigue syndrome?

C2: I think it's right . . . .

LMW: Is he on the money or . . . ?

C2: Everybody thinks that's what I have.

LMW: Yes, but what do *you* believe? Do you think he's accurate and on the money here?

C2: Sure.

LMW: Okay. So, what advice has he given you so far to manage this?

C2: He's saying to "do what you can. Don't overexert yourself. Try to get your schoolwork done." That's probably the most important thing.

LMW: And Dr. J., what does he say to you about how long he thinks this CFS is going to last? Does he give you any idea?

C2: No, it's indeterminate; it could last for like 5 years or 2 months. They don't know. Nobody knows.

In this segment, the clinician checks out this teenager's beliefs about her diagnosis. C2 offers an interesting distinction: She believes her diagnosis but does not believe that anyone knows how long it will last. This is a facilitative belief because it offers the option that if nobody knows when her chronic fatigue will end, perhaps she can learn some strategies for maintaining and improving her health. Her future, therefore, has many more possibilities to be coevolved with the clinician; an alternative diagnosis of "chronic uncertainty syndrome" was cocreated.

## BELIEFS ABOUT ETIOLOGY

It is imperative to draw forth and understand family members' explanations of why they are encountering a particular illness experience in their lives at this time. All people give themselves an explanation about major unusual or unexpected events in their lives. Beliefs about the etiology of illness are as varied as family members and can range from assuming personal responsibility (e.g., my hypertension is due to my obesity) to giving others responsibility (e.g., my mother gave us too much sugar when we were kids, and that's contributed to my diabetes) to blaming external forces (e.g., my life on a farm contributed to my respiratory condition). Family members always have ideas about causes. Wynne, Shields, and Sirkin (1992) helpfully remind us that the Greek root *aitia*, from which the word *etiology* (the study of causes) is derived, means not only "cause" but also "responsibility" and "blame." They offer six classes of "causes" that have been interpreted as explaining illness: (a) supernatural causes, (b) physical–biological agents, (c) unconscious processes "external" to the self, (d) societal processes such as severe poverty and community disorganization, (e) traumatic life events, and (f) family-system processes.

What family members believe about the cause of an illness influences how open or closed they will be to various approaches for healing and treatment. In the following segment, Mark (Research Family 1) was asked a "difference question" (Selvini Palazzoli, Boscolo, Cecchin, & Prata, 1980a; Tomm & Lannamann, 1988) to draw forth his beliefs about how MS had affected his life. Note that this one question immediately drew forth intense affect as this young man's silent tears gave evidence of his grief about his illness. In this important discussion about his explanation of his illness, his beliefs about etiology were revealed.

LMW: What's been the thing that's been the biggest surprise to you about it all?
MARK: [*sniffs*] I don't know. It's kinda hard to believe you could have 29 . . . [*crying*] 29 good years . . . [*long pause*]
LMW: And then some not so good years now. [*nods head*] Yes? Do you see these as not good years?
MARK: [*crying*] Yes.
LMW: Well, it's like I've said, you've been dealt a challenge and a blow in your life, Mark, that most people do not have to face. And I can

appreciate that must be a real struggle for you. How do you make sense out of that for yourself? What thoughts do you have about why you and not other people? How come other people haven't been faced with this challenge in their life? How have you answered that for yourself?

MARK: There's not really any logical explanation for it. It's just the odds or the luck of the draw or whatever.

LMW: It's always one of the things that people really struggle with, I find, especially young people when they have been diagnosed with a serious illness and experience a serious chronic illness . . .

MARK: Yes.

LMW: . . . is trying to make sense out of it for themselves, you know, trying to understand, and they have many different beliefs about it. I'm wondering what your belief is about how it is that you have MS?

MARK: There's not really any explanation I guess. And no one in our family has it.

FATHER: No.

MARK: [*talking to parents*] On either side of your families?

FATHER: That's right.

LMW: So how do you explain it? The luck of the draw? You had a stroke of bad luck? Is that what you say to yourself? Anything else you say to yourself about it?

MARK: Not really. [*pause*] I can't really rationalize . . .

The expression of Mark's grief was again validated by the clinician, who made a connection that grief is tied to one's belief about the cause. It could be speculated that Mark's belief that it is "the luck of the draw" caused him more grief, because this belief places MS so much out of his control. This is a different explanation from that of his parents, who believed that the MS was the result of a virus or measles when he was a boy.

## BELIEFS ABOUT HEALING AND TREATMENT

A strong belief exists in our North American health care culture that eliciting, discussing, and expressing one's illness story and accompanying emotions can be healing. Families also share this cultural belief and have often remarked in our clinical practice how they have appreciated the opportunity to talk with one another about the effect of illness on their lives and relationships. A study by Robinson (1994a) about families, illness, and intervention, conducted within the FNU, has given further validation to the idea that families find clinician's invitations to engage in meaningful conversation about the impact of illness on their lives to be one of the most useful interventions in assisting families to move beyond and overcome problems. The capacity of clinicians to be "witnesses" to the stories of suffering of patients and families is central to providing care; it is frequently the genesis of healing, if not curing (Frank, 1994; Kleinman, 1988).

With Research Family 1, a heart-to-heart conversation between the clinician and the young man experiencing MS later proved to be a turning point in this young man's healing from his intense emotional suffering. In the final session, his parents reported that they believed one of the most useful aspects of the sessions was having their son talk about his illness experience, something they claimed he had never done before. The intense affective sharing began with the clinician drawing a distinction about possible affective responses to illness, specifically anger versus sadness.

LMW: I see you get sad about your MS. Do you ever get angry about having MS? [*Mark nods yes.*] Which emotion is more common for you to feel about your MS? Do you feel more sad or more angry about it?

MARK: Sad.

LMW: At this moment?

MARK: Sad.

LMW: More sad about it. And which one is easier for you to deal with? Which emotion do you feel more comfortable with? Is it easier to be sad about it or to be angry about it?

MARK: Angry.

LMW: Easier to be angry. The sadness is harder? Can you tell me about that?

MARK: Well, it's just letting off steam; it's easier than feeling bad about it.

LMW: [*looks at Mother and Father*] Do you agree with that? Do you think it's easier? Do you notice that it's easier for him to be angry than to be sad?

MOTHER AND FATHER: Yes, oh yes.

LMW: That's a harder emotion. What about for you? What's the harder one for you to see your son experiencing, sadness or . . .

FATHER: Sadness.

LMW: . . . or anger? Sadness.

FATHER: I'm glad when he's angry and shouts and screams and lets it out; then he's good for a while. But when he's sad and sits there and we ask, "What's the matter, Mark?" And he says, "Nothing" . . .

MOTHER: Doesn't say anything, just sits . . .

FATHER: No conversation, just watches TV.

LMW: Actually, in some ways it probably takes more strength to be sad, doesn't it, than to be angry? Because, like you say, when you're angry, it's over . . .

MOTHER: Oh yes, it's over.

LMW: But it takes a lot of strength to be sad. When you're sad, do you cry on the inside or do you cry on the outside, Mark?

MARK: Both, I guess. [*very softly*]

MOTHER: Sometimes he cries.

FATHER: Oh yes, he has incidents of crying . . .

LMW: Because I've had other patients with MS and other illnesses tell me that crying on the inside takes more energy. They find when they cry on the outside and let the tears come, that it doesn't take as much energy. Do you find that?

MARK: Yes.

LMW: It's harder, and it seems like it saps your energy more if you just cry on the inside? So sometimes you allow yourself to cry on the outside?

MARK: Yes.

LMW: Good. That's good. Do you understand what I mean?

MOTHER AND FATHER: Oh yes. I wish he would do it that way all the time.

LMW: That he cries on the outside.

FATHER: Have a darn good cry and then . . .

LMW: Just like anger then, it's out, doesn't take as much energy, but being sad all the time on the inside, you're always being angry on the inside . . .

FATHER: It's eating away . . .

LMW: It saps your energy, doesn't it?

FATHER: Oh, yes, it's hard, yes.

LMW: Do you ever hold back or cry on the inside because you're afraid it might upset your mom and dad? [*pause*] Would you ever hold it back because you're . . .

FATHER: I hope he doesn't. I wish, if he wants to cry, let him cry.

MARK: I don't think I purposely do.

In this short but intense focus on affect, the clinician draws a distinction between anger and sadness, exploring which affect is easier for the son to experience and which is easier for his parents to observe. From the family members' responses, family beliefs that were drawn forth were (a) it is okay to be angry, (b) it is not okay to be sad, and (c) it is weak to cry and weak to be sad. The clinician embeds the suggestion that sadness—a difficult emotion for this family—takes more strength and courage, and she counters societal beliefs about sadness: "Actually, in some ways it probably takes more strength to be sad, doesn't it, than to be angry?" As the parents hear the clinician explore these issues with their son, they are hearing the previously unspeakable (their son's sadness) being spoken in front of them.

The wonderfully facilitative distinction between crying on the inside and crying on the outside (learned from our clinical work with other families) led to further understanding about the son's experience of illness. The clinician combines an exploration of affect with an exploration of cognition and behavior. Note the redundant use of the words *sad* and *sadness* in this segment of the conversation, opening possibilities for the family to make room for the expression of sadness in ways they had not previously been able to. The clinician also had an intense affective experience of sadness while listening to this young man and, for a few moments, suffered with him as well as being a "witness" to his suffering.

## BELIEFS ABOUT MASTERY, CONTROL, AND INFLUENCE

An in-depth discussion about our thoughts and clinical findings concerning control is offered in the section Beliefs About Illness in chapter 2. The following clinical examples illuminate these beliefs. The move of introducing temporal boundaries in the management of chronic illness is one way of offering the idea that persons can have an effect not only on their experience of illness but even on the duration of their illness. In so doing, hope is given to a family that they can influence their illness. An example follows of the use of this move with Research Family 2, experiencing chronic fatigue syndrome.

LMW: What does Dr. J. say to you about how long he thinks this CFS is going to last? Does he give you any idea?

C2: He can't. It's indeterminate. It could last for 5 years or 2 months; they don't know, nobody knows.

LMW: I'm a real believer that people often know how long their illness is going to last. Do you have a best guess of what you think?

C2: I have no idea.

LMW: Like if you were to guess, would you say 6 months, a year, 3 years?

C2: I don't know. I can't tell.

LMW: So, you're just playing it by ear right now, are you?

C2: I have "off" days and "on" days, so it's really hard to tell. Like some days I'm feeling fine, and other days I feel really bad.

LMW: So, you've been struggling with this for about 3 months now?

C2: Yes.

LMW: Is that about right? So would you say you're better, the same, or worse than when the symptoms first started?

C2: It depends on the day.

LMW: It depends on the day whether you're better, worse, or the same. Do you have any days that are absolutely worse than what you first had?

C2: Oh, yes.

LMW: And do you have any days that are really better?

C2: Yes.

LMW: So when you have a good day, what do you do then?

C2: Well, I'm not supposed to work too hard on a day that I am feeling good, because then I could fall back for the rest of the day.

LMW: Really, and do you find that? That has been given to you as advice, eh? And have you experimented with that, to see if that's so?

C2: Yes. [laughs]

LMW: And if you go at it too hard on a good day, then you pay for it the next day? Do you?

C2: Yes, that's right.

LMW: Okay. And on a not so good day, what kinds of things do you do then?

C2: I do my homework.

LMW: Right. Can you get together with friends or go out?

C2: My friends are not really dealing with this very well.

LMW: What are they doing?

C2: Well, they're scared to come and see me because they don't know what I have and they're kind of . . .

C1: They probably think they're going to get it, and it's contagious and stuff like that.

LMW: Oh really. So have you missed seeing them?

Of course, the amount of influence varies depending on the disease. For example, MS is not anticipated to improve over time, whereas with CFS, little is known about the length of the illness; it's as if the illness has no boundaries and therefore the client has little control over it. Regardless, the clinician explores a significant belief about how long the illness will last in an attempt to define the client's perception of the temporal boundaries of the illness. The clinician offers her belief that clients often possess the expert knowledge about the duration of an illness and invites the client through a "best guess" to declare her belief about the length of her illness: "I'm a real believer that people often know how long their illness is going to last. Do you have a best guess of what you think?" When the client claims that she does not know or cannot tell, the clinician persists by offering options of time (6 months, 1 year, 3 years) and thus sends a powerful implicit message that "your experience is credible; you are the expert on your experience." The clinician's question about the length of illness drew forth the client's experience of "good days" and "not so good days." This distinction is pursued by exploring the client's experience with these different kinds of days: "What kinds of things do you do then?"

Throughout this process, the clinician shows that she is interested in both kinds of days. For example, she says, "and on a not so good day, what kinds of things do you do then?" A significant micromove occurs when the clinician suggests that the client is disagreeing with the experts—that the client is challenging the beliefs of the experts about length of time of the illness precisely by the fact that the client cannot guess how long CFS will last. The experts say 2 months to 5 years, but the clinician counters that notion with "but you know your own body best, how long do you think it will last?" This inquiry begins to put a "chink" in the armor of the chronic question mark of CFS. The client's belief is challenged, which provides evidence that assessment may also be intervention. The clinician attempts to expand the small opening by augmenting with perspectives of the sister and mother. This challenges the beliefs that CFS is interminable and that health professionals are more expert than the client and the family.

## BELIEFS ABOUT PROGNOSIS

Family members' beliefs about prognosis provide a glimpse of the future: What do family members anticipate the future trajectory of the illness will look like? Are they hopeful or pessimistic about the outcome of the illness? Is there agreement or disagreement between family members about the prognosis? Norman Cousins (1989) suggested that our beliefs about prognosis affect our physiology, stating that "beliefs become biology." He proposed that a healthy disregard for prognoses pronounced by "experts" can indeed be life-giving, even in the face of life-shortening diagnoses.

Cultural beliefs have been shown to affect life span. David Phillips and colleagues from the departments of sociology and mathematics at the University of California, San Diego, compared the deaths of 28,169 adult Chinese-Americans with the deaths of 412,632 white Americans. Their results are fascinating. They found that Chinese-Americans die significantly earlier than normal—1.3 to 4.9 years—if they have a combination of disease and a birth year that Chinese astrology and medicine consider ill-fated. These researchers hypothesized that "the more strongly a group is attached to Chinese traditions, the more years of life are lost" (Guardian, 1993).

These researchers looked at five types of cancer, heart disease, diabetes, peptic ulcer, pneumonia, bronchitis, and cirrhosis of the liver, attempting to correlate cause of death with birth year. According to Chinese medicine, one's fate is influenced by the year of birth, each year being associated with one of five phases: fire, earth, metal, water, and wood. In turn, each phase is associated with an organ, for instance, fire with the heart and earth with tumors. Accordingly, a person born in 1908 (an earth year) would be unusually susceptible to tumors, whereas a person born in 1907 (a fire year) would be prone to heart disease.

The researchers found that Chinese women lost more years of life than Chinese men, perhaps because Chinese women were more influenced by the Chinese cultural beliefs, being less exposed to countering Western influences. So strong were these cultural beliefs that Phillips and his colleagues concluded that patients with ill-fated combinations of birth year and disease refused to change unhealthy habits, which would lengthen their lives, because they believed their deaths were inevitable (Guardian, 1993).

The following segment is from the first session with Research Family 3. The youngest daughter, experiencing CFS, confidently and repeatedly states her belief that "I will get better." This is in stark contrast to the beliefs of other family members, particularly her sister. (C1 = eldest daughter, C2 = youngest daughter)

LMW: Alright, so your primary hope for coming here is getting some ideas—see if I've got this right—you would prefer some coping mechanisms to provide support and to help the family to pull together.

MOTHER: Yes, because in my work [she is a nurse] and just in my own experience, I found that even the diabetes was a real strain for a while until [C2] could get a handle on it. I think that part of this is so long term, it's just indefinitely knowing that if we don't pull together, we may not make it through as a whole.

C1: I think it's hard on the rest of us because we have to deal with the fact that [C2] may never get better, and I think it's hard for us to see her like that. Like we don't want to see her tired all the time.

LMW: So in terms of her prognosis, you're saying, because it's unknown, you're saying she may never get better?

C1: Exactly.

C2: I will get better. [*Comment offered in a very determined tone.*]

LMW: Does anybody else believe she [C2] will get better? Do you believe it?

c2: I will get better. [*Repeats same belief in an even stronger tone.*]

LMW: You believe you will get better.

c2: That's a fact! I will get better.

c1: But, uh, some people don't.

c2: I know.

LMW: [*to C1*] And you're what, sort of unsure whether she'll get better?

c1: No, I think she'll get better. It's just we don't know when, and so it may be indefinite. I mean we don't know for sure. We think she'll get better, and we're pretty sure she'll get better, but we don't know for sure. I think that's the major thing.

c2: The doctors know that I'll get better. I mean everybody that has this gets better, but they just don't know how long it will take.

c1: Exactly, so that's why I said it's indefinite because it may last years, it may last months, it may last weeks.

This exploration was particularly relevant because of the uncertainty around the temporal aspect of this illness. It was impressive to hear this young girl's confident belief that she indeed would recover from CFS. She just did not know how long it would take. As other family members expressed their uncertainty, this teenager expressed more and more certainty that she would recover from CFS, a very facilitative belief indeed.

Another poignant example of distinguishing beliefs about prognosis occurred with Research Family 1 regarding the young man experiencing MS. The therapeutic conversation quickly moved from one about diagnosis to one of prognosis. More accurately, it moved from the story of suffering at the time of diagnosis to Mark's present suffering about his future.

MARK: They sent me to an ophthalmologist, and he did a vision range or field on a big cloth thing . . .

LMW: Yes?

MARK: And he found I had a blind spot, and he said, "I don't want to ruin your holiday, but either this is something unrelated to anything, just an isolated incident, or that's how MS starts . . . "

LMW: Well, it must have been quite a shock for you to hear this.

MARK: Oh yes, I was on a holiday having a good time . . .

LMW: Yes? So that was the first time and then what happened from there?

MARK: That would have been February . . .

MOTHER: Yes, February, it was.

MARK: And I was diagnosed in December of that year.

LMW: In December of that year.

MARK: So 9 months later.

LMW: Nine months later. Well, you've been dealt quite a challenge in your life, Mark, haven't you, to cope with MS. I think this is of course one of the reasons your mom and dad were interested in coming here [to FNU] is because it's quite a challenge for family members too when there's a serious illness in the family. So I'd be curious to know from you, what problems or concerns do you have at the moment? Either for yourself or within the family as a whole? Either with dealing with your illness or dealing with other things?

MARK: I've just seen how bad some people get.

LMW: Yes.

MARK: And there's no way to know if I'm going to get that bad.

LMW: Is that a worry for you? Do you worry about how bad your situation is going to become? Is that on your mind?

MARK: Not a lot.

LMW: Not a lot but . . .

MARK: But it's a concern . . .

LMW: Yes, so one of your concerns is what does your future hold. How do you understand your MS? What has been explained to you about it?

MARK: Well it's a neurological disorder.

LMW: Yes, so when you think about your future, what do you think about? What do you see for yourself? Like you said, you're concerned. You've seen what's happened to other people.

MARK: I'm not really too worried about the financial end.

LMW: Okay . . .

MARK: Just concerned about how bad it's going to get.

One nodal point in this segment was when the clinician moved to validate this young man's suffering by stating that he had been "dealt quite a challenge in [his] life." In our clinical experience, the deliberate and open acknowledgment of suffering frequently opens the door for the disclosure of other fears or worries not previously expressed. The clinician also embedded the idea that the parents were impacted by this illness experience. Then a couple of questions were asked that refined the son's present concerns by making distinctions between self and family and between dealing with illness and dealing with other things. Offering this opportunity for refinement of his concerns, on the heels of validating the tremendous challenge he has been given in life, moves the son to respond, "I've just seen how bad some people get." For the first time, he now expresses concern about his prognosis. This disclosure reveals that his present suffering is more about the future (prognosis) than about the past (diagnosis). In our clinical experience, we have learned that clients are more concerned or troubled by their diagnosis when their beliefs about diagnosis differ from those of health professionals or other family members. When there is no disagreement about the diagnosis, clients tend to focus on their prognosis, that is, on how their futures will develop.

Beliefs have a tremendous effect on the optimism and hope that individuals experience about their illness. Hope is different from expectations, wishes, and desires. Hope is, as Ronna Jevne (1994) so beautifully expressed, the space between science and compassion. The existence of hope can be ascertained by asking family members their beliefs about their future with the illness. To be able to focus on the future in the face of a chronic or life-threatening illness enables families to experience the healing phenomenon of hope. Some of the most challenging clinical work with families arises when there are divergent beliefs about the future among family members. If a mother believes that her 16-year-old child with leukemia will die soon, conflict will arise when the father brings home university catalogs based on his belief that the child will live and go to college.

Hope is also different from "the will to live"; the latter may be experienced as satisfying or unsatisfying (Jevne, 1994). At a Japanese health center, "meaningful life therapy" assists cancer patients to continue in a satisfying life, even in the face of horrendous illness. In this therapy, the cancer patients contribute to the community each day and set goals, thereby drawing forth hope about the future (Jevne, 1994).

The place of beliefs about hope and optimism in the illness experience has generally not been addressed by the dominant medical system. In many alternative healing systems, however, beliefs about hope and optimism are central (Jevne, 1994). What is the increasing appeal of alternative or complementary healing approaches? Many persons suffering with illness experience these approaches as more positive than the conventional medical approach because the complementary healing approaches do not shy away from some of the big questions surrounding illness: Why has this sickness happened to me? Why do people get sick despite living well? Why do some people die "before their time"?

## BELIEFS ABOUT RELIGION–SPIRITUALITY

The influence of family members' religious and spiritual beliefs on their illness experience has been one of the most neglected areas in family work. Yet our clinical experience with families has taught us that the experience of suffering becomes transposed to one of spirituality as family members try to make meaning out of their suffering and distress. (See chapter 1 for an in-depth discussion of religious–spiritual beliefs.) When exploring family members' religious and spiritual beliefs, health professionals are often concerned about the issue of religious pluralism. C. Everett Koop (1995), the former U.S. Surgeon General, offered a poignant thought on this matter: "I try to find areas on which we all agree—the importance of compassion, the necessity to alleviate suffering and eliminate pain" (p. 6). To understand how family members offer compassion and what efforts are made to alleviate suffering, it is useful to explore religious and spiritual beliefs.

One clinical family we were privileged to know, learn from, and assist at the FNU consisted of a common-law couple and their 9-year-old daughter. The mother's presenting concern was her daughter's behavior problems at school and aggressive behavior toward the mother at home. During the first session (mother only present), the mother's belief about the connection between the child's behavior, the mother's recurrent breast cancer, and the recent separation of the parents was revealed. Also, the mother expressed concern about the relationship between the daughter and father after her death. The following dialogue occurred in the third session, with the mother, father, and child present.

LMW: How much do you think Natasha [daughter] understands about death or about dying?

FATHER: I think Natasha has a peaceful understanding of that because of the church: reincarnation and perpetuation of the soul.

MOTHER: Natasha was born with these ideas.

LMW: [to Mother] And what are your religious beliefs about death?

MOTHER: I don't have religious beliefs. I just have a spiritual philosophy.

LMW: Yes, and what is that?

MOTHER: I believe that my soul is immortal and no one can touch it except me. I am the only one who can change it. It doesn't stop if my body dies.

LMW: [to Mother] And what do you think Natasha's beliefs are?

MOTHER: Christian Scientist Sunday school and prayer can heal headaches.

LMW: Natasha, can you help me understand what your mom is saying? When your mom is sick and if she does die, what do you believe will happen? [long pause] Can you tell me what you think? It's a pretty tough question. A hard one isn't it?

FATHER: [to daughter] Have you thought about it much?

NATASHA: No.

LMW: Natasha, do you believe that when people are sick they can make themselves better?

NATASHA: [*nods yes*]

LMW: Do you think there are ever times when people get sick and no matter how hard they pray or what they do that they can't get better, that their body can't do what they want and they still might die? Can that happen?

NATASHA: Yes.

Later in the session, the following dialogue took place:

LMW: Do you think at this point in time that Natasha is doing quite well with her understanding of your illness and the possibility of your life being shortened?

MOTHER: She has a good basic foundation. But there is some denial there because she believes that if I wanted to get well, then I could. But I'm at peace. I don't mind moving on.

This uncovering by the clinician of the family members' beliefs was quite significant. We learned that this young mother was at peace with the possibility that her life would be shortened but that her young daughter believed that if her mother wanted to be well, then she would be. We later discovered that the father's belief was similar to his daughter's and that he was also concerned that the mother had given up and was not trying anymore. Discussing these ideas openly and frankly with the family members proved to be a useful exercise. This young mother did die a few months later, and we had the privilege to work with the father and Natasha again. At that time, Natasha was concerned about keeping her mother's memory alive, and we discussed ways that she was already doing that and other ideas that she might entertain.

## BELIEFS ABOUT THE PLACE OF ILLNESS IN OUR LIVES

Integration of illness in our lives and relationships can consist of making a place for illness, living alongside illness, putting illness in its place, and overcoming illness. Temporal distinctions are often useful in understanding various approaches to managing the illness experience. In the early phases of illness, particularly at the time of diagnosis, there occurs the need for "making a place for illness."

A 25-year-old woman with whom LMW worked was experiencing chronic pain. This client was asked by LMW to monitor her activities for 2 weeks and rate her levels of pain each day. In the second session, she stated she now realized that she had not made a place for pain in her life—that she had wanted to continue all of her activities without "making a place" for illness. In another family, a 45-year-old woman—a wife and mother—was newly diagnosed with MS. Her husband remarked, "It may sound selfish, but I was hoping we could just carry on with our lives while we adjusted to this news. But now I see that MS requires some time and attention; carrying on with our lives means including MS." Both of these examples highlight one of the greatest initial challenges with any illness, that is, making a place for it in our lives. However, the North American phenomenon of busyness makes inclusion of illness an irritant and an add-on to life rather than an integral part of life.

The place that is made for illness may change over time. For example, the space and place of a newly diagnosed illness in family members' lives will be different from that of an illness diagnosed several years previously. There is also a distinction between "making a place" in a life for illness (as in the case of the early days of diagnosis) versus "living alongside illness" in order to have a life (as occurs with the long haul of chronic illness). In one family, a woman who was successfully living alongside her illness was invited to write a letter to a young woman experiencing MS who was not yet as successful. The letter gave the recipient hope and encouragement. The older woman expressed that writing the letter was a highly "cathartic" experience for her. She also went on to say, "MS is still here, but it does not dominate our lives and occupies only a small space over in the corner." This woman was successful at living alongside of illness. The useful idea generated by White and Epston (1990) of "expanding the audience" enables persons outside of the family to acknowledge the family's progress and competence at living alongside illness or putting illness in its place.

Another useful way to cope with illness is for clients to "put illness in its place" (Gonzalez, Steinglass, & Reiss, 1989; White, 1988/1989). In so doing, clients acknowledge that they experience an illness and have integrated it into their lives. The following transcript segment from Research Family 3 illustrates how a 13-year-old daughter experiencing CFS was successful in taking charge of another illness in her life, diabetes, and how she integrated that illness into her life by putting it in its place. This leads to a useful comparison and notion of balance between the two illness experiences. It also enables the clinician to offer a new reflection, a new facilitative belief, that perhaps what she (C2) has been able to do is keep "diabetes in its place." This precise choice of words by the clinician fosters the belief that illness can be in one's life but does not have to be in one's face. It also embeds the idea that success breeds success, that is, being successful in coping with one illness (diabetes) may predict success in coping with another (CFS).

LMW: What else do you do to keep diabetes in its place? To keep diabetes in its place, you take insulin; what other kinds of things do you do?

C2: Well, my diet.

LMW: Yes, what else do you do?

C2: Blood tests.

LMW: Blood tests. How often do you have to take those?

C2: I'm supposed to do it about four times a day, but I only do it about two.

C1: She doesn't do it every day, usually. She usually does it . . .

LMW: So has your sister been pretty much in charge of her diabetes then?

C1: Yes.

LMW: You don't have to assist her with the insulin, she's pretty much in charge of all that?

C1: Yes, she is. She won't let us draw it up for her.

LMW: Wow! We certainly know of families and other patients with whom we've worked where adolescents that have diabetes don't really take very good charge of it. So, that's terrific!

FATHER: She's very good.

LMW: When did you start taking charge of your diabetes like that?

C2: Oh . . .

MOTHER: Almost right after she got it.

C2: I got it when I was 8, and I was sort of confused and stuff. I just didn't know how to really deal with it and then I sort of relied on my parents to draw it up [insulin] and give it and everything and then . . .

C1: Yes, but that was only for a month.

C2: . . . and then after a while I started getting braver and giving it myself.

LMW: Well, that's impressive! So you must be pretty impressed with your daughter with the way she's . . .

C1: I know if I had diabetes, I would have, well, I like being independent. I don't think I could rely on somebody else drawing it up and giving it for me. I think [C2] is the same way. I think it was the way we were raised. Like not being dependent on others.

LMW: Where did you get this sort of leadership and take charge kind of attitude from? Where did that come from?

FATHER: It wasn't us.

C1: I think that we've just always had it.

LMW: Yes, but you said . . .

C1: Upbringing . . .

LMW: Part of your upbringing.

C1: Because I remember in Fernie, I mean me and my sister were always the most mature out of all the kids we hung around with. We always took charge and stuff like that, so I think it's been throughout.

LMW: [*to parents*] Do you agree they obtained this sort of take charge approach to things from you folks?

FATHER: I think so, in that sense.

LMW: So it sounds like you've really been able to put diabetes in its place, but it doesn't sound like you've been able to put chronic fatigue syndrome in its place yet. You're still trying to figure out how to put it in its place?

This move offers and supports the belief that managing an illness successfully involves "putting the illness in its place." This is an important facilitative belief because it challenges the constraining belief that "managing an illness successfully equals eliminating the illness from one's life." Illness can be included in a life. Illness and a good life can coexist. One way of integrating illness into one's life is to "put illness in its place."

An important developmental question in the history of the illness with the adolescent with CFS was, "When did you start taking charge of your diabetes like that?" This question embeds a commendation for this young woman of taking personal responsibility for her illness. The clinician is broadcasting the success in the context of the therapeutic conversation. Other family members validate the daughter's past success at taking personal responsibility for the illness. The concepts of volition and responsibility are then added on and framed as leadership. Careful use of the words suggests to the client that she has influence over the diabetes. The client and other family members respond quickly to this use of language. There seems to be a fit between the words the clinician uses and the family's experience.

Next, the commendation to the daughter is enlarged to include the parents: Perhaps the daughter obtained this take charge kind of approach to illnesses from her parents. An important connection is then made by the clinician: The daughter has been able to put diabetes in its place but, as yet, has not been able to put CFS in its place. This balancing and comparing of illnesses has remarkable leverage in opening space for the daughter to see the possibility of having some influence over the CFS: the uncertain and mysteriously nontemporally bound illness. The embedding of expectations and probabilities of success on the basis of a client's previous success story offers invitations for confidence in putting CFS in its place.

Through the therapeutic conversation, this teenager's experiences and expertise are elevated using the family's former experience and past successes. This embeds hope for the present situation because the client is distinguished as victor, not a victim of illness. Possibilities for future change are opened through the uncovering of past illness experiences.

It is tremendously useful to offer distinctions to families about making a place for illness, living alongside illness, or putting illness in its place. It removes a common belief in our culture that to have a satisfying life, one must not experience illness. Instead, the clinician offers the more optimistic idea that illness does not need to consume one's whole life. One can make a place for it and can decide how much space the illness is going to occupy in one's life. This notion offers an element of volition in that family members decide what place and space illness will have in their lives. It allows for more acceptance of illness, less blaming for failure to manage the illness, and less blaming for the fact that illness exists or has arisen in the first place.

## CONCLUSION

The macromove of uncovering and discovering illness beliefs of family members involves a purposeful and continued effort on behalf of the clinician to draw forth illness beliefs with curiosity, respectfulness, and appreciation of the expert role of family members in the experience of illness. Art Frank (personal communication, June 1995) offered us the notion that our clinical work could be thought of as an "ethics consultation," that is, dealing with the ethics of illness. This chapter has given a sampling of some of the beliefs that are useful to explore to uncover and distinguish illness beliefs, namely, beliefs about diagnosis; etiology; healing and treatment; mastery, control, and influence; prognosis; religion–spirituality; and the place of illness in our lives and relationships.

Through the micromove of drawing forth illness beliefs, the clinician is able to coassess with family members which beliefs are constraining and which are facilitative in the management or the ethics of an illness experience. Of course, there are no correct beliefs for families coping with illness, only beliefs that are more freeing, useful, and facilitative in the lives and relationships of family members.

# CHAPTER 6

# Challenging, Altering, and Modifying Constraining Beliefs

THE MICROMOVES DESCRIBED in this chapter have been identified from our research and clinical practice with families. Some of these micromoves were developed through our clinical work and have come to typify our practice; others were derived from family intervention literature and presentations at conferences and workshops, particularly on the subject of family therapy. Regardless of their origin, the purpose of all of these micromoves is to invite family members to a reflection (Maturana & Varela, 1992). (See table 6.1 for micromoves.) This is not an exhaustive list of the micromoves that we use to challenge, alter, or modify beliefs, but these best characterize our work with families.

## OFFERING COMMENDATIONS

The offering of commendations is a central micromove that characterizes our clinical practice. Fabie Duhamel (1994) examined the clinical practice provided at the Family Nursing Unit to families experiencing hypertension. Her analysis of the clinical work brought to our awareness our practice of commenting on family strengths. Lorraine Wright chose the word *commendation* to name the clinical move in which the

TABLE 6.1

**Micromoves to Challenge, Alter, and Modify Constraining Beliefs**

Offering commendations

Asking interventive questions

Drawing distinctions

Speaking the unspeakable

Distinguishing incongruence between beliefs and behavior

Offering a hypothetical facilitative belief

Using reflecting teams

Writing therapeutic letters

Offering videotapes

Externalizing problems, symptoms, and solutions

Offering differing opinions: split-opinion intervention

Using research findings

Offering alternative beliefs (new or modified)

Offering sermonettes and storytelling

Using words and voice to invite healing

clinician draws forth and highlights family strengths. We now offer commendations to every family in every therapeutic conversation, both during the interview and at the end-of-session summary of our impressions, ideas, and recommendations. We prefer emphasizing strengths rather than deficits, dysfunction, and deficiencies in family members. Steve Wolin, Bill O'Hanlon, and Lynn Hoffman (1995) have termed approaches that emphasize the latter "damage models."

Wright and Leahey (1994b) have defined *commendations* as "observations of patterns of behavior that occur across time (e.g., 'Your family members are very loyal to one another') whereas a compliment is usually an observational comment on a onetime event (e.g., 'You were very praising of your son today')" (p. 106). Commendations are often connected to the family's story of illness. Two of our former graduate students (McElheran & Harper-Jaques, 1994) adopted our ideas and wrote about and embellished the idea of commendations on the basis of their experience as clinicians.

The deliberate drawing forth and elaborating on family strengths and resources has a profound impact on families. Family members frequently respond to the perturbation in a dramatic, affective manner.

They voice confirmation that they feel heard or understood (sometimes for the first time in years), or they become tearful as they describe how validated the commendation makes them feel.

Through our consistent use of commendations over many years, we have noted that when we commend a family about a particular strength or a resourceful behavior they are showing, they seem to be more open to ideas offered by the clinician. We believe that commendations increase structural coupling between the family members and the clinician and invite the family to open space to new ideas. They are, in essence, conversations of affirmation and affection between the clinician or clinical team and the family and thereby open possibilities for healing.

There are many forms of commendations. In the following example from the first session with Research Family 2, the clinician (LMW) capitalizes on an opportunity within the session to commend the client (Connie) in a comparative way, pointing out how wise she is in comparison to "society." A distinction is drawn between society's beliefs about therapy and the client's wisdom.

LMW: What do you tell yourself about coming for counseling?

CONNIE: Well I thought about it quite a while. I need some help and I want to get it.

LMW: Well I admire you, because we still unfortunately have the idea in our society that going for help is embarrassing or shameful. Yet I look at it quite differently. I prefer to think that it's a sign of wanting to get past the problem—you've exhausted your own resources, you've tried things on your own. You've tried them and, yes, some things have helped somewhat, but it seems like you want to get past the problem. You want to get further with it.

CONNIE: And if I don't, I'm going to end up somewhere, I don't know, 'cause I can't take it anymore.

A commendation that summarizes and highlights the family's story is another form of commendation. This type recognizes more than a single idea. It is a sustained pattern of commendations, an elaborate reflection on the family's story, which confirms for the family that they have been heard and understood. In the first session with Research Family 1, the clinician (LMW) offers an end-of-session commendation to the parents who were caregivers to their adult son experiencing multiple sclerosis (MS).

LMW: First of all I want to tell you that my team and I are just incredibly impressed with the two of you as a couple and as a mother and father. I think you've gone above and beyond what most parents do for their children. You've had an unusual circumstance enter your family. Most families do not have to have this challenge of coping with having a son with MS. It has been an incredible challenge your family has been hit with. You have really risen to the occasion. We're just very impressed by you. For whatever reasons, one of your lots in life and your missions in life seems to be the role of caring for people and taking care of people. How do you do that—how do you keep your own health through that and your own sanity through all the pressures . . . ?

FATHER: Struggle along.

LMW: Yes, it's something we want to talk to you about. We've been very impressed with your dedication and devotion to your son. We've certainly worked with lots of families where there's been health problems, but you're the first family that I've met where the parents have left their home to come and care for their child. More often my experience has been that it's the child who goes back home to care for the parents. Or if the child is not well, then they usually go back to where they grew up or something to make it a bit easier. But you're quite remarkable; to give up your home, your family, your friends, and your social life, your activities and all of that, to come here to care for your son is just quite remarkable. This is the first I've ever heard of this. I've usually seen it the other way.

MOTHER: Well, he's your child, you brought him into the world.

LMW: Oh sure, I'm just saying, it's the first I've heard. You're a very unique couple, you're to be admired. You've just gone above and beyond as parents and sacrificed. You know, if he had gone back home and you were caring for him there, I would have said *that* was a tremendous sacrifice.

FATHER: At least you'd have all your friends . . .

LMW: You'd have your friends, your family. I would have been commending you for that and say it's a tremendous thing you've done to have your son come home and to care for him and look after him as best you can. You would have to make a lot of sacrifices and adjustments, but you'd be around, like you say, you'd be around your family, your friends, and maybe get some relief once in a while. However, here you're pretty much on your own, because I don't know how many people you [know] here. Not really anybody.

MOTHER: No we don't, not really too many.

LMW: So now it seems like even your health is even being sacrificed somewhat. The tension is perhaps having some effect on that—not being able to have breaks together. We were wondering if your body isn't trying to tell you something. Perhaps the sacrifice—

maybe, we don't know, we're just guessing here—is even going a bit too far if it's coming to the point of sacrificing your health, because if your health is affected, then how will you be able to care for your son?

MOTHER: Well, I just pray every night that I'll keep up.

FATHER: Me too.

LMW: Yes, well we can hope your prayers are answered in the positive vein, but I guess the question we as a team have is, "How far are you willing to go to continue to make these sacrifices? Is there any limit to the sacrifices you would make for your son?"

The elaborate commendation not only summarizes the family's story but distinguishes many family strengths. The embellished nature of the commendation paves the way for the clinician to pose a reflexive question that challenges the couple's beliefs about caregiving: "Is there any limit to the sacrifices you would make for your son?"

Commendations that highlight and acknowledge strengths that are outside the family members' awareness have extra potency and therapeutic value. This form of commendation challenges, alters, or modifies constraining beliefs by drawing forth a new identity or belief about the family or about their situation.

In Research Family 4, the single-parent mother of four young children believed that she was a failure as evidenced by her need to seek therapy. At the end of the first session, the clinician (WLW) uses evidence from the mother's life to deliver an end-of-session commendation that challenges the mother's constraining belief about herself:

WLW: The team really wanted to commend you. I wrote down everything they said. Number one, they see you as a very caring mother. They said that they are also really impressed that you knew that now was the time that you had energy to do something about your situation. You know, that's really impressive.

MOTHER: Thank you.

WLW: You've come to a point—even though you define your situation as a chronic crisis—and there's been something that said, "You can go now, get on with it now." They were very impressed, as was I, with everything that you've survived, the abundance of unexpected events, the abundance of violence that you've experienced, and that you've survived all this. And survived some big disappointments. Everything from your marriage to school.

MOTHER: I don't know how well I've survived.

WLW: Well, you're here, and you've got four kids here with you. I'd say that's very good survival. The team is impressed with your willingness to take responsibility for your life. I found this amazing that even though you said to yourself, "My husband's violence is related to his organic brain disorder"—that it's something very organic—that you were able to say, "I want to get out of this relationship. I need to, for myself, and my children. I need to do the right thing—the protecting, safe thing. And that is to leave the relationship." Not a lot of women would have been able to figure that out.

ELDEST SON: She's very intelligent.

WLW: She *is* intelligent, isn't she! The way that she could figure that out.

ELDEST SON: She uses her brains.

MOTHER: Thank you, Son. I appreciate the compliment.

ELDEST SON: I try using my brains too.

MOTHER: And you do a very good job of it.

The commendations offered by the clinician and the clinical team focus on the mother's intelligence, her perceptiveness, and her ability to figure things out that other women could not. This is a deliberate counter to the negative opinions the mother reported she had experienced from her husband, her father, her professors, and other professionals. Notice that the commendation opens space for the son to add to the commendation of his mother, at which point the mother reciprocates. Commendations invited commendations, and thus a conversation of affirmation and affection coevolved.

The commendation also focuses on the mother's wisdom in knowing when to get help and choosing to do something now. Families often present for help when they have bottomed out, that is, when illness burden or illness experience has become unbearable and family resources depleted. In this session, commendations provided an alternative view of the decision to seek help, viewing the mother as insightful, knowledgeable, and clear thinking. In so doing, the commendations challenged the mother's beliefs about herself as incompetent and a failure and offered an alternative view of her capabilities. This is the highest order of commendation.

## ASKING INTERVENTIVE QUESTIONS

We were initiated into the interventive world of questioning through the work of the Milan team (Boscolo & Cecchin, 1980, March; 1980, October). Mara Selvini Palazzoli, one of the original members of the Milan team, was asked by Lorraine Wright, "What is the best way to teach nurses to be helpful to families?" Her answer was, "Teach them to ask relationship questions" (M. Selvini Palazzoli, personal communication, 1985). The beneficial and elegant aspects of interventive questions (i.e., circular, reflexive, and relative influence questions) have been described, typologized, and illustrated elsewhere (Fleuridas, Nelson, & Rosenthal, 1986; Loos & Bell, 1990; Tomm, 1985, 1987a, 1987b, 1988; White, 1988; Wright, 1989; Wright & Leahey, 1994a, 1994b).

Questions assist us in our therapeutic efforts to "structurally couple" with another person in a therapeutic conversation, create a context for changing beliefs, uncover and distinguish current facilitative and constraining beliefs, modify and challenge constraining beliefs, and introduce and solidify facilitative beliefs.

Beliefs are embedded in the questions we ask. As the clinician asks questions, family members reflect on their beliefs, and the process of challenging, altering, or modifying constraining beliefs begins. Three variations on the theme of asking questions that we use in our therapeutic conversations are (a) asking questions that invite a reflection, (b) inviting family members to externalize internalized questions, and (c) inviting family members to ask questions.

## ASKING QUESTIONS THAT INVITE A REFLECTION

Part of opening space for reflection occurs with the seemingly simple lead-ins to the questions we ask. We have found that it is not just the questions that are important but the lead-ins; they embed so much and are rich with messages and meanings. These lead-ins increase the likelihood that the question (the trigger) will be experienced as a perturbation and invite the family member to a reflection.

In the following example, the clinician prepares the family for the move of an unusual and strange question about the benefits of MS: "I'm going to ask you a question that may seem a bit strange but I've been curious; has there been any good that's come out of having MS?" The preparation and the "strange question" that follows acknowledge the problematic, troublesome, suffering aspects of the illness that have been previously discussed and, at the same time, offer an alternative view of the experience of the illness.

As in most issues related to work with families, context is key. It is rarely one question alone that triggers a perturbation but the timing, spacing, placing, and sequencing of questions—the contextualizing of questions—that perturbs and opens space for new beliefs. We agree with Goolishian, who said, "You need to listen recursively; each question is a modification of the answer to the previous question" (Anderson, Goolishian, Pulliam, & Winderman, 1986, p. 115).

The following questions unfolded in the therapeutic conversation between WLW and a woman who expressed suicidal ideation during a session with a clinical family. A dramatic change in the woman's belief sustained her life:

- What if you were able to discover you had 10% more desire to live than you thought you had? What difference would that make?
- If we had a "desire to live" meter and you found out that you were 4 on the scale of 10, instead of 3, what could you do more of that you couldn't do as a 3? (The woman was able to think of several things ranging from associating with people to attending meetings.)
- So very much that has happened doesn't make sense to you. Is there any part of you that says it all *does* make sense? (The woman expressed that she had never thought about it from this point of view. Through her reflection, we uncovered a core belief: "I believe if we persevere or endure through any trial we grow from [it]." The clinician and client called this "Vivian's motto," a belief that she felt in her "heart and mind." Building on this response, the questions to invite reflection continued.)
- What is going to keep you persevering and enduring in the next week or two? (An important question for a woman who had been threatening not to be alive the next day.)
- What could you think about or do this month to tell you that you are persevering and growing?
- If you were to establish a project that shows you are persevering and growing, what project would that be? (She was able to describe something she wanted to do that involved two very concrete steps.)
- What do you want to see yourself doing with regard to the project that will keep you persevering, enduring, and growing?
- What do you predict you will experience as a woman who is persevering, enduring, and growing through this trial? (Her predictions were increased energy, increased positiveness with her children, and decreased irritability.)
- Is there anything else, now that you are acknowledging things about yourself—maybe you have been lonely for yourself? What else would tell you, "I believe in persevering and enduring and growing through trials"? (Three years later, the belief and accompanying changes in this woman's life are sustained by her.)

Having established that "lead-ins" and contextualizing of questions are useful, we also acknowledge times when the therapeutic conversation is going in a particular direction. In those times, no lead-in is given, and a question is asked that seems to come out of the blue and cuts to the heart of the matter. In the following example with Research Family 5, LMW was speaking with the wife, Julie. The conversation had coevolved with the wife describing the husband's violent behavior toward her:

JULIE: It's not just violence. We don't have to go very far into a fight. It doesn't even have to reach a point where it could accomplish something before Robert tells me to get out, pack my bags, he doesn't need me. And you don't have to have much of a fight for that to happen.

LMW: So, are you feeling loved enough in your marriage these days?

This leapfrogging question took the therapeutic conversation into the heart of the matter; the conversation culminated in ideas about how to draw forth loving experiences for both husband and wife and how to diminish the anger and violence. The unexpected timing and sequencing of this question were important, as was the use of language. If the clinician had left out the word *enough* and had asked instead whether the woman was feeling loved in her marriage these days, this woman may have said, "I know that he loves me" or "I know that he doesn't love me," and the conversation would have ended. The word *enough* seemed to be important in opening space for this woman to reflect on her experiences in a different way.

### INVITING FAMILY MEMBERS TO EXTERNALIZE INTERNALIZED QUESTIONS

We agree with Tom Andersen (1991b) that it is important to ask "questions that those we speak with usually do not ask themselves, and which give possibilities for many answers, which in turn might create new questions" (p. 34). However, we also believe that it is important to access the questions that family members *do* ask themselves because of our belief that beliefs are embedded in the questions we ask ourselves. We need to understand the questions clients currently ask themselves and thereby uncover their current constraining or facilitative beliefs. At that point, we can ask them questions they usually *do not* ask themselves and thereby invite them to consider beliefs they have not considered.

To have clients say out loud the questions that are most troublesome to them "inside" is one important step in understanding their biopsychosocial–spiritual structures and the beliefs that constitute those structures. We invite clients to externalize (say out loud) their internalized questions through our clinician questions, such as the following:

• We have a lot of internal conversations, conversations with ourselves. What kinds of conversations have you been having with yourself these days? What kinds of questions do you ask yourself in a day?

- What do you ask yourself on a bad (good) day?
- When you talk to yourself, what's the most discouraging (encouraging) question you find yourself coming back to?

Chapter 8 provides a clinical example of the usefulness of externalizing internalized questions.

### INVITING FAMILY MEMBERS TO ASK QUESTIONS

Another way to access family members' beliefs is by inviting them to ask questions of each other or of the clinician or clinical team (Wright, 1989):

- Are there any questions you wish I had asked you or another family member?
- Is there any question you would like to ask us or another family member?

In the following example with a clinical family experiencing a life-shortening illness, the conversation had shifted to the couple's relationship. The team learned that the husband (Igor) had noticed that his wife (Ivana) was no longer optimistic about her future. She had accepted that she would die and was now focusing on her relationship with her daughter (Natasha) to teach her all she could in the time she had left. Igor felt guilty that this shift had occurred at a time when Ivana gave up hope of reconciling their relationship (i.e., when she discovered he was having an affair). In the middle of a conversation of their beliefs about how two people who cared so deeply for each other got "bogged down" in their relationship, LMW invited them to ask questions of each other. The focus was on this couple's struggle concerning whether or not they should marry.

LMW: If you could look ahead in the future, 10 years from now, say even if you did pass on, Ivana, do you think it would be useful for Natasha to know that her parents did marry, or would that matter? Will it make a difference for her life?

IGOR: I've seen my father and brother get married and divorced. If we did get married, I would be doing it more for Ivana. She's more traditional. A more important lesson for Natasha is love.

IVANA: I think for the future what will make a great deal of difference for Natasha is how we deal with this. She'll probably script her life by how we resolve our problems.

LMW: [*5 minutes later*] Are there any last things you want to say to each other or ask each other?

IGOR: [*to Ivana*] Do you feel it is necessary to get back together to give Natasha the right lesson?

IVANA: Yes.

LMW: Is it essential for Natasha, or is it more essential for you?

IVANA: It's important to me, but it's like I want to leave her some essence of my values, so I should live them. If we just split up and he has girlfriends coming in and out of her life, she won't get that. I want to be sure that Natasha and Igor can get along together when I pass on.

The question that Igor asked Ivana invited a conversation that challenged the belief that they could be helpful to Natasha only if they were married or together as a couple and helped them to join forces in the common goal of helping Natasha.

## DRAWING DISTINCTIONS

Beliefs can arise through the process of drawing distinctions. (For a more conceptual discussion about distinctions, see chapter 3.) In our therapeutic conversations, we are continually seeking to draw forth distinctions through the questions we ask and the opinions and recommendations we offer. As distinctions are drawn, possibilities for new beliefs arise.

In Research Family 1, the elderly parents of an adult son with MS were distinguished as "nurses" in a caregiving situation involving their son. When this distinction was offered, possibilities for respite were opened up.

LMW: [*to son, Mark*] Your parents didn't feel right about taking off, but you got that clarified with them last time. You're very supportive of them having a break. And like we said, your parents really serve two roles with you, don't they? They're your parents but they also do a lot of nursing.

MARK: Oh yes.

LMW: And nurses get days off, you know. Parents don't.

MOTHER: [*laughs with Father*] Those poor parents.

LMW: Parents don't get a day off, but nurses do. You've got a male and a female nurse here, so you have to give them a holiday once in a while.

MOTHER AND FATHER: Yes.

MARK: Right.

By making the distinction that it was the "nurses" who would be taking a break, the parents and son were freed up to explore respite possibilities. Their belief that "good parents providing nursing care to a son with MS never take a vacation" shifted to "good nurses taking care of a young man with MS take a vacation." The outcome? Mark took initiative and discovered that he had $50,000 per year of nursing coverage through his employer. The parents took a trip to Reno and won the door prize: a trip to anywhere in Canada, the United States, or Australia! The distinction between "nurses" and "parents" had dramatically opened possibilities for this family experiencing MS.

With this same family, other distinctions were drawn that proved particularly useful: crying on the inside versus crying on the outside, making a place for illness in one's life versus putting illness in its place, the expression and experience of anger versus sadness, and the unfolding and number of good days versus bad days.

Differential diagnosis is a common practice in the health care field. What we find useful is drawing distinctions between the medical diagnosis and the "family experience diagnosis." In one clinical family, the 13-year-old had been diagnosed with attention deficit disorder (ADD). WLW uncovered that it was not ADD that was affecting his "mind" but rather that it was D-A-D, his dad, that was on this young boy's mind. The "diagnosis" of "sad for dad" fit for the boy and opened space for him and his mother to talk about how to get his out-of-state, divorced father to be more involved in his life. The distinction in diagnosis made a difference.

We have also found it useful to make a distinction between depression and exhaustion. In Research Family 5, the wife (Julie) had been telling LMW about the many things she was "coping with," including her husband's two heart attacks. LMW offered the following distinction:

LMW: Can I tell you another thing I think about you? I think you're exhausted.

JULIE: I am!

LMW: And you know sometimes I wonder if we confuse exhaustion with depression.

JULIE: Well, it's funny that you should say that because I've been wondering if I'm suffering from depression. Because when I go out and get away from it all, I feel so good. And yet I know ever since Robert [her husband] was sick, all I want to do is rest. I just want a break, and I feel like I've never had it. I don't know how to explain that . . .

LMW: I think you've explained it very well.

JULIE: That's not verbatim what it's like.

LMW: I think you've explained it very well. I mean, I really wonder if you're exhausted and not depressed. Sometimes I think depression and exhaustion can be confused, that you can get so exhausted you think you're depressed but it's actually being really exhausted.

JULIE: It's been a strange year of coping. I had to, you know. Robert was sick, and I had to come home and cope with the children, and I had to keep things cool so that my son wouldn't have an asthma attack, and my daughter was having problems with her Ritalin, and my mother was trying to have another heart attack.

The distinction fit for this woman, and in our follow-up outcome study, Julie reported that she was taking better care of herself, getting more rest, and that she felt less moody.

It is important to assess women's workload, the busyness of their lives, and the responsibilities they carry when illness is present (Robinson, 1994a). Is this a depressed woman or an exhausted woman? Would it be useful to move beyond labeling women as depressed and perhaps offer a diagnosis of "unhelpful husband and ungrateful children"? Because diagnosis leads to treatment ideas, the distinction is important: Depression versus exhaustion may translate to Prozac versus sleep!

Another distinction we find useful is the distinction between "this" family and "other" families. As we draw distinctions between how we believe other families would handle a situation and how we experience the family in front of us doing so, the remarkableness of the family is noted: Most women in your situation would not be able to . . . . We usually see that couples who are trying to blend families have problems with . . . . How have you been able to work those out?

The remarkableness of the family is marked through concrete examples from the literature or experiences with other families juxtaposed with distinguishing examples from this family. Through the distinctions that are drawn, this family is truly distinguished! The therapeutic move of drawing distinctions sets this family apart from the "norm." It is the antithesis to the therapeutic move of "normalization."

## SPEAKING THE UNSPEAKABLE

Therapeutic change occurs when the belief that is at the heart of the matter is distinguished. (See chapter 3 for a discussion of beliefs about change and clinicians.) Speaking the unspeakable is a powerful therapeutic move used to uncover beliefs that are central to the problem with which a family is struggling. These core beliefs may be outside a family member's awareness or may be too explosive, frightening, or painful for family members to articulate. When the clinician deliberately goes against social convention to raise these issues in a therapeutic conversation, the family's constraining belief about their inability to discuss sensitive issues is challenged, and new, facilitative beliefs may arise.

In Research Family 1, the clinician (LMW) learned that the caregiving parents had not been able to take a holiday together since they began caring for their chronically ill, adult son (Mark). In the following dialogue, the clinician explores the parents' belief about what constrains them from taking a break together. After learning that the parents believe they need to ask their son's permission to leave, the clinician uncovers the core belief that constrains them.

LMW: But you would have to ask your son first, you're saying, to see if he would be okay about that, if he would give his permission to that?

FATHER: I wouldn't just bring somebody in and say, "Here, we're going away."

LMW: When do you think you would be, like, what do you think you would be comfortable asking Mark about that, his permission on that, for the two of you?

MOTHER: That's it, you don't know how to . . .

FATHER: . . . approach him.

LMW: Approach him on that?

FATHER: Yes.

MOTHER: Like if—and like I don't like to upset him.

LMW: Aha, because what would happen if you did?

MOTHER: Oh, I just feel that, you know, maybe it's not good [*Father speaking in agreement at the same time*] to be upset with. . .

LMW: So you think it could make his illness worse if you upset him?

FATHER: Possibly, yes.

LMW: Okay, have you been told that, or is that something . . .

MOTHER AND FATHER: No! [*both talking*]

FATHER: No, it's just something that I would think, ah . . .

LMW: Something you believe that, perhaps, it could make his illness worse . . .

The clinician speaks the unspeakable when she suggests the parents think it could make his illness worse if they upset him. By persistent and sensitive probing (what would happen if you did?), the clinician uncovers the fear that constrains the parents from seeking respite together. The very nature of uncovering the core belief and saying it out loud—that the parents could make their son's illness worse by taking a vacation and upsetting him—invites the couple to examine the belief: Where did the belief come from? What impact does the belief have on them? The process also invites the couple to reconsider the usefulness of the belief. The act of speaking the unspeakable out loud reduces its clandestine power and fearful grip over families.

Speaking the unspeakable around the issue of violence is a situation frequently encountered in clinical work with families. In the following example with Research Family 5, violence was even more unspeakable than usual: The couple had presented with concern about the husband's cardiac illness, not spousal violence. Notice the nonthreatening, nondefensive curiosity of the clinician (LMW). At the beginning of Session 3, the wife (Julie) shows sadness and discouragement. The clinician is persistent in exploring what the wife is troubled about and uncovers the belief that Julie thinks the clinician is allied more closely with her husband than with herself. As the clinician states a position of advocating for the relationship rather than for either person, Julie seems to feel it is safe to disclose a violent incident that is troubling her:

JULIE: I was really afraid to say what I said because I know it's going to make him angry. And yet that's what I see happening. I didn't come in here to say he's a "bad guy" and he did this and he did that, but unless I do some of that, I'm not giving you a clear picture of how I feel either.

LMW: Well, I'm trying to understand what would constrain you from getting your anger out.

JULIE: Well, first, I don't want to make him mad. I don't want to hurt him. [*crying*]

LMW: So what would be wrong with getting him mad? So what? So he gets mad.

JULIE: It's really unpleasant when he's mad.

LMW: Oh, it's unpleasant. Well, that's different then. So, you're saying if you come in here and tell me some not nice stories about your husband, that you don't want him to get mad. But you're saying, it's not just that you don't want him to get mad—he's not nice when he's mad. Is that right? So what's the worst thing he does when he's mad? [*long pause*]

JULIE: He loses his, loses control.

LMW: He loses control.

JULIE: I already told you when I made the first appointment. Things had been really bad ...

LMW: Yes.

JULIE: And I don't want to give the impression that it happens all the time, but he grabbed me and tried to throw me out of the house. And our kids heard and saw that, it was awful, and I won't ever have it happen again.

LMW: And nor *should* you. . . . Is this the worst thing about Robert that you want me to know? [*Julie is crying.*] Okay, and is this the balancing that you're trying to help me to understand, that last time you were concerned that I would walk away thinking he's Mister Good Guy when he does not-so-nice-guy things to you?

Throughout this segment, we see the continual persistence and curiosity of the clinician, which uncovered the spousal violence by the husband. Notice the particular questions that helped the wife speak the unspeakable: What would constrain you? What would be wrong with getting him mad? What's the worst thing he does when he's mad? Is this the worst thing you want me to know about your husband? This is accompanied by a clear declaration by the clinician that violence is not acceptable. Virginia Goldner, Peggy Penn, Marcia Sheinberg, and Gillian Walker (1990) suggested that "we could interrupt the cycle of violence, and thus make love safer for women and less threatening for men" (p. 344). Perhaps the same could be said for therapeutic conversations about violence. By offering opportunities to speak the unspeakable about violence, the clinician makes therapy safer for women and less threatening for men. Speaking the unspeakable challenges the wife's belief that discussing the violence may have negative consequences for her husband's health. By reducing the grip of this constraining belief, she begins to view her husband as capable of handling conflict.

The "unspeakable" takes as many unique forms as there are families. Over the years of seeing families experiencing difficulties with illness, we have come to appreciate that the unspeakable issue surrounding illness frequently centers on death and mortality. This is not surprising. Family members and health care professionals alike often enter into "conspiracies of silence" (Wortman & Schetter, 1979), motivated by a belief that withholding conversations about death may serve to protect the ill family member. Having worked with many families experiencing life-shortening and life-threatening illness, we have learned that it is useful to make a distinction between dying and death. Speaking about the process—the anticipation and knowledge that one's life is being shortened—is very different from trying to have knowledge about the time of death (Wright & Nagy, 1993). Once this secret of time is acknowledged as being undetermined, families are more able to talk about the knowledge of dying and the associated suffering of pain and grief.

In a recent therapeutic conversation with a clinical family, various family members reported their grave concern about the health habits of the 55-year-old father, who had experienced a heart attack and cardiac bypass surgery. Their concern was shown through their disapproval and nagging when the father indulged in behaviors such as overeating, not exercising, and smoking. In fact, the 25-year-old son reported his disapproval had escalated to intense anger and fighting with his father on several occasions. Notice the clinician's (LMW) deft probing for beliefs at the heart of the conflict.

LMW: Do you think your father knows he can count on you folks to worry?

SON: Definitely.

LMW: Have you decreased your worry for him?

SON: No, but I try to handle it better. I used to bug him and he'd bite back at me. I just care about him. I want him to be around forever. My Dad's the strong man . . .

LMW: And your biggest worry is what?

SON: I just want him to be around forever.

LMW: So your biggest worry is . . . ?

SON: [crying] I just want him to treat himself better. I just want him to be around till he's 70 or 80.

LMW: So your biggest worry is that he'll die prematurely?

SON: Yes.

LMW: That's an awful worry isn't it?

SON: And he's a great person. He has a lot to show me still. [All family members are crying, including the father.] I have a lot to learn from him in terms of business and getting my career in line. And I don't want my mom to be by herself; she loves him dearly. . . . I know he can't live forever.

LMW: So you get sad about this and discouraged. Does he know you have felt this strongly? Does he know the depth of your worry for him?

SON: No.

FATHER: No, I knew he cared, but I never knew he worried this much.

SON: I want my dad to be there. He's my buddy.

By inviting the son to speak the unspeakable, the family members' worry became more easily understood. The son feared his father would die. The opportunity to speak this fear aloud altered the meaning of nagging and fighting and created new understanding and appreciation between family members. The belief that drew forth conversations of accusation and recrimination concerning the father's noncompliance was, "he doesn't care enough about his health or our family." This belief was transformed into a belief that invited conversations of affirmation and affection: "I love my father and worry about him because I want him to live forever."

## DISTINGUISHING INCONGRUENCE BETWEEN BELIEFS AND BEHAVIOR

Another move that is useful in challenging constraining beliefs is to point out the discrepancy between what a person believes and how a person behaves. This is especially useful around issues of physical or mental violence, discipline, or the imposing of one's will. The challenge is to expose the contradiction, not in an accusatory way but at the level of beliefs. Rather than asking Robert, the husband in Research Family 5, whether he felt remorseful about hitting his wife, his behavior is juxtaposed with his beliefs about hitting in the following conversation:

LMW: What are your beliefs about violent behavior in a couple relationship?

ROBERT: I don't believe in hitting.

LMW: You don't believe in hitting.

ROBERT: I came from a background where my parents were physical and I don't agree with it. I don't agree a boy should hit a girl, like my son hitting my daughter, yet I act the opposite toward my wife and that's stupid.

LMW: So you don't believe that you should . . .

ROBERT: No, I don't think so.

LMW: . . . use physical force to deal with conflict. Do you ever feel it's acceptable, Robert, or justified to . . .

ROBERT: No.

LMW: . . . shove your wife or—never?

ROBERT: No.

LMW: So when you do it and you go against what you believe or what you think, then where does that leave you?

ROBERT: I felt bad.

LMW: How do you account for that?

ROBERT: I think that you can be pushed to a point. I mean I controlled myself to that point where I didn't do that and I stopped myself, but I mean I was pushed to a point where, and it got me there. It makes me sick in the sense, because I came from a background where that was part of my family life. Like I remember [lying] in bed with my sister with our arms wrapped around each other when my father beat on my mother. I can't watch TV shows that have any violence like that in it. I get teased about it, but I can't do that.

LMW: So, how do you reconcile with yourself then that it came to that point? You're saying because you were provoked to that point, or how does it make sense to you?

The key process of altering beliefs about violence is not just to draw forth affect—remorse or shame—but to invite the person to take responsibility for the incongruence between beliefs and behavior. In the preceding segment, the clinician first explores the beliefs about violence in a reflexive way to determine whether there is an incongruence between beliefs and behavior. Next, the clinician points out the discrepancy and seeks an explanation for the incongruence. The consequences of the incongruence may also be explored. If the client believes that violence is justified, the origin of the belief should be explored. An invitation could then be extended to the client—Would you be willing to be even 10% less loyal to your cultural beliefs [family beliefs, religious beliefs]?—to open space to entertain alternative options to violent behavior. We have found that this type of exploration of beliefs has been successful in inviting individuals to take responsibility for their violent behavior and to adopt more acceptable behavior in the future. The behavior then coincides with their moral beliefs of how to treat their partners appropriately and respectfully. By reflecting on the gap between their beliefs and behavior, we have witnessed remarkable changes in behavior.

## OFFERING A HYPOTHETICAL FACILITATIVE BELIEF

In this micromove, a hypothetical question related to a core, constraining belief is asked. The question offers or embeds a facilitative belief and is an indirect way of challenging or altering a constraining belief. The hypothetical nature of the question invites a sense of playfulness and experimentation with a new way of thinking. We experience that there is something about the hypothetical subjunctive mood of the "if you were to believe ..." question, developed by WLW, that invites people in a gentle yet powerful manner to consider an alternative facilitative belief, a belief often diametrically opposed to their current constraining belief. The question also embeds the suggestion that altered beliefs may give rise to new behaviors. In that process of suspended speculation, we observe changes: changes in affect, behavior, and ideas. As people hypothetically entertain a belief that is an alternative to the constraining belief that is at the heart of the matter, we believe internal changes in their biopsychosocial–spiritual structure occur. We find that through the asking of the "if you were to believe ..." question, eyes change, minds change, and hearts change. We have found that it is often sufficient to ask family members questions such as the following:

- If you were to believe . . . , what would be different? (This question opens space for new ideas and offers a nonthreatening reflexive view of the present problem.)
- What would need to be different for you to believe . . . ?
- What part of you already believes . . . ?

Temporal distinctions also assist in the offering of the "if you were to believe . . ." question. When the conceptual leap that is offered through the new embedded facilitative belief is large, couching the question in small time increments facilitates the perturbation: If just for the next 10 minutes you were to believe . . . , what difference would that make?

In a recent therapeutic conversation with a clinical family, the couple reported feeling overwhelmed by the husband's arthritis and believed they could do nothing to influence the illness, particularly the husband's experience of pain. It was hypothesized that this lack of influence invited the couple to withdraw from each other, which invited conflict. The following hypothetical questions were offered to them: If you were to believe that you could have 10% more control over the pain, what would be different in your marriage? If you were to believe that you could unite as a couple against the arthritis, what do you think might happen to the pain? Several weeks later, the couple reported more communication and an increased sense of "team effort" around pain management, in contrast to their previous experience of withdrawal and isolation.

A wife was exhausted and demoralized by her efforts to help her husband (John) grieve the suicidal death of his brother. The wife's creativity and energy were increased when WLW asked the woman to ask herself the following questions: If I were to believe that John cares about my efforts to help him grieve, what would I do more of [less of]? If I were to believe I have compassionate feelings for John, what would I do? If I were to believe that I influence John's grief, what would that invite me to do?

Great changes occurred for a middle-aged woman (Andrea) who experienced being perpetually criticized about the quiet nature of her voice by a "friend" (Maxine). "Speak up! You're too soft-spoken!" were the words Andrea heard from Maxine. Andrea was the leader in a woman's organization in which Maxine participated, and she was considering leaving her position because of the undermining she experienced from Maxine's comments. WLW invited Andrea to ask herself a question from time to time to see what answers came to her mind. She could then either contemplate the ideas or act on them. The question was, "If I were to believe that my voice matters in Maxine's life, how would I handle my interactions with her?" Andrea's answers and her acting on them brought about a cessation of the escalating vicious cycle of soft talking, being criticized, feeling anxious, softer talking, and so on. Andrea continued as a strong leader with a stronger voice—on many levels.

In working with aging families, WLW has found that the "if I were to believe . . ." question opens many possibilities. In the following example, the question gives permission to speak about difficult topics, as an alternative belief is offered: that speaking up and loyalty go together. The clinician (WLW) said the following to the elderly parent: "Some parents feel that loyalty and silence about difficulties go together. However, many parents find that they can be most loyal and helpful to their family by speaking up about a problem. If you were to believe that as the parent of this family it was an important job for you to speak up, what would you speak up about?"

The "if you were to believe . . ." question can be used by itself, as in the preceding example; nested in a fuller therapeutic move; or as the punch line of a therapeutic offering, as in the following letter sent to a young couple experiencing marital difficulties. The couple kept comparing their marriage to others' and coming up short on their assessment of themselves. Part of the letter WLW sent to them follows:

Dear Bill and Barbara,

After a lengthy discussion, the team came away with the impression that you are a couple who love each other and have a form of intimacy that is unique to your relationship at this time. Your connectedness, at times, may look and feel different from that of others and from what you might have expected if you only look[ed] to others for "how things should be."

The team were struck with the story of your Valentine present, Bill, to Barbara. They wonder if the experience of the Valentine present may be a metaphor for each of your experiences to this point with your marriage.

Bill, you gave Barbara a big beautiful box for a Valentine present, which she opened—only to find another box—a smaller box—and a smaller—and a smaller—down to a ring-sized box, which she opened to find—NOTHING! What was that experience like for her? Anticipation, hope, excitement—dissolving into disappointment and emptiness? The true precious gift was found only when, with your help, she looked in an unusual place—UNDER the box! There was the treasured ring!

The team wondered if, before you were married, you as a couple were given "a big beautiful box of marriage," i.e., an image of what marriage was and should and would be. Perhaps as you commenced to open your "big beautiful marriage box," it suddenly looked smaller than you thought. Some ups and downs of life made your "big beautiful marriage box" shrink even further. As the boxes became smaller . . . [*the letter continues and closes with the following "if you were to believe . . ." question, itself enclosed in a box*].

The team wonders what you would discover/uncover if you were to ask yourselves the following question every day for one month:

> If we were to believe that we have a unique form of intimacy that many other couples have not yet developed and may never develop—and therefore we cannot look outside our marriage for examples of our kind of beautiful marriage—what would we do today to find and appreciate the beautiful and precious marriage that is ours, that belongs uniquely to Barbara and Bill?

> Sincerely,
> Dr. Wendy L. Watson and members of the
> Marriage and Family Therapy team

The "if you were to believe . . ." question is also useful in challenging clinicians' beliefs and expanding options for therapeutic interviews. WLW offers family therapy graduate students the following assignment to help them come up with their own answers to their question of, "What will I do in the next session with this family?" The students are offered the following question:

If you were to believe that your role as a family clinician is to coevolve various kinds of therapeutic conversations with the family–client, what questions would help you coevolve the following conversations with this family at this time?
- Conversations that clear away obstacles for therapeutic progress
- Conversations that open space (for what?)
- Conversations of healing (between whom? of what?)
- Conversations that invite family members to a reflection

Although the questions are not always used in the family session, the thoughtful preparedness and facilitative belief carry the student clinician into new ways of being with the family.

We believe that the following "if I were to believe . . ." question is important for all family clinicians to ask themselves to continue coevolving therapeutic moves that are useful to the family: If I were to believe that each person in this family is experiencing the Alzheimer's (depression, cancer; insert the presenting problem) along with "the patient," what questions would I ask and of whom? Whose ideas would I want to commence gathering? Whose suffering would I be most drawn to?

## USING REFLECTING TEAMS

A reflecting team is a therapeutic medium for offering a variety of ideas from which family members may select. Andersen's (1987; 1991a) approach to dialogues about dialogues has flattened the clinician–family hierarchy, facilitated multiple levels of reflections, and made a tremendous contribution to clinical work with families. Team members behind a one-way mirror observe the conversation between the clinician and family members and then reverse vantage points. The team comes into the therapy room, and the clinician and family members go behind the mirror to listen to the reflections of the team—i.e., their conversations about the clinician–family conversations. Subsequently, viewing angles are shifted once again, and the clinician and family return to the room to hear the family's reflections on the team's reflections. In this way, reflections on reflections and dialogues about dialogues continue.

Many variations on the original format of reflecting teams have been documented in the literature (Friedman, 1995). In our clinical practice, we have found variations on the traditional format to be usefully perturbing for all involved. Presession reflecting teams offer the family involvement in the views of the clinician. In our educational settings, presession includes the following: presentation of the genogram, presenting problem, related concerns, highlights from two key articles related to the family situation, generation of hypotheses about the connection between possible constraining or facilitative beliefs and the problem or solution, and questions the clinician could ask to validate or discard the presession hypotheses.

The family is invited to collaborate with the clinical team. The session commences with family members' reflections on what the team or clinician has offered in the presession. We also encourage family members to call into the team, from behind the one-way mirror, to add input, correct, and clarify.

We believe that the one-way mirror is often a magnifying glass and amplifier, enabling family members to see and hear things they do not normally select out of the environment when in the room. Recently, however, WLW has been experimenting with what she is calling "to the side" reflecting teams. In this instance, the team is in the room interjecting from time to time a commentary and questions as the therapist and family members talk. A spatial separateness is created between the team and family in that the team members do not look at the family members but rather look at and talk to each other.

As clinical supervisors and educators, we experience that inviting graduate students to participate in a reflecting team is one of the quickest ways to invite systemic, nonblaming, nonjudgmental conversations of "what is happening in the family" and avoid the "wicked witch of linear thinking."

Although there is no one right way to participate in a reflecting team, there are certain behaviors of team members that are more useful to the meaningfulness of reflecting teams. Some of the suggestions we offer to initiate a new team member include the following:

- Validate one family member's position (I can understand that point of view because . . . ). Other team members will validate others' positions.
- Offer alternative views and beliefs about family members' lives, relationships, and experiences of illness.
- Offer personal experience that is triggered by the family's stories and beliefs.
- Offer ideas from research or literature review.
- Offer commendations that are based on evidence from the family session or from research or professional or personal experiences.
- Offer alternative views concerning questions family members have posed to the team.
- Offer answers to the question, "What will you never forget about this family?"

What are the reflections of family members about the reflections of the team about them? Following is one experience with Research Family 4, a single mother with four children:

WLW: What stays with you from what the team has just talked about?
MOTHER: I think just the general idea that I'm impressive! Honestly, I've never thought of myself as impressive . . .
WLW: You didn't?
MOTHER: No.
WLW: How did you manage to miss that all these years?
MOTHER: I never thought of myself as special or impressive or extraordinary or anything else. I've always just looked at myself as, oh well, I'm just this stupid cop-out that flunked out in marriage and didn't do too well in school and, you know, I've looked more at the negatives I think.
WLW: But when you hear the team talking about you today, what do you believe today?
MOTHER: Well, there must be something real neat about me because I hear this from people.
WLW: Do you? So, this is not the first time you've heard this?
MOTHER: I've heard it a couple of times. I just haven't believed it.

Something about being behind the mirror and hearing the team opened the possibility for the mother to "believe it" more that day; clearly, this woman benefited by being behind the mirror and hearing the team. The benefits of the reflecting team have recently been evaluated: Consistently, family members and clinicians report their appreciation of the multiple perspectives, opinions, and comments of the reflecting team (Sells, Smith, Coe, Yoshioka, & Robbins, 1994; Smith, Sells, & Clevenger, 1994).

## WRITING THERAPEUTIC LETTERS

The postman is a cotherapist for David Epston of New Zealand and Michael White of Australia. Although many clinicians have written therapeutic letters to clients to invite family members to sessions, offer interventions, summarize therapeutic work, or solidify change, it was White and Epston's (1990) creative and elegantly written book *Narrative Means to Therapeutic Ends* that catapulted letter writing into the therapeutic mainstream.

The power of the pen and the influence of the written word struck us in our work with an estranged mother and daughter (Wright & Watson, 1988). We wrote a three-way split-opinion letter highlighting their dilemma. The mother returned to the following session, waving the much-read letter in her hand, pronouncing, "This is the most wonderful letter I have ever received." The daughter had an equally profound experience. She read and then destroyed the letter because she believed her husband was unaware of the mother–daughter conflict. Each had been perturbed by the contents of the letter, and subsequently their relationship and, we believe, their structures changed. They returned with different beliefs about the situation and each other, and dramatic change continued.

We have found therapeutic letters to be a marvelous medium for carrying into the homes, minds, and hearts of family members, in sealed personally addressed envelopes, such things as:

- Commendations
- Questions we would have or could have asked in a session
- Words, phrases, and ideas that particularly stood out for us from a session
- Highlights of our work with a family and what we learned from our work with them
- Any therapeutic move

Therapeutic letters can do some things that a therapeutic session cannot do, such as invite nonparticipating family members to a session, follow up on "no shows," and help students or supervisees to articulate more clearly their own constraining beliefs about a family. A therapeutic letter also can do many things that a therapeutic session *can* do. We have used therapeutic letters to create a context for changing beliefs, challenge constraining beliefs, and solidify facilitative beliefs.

In Research Family 4, individual letters were sent to the mother (Linda) and eldest son (David) after the second session. The letters focused on solidifying the major shifts in beliefs that had occurred during the session. The letter to the mother read:

Dear Linda:
We mentioned at the end of the session on Tuesday that we wanted to send a letter to David. He is a delightful young man. Often, we have found that the eldest child in a single-parent family assumes a psychological burden of responsibility within the family. However, we do not believe that this has happened to David, and we see this as a tribute to you and your parenting.

As a team, we also wanted to write to you to emphasize something that we learned about you. We were very impressed by you as the session unfolded. You came to the session with a significant concern about David, and you listened to his comments and perceptions with great attention. Because of your openness to his comments throughout the session, you changed your point of view and your impressions about him. This demonstrates tremendous flexibility on your part and is very impressive to us. You seem to us to be the kind of mother who is willing to entertain other ways of understanding your children when you hear their ideas. We were impressed with your ability to give up some worries about David, and to consider when to worry and when to let go of worry.

You have been working very hard on concerns that you have for your family. However, we were also very impressed by your willingness to discard the "problem glasses" and consider following up this session by having a discussion with your family to come up with a list of things that are going well!

We look forward to seeing you again next Tuesday.
Sincerely,
Dr. Wendy L. Watson and members of the
Family Nursing Unit clinical nursing team

The letter to the son read:

Dear David:
The team behind the mirror was so impressed by what we learned about you during the session last Tuesday that we wanted to write you a letter describing our understanding of you.

We were very serious when we asked Dr. Watson to tell you that we see you as a very caring, sensitive and mature young man. You are very perceptive—you described in detail what other people in your life think about you and you participated very attentively throughout the entire session.

We were impressed that you know what you want in your life right now and that you have many interests. We were all very interested in your enjoyment of your drama classes, your collecting hockey cards, and your interest in basketball as a sport that you most like to play right now.

You suggested that you were also interested in having 7 or 8 more friends in your life at this time. You also provided us with a list of people who are already your fans: Mom, Dad, Brother Brandley, Shelly, Micah, Miranda, and Tim. As Dr. Watson mentioned, there were 8 of us watching from behind the mirror and we were also so impressed by you that we would be proud if you wished to add our names to your list of "Fans of David." Dr. Watson wants to join this team of fans too, so that makes an additional 9 names that you could add to your team! All of our names have been included with this letter.

Of course, our compliments to you in this letter are personal and private, and you may not wish to share them with anyone else. However, if you are not feeling too modest and would like to share our ideas with other people in your life, you are most welcome to do so.

We look forward to seeing you again, seeing your hockey cards and hearing about your experiment of sharing your thoughts and feelings with your Mom in the "game": I feel mad/sad/bad/glad about . . .

> Yours truly,
> Members of the Family Nursing Unit clinical
> nursing team [the 9 names were listed]

Therapeutic letters are ironic entities. They are time consuming and time saving. The time it takes to weigh the words and phrases is more than compensated for by the therapeutic leaps that follow. Michael White, at a recent conference on narrative therapy, asked a group of clinicians, "How many sessions is a therapeutic letter worth?" The answers ranged from 5 to 10!

In exploring the therapeutic influence of the therapeutic letters with Research Family 4 (Linda and eldest son, David), we came to appreciate the double reflection that therapeutic letters afford. The first reflection occurs when the family member reads the letter; the second comes when they share that reflection with the clinician. Multiple levels of reflection also occur for the clinician as she writes the letter and then hears what stood out for each family member. Note the clinician's careful inquiry about the impact of the letters in the following dialogue.

WLW: And did you get the letters?

LINDA: Yes. Thank you. That was really nice . . .

WLW: Well, you can imagine that my team is pretty excited to hear what you thought about the letter. What stood out for you?

DAVID: Oh, I liked it!

WLW: You liked it? What do you remember about it?

DAVID: I like what you said about me. Like you're serious about what you said.

WLW: That I was serious about which part?

DAVID: That I'm kinda nice.

WLW: Kinda nice? Okay, and that's what you remember from the letter? Did you share it with anybody or . . .

DAVID: No.

WLW: No. You kept it private.

DAVID: Except that I showed it to my mom.

WLW: Okay. Anything else that you remember from your letter?

DAVID: Just that you and the team liked me.

WLW: Okay. And have you got it stuck away in your drawer now?

DAVID: It's sitting up on my piano.

LINDA: We're going to put it in some special letter drawers.

WLW: Really. And when did they arrive, Linda?

LINDA: Yesterday.

WLW: And what stood out for you from your letter?

LINDA: Oh, sometimes I feel like such a failure as a mom, and it was kind of nice to have somebody say, "Hey, you're pretty good." I need to hear that because I knock myself a lot.

WLW: So you did hear that?

LINDA: Yes.

What stood out for us in hearing the family members' reflections was that both Linda and her son David felt validated as persons. It was not a particular characteristic that they commented on but rather their whole perception of self by another, whose opinion mattered. A global validation of self, a major shift in belief about themselves, had occurred: "I'm kinda nice" and "[I'm] pretty good."

The writer and recipient of the therapeutic letter may vary according to creativity and need. In addition to clinician-to-client letters there can be the following letters:

- Client-to-clinician letters
- Client-to-self letters

- Client-to-other-client letters
- Client-to-other-family-member letters (living, dead, not born, and so on)
- Client-and-clinician-to-larger-system letters

We wonder if the "medium is the message" (McLuhan & Fiore, 1967); that is, is there something therapeutic about the paper, stamp, and ink of a therapeutic letter, or will therapeutic faxes and therapeutic E-mail be as potentially perturbing?

## OFFERING VIDEOTAPES

When family members are offered the opportunity to review a video-taped session, they are invited to a reflection as they observe themselves (in freeze-frame, using fast forward, rewinding). These observations may include family members interacting with each other, family members interacting with the clinician, the clinician questioning and commenting, and the reflecting team offering ideas.

We have found that family members of all ages appreciate the videotapes, from children who are fascinated by watching themselves and by hearing family members comment, again and again, on something wonderful they did, to the elderly who want to hear and see one more time the comments made by the reflecting team.

Early in our clinical practice, we occasionally offered videotapes as a special gift to families, and we attached a therapeutic letter summarizing what we had learned from working with the family. For one clinical family, the videotaped family session depicted the last time they were with their father, who died only days later of Lou Gehrig's disease. With the prevalence of VCRs and high-tech sophistication of family members, offering a videotape of a session or edited version of several sessions increasingly has become a regular occurrence. We also find that families spontaneously request videotapes of the sessions. In accordance with our desire to flatten the hierarchy, we request that families write a consent form regarding viewing their videotape, which *we* sign, just as we have *them* sign a consent form for the videotaping. The consent form regarding viewing includes how the family will use the videotape, to whom they will show the videotape, and so on. Following is an example of such a consent form from a clinical family:

VIDEO CONSENT FORM:
Re: Video of Family Nursing Unit, University of Calgary, session on April 17, featuring Anthony and Sonia Schmitt; Anne Marie Levac, clinician; and other members of the Family Nursing Unit clinical team.

We authorize Anthony and Sonia Schmitt to use or show this video-tape for the following purposes:

_____ 1. For personal viewing.

_____ 2. For showing to friends/family members (upon mutual agreement of Anthony and Sonia).

Date: _____

Signatures of clinical team: _____

The James family is another example of a clinical family who *loved* videotapes! They borrowed the tapes after each session and requested copies of the entire series at the end of our work together. The couple had requested help in coping with the husband's multiple chronic and life-threatening illnesses (fibromyalgia, leg amputation 10 months earlier, prospect of amputation of his other leg, heart condition, lupus). The idea of offering the videotapes arose in the postsession following the first session. The couple had been unclear during the session about what the problem was that brought them to the Family Nursing Unit. During the session, they were invited to think about the "miracle question" (de Shazer & Berg, 1988) in order to consider what changes might be helpful to them. The team wondered if reviewing the videotape might also help the couple clarify the problem.

The major thrust of the clinical work with this family was working with their differing beliefs about how to deal with the future regarding the husband's prognosis and his possible death. Each spouse held different beliefs about the usefulness of talking about the future. The husband (Bill) expressed his belief by saying, "Don't worry, it doesn't help, accept fate," whereas his wife (Carol) believed that "sharing worry makes it easier to face." This created an escalating pattern of worry, withdrawal, and conflict. At the beginning of Session 3, they commented about what stood out from viewing the videotapes.

BILL: What we talked about—the way we talked—we're more open and doing more of that at home. We see it on the videotape and it reinforces it.

CAROL: It's good for my self-esteem.

In the fourth and final session, the couple reported that they were having more open conversations at home about sharing worry, anger, and concern for the future. They noticed that these conversations were similar to the kinds of conversations they had been able to have at the FNU. Bill was sharing his feelings more; Carol was expressing her worry more. They felt that they understood each other better, and they were feeling closer. Carol had some difficult run-ins with health care providers and found that the videotapes offered convincing evidence that she could communicate knowledgeably and effectively with health care providers: "Health care professionals are very intimidating; I know now that I did handle myself in a very appropriate way." Bill said he also noticed that Carol showed less self-doubt. Constraining beliefs can be challenged and facilitative beliefs solidified with the reflections afforded and invited through the review of videotaped clinical sessions.

One constraining belief that videotaping can challenge is the belief that "we need therapy . . . forever!" When families begin to organize their lives around going for therapy, instead of reorganizing and recalibrating their lives with the help of therapy, demoralization and disempowerment of the family and the clinician occur.

Recently, WLW was supervising a doctoral student who was seeing a family who had worked with two previous clinicians. WLW's first supervision session with the student was his 40th session with the couple, who were on their 110th therapy session! To say that the momentum of therapy was lacking in this "interminable-therapy-hand-me-down-therapy" case was an understatement. The student clinician and the family experienced being "stuck": stuck together, stuck with each other, and stuck in their therapeutic process. However, something unusual happened during a supervisory phone-in. While WLW was talking with the student, the couple spontaneously commenced having a lively conversation. This was a difference; up to this point in the therapy session, the spouses had shown varying degrees of lethargy and mutism. When the same unusual event occurred during the next phone-in, WLW went into the room and offered her observation: She wondered if it were time for an experiment with "no therapist therapy": two sessions of therapy without the student clinician present. This supervisory intervention was created on the spot in an effort to assist both the couple and the student. The couple and the student showed enthusiasm for the experiment. The student booked the couple "their" therapy room complete with videotaping.

For Session 1 the spouses met and talked about changes they had experienced up to this point and others they still desired. For Session 2 the spouses met and reviewed the videotape from Session 1, noting things they appreciated about the other during the conversation of Session 1. For the third session, the student clinician, having reviewed the videotapes from Sessions 1 and 2, met with the couple to exchange views about the process. The student saw things about the couple he had never seen. He was invited through the nonthreatening and noninstructive interaction process of the videotape review to reflect on how his beliefs about therapy and families who present for therapy had constrained him from drawing forth this couple's strengths and problems and how he and the couple had coevolved a systemic stagnation. The best part was that the student recognized his own constraining beliefs and how to free himself in the future, on his own. The couple returned to the joint session ecstatic, a condition the student had not experienced with them previously. The spouses had enjoyed the two sessions and requested three more "no therapist therapy" sessions. Following these three sessions, a termination therapy session was held, celebrating the changes in the couple and the student clinician.

## EXTERNALIZING PROBLEMS, SYMPTOMS, AND SOLUTIONS

An innovative move, developed by Michael White of Australia, is the externalization of a problem (Tomm, 1989; White, 1984, 1986, 1988/1989; White & Epston, 1990). This move has had an enormous positive impact and influence on the family therapy field and, more recently, on the family health field. *Externalization* involves separating the problem or symptom from the personal identity of the client. Instead of viewing the problem as residing in the person, the problem is externalized and viewed as being outside the person. Rather than a client being objectified, a problem, symptom, or solution is objectified (White, 1988/1989). In this manner, constraining beliefs can be "put out there" to be challenged, altered, or modified.

Externalization can be achieved during a family interview by introducing questions that encourage family members to map the influence of the problem on their lives and relationships and conversely, their influence on the life of the problem. This is called *relative influence questioning* (White, 1988). A family member may be asked how much influence he has over the problem or illness and, reciprocally, how much influence the problem or illness has over him and his relationships.

A useful idea about externalizing the problem of illness has been offered by Wynne, Shields, and Sirkin (1992). They suggested that when a problem is looked at by more than one person, illness is psychologically "outside" the client as well as "outside" for other "observers." They explained that when an illness is psychologically externalized, the illness is afflicting the self but does not constitute the self. This is a significant distinction. A problem that is perceived as "external" is experienced as more manageable, and this implies more possibilities for taking effective responsibility.

Once the problem is externalized, the clinician identifies times when the problem was less distressing (de Shazer, 1985). When the clinician draws forth and distinguishes the times when the distress was less severe (i.e., exceptions to the problem), family members are enabled to

adopt new beliefs about their abilities to manage the problem and consider how small changes can be repeated and amplified.

In our clinical practice, we have externalized chronic pain, phobias,
and depressions, with dramatic, positive results with adults.
Externalization of the problem is also particularly useful with children
experiencing phobias, encopresis, enuresis, behavioral problems, and
chronic pain. Externalizing the problem was even useful with a
teenager who was experiencing depression related to her jealous feelings about a friend who reminded her of Marilyn Monroe. In this case,
the problem was externalized as "a case of Marilynitis"; there was an
extremely positive outcome (Wright & Park Dorsay, 1989).

Another useful effort to externalize a problem occurred in working
with Research Family 4. The following dialogue with the mother
(Linda) is an example of externalizing a behavior and giving it the ability to talk. The clinician is externalizing the behavior of the youngest
son (Timothy).

WLW: When you say, "What does this behavior mean?. . . " If the behavior could talk, what do you guess, or what do you fear, or what do
you worry it might be saying? You have thought about this a lot,
I'm sure.

LINDA: Well I guess it's saying, "I'm hurting Mommy, I need attention."

WLW: So, "I'm hurting, I need attention. Love me?"

LINDA: It could be saying, "I worry and am concerned about something." It usually happens after his dad's been around. When I was
going to school, I was going to school in this full-time program. I
wasn't just part-time. With four kids, my husband was supposed
to do the looking after. I didn't realize at the time that he was sick
and that he was abusing Timothy. The other kids were in school; he
wasn't. I think there was some abuse at the preverbal stage.
Timothy was acting out and trying to tell me, but I just don't know
how to cue into it.

WLW: When you ask yourself some of those questions—"How come
Timothy is showing these behaviors?"—is your best guess that he
might be saying, "I'm hurting, I need attention, love me, I'm angry
about my dad hurting me, I'm angry at you for having allowed it"?
Is there any other explanation that fits for you, that he's doing
these hurtful behaviors?

In this segment of clinical work, through the process of externalizing
the problem, the constraining beliefs about the problem become accessible and palpable. Specifically, the clinician invites the mother to share
her concerns about her children: "If the behavior could talk, what do
you . . . fear . . . it might be saying?" The mother believes that she is

responsible for not protecting the children from the abuse of their father. Through this process, the mother's stories, fears, and problem-saturated view unfolds. The mother discloses her concern about not being available to her children; however, the clinician is accepting and nonjudgmental and commends the mother for coming to some of these realizations on her own. The clinician offers the mother a commendation about this realization through the asking of a question: "Have you just come to these realizations on your own?" Ways to show nonjudgment include showing that an explanation has been heard and understood and inviting consideration that there may be another explanation, that there is more than one right answer. The externalization of this mother's belief about a problem reduced her self-blame and invited her to consider another view.

Although we have been extremely impressed with the creativeness and effectiveness of the process of externalizing problems, symptoms, and solutions, we have also had to use prudence with this clinical micromove when working with families experiencing illness. Clinicians need to assess and evaluate carefully what problems or illnesses can appropriately be externalized.

## OFFERING DIFFERING OPINIONS: SPLIT-OPINION INTERVENTION

When family therapists began working with clinical teams and one-way mirrors, it became possible to use the team, rather than just the clinician, for deliberately targeting or challenging family beliefs, rules, or interactions (Breulin & Cade, 1981). Team members could report and elaborate on split opinions within the team to highlight themes or issues in the family or in the process of therapy (Cade & Cornwell, 1985).

The theoretical premise of offering a split opinion is based on Bateson's (1979) idea about the "method of double or multiple comparison" (p. 97). By comparing what is seen in each eye, Bateson suggested we disclose another dimension or depth. Peggy Papp (1980), in a classic article on paradoxical therapy, contended that the therapeutic usefulness of a split opinion stems from the triangulation of the clinician, family, and observing team; that is, the team members support or challenge family members, with the clinician free to agree with them or oppose them. Maturana and Varela (1992) would likely offer that the split opinion is but another form of perturbation, another way of inviting family members to a reflection and thus opening space to new ideas.

We have used split opinions for some time to challenge beliefs in our practice with families experiencing illness. An example of the usefulness of this intervention has been documented in a previous publication (Wright & Watson, 1988) in dealing with intense conflict between an elderly mother and her daughter. It is interesting to note that, in this clinical example, the debilitating angina experienced by the elderly mother dramatically decreased in frequency and severity when the intergenerational conflict with her daughter subsided.

With a recent clinical family, the split-opinion intervention was used in the second session to challenge the constraining belief of a young mother whose 12-year-old daughter was suffering from a rare, life-shortening, pituitary tumor. After dealing with many challenges over the 2½ years since her daughter's diagnosis, the mother felt worn out and was taking the antidepressant drug Prozac to cope with the uncertainty and stress of her daughter's illness. She felt her coping skills had been exhausted, causing her to feel extremely tired and depressed about the future. She was concerned about her reliance on the drug and wondered whether she could "cope" without it.

In the reflecting team at the end of the session, the team members offered differing perspectives on the helpfulness of Prozac. These differing views were based on their own beliefs; they were not contrived or feigned. One team member proposed that Prozac might be just what the mother needed to get through this particularly tough spot, suggesting the drug likely gave the mother more energy to cope with the demands of the illness experience. Another team member offered the idea that the mother should take some credit away from Prozac and give it to herself. This team member pointed out the mother's long history of strengths, including raising a child as a teenage single mom, completing a university degree, enrolling in graduate school, and dealing with many instrumental as well as emotional issues of her daughter's illness.

At the third session, when asked what stood out for her from the previous session, the mother stated that she had thought a lot about the idea that she could give herself more credit for coping rather than give all the credit to Prozac. She reported worrying less about when, in the future, she might stop taking Prozac. She also reported many positive developments in her thinking about her ability to care for her child and to learn from this difficult experience in the "book of life" without feeling resentful about taking a temporary absence from her graduate school studies. By challenging the mother's belief about her dependence and reliance on a drug, the mother's strengths and abilities were drawn forth in a manner that allowed her to entertain the idea that she was capable of dealing with her tragic situation.

## USING RESEARCH FINDINGS

Given the preeminence of science and technology in our society, knowledge derived from research has been given powerful status. This privileging of research has created novel opportunities to use both research findings and the process of research to challenge, alter, or modify beliefs. In 1990, Wright asserted that "the research process may be termed an intervention if it perturbs subjects' thinking to the point that they alter their beliefs regarding problematic issues" (p. 477). The article described a family our clinical research team worked with within the Family Nursing Unit. Family members became more open to the ideas of the team when we invited them to help us learn about the impact of chronic illness on their family as participants in a research project rather than as recipients of therapy.

We have continued to experiment with the use of research findings to draw new distinctions. The clinician must first determine the family members' beliefs about the influence of research by directly asking, "Do you believe in research?" If the family members value research, the clinician may use specific, relevant research reports to challenge constraining beliefs. Efforts are consistently made to have family members open space to the ideas offered by the clinician. If a family does not "believe in research," the offering of ideas from research will not be a fit and no beliefs will be altered or challenged.

In the second session with Research Family 3, the clinician (LMW) used research findings to challenge the family's belief that they had little influence or control over the uncertain illness, chronic fatigue syndrome, experienced by the younger daughter (C2). Notice the way that the clinician drumrolls the move and heightens the anticipation of the research information when she introduces the idea to the family. The clinician does not impose her ideas through instructive interaction: "Here is what you need to know and how you must behave in the future." She builds up and heightens the need to know, culminating in an offer: "Do you believe in research?" This is similar to other invitations such as, "Would you be interested in my ideas?" or "Is it useful at this time to hear an idea?" Other possibilities include, "Are you in the mood to hear this idea today?" or "Would you like to wait till next week?" We hypothesize that this buildup, or drumroll, increases family members' curiosity about what will be offered and invites them to open space to the ideas.

This paced introduction of a therapeutic offering is also an intervention for clinicians. It slows clinicians down and tempers their enthusiasm for their own ideas. It keeps clinicians from plunging in prematurely, imposing their ideas, being invested in the rightness of their opinions, or becoming too enthusiastic or passionate about the direction, pace, or outcome of change. (But we are enthusiastic and passionate about the *occurrence* of change.) If the family agrees to listen to the idea, the perturbation may be experienced differently because they have *chosen* to listen rather than *being forced* to listen. There is an underlying assumption of respect: that the listeners have a choice about receiving the opinion or information and will take in what fits for them. (In the following transcript, Nicole = mother, John = father.)

LMW: There's a couple of research studies that were brought to my attention by my students this last semester in class that were so interesting. The researchers were looking at families who were experiencing chronic illness and trying to see how come some families seem to adjust to the chronic illness and seem to live alongside of it or manage it, and other families don't. I just want to say you match what the research is saying. And what the research is saying is, families that start to feel that they have a sense of confidence and mastery over the illness adjust to the illness better than families that feel like the illness is ruling them. These families have no sense of mastery or any sort of confidence to live alongside this illness. And all the things you've been telling me today validate that piece of research. You're [daughter] saying, "As I'm feeling better, and as I feel like I'm mastering this more, I'm not worrying about it as much and we're adjusting to it." And you're saying, "I'm not as anxious." People are giving you different ideas about what you can do to set the date for the uncertainty about this illness to be over, and you're all coming up with some good ideas about what you could do.

NICOLE: I agree with that too, because the feeling that I had when she was first sick, we didn't know what it was and then we did know what it was. But then that's what we felt like, this illness was like a blanket that was smothering us all. You know, it was like being claustrophobic; there was no way out.

LMW: Sure, it just feels like it's oppressing you and it's ruling you. When you feel like that, you're not having a sense of mastery or confidence. It doesn't mean that you're going to cure your illness necessarily, but at least if you feel like there's some areas that you have some control in what you're doing, the research is saying people seem to be able to live alongside the illness better.

NICOLE: Well I think that's true.

JOHN: As long as you don't get too overconfident.

The family's experience, expertise, and curiosity are elevated by the posing of the question, "Do you believe in research?" The content of the research findings about mastery is customized to fit exquisitely with the family's constraining belief, "We have no control." This new distinction is offered in a manner that gently embeds the suggestion that if they were to have more influence over the illness, they would experience more mastery. It is important to note that this move has three stages: opening space by heightening curiosity, embellishing the idea through research findings, and inviting family reactions to the ideas offered. When family members are asked to respond to an idea and verbalize it, the languaging of the idea helps the family to remember it.

Later in the second session, the clinician asks the family to elaborate on the degree to which they believe they can influence the illness. The mother's response is to acknowledge change: "I think now I can see that we're getting there." This statement is in sharp contrast to her earlier comment about illness smothering the family like a blanket: "There was no way out." The clinician punctuates the shift in beliefs by again referring to the research findings. This time she commends the family by offering, "You are the family that validates the research findings." Research is again used to draw a new distinction. The implication is that the family is more expert than the research.

Another useful example of using research findings to challenge beliefs is demonstrated with Research Family 5. The wife (Julie) believed she could trigger another heart attack in her husband (Robert) if she raised conflictual issues or burdened him with her worries. She kept these concerns to herself, thereby protecting her husband but increasing her own stress. In a reflecting team discussion at the end of Session 2, team members used research findings to challenge the wife's belief.

LMW: [*to graduate student team members specializing in families with cardiac illness*] What ideas does the research have about how to help families get out of this? How protective do spouses have to be around each other?

TEAM MEMBER 1: Actually, there isn't a lot out there [in the cardiac research literature] that has concrete solutions for cardiac couples. It is very much a matter of openly discussing concerns and openly discussing feelings about all of the changes that they've been experiencing so they understand where each other is coming from. There is very little in the literature that would substantiate that stress from a marital discussion will aggravate a heart attack.

LMW: There's little to substantiate that? Say that again. I think they really need to hear this one.

TEAM MEMBER 1: Sure. There's little in the cardiac literature that substantiates that a heart attack will be triggered by marital disagreement. Marital conflict is very common following a heart attack, but it's not something that is seen as a cause of a recurrence of a heart attack.

TEAM MEMBER 2: In fact there is evidence that trying to protect each other is, in fact, much more stressful than having open communication.

TEAM MEMBER 1: Yes, that's a good point.

TEAM MEMBER 2: And I think that's important for people to know because you're spending all this energy trying to protect each other.

LMW: Yes, that's certainly been my experience in working with families where there has been a coronary like this: They get more stressed trying to protect each other than if they could just deal with the issues more frankly. I think, in a very curious kind of way, [this family is] doing that today. They are being very frank with each other today, and they're even being frank with their compliments today. I mean Robert says he thinks these very nice things about Julie but he doesn't say them. And even today, he's saying them, and she's being very frank about wanting him more involved in family responsibilities.

The team used research findings to challenge the wife's constraining belief by identifying the lack of evidence for the idea that stress could trigger another heart attack and offering the idea that protecting each other might be more stressful and take more energy than being open with each other. On the basis of this new information, the couple wrestled with the question, "Is stress that is shared doubled, or is stress that is shared halved?" At the fifth and last session, the couple provided evidence for a shift in the constraining belief. The protective pattern they had been using in their marriage had changed. The wife reported that there was "less conflict—I'm not backing off anymore."

## OFFERING ALTERNATIVE (NEW OR MODIFIED) BELIEFS ABOUT FAMILY MEMBERS' LIVES, RELATIONSHIPS, OR ILLNESS

The clinician's offering of alternative beliefs about an illness or relationships can be an extremely useful micromove after a context for change has been created. Families frequently privilege the voice of health professionals; consequently, if it is wisely used, the professional voice may alleviate suffering. We have found that family members most often open space for new ideas or beliefs when the ideas are framed in a manner that makes them inviting. One way we have found useful to begin offering a particular idea is to recount for families that we have embraced and learned this knowledge from our work with other families. With children, we have also found it useful to invite the parent to confirm the new belief that is being offered. The following clinical example illustrates this point.

A clinical family presented at the FNU with the mother's primary concern being her 9-year-old daughter's behavior problems at school and aggressive behavior toward her mother at home. During the first session with the mother only, the mother revealed her beliefs about the connections between (a) her daughter's (Natasha's) behavior and her own struggle with recurrent breast cancer and (b) Natasha's behavior and the separation of her parents.

During the second session, the clinician spent the first half hour creating a context for change with Natasha. After exploring what Natasha had been told about her mother's illness, the clinician offered the idea that Natasha might be blaming herself for her mother's illness and invited the mother to challenge that belief:

LMW: Some kids have told me that when their mom and dad stop living together that they think it is their fault. Do you think that?

NATASHA: Yes.

LMW: And sometimes kids have told me that when their mom or dad gets sick, they think it is their fault. Do you think it is your fault that your mom has got sick?

NATASHA: Half and half.

LMW: How would it be your fault?

NATASHA: With my dad fighting with my mom, it is hard to raise me.

LMW: You think that caused her cancer?

NATASHA: Yes.

LMW: So that half of you thinks it's your fault? A lot of kids think that. I would really like your mom to tell you what she thinks. Would you like to hear from your mom?

NATASHA: Yes.

MOTHER: Cancer is nobody's fault. It's a sickness like you catch a cold, you don't blame it on somebody, it's nobody's fault. An illness is like that. And I certainly don't think that you are to blame for me being sick, not even a little bit. You make me feel well. You have helped me to get better every time I'm in the hospital.

LMW: Your mom has told you something really important. Do you believe her when she tells you that?

NATASHA: Yes, I do.

MOTHER: And it's not your fault that your dad and I split up.

LMW: Something else I have learned from other kids is that even though mom and dad tell them this, they tell me that it helps them to hear about this more than once. Are you like that or is once enough?
NATASHA: Sometimes, I like to hear it more than once.

The clinician then invited the mother to ask Natasha in a couple of days if she wanted to hear again that she was not to blame for either the mother's illness or the breakdown of her parents' relationship. The clinician offered the idea that family members, particularly children, frequently feel they are to blame for illness or marital breakdown. But the clinician carefully offered this new idea by informing the family that this notion was gleaned in work with other families. The process of this micromove continued with the clinician inviting the mother into the conversation to offer the alternative belief that her daughter was not to blame for her mother's cancer. Beliefs about etiology have a powerful influence on family members' healing and treatment. It is particularly crucial to offer an alternative belief about how an illness may arise when one family member believes she is to blame for an illness. This latter belief can be far more destructive to family members than the belief that illness just happens or is due to fate or some external influence such as pollution.

## OFFERING SERMONETTES AND STORYTELLING

The micromove of offering sermonettes and storytelling was revealed as a characteristic aspect of our approach through the analysis of our hermeneutic research. Sermonettes and storytelling offer families the beliefs of the clinician, most frequently alternative beliefs to those currently held by family members. The offering of sermonettes occurs in our clinical work when we believe there is a need for information that goes to the heart of the matter. Families are invited to open space to information by being offered the option to hear the information. This information is often stated through questions such as, "Would you be interested in a story of another family?" The rationale for asking is to avoid imposing the clinician's view and to create a dialogue rather than a monologue. If the family says *no*, the information is not given. The idea is to give a choice whereby the client selects what fits and what does not. The respectful offering of the option of receiving or not receiving information is, we have learned, the most effective way to help families to open space both to hearing information and to being receptive to it.

One example of offering and giving a sermonette occurred with

Research Family 5 in the third session. In this session, the clinician chose to have a therapeutic conversation with the husband (Robert) and wife (Julie) individually. The following transcript illustrates how sermonettes are presented. First, there is the question of whether to offer ideas and the consideration of whether they will be useful.

LMW: Well, should I offer a couple of more thoughts?

ROBERT: Sure.

LMW: Or not? We run the risk again of you trying and it may not be that useful. I do appreciate your efforts in doing more housework, which seems to be a big, a really big area for her. But I have two thoughts for you; whether that makes it better or not I don't know. But they're two things that if you would be willing to try, I have the belief, Robert, that you have the ability to make a very big difference and to influence her happiness. And I'll tell you what really stood out for me. I mentioned it in our presession discussion: your compliment to her last time that she does a good job, she was just hungry to hear that from you . . .

ROBERT: Yes, I can see that, 'cause I'm not good at that.

LMW: . . . to know that.

ROBERT: It's one of those things that I've never been able to do, and I think it probably stems from my past, the emotional things I never had. I never was hugged. I never had a close relationship with my parents, so it's very difficult. It's always been difficult for me to show that side, that emotional side. I've never been good at it, and it's got to stem back, I think, from how I was brought up. My father told me how stupid I was, that I would never amount to anything, and my mother never paid any attention to me. I grew up in that. I left home at 16 because there was nothing there, there was no relationship, family relationship. My father was an alcoholic, so I think for me, I've never been able to show emotion.

LMW: But you do show emotion in here. So, I don't know what kind of emotion you mean.

ROBERT: Well of gratitude, thanks, love.

LMW: Oh, okay.

ROBERT: Anger, I can show.

LMW: Yes.

ROBERT: Because that's a defense mechanism in a way, I think.

LMW: I think this is the core for your wife. I think she's hungry for that from you. This is why I wanted to meet you individually; I didn't want to be saying these kinds of things in front of your wife because I don't want her saying at home that you're just doing this because . . .

Robert: That's what I'd be afraid of too, all of a sudden she sees this change . . .

lmw: Dr. Wright is saying this to you.

Robert: Yes.

lmw: But, I wanted to point out to you that you do have an incredible influence on her. I believe it is because she is hungry for affirmation and affection from you, a compliment, an affirmation that she's doing a good job at home, that kind of thing. So, I had two things in mind for you. I know it's asking you to do the very thing that you're saying you're not good at. That's a bit paradoxical, isn't it, but I think that's where the greatest assurance can come. I think she needs reassurance from you that she's loved and cared about and appreciated. And I don't think it matters what I say or the kids say, she needs to hear it from you. Just the way she responded to your one idea that you thought she did a good job; she sat up and commented on it. It obviously really stood out and meant a lot to her. So, what [I am] asking is, can you look for more opportunities to do that? Maybe it won't be easy and maybe it won't be like falling off a log, but if you can work at that, to get into the habit of that, I think it would have great payoffs for her. And I think she would feel a lot better, because then she'd know what you think about her and how you feel toward her. But I'm asking you to do the very thing that is the hardest for you.

Robert: Yes. Well, you know, I mean, it just takes trying to do it.

lmw: Yes, and there's many ways to try and do it, eh? Sometimes you can learn to do it more by writing a note: "Thanks for doing this" or "I appreciated your efforts on that" or whatever. It's just trying to be more conscious about saying something at least every other day to her, something that will build her up so that she knows that she's cared about by you. Because, we can know that in your heart . . .

Robert: Yes, you tend to take it for granted in a way because you know what they know and . . .

lmw: And I think your wife is a woman that needs to hear it and really feels good when she does hear it from you. So that was the one idea I had. And I didn't realize I was asking you, till we've now talked a bit more, that I'm asking you to do the very thing that's the most difficult. But you've done a lot of difficult things, haven't you?

Robert: Yes.

lmw: You've overcome a lot of difficult things. I admire you—with the kind of family background you describe—the type of person you've become, how you have matured in spite of your family.

Robert: I didn't do it alone; I had help along the way from different people.

LMW: Yes, and the second thing that I would like you to consider is to apologize for the two incidents of physical abuse. Whether you felt justified, whether you felt . . .

ROBERT: Oh, I never felt justified.

LMW: . . . provoked, but I think it's an area that she needs an apology. And I'm saying that to you as a woman and as your counselor. I think that would also mean a lot to her. . . . So when the time seems right, you know when that would be, what the situation would be, that you could offer her an apology.

ROBERT: Okay.

LMW: I'm not saying these are cure-alls. But I'm trying to get to some of the real core issues of concern. We can talk about housework and doing this and that . . .

ROBERT: It's not the cause of what's going on.

LMW: Exactly. All of that can be worked out when someone knows that they're really loved and cared about. We all can put up with a lot more and tolerate a lot more when we know we're really loved and cared about, and I think she needs that . . .

ROBERT: And I should know that.

LMW: . . . so much from you. She needs, I believe, to hear those words and she needs to hear it from you. So, are you willing to . . .

ROBERT: Yes.

LMW: . . . give it a try? Great. And for the moment, I would put a moratorium on the kinds of things we talked about here today. I don't think rehashing it and going over it again and again is helpful.

ROBERT: No.

LMW: I think you should, and I'm going to say that to Julie as well, I think you just need to press on from here and say, "That was difficult, it was hard." You both obviously have a lot of hurts and resentments from the past and different ideas and perceptions about them but you need to try and press forward and do some things differently. Except for that one piece of the past, that I think offering her an apology would mean a lot to her.

ROBERT: Okay.

LMW: Okay, great. Well I'm going to see Julie now for a few minutes.

In 4 minutes of a therapeutic conversation, the husband transforms from a man telling the clinician he does not know what his wife wants to a man who says he is willing to do the hardest thing for him: to offer affirmations to his wife. He also convincingly tells the clinician that "it just takes trying to do it." How did this transformation take place? It began by the clinician increasing the husband's curiosity and thereby decreasing his resistance and by the clinician declaring the uncertainty of the usefulness or outcome of her "two thoughts." The first idea is given credence, however, by the clinician's providing evidence from a previous session that the wife is experiencing affirmation deprivation. The clinician also challenges the husband's family-of-origin explanation of his belief that the past rules the present and future. He says, "I've never been able to show emotion," but the clinician points out with direct evidence from the session, "but you do show emotion in here" and then invites a distinction about what kinds of emotion he shows.

In our hermeneutic interpretation of this change segment, we thought this sermonette could by titled, "Blessed are those (husbands) who feed others (their wives) who are experiencing affirmation deprivation." The clinician acknowledges the husband's difficulty by stating, "I'm asking you to do the very thing that is hardest for you." The client responds to this acknowledgment with a minisermonette of his own: "It just takes trying to do it." The receptivity of the husband enables the clinician to offer ideas of how to implement the message of the sermonette by suggesting that there are many ways he could affirm his wife; she concludes with significant words for this couple experiencing cardiac disease: "We know that [you care about her] in your heart."

Another micromove used a former constraining belief of the husband to open space to a new behavior. Specifically, the husband's belief that the past rules the present was offered back to him as, "You've done a lot of difficult things, overcome a lot of difficult things . . . in spite of your family." This sermonette also embeds beliefs about relationships: the positive correlation between tolerance and love ("We can all tolerate a lot more when we know we're really loved . . . "). Finally, this sermonette gave the suggestion to put a moratorium on conversations of accusations and recriminations while the couple move toward more conversations of affirmation and affection. Sermonettes can embed useful ideas that can alter, modify, or challenge constraining beliefs when approached from an "offering" and "inviting" stance.

Telling stories of oneself or, more frequently, telling stories of other families with whom one has worked changes the conversational flow: The clinician stops asking questions and begins telling stories. This change in conversational behavior by the clinician invites family members into a listening mode. We have found this micromove to be extremely useful for embedding alternative beliefs and validating one family's experience through the telling of a story of another family.

The following example of storytelling occurred in the second session with Research Family 5. Family members were expressing their apprehension about Ritalin being prescribed for the daughter.

LMW: So are you of the belief now that your daughter's problems are more psychological, biological, or both?

ROBERT: Probably both, but we have to do something. I've got reservations as anyone would with drugs. I mean I think most drugs can have both good and bad about them, but the thing with our daughter is, the drugs help her because she has a hard time . . . it's not a good life, you know what I mean?

LMW: Would you be interested in hearing about an adolescent I just saw yesterday who's on Ritalin? Would that be of interest to you?

ROBERT: Mmhm.

JULIE: Especially for him [*referring to husband*]; I've heard lots of stories . . .

LMW: This is just so timely. I just saw this young person last night. I've been working with her parents, and they like me to see their daughter from time to time individually. So I did last night. I hadn't seen her for probably 5 or 6 months. One of the real concerns of the parents is that this young woman had a dreadful history in school all of her life. She'd had just a horrendous school career, failure after failure, poor grades, and she was a very big girl. She had just turned 16, but even when she was 14 and 15, she was very large. So socially, she hasn't really fit in. So they've had this long history. Well, she came back yesterday. I hardly recognized her.

JULIE: Yeah?

LMW: Because she'd lost weight, because of the Ritalin, and she felt good about herself. But the other thing that was far more fascinating to me was that she was so focused. She was right with me, and I said to her, "There's something different about you? What is it that's so different about you?" And do you know what she said? "I can concentrate now, I can concentrate!"

ROBERT: We've heard it put "that I can hear with one voice now."

LMW: Yes. She said, "Now I'm able to focus," and I said, "Well, just talking with me, I notice a difference in you." Well, she was so taken by my comments. I said to her, "I'm so happy for you. This must be just wonderful. That must really do a lot for you," and she said, "Yes."

JULIE: See, that's the thing, if it can do that.

LMW: If it can do that. So here she's had years and years of history of this, and because I think I was so pleased with how she was doing, and I was so thrilled for her that she said to me, "I can really work on things with my family now." So, I don't know, I mean that's just one example.

The "are you of the belief . . . ?" question was followed by a story. The story was meant to open space for the consideration of options about

Ritalin. This conversational sequence was followed by the lead-in question, "Would you be interested in hearing . . . ?" If the family responds with *yes*, the conversation is very different than it would be if this question were not asked. The family is shown respect by the clinician's words, "This may or may not fit for you."

The storytelling in this clinical vignette enabled the parents of this young daughter to hear a success story of a young woman who was taking Ritalin. It enabled the clinician to be enthusiastic about the change of another young person, but it also embedded a little cautionary note by offering the idea that this was "just one example." The whole intent of this storytelling is to offer hope to the family that this might be one solution to their daughter's difficulties and thus alter their present constraining belief that the option was not to be considered.

Another clinician belief becomes evident from this therapeutic conversation. The belief is that "if clinicians are too passionate about change, they can begin imposing their ideas and thus close space to change." By offering the option to hear an idea—"Would you be interested in hearing my idea?"—a domain of requests evolves rather than of demands. If a family member agrees to listen, the resulting perturbation is totally different in nature because the person is listening differently. There is an underlying assumption of respect that family members can absorb only what their present biopsychosocial–spiritual structures will allow.

## USING WORDS AND VOICE TO INVITE HEALING

If the world is constructed through language, then of course one powerful way to destroy the world is to destroy people's language. Consider the Tower of Babel. The people could not build a tower to heaven, nor construct anything else, because their real "tool," language, was gone.

Our words give away the stance we take toward our relationships, our own lives, and our experiences of illness. An objectivity-without-parentheses stance uses words like "you must do this." We prefer using the word *experiment* with families. When a clinician invites a family to do something as an experiment, it can be inviting and enticing, perhaps even exciting. The word *experiment* opens space and is not in the realm of instructive interaction.

Words can hurt, and words can heal. When we listen to our clients, they not only speak the words they need to, they also teach us the impact of words on them, as in the following example of a graduate student's conversation with a clinical couple:

CLINICIAN: So his words are hitting you.

WIFE: Oh, they hurt so much. [*crying deeply*] I think the word *stupid* is the meanest word in the whole world, because I've heard it so much and I'm not stupid. I know I'm not, but still it hurts because this is the person I love, and when he says that, it makes me feel so bad. It hurts. It hurts so much. It hurts my soul. My soul wants to run away and hide. But I can't because this is my marriage.

We often ask ourselves as clinicians, "How is it that this person's own voice does not have more influence on her life? Whose voice is the voice of authority in this person's life?" We want to discover the voice in a person's life that matters and increase the likelihood that the person's own voice will increasingly be that voice.

Maturana (1992, May) stated, "If you don't use the right words, you don't draw forth the reflection." We wonder if it is an indication that structural coupling has taken place when clinicians are increasingly able to use words that open space for a reflection by clients. In the following clinical family, a young couple had been struggling with difficulties with their sexual relationship from the beginning of their 18-month marriage. WLW invited this couple to a reflection about the impact of words.

The husband (Ramon) related that he said harsh words to his wife (Maria) about how she was performing sexually and raised his voice in doing so. Maria said that the actual words spoken were more hurtful than how they were said, i.e., the tone and volume. As Maria reflected on the pain caused by those words, she became tearful. Maria said that the pain she felt from Ramon's stinging words was the most pain she had ever felt. She also said she never wanted to feel that pain again. She could not recall the words Ramon spoke, but she vividly recalled the intense feelings associated with them and was afraid of feeling the pain again. A doctoral student was interviewing the family while WLW provided supervision for this session. WLW entered the room to offer the couple an opinion, because it was too lengthy to offer through a supervisory phone-in.

WLW: Do either of you know of the poet laureate, Dr. Maya Angelou? Have you heard of her?

RAMON AND MARIA: No.

WLW: She is an African-American woman, incredibly amazing, who at about the age of 7 was sexually abused. She told the townspeople, and they killed the man. She then believed that her voice killed this man, and so what did she do? She became mute for the next 7 years. She said that she realized, and this is certainly something that we believe, just like what you are saying, Ramon, that words can have a tremendous impact. Nonverbal behavior can have a tremendous impact also. You're saying, "We'd love to have this wonderful, nonverbal intimate way of communicating." This would be lovely. And you say, Maria, "I desire to desire it."

MARIA: [*responds affirmatively*]

WLW: And Ramon, you're saying, "Yeah, I know there was a time when I didn't really like the words that were coming out of my mouth." I was thinking of this metaphor, trying to figure this out as I heard. . . desperation [in both of you]. Your tenacity to make it better. Your tenacity and patience to say, "Hey, it'll happen, it [your sexual happiness] will come at some point." But, I wonder if the two of you, just even for the next 5 minutes, thought that the problem wasn't you. It wasn't you [*pointing to other person*] but that the problem was somehow, that through the words and nonwords, that you had formed a sort of barrier where, literally, penetration was not possible, not pleasurable, not desirable. Does that make sense?

RAMON: [*responds affirmatively*]

WLW: That Maria experienced your words lodging in her. Do you know what I mean? Because this is one thing that Dr. Maya Angelou really believes: that words get stuck in the walls of our homes and in our cells. That's when she says, "We really need to watch how we talk to each other." Words can hurt and words can heal; words can lubricate, right? Words can cause your blood pressure to go higher; words can cause your hearts to beat together or separately. If you were to think about the words that you shared, if you think that somehow those words got lodged, literally, in your vagina, what would the two of you—it is not just one of you that needs to work on this—how would the two of you dislodge that? It sounds like you have tried a lot of different things. You have tried discouragement and that hasn't really worked a lot, right? What if you were to believe that it's not a problem of lack of desire, it's not a problem of wanting it too much, it's not that there's some deficit in either of you. So because of this unfortunate thing that took you by surprise, some words—and I don't believe that people say awful words just on their own—I'm sure that . . .

MARIA: It was a two-way thing.

WLW: I'm sure you helped. You could probably think of some ways that you invited him to say some pretty awful things.

MARIA: [*agrees*]

WLW: That through the working of the two of you together, you almost stuck a big clog of words up there that really prevents the natural lubrication, the natural coming together, because you just can't get in there, literally, nor can you literally open up because you're filled. Those words are stuck there. How would the two of you think about it? What would be different for you? Let me just ask it as simple as that. I wonder what comes to your mind when you think about it that way? What would be different?

RAMON: What do you mean? What would be different if those words weren't lodged there?

WLW: No, what would be different if you were to think about this as a "words-stuck-in-a-vagina" problem, not as a "lack-of-desire" problem. You have been aroused before; now you desire to desire. There has got to be something else. That is why I wonder if I could check that out. If you were to think of it as a "word blockage" problem.

RAMON: Well, I would try to unclog it then. I would look at Maria and I would say, "Maria, I'm sorry for what I said and I'm sorry for what happened," and try to, somehow we've got to break it up and through remorse and through. . . . Look, we made some mistakes and if that's the problem, jumble it up a bit and fill it with words of love and words of compassion and things like that.

WLW: Okay, so you are ready for action right here. Does it change at all how you would approach it, if you thought you had to draw those words out, almost soften or melt, or what other word, but almost sort of . . .

GRADUATE STUDENT CLINICIAN: Dissolve.

WLW: Dissolve, that's a perfect word. Dissolve them. Does that open up any other possibilities for you? Would your approach be different do you think? With yourself even? Would your approach with yourself about all this be different?

RAMON: If I understand what you're saying to me, just by what you've been saying the past couple of minutes, I feel some relief.

WLW: So, for you, there's a little immediate relief about this? I wonder what would happen if you asked yourself, "Is that word adding to the blockage or dissolving it? Is it dissolving or is it firming that up even more so that I can't be part of her—these words are so stuck in there."

MARIA: Well, I think we've both been so worried that we're not normal. That we're having this very unnormal, unnatural thing. I mean, it scares me to death. I've told Barbara [graduate student clinician] before, I told Ramon, I said, "Why does Barbara want to see me alone? Am I just this whacked-out, crazy woman who has no bearing on life? Why are we experiencing this? Why isn't it a normal thing?" It's hard because I've blamed myself, I think we've both blamed each other at times and, just like Ramon says, it's nice to view it metaphorically. It's nice to see that it's not that I am a crazed, unhormonal woman. It's nice to view it in a different light.

WLW: Is there anything that comes to your mind, Maria? Is there anything you would like to do differently if you were to think about it as a word blockage that the two of you cocreated because of some unfortunate experiences? How would you approach showing love? Let's not talk about sexual intimacy. Let's talk about how would you approach showing love to Ramon so it might dissolve, ever so slightly, maybe even just 1 percent, maybe just a little softening there. Think of a blockage up there. It's that softening effect. It's that dissolving. It's that melting. It would be interesting to see how that comes out.

MARIA: I think my approach would change in that by viewing it as, here is the problem, here is the block, here we are [*indicates through hand movements the separation of the problem from them as people*]. I think instead of me being so concerned about me, so concerned about how I'm feeling, how it's going, how everything, I think I would be able to view us more as a little team over here tackling this little thing, rather than me going, "Oh, Maria, I am the problem. I am not doing this right, and this is a problem and our marriage is doomed because I am not keeping his needs satisfied. And he is going to go to work in 30 years and have a secretary and cheat with his secretary." I think I would be able to view it more as a team tackling this little thing.

WLW: Against this little thing over here. It doesn't even have to be a big thing. I mean, you think about that little vagina that can grow and stretch, just like your love together. But it wouldn't take much, would it, to get up there and block it and give you folks the notion that there is some huge, gigantic problem here or some deficit in you or something wrong about you that you cannot solve?

In this example, words were used in a powerful way to invite the couple to a reflection and eventual healing. This micromove was not just a reframing of their presenting problem of lack of sexual desire. It was drawing the family into a particular word usage that was dramatically different—"words stuck in a vagina"—from their previous conceptualization of the problem. The words themselves altered the couple's beliefs about the problem. The novel conceptualization of the problem offered by the clinician fit for this couple. There was a transformation in their beliefs and in their behavior toward each other as evidenced in the following session, 1 week later. The graduate student asked the couple about the impact of the therapeutic conversation with the supervisor. Here are their words:

MARIA: I felt great. I left feeling good. It was very good. I was very, very, very apprehensive about coming and having people watch. But when I came, I was very comforted by the concept. It was very comforting to me to view it in a different light. It took away the blame. I now view it as this kind of a thing over here, and here we are over here trying to deal with this little thing, rather than, "What's wrong with me? Why can't I . . . ?" I thought it was very good.

GRADUATE STUDENT CLINICIAN: [*to husband*] How did you experience it?

RAMON: I thought it was great. I felt really good about it. I felt "truth" was being spoken. I haven't felt peace before when I've talked about this. I really think this is the problem. After the session, we both got in the car and said, "I feel more peace than I ever have before."

GRADUATE STUDENT: Well, this is a new paradigm for me. I liked the way it worked. It was the first time for me. It was powerful and I was very affected by it. It felt very real to me. It moved it out of an intellectual level for me.

MARIA: Such a burden was lifted. That alone has helped to dissolve the problem. It has taken the pressure and stress off both of us.

RAMON: It has been so interesting to see how our words affect one another. And we've known it. Instead of harsh words, we are being especially kind with our words. If we don't understand, we are trying to communicate more about it.

MARIA: And with the act of intimacy, we are trying to be more aware of one another. I'm trying to be more open and honest with him and let him know how I'm feeling. It's hard for me to say, "I like this," but I'm trying and he is trying to be as patient.

In this clinical example, the clinician's creative and innovative metaphoric use of words altered a constraining belief and paved the way for new behaviors and new affect to emerge. In the process, as evidenced in the next session, this couple was healing from their hurtful words and conscientiously "being especially kind with our words."

## CONCLUSION

This chapter on challenging, altering, and modifying constraining beliefs has offered the micromoves that are most salient to our clinical work at this time. We believe that new, serendipitous, spontaneous learning occurs with each family with whom we work. Because of the unique coevolution of these micromoves among the clinician, family members, clinical team, and existing literature and research, the micromoves offered in this chapter are current only until we see the next family!

CHAPTER 7

# Distinguishing Change: Identifying, Affirming, and Solidifying Facilitative Beliefs

C
HANGE NEEDS TO BE distinguished to become a reality. According to Humberto Maturana, reality is brought forth; therefore, something becomes "real" through the observing and distinguishing of it (Maturana & Varela, 1992). If change is not distinguished, noticed, observed, and languaged by a person, it is not present for that person. To distinguish change is to bring change forth: to bring change forward from its background, to "see" change, to determine what change has occurred. To distinguish change is to make change real.

Distinguishing change involves therapeutic moves that identify, affirm, and solidify facilitative beliefs. These therapeutic moves are key to client experiences and reflections on change as expressed in the following quotations:

- Research Family 1: I didn't know how I could say this to him [my son]: "Can we [your father and I] go away somewhere together?" It's just wonderful. It's changed our life completely. (Mother of son experiencing multiple sclerosis, fourth and final session. Previous constraining belief: Good caretaking parents of a son cannot take a holiday.)

- Research Family 3: I now realize there are always solutions if we can just keep talking. (Mother of daughter with chronic fatigue syndrome, fourth and final session. Previous constraining belief: We are sick and tired of being tired and sick. There is nothing more we can do.)
- Research Family 5: Things are going better. There's not the conflict; I'm not backing off anymore. I don't believe I have to protect him. I believe he can take it. (Wife of man who experienced heart attack, fifth and final session. Previous constraining belief: If I upset my husband, he'll get angry and have another heart attack.)
- Research Family 3: I can control my illness. It doesn't control me. (13-year-old experiencing chronic fatigue syndrome, fourth and final session. Previous constraining belief: My illness controls me. I am a victim of chronic fatigue.)

## PASSIONATE PERSISTENCE IN PURSUING CHANGE

The distinguishing of change requires passionate persistence by the clinician. The beliefs that undergird our clinical approach in distinguishing change include the following:

1. Change is always happening.
2. Families are frequently not aware of changes they are making.
3. Families are frequently not able to talk about the changes they have made.
4. Through talking about and reflecting on change, change is drawn forth as a reality; that is, change is distinguished.
5. Through the distinguishing of change, change is solidified.
6. There is always more change to uncover, discover, and distinguish.
7. Change is awesome and well worth distinguishing.
8. Distinguishing change is not only key to the therapeutic process, it is joyous!

These clinician beliefs invite wonderment, awe, and an insatiable curiosity with respect to change. Passionate persistence in pursuing the change naturally follows and flows. The clinician anticipates and distinguishes changes. Change is encapsulated, brought to the fore, and highlighted. Every possible aspect about change is rolled over, described, explored, amplified, and magnified to make it real, to demonstrate that it exists.

It is not just one aspect of the change that makes it stand out, it is the composite of the distinctions that makes it real. The passionate persistence in pursuing change is a process in the therapeutic domain of coevolving and bringing forth a particular entity called *change*. At that particular point in time, that is the only thing that matters, the only reality that exists. Like all passions, when change is being distinguished, it is "the only game in town," making other concerns and pleasures pale.

## SEEING CHANGE

What do you see? According to Humberto Maturana, it is what we select out of our environment, what we "see," that influences us (Maturana, 1988b; Maturana & Varela, 1992). What we are structurally able to see influences our relationships with others. In turn, our relationships with others influence our structure and thus what we are able to see. From our clinical approach, what people see can be a clue to their present biopsychosocial–spiritual structures and to their beliefs. (For further discussion of these ideas, refer to chapters 1, 2, and 3.)

In some families, members spontaneously offer what they see. One example occurred with Research Family 5, the couple who were suffering with marital conflict in the context of the husband's heart attack. In the fourth session, when the clinician asked about what had happened since the previous session, the wife offered the following: "I *see* [my husband] making efforts. . . . I *see* him stopping short when he would have said something and thinking about things."

This wife has been able to distinguish her husband's efforts. His changes have been noticeable to and noticed by her. His different behavior has been a difference that has made a difference to her and has emerged out of the background of "no change" for her. For this woman, her husband's changes are real!

In the following example with Research Family 3, in which the youngest daughter (C2) has been experiencing chronic fatigue syndrome, the clinician (LMW) follows up, during the second session, on a conversation about "putting uncertainty in its place." The mother spontaneously comments, "I *feel* that she [C2] is making some progress." Neurolinguistic programmers would say that the clinician should use the word *feel* to continue the conversation with this kinesthetically oriented woman. But look at how readily the mother and, sequentially, other family members respond when the clinician asks a question using a visual word:

LMW: What do you *see*?
MOTHER: I *see* her up for longer periods. I see her able to interact. Like if a friend comes over, she may be tired but she'll stick with her friend for a long time and she may fall into bed after that.

LMW: So up for longer periods? Socializing longer?

FATHER: I think she bounces back quicker, don't you find that?

MOTHER: Yes, and it doesn't take her as long.

LMW: Really! Wow! [*then to C2*] Do you *notice* that yourself?

C2: Mmhm.

LMW: Are you up for longer periods, socializing longer?

C2: I was going to try to go to school today because I was feeling not bad for a while. But this morning I got up and I just knew, no way, I couldn't.

C1: Her attention is coming back too. She has a longer attention span.

MOTHER: Because her attention is coming back, she can read for longer periods, but her memory is getting worse.

C2: I'll read a book then forget about it.

LMW: But your memory is—you don't remember sometimes just what you've read?

C2: No.

LMW: Wow. This is a lot. So, what else?

The clinician discovers what changes various family members are selecting out: what changes they are able to "see" and what changes they are each able to distinguish. In this process the clinician learns that the changes family members are seeing range from positive changes of the daughter socializing longer, bouncing back quicker, and attending school longer to a negative change in the daughter's memory. The clinician expresses her own amazement at the amount of change that the family members are able to see after only one session, and in a "true," ever-curious therapeutic style, she inquires about what else they are seeing these days.

## EXPLORING CHANGE

Change is not linear, nor is the exploration of change. The systems theory axiom that "a change in one part of the system affects other parts of the system" implies that when change is being distinguished, it needs to be explored in different areas of the system and from different points of view. To distinguish change, the exploration of change is thorough, systemic, and nonlinear. No turn in the loop of change is left unexplored.

In the following change segment, the clinician (LMW) distinguishes change with Research Family 5 by exploring change from the husband's point of view, exploring the wife's view of the husband's view, and exploring the wife's view. Change becomes real as the clinician turns the change that is being described over and over, looking at it from various angles and points of view.

LMW: Well, tell me, how are Robert and Julie doing together as a couple? You've told me a lot about the kids and how you're doing individually. How are you doing as a couple?

JULIE: [*Something about "doing" catches the wife's attention and she responds.*] What do we really *do* together? We're always with kids and family. We don't do a whole lot just as a couple.

ROBERT: No we do it as a . . .

JULIE: [*The wife continues with the theme of what they are not doing as a couple, which begins to distinguish change*] We're not fighting.

LMW: Well, okay. Maybe I don't mean doing activities together.

ROBERT: I've become more comfortable.

LMW: Let me ask you this question then in a different way. . . . How are you getting on together?

ROBERT: I'm happy. I'm comfortable. I'm in love. I'm in admiration.

LMW: [*The clinician turns over the husband's vivid and poignant description of change in himself and explores how his comments impact on his wife.*] She's looking at you like . . .

ROBERT: I like the relationship. . .

LMW: Julie's looking at you like . . .

ROBERT: . . . that we have.

LMW: But Julie looked kind of quizzical when you said *admiration*.

The clinician explores the explanation for the wife's quizzical look, discovering that this is the first time the wife has heard that her husband is "happy, comfortable, in love, in admiration." The clinician then draws forth the wife's experience:

LMW: And what about for you, Julie? How are you? How do you feel things are going for you in your marriage?

From a variety of angles and with an undaunted stance, the clinician explores change, never assuming that one family member's experience is the same as another's, always curious about the impact of one person's description of change on another.

## INVITING OBSERVATIONS OF OTHERS' OBSERVATIONS

"Everything said is said by an observer to another observer" (Maturana, 1978, p. 31). This statement by Maturana, himself an observer, makes the term *observer perspective* a nonuseful term for us. If everything said is said by an observer, our interest becomes, "Who is the observer that is making the statement?" Accordingly, an "observer-perspective question" (Tomm, 1988) becomes any question that draws forth any person's perspective, because all are observers.

Operating from a systemic stance, the perspective of multiple observers is critical. In the previous example of Research Family 3, in which family members were experiencing the chronic fatigue of the daughter, each offered his or her perspective on changes observed. Directly or indirectly, we inquire about such aspects as (a) others' perspectives on changes "seen," (b) others' explanations of how changes have occurred, and (c) others' perspectives of the effects of change.

To thicken the descriptions, we also inquire about observers' observations of other observers' observations. We are curious about one person's reflections on another's reflections. Possible questions are as follows: What change has caught your mother's attention and meant the most to her? What would your sister need to see or experience that would convince her that you are on her side?

In Research Family 2, the client (Connie) was challenging beliefs about herself and experiencing a decrease in her anxiety. The clinician (LMW) invites the client to notice others' noticing of her changes:

LMW: Well, I'm wondering if anybody else noticed this change in you?
CONNIE: No.
LMW: Nobody's noticed. You don't think that they did? Were you pretty good at masking your anxiety?
CONNIE: Yes.
LMW: So your friends, your husband, your kids wouldn't have picked up on this [change]?
CONNIE: Oh, I think my husband knows. I'm not so crabby all the time; you could put it that way.
LMW: Ah. So, that's one difference. If he were here, he may not comment on the anxiety, but he would notice that difference in you?
CONNIE: Yes.
LMW: Not as crabby? Anything else that your friends and family would notice about you?

Here the client's view of her changes is shored up when the clinician solicits the client's view of others' views of her changes. When the client initially says no one has noticed, the clinician explores the hypothesis that no one has noticed the dramatic changes because the client was so good at masking her problem. The question embeds a commendation about the amount of change: The client would have to be "pretty good at masking the anxiety" for others not to notice now the change in her anxiety. Following this question, the clinician gives the client another opportunity to view others' viewing of her. This time her view has shifted, and she is able to notice that her husband would notice less crabbiness. We believe that the family at the end of the session is different from the family at the beginning of the session because of structural coupling with the clinician and among the family members, which changes the biopsychosocial–spiritual structures of family members. The same question can be asked at two points in a family session, and two different "truthful" answers may be given.

## EXPLORING THE EFFECTS OF CHANGE

When changes have happened, one way to solidify them is to explore the effects of the changes on various family members. Exploration and reflection are involved in this process. Research Family 1 presented with respite issues concerning managing the 34-year-old son's multiple sclerosis (MS). Sessions 1 and 2 focused on creating a context for change, identifying constraining beliefs, and challenging constraining beliefs. Beliefs constraining these family members included the following:

Good parents of a son with MS sacrifice all they have, including their own health, for the well-being of their son.

Good parents of a son with MS need to do all the nursing care themselves.

Good parents of a son with MS can never take a holiday, especially without their son's permission.

While masterful therapeutic moves were involved in identifying and challenging the constraining beliefs, equally important to the work with this family were the therapeutic moves to draw forth and solidify the facilitative beliefs. Sessions 3 and 4 were focused solely on distinguishing change: drawing forth and sustaining facilitative beliefs and the corresponding affective and behavioral changes. During the course of four sessions, the issues of family members shifted from worry about the son's trips to the bathroom and the parents' fear of his tripping and falling down in their absence, to the parents' making plans for respite: their vacation trip to Las Vegas.

In following up on an assignment from Session 2, the clinician (LMW) heard the report from the 34-year-old son that he has made phone calls securing information about nursing services available for himself, which would allow respite for his caregiving parents and a change for him in being cared for by someone other than his parents. The son could receive respite from his parents' caregiving just as the parents could receive respite. LMW's efforts to draw forth and solidify facilitative beliefs involved pursuing the effect of this new information ("new" on many levels) on family members.

One seemingly small but important aspect of exploring the effects of change is sequencing. Sometimes "who's on first" matters. To whom do you address the first question? To solidify the facilitative belief that the son can manage his illness, the clinician initially addresses questions to the son, asking his opinion first, a move that is not minor but is saturated with meaningful messages. By addressing questions initially to the son, the clinician supports his newly claimed leadership position in the family. The young man comes to the foreground, deranking the debilitating illness to the background. These changes serve as possible perturbations for other family members and their relationships.

The following segment demonstrates sequencing while exploring the effects of change. The son (Mark) has just told the clinician of his accessing the life-liberating information regarding nursing care services available to him.

LMW: Congratulations! That's wonderful. I'm really pleased to hear that. What do you think this information has done for your parents? Do you think it's done anything for them? [*The clinician invites the son to a reflection about the impact of the change on his parents.*]

MARK: Well, it's taken a load off their shoulders, I would think. They want to go . . .

LMW: Knowing that they have that option now and knowing that you're supportive of it. Remember last time we met, you really were very clear about that, that you're very supportive of them having a holiday. And now knowing how they could arrange it.

MARK: Yes.

LMW: [*to parents*] Is that so? Has it given you . . .

MOTHER AND FATHER: Yes. It's a big relief . . .

MARK: Having that registered nurse or whatever . . .

LMW: Yes.

MARK: They know I'll be in good hands.

LMW: Yes. So is Mark accurate when he says it's taken some pressure off?

FATHER: Oh, it sure has . . .

LMW: Knowing you've got that option now, being able to . . .

MOTHER AND FATHER: [*speaking in unison*] Yes.

LMW: [*turning to son and checking the effect of the information in another way by bringing up the formerly forbidden topic of travel*] When do you think they're going to take off?

MARK: I think they . . .

MOTHER: [*interrupts*] October.

MARK: . . . said October.

LMW: Ah, so you're planning. Great!

The clinician then invites the parents into a conversation about the holiday they might take, allowing them to create a new belief about themselves right in the session. The new belief is about themselves as a traveling couple instead of as permanent, full-time nurses. LMW then reciprocally pursues the information from the parents' points of view: "What do you think this information has done for your son? Do you think it's made any difference for him?" The clinician then provides the son an opportunity to give his reflection on his parents' reflections. In this manner the son has had the first and last word, and the belief that the son can take leadership and manage his illness is gently solidified.

## INVITING EXPLANATIONS OF CHANGE

Persistently seeking the explanation for how change has come to be is another way to distinguish change and make it real. As family members are invited to offer explanations about their changes, they are concurrently invited to stand still for a moment and look at the changes in perhaps a new way, happening for a new reason. In noticing and attending to the changes to explain them, a new level of valuing of the change emerges. Both the change and the family members' efforts become more real. Our belief is that if change can be explained, it is more likely to be maintained.

In the following example concerning Research Family 4, the single-parent mother (Linda) has just told the clinician (WLW) that since the last session her formerly obstreperous children have initiated speaking positively about her. In an effort to help that change become more real, the clinician asks the mother how she accomplished this notable difference. The way the clinician's initial question is phrased implies that the mother has a part in the children's change, thus opening up the possibility for her to sustain the change. If she is part of the change and can offer an explanation for how this change came to be, both the change and her influence on her children become more real.

WLW: How did you invite your children to be able to talk so positively about the family and about you? That's quite a remarkable thing.

LINDA: We're quite open in our family because what we do at dinnertime is we have a time when each member of the family is allowed their time to talk a little bit about what their best part of the day was, if they've had any problems at school, that sort of thing.

The clinician continues to be curious to keep the explanation coming and to seek distinctions about what was different about the children's talking this time, when was it different, where, and so on.

WLW: Okay. That was always in place. Now I'm trying to understand, you said, "Something different happened this week where suddenly we were sitting around talking about showing our love, sharing our love, and the kids let me know how important I was to them," and that was different for you.

LINDA: It was different for me because I've always been the head and said, "Okay, it's your turn. It's your chance." And I didn't realize until just a while ago that I wasn't taking my chance to say, "I had this happen today and I felt this way about it."

WLW: When did you realize that?

LINDA: It was just a few weeks ago. I thought, "Gee maybe I better start talking about my day too."

At this point the clinician invites the eldest son into the conversation to see if he experienced the dinner-table conversation in a manner different from usual. When the son says it was not different for him, the clinician does not allow him to diminish the experience of his mother and persists with the curiosity about the change.

WLW: [to Linda] So you experienced it as different. There was something different there for you.

LINDA: I don't know what it was. [And then she tells about something she has always believed rather than something different, so the clinician persists.]

WLW: Can you think of anything else that allowed you to hear your children's comments?

LINDA: I don't know what was different, because we just sat around and . . .

WLW: This was last night . . .

LINDA: Mmhm. [Now Linda describes her efforts to invite her children into a conversation based on two experiments offered at the end of the previous session.] And I gave each of them an opportunity to say what their feelings were, if they feel mad, sad, glad, and I gave each of them the opportunity and asked each of them what's important to them in our family. I asked them, "What do you want to keep the same?" And each of them said, "You're important, Mom!" I have never heard that from my kids.

WLW: So clearly or ever at all?

Look at the change that is distinguished by clarifying the distinction between the following two questions: Has the mother never heard "you're important" so clearly from her children? Has the mother never heard "you're important" from her children at all? The mother's description of her past feelings becomes more and more vivid, magnifying the difference between how she felt previously and how she feels now.

LINDA: I've never heard it at all. I've always felt sort of violated by my kids and run over by my kids and overrun. I mean just literally overrun!

WLW: Overrun by your kids?

LINDA: By children. Yeah, infested with them and . . .

WLW: And last night . . .

LINDA: I had never realized until they said that, "Mom's important." I'd never really heard that from them.

WLW: That's a big difference, from feeling overrun by children, taken for granted, to suddenly hearing, "You're important to us, Mom." What other thought fit with that? You know, like a puzzle. You find a piece of the puzzle and then other pieces fit in. When you heard last night, "You're important to us," that's a big piece of the puzzle. What else fits with that, for you? [*The persistent exploration for an understanding of the difference now yields the following.*]

LINDA: Maybe what happened was that over a period of time they have become important to me. And maybe it's because I have taken an interest in them and taken them aside and said, "Okay, so what's going on with you? What's happening with you?" And maybe it was because I have been willing to recognize them, where in the past when I was busy with school and had all this busy stuff, a lot of it was just, "Go. I don't want to talk to you right now." And over the past 6 months I have taken a more active interest in them and in their feelings. And I've tried to put myself in their shoes, and I've tried to be kind with them. And more compassionate. And maybe that's what's happening. Maybe it's paying off, because I'm giving them compassion so maybe they're in turn saying . . . [*One of the children comes into the room, but the point of the reciprocal influencing of mother on children and children on mother is completed.*]

The evidence that change became quite real for this single mother and her children is that the following session, 6 weeks later, was their last session. Change was reported in a variety of areas including the following: Positive interactions between Linda and her children continued; unusually positive interactions took place between Linda and her own father; Linda underwent body-shaping surgery and lost 30 pounds; and she now believed, "We are a loving family" and "I am a neat person."

## DISTINGUISHING FACILITATIVE BELIEFS

Distinguishing change involves therapeutic moves that identify, affirm, and solidify facilitative beliefs. Facilitative beliefs are those that open the possibility for a greater variety of solutions and new and empowering ideas about one's self, relationships, and abilities.

How does one invite clients to reflect on and articulate their beliefs so that further refinement and solidification of change can happen? Sometimes it can be as simple as asking, "What have you come to believe about yourself [your spouse, your marriage, life] through our work together?" And by further exploring, "What else have you come to believe?" If a change in behavior is noted by the client, family members, or the clinician, it is possible to pursue facilitative beliefs by asking, "What do you think this new behavior says about you? What other beliefs and behavior fit with this new behavior and belief?" The therapeutic conversation that unfolds provides an opportunity for family members to view other family members differently, in a new light, generating and distinguishing new beliefs.

An example of this process occurred with Research Family 4, when the mother (Linda) was listening to a therapeutic conversation between her 13-year-old son (David) and the clinician (WLW). The clinician wanted to assess the impact the conversation had on the mother's beliefs about the problem. The mother was initially concerned that her son was depressed and believed he was "not normal socially."

LINDA: I've been worried about his [her son's] self-esteem.
WLW: And have you heard him say anything today that makes you worry more or that makes you worry less?

The clinician does not want to assume the direction of change. Asking on both sides of the possibility of change allows the client to language out loud, out of her own mouth, the impact hearing her son's story has had on her.

LINDA: Well, it makes me worry less. [*turning to son*] Okay, so you're normal [*laughs*]. Okay, so you're tired.
WLW: But what gave you that idea? I really want to say this very sincerely to you. I do not want to minimize your concerns. I think your son is really lucky to have a mom who is concerned enough to say, "I'm concerned. Let's figure this out." But I'm saying, what

did you hear David say that would make you say, "Yes, I see you as a normal kid"? What happened here that gave you that idea? [*By not minimizing the mother's concerns, the clinician decreases the mother's need to defend her position, whereas her ability to hear, speak, and believe differently is increased.*]

LINDA: I just heard him being frank and saying, "Well, yes, of course I collect hockey cards. I like hockey cards." I guess that's not so bad. I was concerned because in some of my psychiatric training, one of the things they talked about is that excessive interest in something can indicate deeper psychological problems. So, maybe I'm just kind of like the nursing student that figures she's got everything. [*This spontaneous reflection with an offering of the origin of her constraining belief provides more evidence that the mother's original belief about her son has been challenged.*]

WLW: Got every disease going? [*laughter*] And you've got four kids! Just think about that. You could have them all. You could have every disease going.

LINDA: Yes, I could have . . .

WLW: You're bringing up a really good point. Oftentimes what we're reading we do see. Believing is seeing. Right? We believe what we read, and then [we] see it. I could show you an equal number of books, and this is why we needed to check it out with David and you, that say having a really keen hobby, having something a boy is really keen about, is a really healthy thing. Right?

The clinician seizes the moment to support the belief that believing is seeing. The converse is also true: that seeing is believing. In this session, the mother has "seen" her son differently and now believes differently about him.

LINDA: Yes.

WLW: So, it's trying to draw that distinction, isn't it?

LINDA: Yes.

WLW: What else have you come to believe about David through our conversation here today?

LINDA: Just that he's a really perceptive kid. I didn't think that he had the depth of perception [about] me. You know I didn't realize that.

WLW: And what gave you that? What helped you realize that this is a son who has a "depth of perception," to use your words?

LINDA: Just some of his answers that he's given me plus his being attentive to me.

In this segment of the therapeutic conversation, the mother shifts from her constraining belief, "My son is depressed and not normal socially," to a facilitative belief, "My son is perceptive, loves hockey, and is sometimes tired." Possibilities for facilitative mother–son interaction have been opened up through the experience of distinguishing this facilitative belief, and the distinguishing of one facilitative belief increases the likelihood of distinguishing another, and another.

## CELEBRATING CHANGE

When change has occurred, change needs to be drawn forth, languaged, commended, even celebrated. Unfortunately, the best kept secret of some clinicians is how enthused they are about the changes that have occurred between and within family members. Some clinicians have erroneously interpreted the Milan team's concept of neutrality (Selvini Palazzoli, Boscolo, Cecchin, & Prata, 1980a) to mean that there should be no analogic leakage by the clinician about wonderful things that have happened during the session or since the last session with a family.

How does one invite a family to celebrate change? How can a clinician provide opportunities for conversations of commendation and celebration? The following are some of the ways:

- Use celebratory language: wow, really, incredible, fantastic, terrific.
- Refocus back to the celebration of change.
- Repeat the client's words.
- Concretize change by audible note taking.
- Elevate, specify, and celebrate client effort, attributing the change to the client and specifying client behavior that led to the change through persistent inquiry.
- Do not allow diminishing of client effort.
- Offer comparative commendations: commendations pointing out, for example, how wise or courageous the client is in comparison to others in the situation.
- Offer global affirmation of the whole being of the person (whole-person validation).

We make conscious efforts to celebrate change. The following segment of the fourth and final session with Research Family 3, who were experiencing difficulties with the younger daughter's chronic fatigue syndrome, is a typical example of our efforts. Listen as the accolades abound and sincere commendations are offered with enthusiasm to solidify the changes. None of the celebration can be feigned. The clinician must believe at a deep "cellular–soulular" level that she is witnessing amazing change. When the clinician believes in the celebratory worthiness of the change, corresponding palpable emotion and therapeutic cheerleading behavior will be present. Change is magnified through therapeutic inquiries—What did your family say?—and by pursuing the client's internal conversations: How did you make the decision to go each day like that? What did you say to yourself while doing this? What does this tell you about your ability to control the disease? Following is a segment of therapeutic celebration from LMW's consultation with the 13-year-old daughter (C2) in this family:

LMW: And anything else new since I've seen you last, before we talk about your assignment?

C2: The week I saw you, what day was that?

LMW: That was the 26th of May.

C2: Yeah, well I think I didn't go to school that week, but then the next week and the week after and the next week and the next week I went for about the whole week.

It is interesting that the daughter who has been immobilized by chronic fatigue has been going so regularly to school that she now " doesn't think" she went to school that first week. School is such a part of her repertoire of behaviors, she cannot remember when it started to be so.

LMW: Did you?

C2: Yeah, in the mornings.

LMW: Wow! Congratulations! That's fantastic! Let me get this down. So, not the week I saw you, but the next week and the week after . . . [*Audible note taking is one way to underline and send the message "this is important." Distinguishing what is important is important. Family members feel valued for their comments.*]

C2: Yeah.

LMW: You went in the mornings? Dynamite!

C2: And there was a dance and I really wanted to go, right? So I asked the counselor and everything and the principal and they said, "Yes, that would be okay." So I went, and then I was really tired for the next week.

LMW: So you went to the dance. Well, I can imagine after not being out dancing for a while, that you would be tired. Did you actually get up and dance?

C2: Not really. I just sort of hung out.

LMW: Hung out, yes. Just hung out and visited with your friends. Well that's incredible! That's really terrific! What did your family say?

At this point, the clinician shifts to enlarge the celebration, exploring the client's view on others' views of her accomplishment. She explores responses of family members by broadening the audience of change.

c2: They were happy with it.

LMW: Yes? And how did you make the decision to go each day like that, because we talked about, um ... [*Here the clinician is embedding volition by strengthening the client's belief about herself. Note the wonderful response of the client, who now, from a position of strength, interrupts the clinician and says:*]

c2: Me controlling the disease instead of the disease controlling me! [*This client-initiated interruption is rich evidence of significant, meaningful change. It shows the client's understanding of the change and clearly puts forth the new facilitative belief.*]

LMW: We talked about pacing it, maybe every other day. How did you figure out that you could handle it every morning? [*Again, the clinician is embedding and inviting the client to a reflection.*]

c2: Well, I just, I don't know, I was feeling good. Like I was feeling better than I was, so I thought that I could add to it. [*The client's structure is being perturbed. Perhaps this "trying-to-sort-it-out, quasi-confused" languaging is an indicator of the beginnings of a structural change, a change in beliefs.*]

LMW: Well that is just fantastic! That's a real accomplishment! What did you say to yourself when you were doing this?

c2: Oh, I thought, well, I just wanted to get back to school . . .

LMW: Yes, I know.

c2: I was tired a little bit, but I was better than I was, I think.

LMW: Well, I'm sure you would be a little bit, but that's just a tremendous accomplishment. So what does this say to [you] about your ability to control this disease a little more instead of it always ruling you? What does this tell you?

In these few minutes, change has been distinguished through celebration, and the possibilities for more change have been opened.

## PUBLISHING CHANGE

Sometimes celebration of change involves publication of change. We first encountered this move through the clinical work of White and Epston (1990) and have since expanded on these ideas. Publishing change involves (a) exploring the desirability of publicity (e.g., Would you like anybody else to know of your success?) and (b) elevating clients' experiences of success and expertise by connecting the experience to the clinician's future work with families. This is done in a manner that recaps the client's whole story, validating, amplifying, and solidifying the changes. The clinician pursues by saying, "What advice would you suggest I give to another person who is struggling with . . . ?"

Another powerful way to publish the change is to put it on paper, to have the changes communicated through text rather than through spoken words. Recording changes in the form of written words concretizes the changes for the client. The written word can be read, reread, and shared with others and thus published over and over again. Following is an example of a therapeutic letter that draws forth the significant changes of a clinical family; it was written by WLW to a 52-year-old woman who had presented with hypertension and marital conflict:

> Dear Michele:
>
> Further to our interview last week, I want to reiterate our thanks for the gift you have given us: the privilege of watching you change from a cocoon into a beautiful butterfly. To reciprocate, we would offer you a gift as well: your own "Pearls of Wisdom." These pearls include your wise statements, beliefs and advice.
>
> Michele's Pearls of Wisdom:
> - We have lived in a man's world.
> - Let it be heard, women do have a voice.
> - Women have contributed to their own oppression.
> - We have let the men dominate us.
> - Get involved to help change things for women.
> - It's okay to show it "like it is."
> - Be yourself. Don't let people tell you how you should behave.
> - I can do difficult things.
> - There is no perfect family.
> - We are grateful for what we have.
> - Things aren't as bad as you think they are.
> - We can work them out.
> - It's okay to have, and express, a difference of opinion with your husband.
> - Nothing is ever the way it appears to be.
>
> Michele's Advice to Younger Women:
> - Be yourself.
> - Get a career and be able to provide financially for yourself.
>
> Michele's Advice to "Seasoned" Married Women:
> - Don't be an extension of your husband.
>
> Michele, it has been a privilege to work with you and your family. We wish you every success as you continue to co-author new chapters in your book, "The Marriage of Michele and Steve." Again we thank you for your Pearls of Wisdom and advice which will help other women and their families.
>
> > Sincerely,
> > Wendy L. Watson, and members of the clinical nursing team

By distinguishing Michele's changes through the writing of the therapeutic letter, the clinician helped make the changes more real to her. Her change was published, and subscriptions to the "publication" were increased, as was the reality of her change when she shared the letter with family members and friends, of her own volition.

## CONCLUSION

We want to distinguish change, to draw it forth from its background in a manner that identifies, magnifies, and sustains change. It's all about bringing change to life!

We bring change to life in the following ways:

- We are passionately persistent in pursuing change.
- We see what change family members are seeing and help them see more.
- We systemically explore change.
- We invite observations of others' observations of change.
- We systemically explore the effects of change.
- We invite explanations for change.
- We distinguish facilitative beliefs.
- We systemically celebrate change.
- We publish change.

By bringing change to life, we increase the possibility for the continuing presence and influence of change in family members' lives.

# PART III

# Clinical Exemplar

CHAPTER 8

# Clinical Exemplar:
# Taking One's Own Advice

T HIS CHAPTER IS A case presentation of the clinical work with
Research Family 2 (see Appendix A for the genogram). The goal
of this chapter is to portray in detail the evolving therapeutic conversation between the clinician and the family. In this particular case,
only one family member, the wife–mother, participated in the sessions.
In presenting one research family in detail, we hope that our clinical
approach will be even more transparent and illustrate many of the theoretical underpinnings as well as macromoves and micromoves. This
particular research family was chosen because the clinical work seemed
to be unusually condensed and compressed. Dramatic change was
experienced by the client after only two sessions, which were held 8
weeks apart.

The client, whose fictional name is Connie, was 39 years old. She
lived in a small town 3 hours from the Family Nursing Unit (FNU) with
her second husband, with whom she had been married for 10 years.
Their children consisted of an adolescent son from Connie's first marriage and two children from the present marriage. Connie had experienced a myocardial infarction (heart attack) within the past year and
was currently taking medication for heart disease, rheumatoid arthritis,
and hypertension. She reported a strong family history of heart disease,
including her mother's experience of four heart attacks and recent

249

triple cardiac bypass surgery. Connie was presently experiencing occasional angina and was suffering from panic attacks. Connie's aunt, a former client at the Family Nursing Unit, had referred Connie to the FNU. Connie was the only member of her family who attended the sessions over the 8-week period. The clinician was Dr. Lorraine Wright (LMW). The clinical team consisted of Dr. Wendy Watson (WLW) and graduate students.

## FIRST SESSION

Just before the first interview, the clinical team met for a presession discussion. The intake information, which had been obtained from Connie's aunt over the phone, was reviewed. Connie's history of a heart attack and arthritis was noted as well as the recent triple bypass surgery of her mother. The presenting concern, according to the intake information, was anxiety and panic attacks. Literature related to the intake information was reviewed. In this case, John Rolland's (1987) article on life cycle and chronic illness was included as part of the team's presession discussion, along with the Milan team's article on the subject of the referring person (Selvini Palazzoli, Boscolo, Cecchin, & Prata, 1980a). From previous clinical work with families experiencing life-shortening illness, several hypotheses emerged, one being that life-shortening illness invites questions about life and death.

Although the clinician's job is to invite family members to a reflection on a belief that will facilitate getting past a problem, the family member's job is to invite the clinician to an appreciation of the problem. Between the two, a therapeutic conversation coevolves. With this principle in mind, the interview commenced. The clinician (LMW) introduced herself and explained the context of the FNU including the format and length of the sessions, the physical setting such as the one-way mirrors, the use of the clinical team, and the videotaping of the sessions. These moves are routine but are important ones for engaging the family and "preparing the ground," as described in chapter 4.

These were the last "routine" moves of this clinical work. From the commencement of the first session until the end of the second session, there was a touching here, touching there, moving here, circling back there. An intensity of moments characterized the therapeutic conversation in the first session. The therapeutic conversations did not progress tidily from genogram information gathering to exploration of the presenting problem to exploration of attempted solutions. Rather, it was a vigorous zigzagging from engagement involving obtaining data for the genogram, to touching on a constraining belief, followed by more genogram information, crossing over to affective issues, up to the pre-senting problem, back to more information about names and dates for the genogram, over to previous successes of the client, and onward, upward, and backward—but always forward in the therapeutic process.

The therapeutic conversation unfolds from seemingly small thera-peutic moves that inform the client what to expect next (e.g., LMW: I like to start by getting a family diagram right off the top) to quantum leaps that neither the client nor the clinician can anticipate (e.g., LMW: What would be an acceptable age [for you] to die?).

Names and ages obtained for completion of the genogram turn into life events, and a continuing systemic clarity unfolds as these events are written down, and events that are salient are momentarily explored for their impact on Connie. How did she respond to the event? How old was she? What memories does she have of the event? One example is the death of Connie's sister from cancer at only 37 years of age. This key and tragic event is drawn forth by the clinician for its possible connec-tion to the present. Following are examples of LMW's questions and comments:

- Well that must have been a great loss for your family.
- Was that difficult for you to adjust to?
- So you would have been how old?
- That's very young to lose a sister. Very shocking, not what you'd expect. (Connie: No, she was my favorite one.)
- Oh, wow! So probably even a greater loss. So her memory and the memories you have of her must be very precious to you.
- Wow, that's a very sad loss for you. Do you think about her?
- So what do you do to keep her memory alive? (And then back to the genogram.)
- So you are the fourth of five children and you were closest to your sister. And now? (Connie says she is now closest to her youngest brother.)

Names and dates can be asked by anyone, even a computer. But look-ing for themes, noticing affective arousal, and tracking constraining beliefs all require therapeutic competence and an ability to coevolve a conversation with the client that allows the clinician and the client to go where computers cannot go: into the heart of the matter. Thus the genogram is so much more than names, dates, ages, and occupations.

The genogram is also evidence that Connie is not alone in her expe-riences of illness. Connie may be the only one visibly present in the room, but perhaps not palpably so. Who else is "with" her? Who else influences her biopsychosocial–spiritual structure and vice versa. With whom is she having conversations of affirmation and affection, conversations of accusation and recrimination? This is what a genogram begins to demonstrate. With whom does she have a passion for living together or lack thereof? Whose beliefs influence her illness, and what beliefs of Connie's influence others?

As the names and dates of the genogram unfold, the clinician takes the opportunity to explore relevant beliefs and always demonstrates therapeutic curiosity, never assuming anything. Look at the following questions that LMW asks while obtaining the genogram information:

- How long have you and your husband been together? Are you married?
- How do you account for the divorce from your first husband?
- How much contact do your son and his father have?
- Is that enough [contact] for Sean [son]?
- How do Mike [second husband] and Sean get on together? Sean was 7 when you were remarried? How was that for Sean?

When Connie indicates that problems around her son's last name arose, the clinician pursues:

- What is your belief about all that? Do you believe they should try to be closer or do you think it's okay when they're not?
- What is your husband's belief that constrains him from saying anything to your son?
- Has it been a problem for you that they are not closer?
- Who does that affect the most?
- What were you thinking about just then when you started to weep?
- Do you think that Mike believed you wanted him to discipline or for him to leave that to you?

We now offer segments of the therapeutic conversation that we believe were salient to the process of therapeutic change with Connie. Guided by the belief that family structure and development may influence both family relationships and health, the clinician was constantly looking for opportunities to confirm or discard this hypothesis. She starts by saying, "So, how it becomes a problem for you is getting caught in the middle [between her husband and her son from a previous marriage]." This statement by the clinician embeds one of our favorite systemic questions: How is it a problem for you? This question invites family members to reflect on where they are in relationship to the problem rather than pointing at others. It quickly cuts through possible linear blaming of other family members. The question also clarifies how a problem somewhere else in the system impacts on clients in such a way as to be a problem for them.

CONNIE: Yes, because I don't know what to do. I understand both sides.

LMW: Who pulls you the most? [*The clinician quickly follows to explore distinctions for increased clarity.*]

CONNIE: My husband.

LMW: Your husband pulls you the most, okay. In terms of trying to get you, to what, to see his point of view?

CONNIE: Yes.

LMW: To discipline your son in a particular way or to . . .

CONNIE: I think just to see his point of view . . .

LMW: To see his point of view. Okay, well that is tough. It's always one of the big challenges of remarriages, when there's stepparents and stepchildren. It's trying to come together, and you're experiencing all those things that are challenges, aren't they?

CONNIE: A million times, yes!

LMW: I've heard other parents talk about similar challenges. Every family has to try and sort that out as best they can for themselves.

CONNIE: Yes.

LMW: But, you've experienced firsthand some of those challenges. So I can appreciate, very much, from other families and the stories they've told me too, that these are the challenges. But there's joys also. I'm sure that you experienced . . .

CONNIE: Oh yes.

LMW: You say for the most part, a lot of times, they do get along, but for you, it's that being caught in the middle.

CONNIE: Yes.

LMW: It makes it difficult. Sure. So just to go back, then so far as you're aware with Mike and Sean, you wish they could be a bit closer but you've sort of come to accept that . . .

CONNIE: That they'll never be close.

Even in this very early segment of the therapeutic conversation, the clinician offers an alternative view, a new frame: a view that may be additive or may provide a contrasting perspective to that of the client. In this segment, Connie implies she feels that family members have failed in coming together as a stepfamily. There is a slow recalibration; metaphorically we could say the client looks south. The clinician does not offer a north view initially but rather offers a comment, an observation, or a question that offers another explanation of the client's experience. In this case, the clinician offers an alternative view: that similar family structures experience similar challenges. Many clinicians might call this normalizing: "I've heard other parents talk about similar challenges." This is intended to help the mother realize she is not alone in the challenges she experiences in a stepparent family. We prefer to think the clinician is connecting the mother to others in a similar situation when the clinician refers to her clinical experience with other stepfamilies and the similarities of this woman to a larger group of stepfamilies. The mother is similar but she is unique; she has "experienced these challenges firsthand." The clinician then moves to offer another distinction in a positive frame: that there are challenges but there are also joys. We could call this a "trial balloon" that explores how open the client is to new views. Will it fly? Will Connie open space to this opposite view? The clinician also embeds the commendation that the client is not a failure. If we could freeze the therapeutic conversation at this point, which is just a few minutes into the first session, how might Connie answer the question, "What do you believe your clinician believes about you and your situation?" We hope Connie is experiencing the clinician as nonjudgmental and validating. The clinician then offers her beliefs transparently and tentatively through the hypothesis of a connection between family relationships and health:

LMW: Okay, let's just go back and finish up [the genogram]. That was very helpful to me because this is an important aspect of your family life and other challenges it sounds like you have, in addition to your health problems. Sometimes other problems can affect your health problems, sometimes not. Would you guess that some of your other problems affect your health problems—some of the [stepparenting and family relationship] issues that go on?

CONNIE: It's hard to say because it's been like that for so long. I don't know.

LMW: It's like the old chicken and the egg, we don't know which comes first. Your family problems get exacerbated or become worse because of health problems, or do the health problems become worse because of your family problems?

CONNIE: Yes.

LMW: Sometimes there's no connection.

CONNIE: I don't know, because it's not a constant problem, you know.

The clinician offers professional beliefs about possible connections between the health problem and family problems, about the direction of the influence or the lack of influence. By posing the possibility of influence coming from either or neither direction, the clinician's neutrality is demonstrated. It is a therapeutic offering. How the client responds at the present time and how that offering may later perturb the biopsychosocial–spiritual structure of family members is not known at this point.

The therapeutic conversation proceeds with more genogram construction; the clinician gathers information about Connie's parents and their ages, occupations, health status, and so on. The clinician learns that Connie's mother was only 48 years of age when she had her first heart attack and that Connie's father is deceased, having died 20 years ago when Connie was 19 years old. During the gathering of the genogram information, the therapeutic timing we call "gambler's rhythm" is vital. As in the Kenny Rogers's song that advises, "You've got to know when to hold 'em, know when to fold 'em, know when to walk away, know when to run," LMW chooses to "hold 'em" and explore more about Connie's father's death:

LMW: How did that affect you? [referring to the death of Connie's father].
CONNIE: I didn't like my dad very much, so I wasn't that sad.
LMW: How was it that you didn't get on so well? [*Connie explains that her father had "lots of problems with drugs and alcohol."*]
LMW: So it was pretty despairing to see your father like that. [*Connie nods and sobs. The clinician assesses how entrenched Connie's beliefs are about her father.*]
LMW: Have you been able to think differently of your dad as you've gotten older? [*Connie shakes her head indicating no but is unable to speak because she is choking up with tears. The clinician continues to pursue Connie's beliefs about her father.*]
LMW: What are your beliefs and feelings about him now? If I asked you to describe your dad in a sentence to me, you'd say . . .
CONNIE: I hate him.
LMW: So, that hasn't changed much over the years?

The clinician then embeds a facilitative belief to see if Connie is currently open to entertaining alternative facilitative beliefs about her father. We make a therapeutic judgment that there is a need for altering current beliefs about the past when there is strong negative affect present. We believe this ongoing emotional suffering may contribute to present physical symptoms.

LMW: Because sometimes I've heard people say, "I've come to learn other things about him, and it's softened my feelings toward him." [*Connie agrees that it is possible for others but says it is not true for her. The clinician continues seeking possible origins of the belief.*]
LMW: You feel like he let your family down?
CONNIE: No, I just feel like he was an awful person.
LMW: And what is your understanding of why he was so awful?
CONNIE: Well, I realized he was sick. But he never tried to be different, and it was terribly hard on us kids.
LMW: So, how mean was mean? How mean was he? [*Connie explains that he was physically abusive.*]

CONNIE: Mostly I picture him being drunk or crabby. You couldn't look at him sideways.

LMW: So, your memories are not very pleasant. His abuse to your mom and to you children. That's not a great legacy. [*The clinician now broadens the conversation about the father to include other family members' perspectives.*] How does your mother talk about him?

CONNIE: Well the stress is gone. She says she loved him. She has some beliefs that she could have done something different.

We believe in the importance of speaking the client's language. Here the client spontaneously uses our language of "beliefs." The therapeutic conversation then shifts from this affect arousal and exploration of a belief back to concrete genogram information about the cause of the father's death and his age at death.

CONNIE: He was just in his chair. My mom said he snored a couple of times, she went over, and he was gone.

LMW: My! So, how old was he? I missed that.

CONNIE: Forty-seven.

LMW: Forty-seven! Wow! [*The way has now been paved for Connie to pronounce a startling belief about her family.*]

CONNIE: We don't have a very long lifeline in our family.

LMW: He [Connie's father] was a very young man, wasn't he? [*Then the clinician seizes the moment to speak the unspeakable and further explore the belief.*] So when you say you don't have a long lifeline in your family, what do you think about that for yourself?

CONNIE: I don't think I have one either.

LMW: You don't? When did you start believing that?

CONNIE: When I had my heart attack.

LMW: Which was?

CONNIE: Last year.

LMW: Last year. Okay. Well I'd like to, that's very helpful for me, what you've given me about the picture of your family. I guess I didn't ask you about brothers and sisters though yet . . .

This segment of therapeutic conversation seems to be right at the heart of the matter, confirming a presession hypothesis that the experience of a life-shortening illness invites questions about mortality and death and, therefore, constitutes a wake-up call about life. The clinician acknowledges the belief about not having a very long lifeline, inquires about it briefly, and then resumes the genogram discussion. The gambler's rhythm is apparent again. Observe how the clinician showed curiosity about this important belief and then, in a surprising shift back to the genogram, left the topic. LMW's choice at this point to "walk away" from a therapeutic moment that appeared so "hot" and "right on" was influenced by her belief that a context for change had not yet been fully created, the presenting problem had not yet been distinguished, and thus exploration of this important belief would have been premature.

Once this segment of the genogram was finished, the clinician began the important work of distinguishing the problem by asking the client what she perceived the problem to be. This phase of distinguishing the problem began 25 minutes into the interview.

LMW: Well, that's very helpful. I'm sure you can see how all that comes to play, the struggles and challenges of life that you've had. So now what is the main concern that brought you here to us?

CONNIE: I'm just a bag of nerves, and I just can't shake it. This all stems from my mom getting this operation. I don't know if I've come to terms with my own mortality. Ever since I knew she was getting this [operation], I've been upset, and it won't go away. And then the panic attacks started [*crying*] so I put up with that, and at first I thought, "Oh, I'm going to have another heart attack," and it's been like that ever since. I settled down somewhat for a while, and then mom had her operation [*still crying*] and here I am.

LMW: And so, even though you've seen your mother progressing, it hasn't made you feel less anxious.

CONNIE: No.

Her mother's progress is not a difference that makes a difference for Connie's beliefs and fears. The clinician now chooses to return to the issue of mortality and speaks the unspeakable again by reintroducing the idea of a possible fear of death. This ability to bring up difficult issues again and again, at different points in the session, compresses the work. We wonder if the repetition softens the biopsychosocial–spiritual structure through the multiple perturbations.

LMW: And how do you explain it to yourself? One explanation you started to give me was you're coming to terms with your own mortality. Is that part of the explanation, or how do you explain to yourself that you're, as you say, "a bag of nerves"? [*The clinician facilitates talking about something that is very difficult by using the client's own language.*]

CONNIE: I'm always waiting for what's going to happen to me next.

LMW: So, you're more worried about yourself than your mother right now? [*Clinician draws distinctions about the object of Connie's anxiety in another effort to bring forth the belief at the heart of the matter.*]

CONNIE: I'm not so worried about mom any more because she's doing
good. She's coming along fine.

LMW: Yes?

CONNIE: And now it's me I guess, and I can't think of anything else
[*crying again*].

Seeking the family member's explanation of her illness—"How do
you explain to yourself that you're, as you say, a 'bag of nerves'"?—also
opens space for the illness narrative and the client's story of suffering
to unfold rather than a continuation of the medical story. The deliberate
focus on the illness narrative versus the medical narrative is further
elaborated in chapter 5.

Although the medical story of the anxiety attacks is important (the
symptoms of anxiety, the frequency, the length of time the symptom is
experienced), it cannot be explored to the exclusion of the personal
story of suffering. Uncovering this woman's beliefs about the anxiety
attacks revealed that her primary concern was about dying. Her
thoughts about herself dying triggered her anxiety attacks; reciprocally,
the anxiety attacks reinforced her fear of dying. She was trapped in the
worst possible constraining belief of, "I am going to die as a result of an
anxiety attack." One way for the clinician to begin to free her from the
oppressively constraining belief that perpetuated the problem was to
speak the unspeakable with these words: "You're coming to terms with
your own mortality." This was the nodal point of the woman's suffering, and until now she had been suffering alone with her belief. This
very frank disclosure makes it possible for alternative views, beliefs,
and solutions to be offered.

At this point, 30 minutes into the interview, WLW phoned in to the
session with the following suggestion:

WLW: Could you ask her [Connie] the question, "What questions do
you find you ask yourself in a day?"

LMW: Okay. The team was just wanting me to ask you, when you have
fears like this or anxiety, of course you're having a lot of conversations with yourself. We have conversations like you and I are having with each other, but we also have a lot of internal conversations
with ourselves. So the team is just wondering what kinds of conversations you've been having with yourself? Like what kinds of
questions do you ask yourself in a day?

We believe that beliefs are embedded in the questions one asks oneself, as well as in the stories one tells. The question about the questions
the client asks herself also provides an opportunity to talk about her
suffering, to share more of her illness narrative.

CONNIE: Well, I get up in the morning and I think to myself, "Now am I going to be able to get through today?" Or, "Is this going to start?" And sure enough, 15 minutes after I'm up [*still crying a bit*], I get that gut feeling in my stomach and I'm trembling inside and I'm trembling outside and I'm past the stage of, like at first, like I said I felt like I was going to have a stroke because the physical symptoms are so strange . . . that you just wonder what's going to happen. I've been to the doctor and that's what he thinks it is.

LMW: So you ask yourself the question, "Am I going to get through the day?"

CONNIE: Like am I normal today?

LMW: Or, "Am I going to be normal today?" Okay, and then, I'm sorry I didn't catch the last part of what you said. When you went to the doctor . . .

CONNIE: Well he said he thinks it's anxiety too.

LMW: And you had thought that's what it was, or did you believe that before you went to see him?

CONNIE: No, I didn't know what it was.

LMW: You didn't know what it was? Okay, so he gave you this idea that it was anxiety.

A further distinction the clinician makes is about the origin of the diagnosis. Where did the idea of "anxiety attacks" come from? Whose voice has been the voice of authority regarding the pronouncement of the diagnosis? The distinction between a physician-generated idea about diagnosis versus a client-generated idea provides the clinician with information about how tenacious the client's belief about the diagnosis may be.

Connie describes the physician's belief about the etiology: "He said, 'You're sitting on an edge and something pushed you over the edge.'" The clinician then shifted the conversation back to exploring how Connie had managed one of her other health problems, her arthritis.

The following segment demonstrates how important it is to ask a question several times. We believe that a therapeutic offering, be it in the form of a question, story, or opinion, has the possibility of being selected as a perturbation and that the perturbation changes the biopsychosocial–spiritual structure of a family member; this belief invites clinicians to give clients an opportunity to be perturbed and to explore those perturbations by asking a question again and sometimes again. Notice in the following segment how Connie's answer shifts from an enthusiastic *no* to a shaking of her head and a "well, I wondered" to "Yeah, I talked to myself many times, saying, 'I'll bet I'll be having one [coronary]'":

LMW: So you'd been struggling with that [arthritis], but I guess you've never thought about heart problems.

CONNIE: No, that's for sure!

LMW: Even with your mother having her coronaries? You never wondered if anything like that would happen to you?

CONNIE: [*shakes her head*] Well, I wondered. [*The clinician witnesses a little chink in the armor and pursues.*]

LMW: Did you? Did you ever ask yourself, "I wonder if I will have a coronary?"

CONNIE: Yeah, I talked to myself many times, saying, "I'll bet I'll be having one."

LMW: Oh, you did. So you did have that belief that "maybe I would too," but maybe not at 37 years old.

CONNIE: No, it was devastating to say the least!

From the point of view of what this interaction revealed, there is no need to apologize for what seems like redundancy. Therapeutic redundancy appreciates that family members are able to peel back their beliefs like an onion skin to reveal the belief at the heart of the matter. The therapeutic conversation shifted to Connie's beliefs about her prognosis when the clinician commended Connie for her efforts to take care of her health:

LMW: You've gone about this in a very ambitious way, taking care of your heart.

CONNIE: Because I don't want to have another attack, and I know I'm probably going to. I'm not being very logical. I know there's nothing wrong right now.

LMW: What do you think is ahead of you down the road?

CONNIE: Like Mom . . .

LMW: Which means?

CONNIE: I don't know how many more heart attacks I'll have. Hopefully none. Maybe not. But chances are . . .

LMW: And do you view this as a terrible thing that is happening to your mother? [*The clinician never assumes but rather asks.*]

CONNIE: No, not a terrible thing.

LMW: Do you say, "That's life; we all have to have something?" How do you think about it, when you say, "I'm going to end up like my mother"?

CONNIE: Well, I'll probably end up having what she's had.

LMW: What has been explained to you about your prognosis? You're saying what you've been guessing. What are the medical people saying?

CONNIE: That I should be reasonably well, whatever that means.

LMW: Reasonably well. So did you pursue what it meant? [*The clinician embeds the expectation of the client's voice being heard. The client explains that "reasonably well" means she will tire more easily, and so on.*] So how did you make sense of the fact that here you are, 39 years old, and you're having a coronary as a young woman. How did you explain that to yourself? [*The clinician makes a shift from beliefs about prognosis back to beliefs about etiology.*]

CONNIE: Well, I smoked.

The therapeutic conversation coevolves about the client's efforts to give up smoking and her belief about the family–hereditary factor. Once again Connie expresses her belief: "People die so young in our family for some reason." The clinician gently challenges that belief by asking again how old her mother is.

CONNIE: Sixty-nine.

LMW: Do you think that's a young age? Would you be happy if you lived to 69?

Connie responds that living to 69 would be great and would not constitute dying at a young age. The clinician remains curious about the client's beliefs about her anxiety attacks. Another distinction is drawn by the clinician: Is it important for the client to understand the etiology of the illness?

LMW: Is that important to you to find out why it's [the anxiety attacks] happening?

CONNIE: No, I just want to get rid of it.

LMW: You just want to get rid of it? Okay . . .

CONNIE: I want to get back to normal.

LMW: Okay, that's helpful for me to know because some people that I meet, they want to know why they have a problem.

CONNIE: Oh.

LMW: They're not going to be happy, it's like they're on a search and they're not going to be happy until they find out why they have a problem. And other people are like you. They don't care why they have it. They just want to get rid of it.

CONNIE: I just want to get rid of it.

LMW: So that helps me to know.

Distinguishing the client's disinterest in etiology from her interest in "getting rid of it" is important, because it will guide the focus of the clinician's attempts to coevolve therapeutic solutions. The strength of

Connie's desire to "get rid of it" rather than to understand "why" is explored through the clinician's mentioning of others who want to know why. Connie's persisting clear declaration that she wants to focus on getting rid of the problem prompts the clinician to explore attempted solutions. The clinician asks, "Okay. What have you been doing to try to deal with this?"

A list of attempted solutions emerges: involvement in a cardiac rehabilitation program after her heart attack and attempts to modify her diet, get more exercise, and stop smoking. Since the onset of the anxiety attacks, she has tried listening to relaxation audiotapes, reading self-help books, receiving acupuncture treatments, taking tranquilizers, keeping busy, and talking to her husband and friends about her concerns. The clinician shows great interest in and curiosity about the various things that Connie has tried in her attempt to eliminate her anxiety attacks. The clinician emphasizes her interest by audible note taking (White & Epston, 1990), writing down the attempted solutions as the client describes them, and by persistently asking, "What other things have you been trying?" Audible note taking underscores the efforts the client has already made and gives a strong implicit message that her words are important because they are recorded. Audible note taking evolves out of our cultural context, which tends to value the written word more than oral stories.

The usefulness of each attempted solution is pursued: Do you believe that helps? What did you experience when you tried that? Understanding what the client has tried provides the clinician with information about the resourcefulness of the client as well as what to avoid by way of suggestion or opinion that the client may have already attempted. This exploration embeds the clinician's belief that the client is capable of choosing, implementing, and evaluating solutions.

Another therapeutic move that is focused on further distinguishing the problem is the clinician's question, "Do you ever get a break from the anxiety attacks?"

CONNIE: Yes, lately I have been.
LMW: You do! And when do you get breaks from it? When do you notice it?

The clinician is interested in what change catches the client's attention and when it occurs. (See chapter 7 for a discussion of distinguishing change.) Connie reports she does not have anxiety attacks at night. A phone-in from the clinical team directs the clinician to ask, "What areas of your life have been affected and which areas have been untouched by the anxiety attacks?" The clinician invites the client to consider a distinction about what to name the client's experiences.

LMW: Do you call them panic attacks? We've been saying anxiety and panic attacks. Which would be the best description?

CONNIE: Well, they're both. To me anxiety is, well I don't know if you call it anxiety but I have this scared feeling inside all the time, like you know, how you are on a blind date, you get that nervous scared feeling in your stomach.

LMW: Yes.

CONNIE: Well, I have that all the time. The panic attacks—at first when they came, like I didn't know what they were and they were overwhelming. Fear just came over me and I figured, "This is it. I'm gone. I'm going to die." You know what I mean?

LMW: Yes . . .

CONNIE: And, it would be for no reason, or else I'd be shopping in a mall and it would come over me and I'm telling you it scared the living daylights out of me.

LMW: It must be very scary. It must be very scary to have the thought that you feel so anxious that you think maybe your life is over.

This clear empathic offering perturbs Connie. It is almost as if she thinks, "She now understands how difficult it has been. Now I can tell her how well I am presently doing." Note the very next statement that Connie makes:

CONNIE: Yeah. Really. It is just terrible. But they have quit basically.

LMW: They have quit?

CONNIE: Thank heavens.

LMW: So when you say they have basically quit, now would it be more accurate to talk about anxiety. . .

CONNIE: Yeah.

LMW: . . . than panic attacks? So when you say they've quit, that overwhelming feeling of "maybe I'm not going to make it" has quit? [*The clinician speaks in first person singular to intensify the experience of the client that the clinician understands.*]

CONNIE: I haven't had one for a couple of weeks or so.

LMW: Oh, wow.

CONNIE: But reading that book [a self-help book on how to cope with anxiety].

LMW: Yes . . .

CONNIE: She [the author] was saying to go with it [the anxiety attacks]. Like try and go with that, which I have tried to do and I think it's helped, like to think to yourself, "You're not going to die or you're going to be okay." Just let it go and it'll pass.

As the therapeutic conversation continues, the clinician persistently yet gently seeks ways to offer a facilitative belief and to distinguish the change that has occurred through Connie's own efforts.

LMW: I see. Instead of trying to fight it, it sounds like you've changed your thoughts while you're having it.

CONNIE: Yes.

LMW: You try not to say, "Gee I'm going to die."

CONNIE: Yes, at first that's what it was like and then I . . .

LMW: You have a different conversation with yourself now, do you?

CONNIE: Yes.

LMW: Wow, anything else that you are trying? The acupuncture did improve things a bit . . .

CONNIE: A little bit.

LMW: One of the books, some of those ideas, anything else that . . .

CONNIE: Yes, the medical books and talking. I talked to my girlfriend quite a bit.

LMW: Yes.

CONNIE: But. . .

LMW: So which of these different things do you think helped you, or is it a combination of all these things? Is there any one thing that's helping the most right now?

CONNIE: Right now?

LMW: Yes.

CONNIE: No, the only thing I can think of is maybe I'm looking at it a little different than I used to.

Here is the first evidence of the impact of the clinician's efforts. Recalibration in the moment has occurred. The clinician, of course, asks one more question to shore up this in-the-moment change:

LMW: Can you tell me, how are you looking at it now?

CONNIE: Well, I'm not so, I can take it more calmly, you know what I mean?

Through the process of considering all that Connie has done and accomplished to deal with the anxiety attacks and evaluating the degree to which each attempted solution has been helpful, the client's belief that the anxiety attacks are involuntary and uncontrollable seems to be challenged. The clinician seizes the opening to punctuate the change by distinguishing the frequency of the anxiety attacks. LMW suggests to Connie that the involuntary behavior is now more controllable because of a voluntary change in her cognition: When she thinks less about dying, she experiences anxiety attacks less frequently. Notice how the clinician punctuates this success with "wow," an expression of wonderment and delight. Evidence for a beginning shift in the client's belief is provided in her response to the clinician's "difference" question, "Is there any one thing that's helping the most right now?" The client offers that maybe she is now looking at things differently. The therapeutic conversation is now 48 minutes into the first session.

The clinician then shifts to asking about the best and worst advice that the client has been given. As with attempted solutions, knowing what advice has been useful or not useful provides the clinician with information about pitfalls to avoid. The client offers that the best advice was from her family physician, who recommended she seek counseling. The clinician again makes the distinction between what the client has been told by others and what she tells herself. The therapeutic intent is to strengthen the client's voice, which in turn will strengthen her beliefs about her ability to master her anxiety and panic attacks.

LMW: So what do you tell yourself about coming for counseling?

CONNIE: Well I thought about it quite a while. I need some help and I want to get it.

LMW: Well I admire you because you know, we still unfortunately have the idea in our society that when we go for professional help we should be embarrassed or we should be ashamed, and yet I look at it quite differently. I prefer to think that it's a sign of wanting to get past a problem. You've exhausted your own resources. You've tried a lot of different things on your own. Some things have helped somewhat, but now you want to get past the problem. You want to get further with it.

A distinction is drawn between society's ideas about therapy and the client's wisdom. In an elegant manner, the clinician compares the client's wisdom to society's constraining beliefs about therapy and uses this comparison not only to validate the client's idea that therapy might be useful but to commend her for her view. Her efforts to "get past" her problem are also commended. The idea of "getting past" embeds the suggestion that the client has a vision of how her life might be without the problem.

CONNIE: And if I don't, I'm going to end up somewhere, I don't know. I can't take it anymore.

LMW: Okay, let me just ask you a couple of other things. [*The intercom rings; the clinical team phones into the interview room and asks the clinician to explore Connie's catastrophic fear.*]

WLW TO LMW: What does she believe would happen if she did not get counseling at this point?

LMW: They just wanted me to follow up on your comment of your fear—if you didn't get help at this point, what would happen?

CONNIE: I think I'm going to end up having a nervous breakdown or something, because I can't think of anything else, I can't focus on anything. People talk to me and I don't hear them.

LMW: Okay, so just let me go back then for a second, Connie, because that's a scary thought for you to have right now, that you'd have a nervous breakdown. I don't know quite what that means for you; what would that mean?

CONNIE: Well, I just feel like I'm losing it.

LMW: Like you're losing it.

CONNIE: Yes.

LMW: Okay. In terms of being able to concentrate or to . . .

CONNIE: To function.

LMW: To function?

CONNIE: Yes.

Exploration of the catastrophic fear helps the clinician appreciate the immensity and intensity of the client's experience. Exploration of the meaning of a "nervous breakdown" is done in a careful and empathic manner. The next series of questions provide further opportunities for the client to give voice to her illness experience.

LMW: What are you not doing that you would most like to be doing right now? What are you not able to do that you would like to be able to do?

CONNIE: Ah, I'd like to stop thinking about myself.

LMW: Stop thinking about yourself.

CONNIE: What's bothering me? I don't even know what's bothering me anymore.

LMW: So you're doing a lot of self-therapy, are you, always trying to help yourself and having conversations about this and . . .

CONNIE: You know, even when the feelings pass, like in the evening or whatever, I'm still thinking to myself. I'm still thinking about it all the time. I'll think to myself, "Well, I really feel a lot better now, but I wonder when it's going to come back." I want to get past that.

LMW: Yes. You want to get past that. And it's getting past some of those questions that you're asking yourself. [*The clinician then returns to inquiring about the best and worst advice.*] Can I just go back? You told me what was helpful—some of the best advice you've received. What's some of the worst advice that you've been given in terms of trying to get a handle on this anxiety, these panic attacks?

CONNIE: To not think about it. It's one of the worst things people tell me. I mean that's unbelievable.

LMW: So the worst advice was, "Don't think about it."

CONNIE: Yes. "Think positive thoughts." Believe me, I've tried. And being told, "You have everything you want in your life; what do you have to complain about?"

The client points to an important distinction that we have uncovered in our work. "Thinking positively" is not the same as solidifying facilitative beliefs; neither is "stopping stinking thinking" the same as challenging constraining beliefs. The stance of (objectivity) taken in our clinical approach is substantially different from the objectivity-without-parentheses worldview that influences the "think positive, stop stinking thinking" approaches.

The therapeutic conversation in the first hour of the first session has centered on creating a context for changing beliefs. The clinician has carefully prepared the ground and used the genogram to begin engaging the client. The problem has been distinguished using a variety of questions related to internal conversations, attempted solutions, best and worst advice, and any openings to link behavior to cognition. Most important, efforts to track constraining beliefs were commenced.

At 58 minutes into the first session, the clinician asks the "one question question." The following interaction illustrates that the "one question question" involves more than just asking it. There is a process—a persistence and a tracking—involved.

LMW: Well, I guess that brings me to a question that we always like to ask in our first meetings with people we see here. If there was just one question that you could have answered during our work together, what would that one question be? What is the question that you would most like to try and get some help with or to get answered? What is the question that you would have for myself and the team to try and help answer for you?

CONNIE: How I can either get over this or how can you help me deal with it? Like put it in perspective or something.

LMW: Well now, that's a very important distinction, isn't it? Is your question how can I get over it, which means getting total control of it, or how can I deal with it?

The invitation to make a distinction has the potential not only to assist the client with what she really wants and needs but also to serve as another perturbation for the problem.

CONNIE: Well. . .

LMW: Which do you want? Do you want to be totally over it or do you just want . . .

CONNIE: I want to be totally over it.

LMW: You want to be totally over it. So you don't want to just learn how to live with it like you do with your arthritis?

CONNIE: No.

LMW: No, you don't want that for this, you want to be rid of it?

CONNIE: Yes.

LMW: Okay, should we say it that boldly?

CONNIE: [*laughs*] Yes, get rid of it!

LMW: Okay, "be rid of." [*Clinician is audibly note taking.*] And what exactly do we want to be rid of?

CONNIE: I want to be rid of these physical feelings I have all the time.

LMW: To be rid of the physical feelings.

CONNIE: Physical. Well once they're going, or once they're gone, hopefully it'll be gone up here. [*Client points to her head.*]

LMW: Okay, so the physical feelings of feeling so anxious inside, I just want to be real clear . . .

CONNIE: All the time, just like I could be on the ceiling, you know . . .

LMW: Okay, how about if I write, "Get rid of the physical feelings of being anxious inside?" Is that right?

CONNIE: Yes.

LMW: Because you're hoping that if we can do that, then you'll be thinking differently about it.

The client's answer to the "one question question" distinguishes the problem even more clearly. Note the process of asking the question and the persistence and tracking of the client's answer. Although the clinician has previously floated several "trial balloons" in terms of offering new connections between behavior and new perspectives, she makes no direct attempt to challenge or modify the client's beliefs until she has a clear understanding of what the beliefs are and has coevolved a context for changing beliefs. With the answer to the "one question question" and the distinctions that have been carefully coevolved about the nature of the problem, the clinician senses a context for change has been created. She seizes the opening and continues her previous sentence focusing on the reciprocity between thinking and behavior. With this deliberate shift, the clinician crosses the line from creating a context and distinguishing illness beliefs to challenging, altering, or modifying constraining beliefs at the heart of the matter:

LMW: Because you're hoping then that if we can do that, then you'll be thinking differently about it. Do you think it's possible that if you could change the way you think, that the physical feelings would go?

The client offers that if she could be rid of the physical feelings of anxiety, she would be rid of the troublesome thoughts in her head. Here the clinician invites the client to consider the converse: that changing her thinking might influence the physical experience of anxiety. This is a micromove of offering an alternative belief in a variation of the "if you were to believe . . ." question. (See chapter 6 for additional discussion of this micromove.)

CONNIE: Yes.

LMW: Which way do you think we have to tackle it?

CONNIE: Actually, I think if I could change the way I think, then the physical feelings will go away.

LMW: Okay. And what's the biggest challenge do you think to [changing] your thinking? What's the one thing that you think that's going to be the hardest to get rid of? What thought do you think is the hardest one to kick out of your mind?

The clinician uses these difference questions to distinguish the core belief: the belief at the heart of the matter. It is as though the clinician has a camera and once she sees a belief that intrigues her she zooms in, gently yet relentlessly drawing distinctions until the belief emerges.

CONNIE: I'd have to say from all the thinking I've done it has to have something to do with me having a heart attack—what triggered it. And maybe I have to just learn how to accept that better.

LMW: Well, okay, I just want to ask you a couple of more questions around that, and then I'd like to take a little break with my team. But I'm just curious to know, when you think about your fear about another heart attack, is it the fear about another heart attack or is it the fear about dying?

The clinician has had several indications from the client that a hypothesis about life-shortening illness and death may be useful to explore. She now invites the client to look death in the eye and explore all aspects of it.

CONNIE: I think dying.

LMW: You're more afraid of dying than you are about having another heart attack. Now when you think about dying, what about that is scary for you?

CONNIE: Ah [*starting to cry*] that I won't see my kids grow up.

LMW: So it would be a great loss for them and a great loss for you too. You want to be able to fulfill that dream for yourself, do you?

CONNIE: Yes.

LMW: Well, not dream—that goal, that desire that you have.

CONNIE: Yes. I don't expect to live till I'm 105, but I don't want to die at 43 either.

LMW: Do you have an idea in your mind of what age would be accept-able to die for you? [*This is a marvelous and courageous therapeutic question that speaks the unspeakable in total innocence and continues to explore the formerly unexplorable.*]

CONNIE: [*speaking through her tears*] Well, 70 I guess.

LMW: Seventy, so around your mother's age?

CONNIE: Yes, I'd be happy.

LMW: So if you could live as long as your mother, you would say that you would think of that as fair, because it's not the most fair that your sister and father died so young. But for you, if you live to 70 you'd say, "That was a reasonable length of time, it was fair."

CONNIE: I could be happy with that.

LMW: You could be happy with that. But dying now, dying between now and 70, you think that you would feel cheated?

CONNIE: Yes.

LMW: You would have felt you were cheated of some of your life.

CONNIE: Yes, I would.

LMW: So it's the fear of dying more than the fear of having a coronary [a heart attack]?

CONNIE: Oh, I don't know. Both. . . . The biggest thing I guess I often think to myself is, "How long am I going to live?" And I think that's what it is. [*Here is the core constraining belief, again, embedded in the question that she asks herself.*]

LMW: Well that makes perfect sense to me, then, why you're so darn anxious.

CONNIE: [*laughs*] But I don't, like, I'm not thinking about it all the time . . .

LMW: No, it's hard to have one thought, 24 hours a day. We all get dis-tracted by different things. I'm curious what percentage of the day is it troubling you, 'cause you're quite right, it's hard to think one thing all day long. What percentage of the time during the day does it trouble you?

This is an example of another micromove related to challenging, altering, or modifying constraining beliefs called "externalizing the problem" (for further elaboration, see chapter 6). The clinician uses a relative influence question to invite the client to consider how much influence she has over her illness:

CONNIE: You mean, how long am I going to live?

LMW: Yes, I mean . . .

CONNIE: Or the anxiousness?

LMW: Yes, the anxiousness and being troubled by that. Is it 50% of the day or 80% or 20% of the day that it troubles you?

CONNIE: Lately, probably 50% of the day . . .

LMW: Fifty percent.

CONNIE: Before, it was 100% of the day.

LMW: One hundred percent. Wow! So you've come down from 100% to 50%.

The client provides evidence of change, and the clinician deliberately begins to distinguish the change to make it more real, understandable, and sustainable (see chapter 7 for further elaboration of the macromove distinguishing change). The clinician shows amazement and curiosity at the accomplishment and invites the client to articulate what she has done to achieve this. Until this point, the client has been unaware of the substantial progress she has made. By distinguishing the change, the clinician embeds the idea that the client *does* have control because she has already had considerable influence over the problem.

CONNIE: Yes, like maybe whatever's bothering me is easing off, I don't know.

LMW: But how did you accomplish that? Going from 100 to 50%, that's terrific!

CONNIE: Because—from reading books and that I guess I understand more what it's about.

LMW: Okay, well that's a tremendous accomplishment . . .

CONNIE: Instead of wondering what's happening to me all the time.

LMW: But you see what I mean? Do you see that? I mean, that's a tremendous accomplishment. Do you think of that as a tremendous accomplishment to go from . . .

CONNIE: I never thought about it that way; I know I felt a little better.

LMW: Yes, to go from 100 to 50%, and the other thing I thought was a terrific accomplishment is that you haven't had a panic attack for 2 weeks.

CONNIE: Yes.

LMW: I mean that does say that you have really discovered some things that work for you.

CONNIE: But I don't know what it is.

LMW: Well, like you said, maybe it's a variety of things. Some of the things that you've read in the books, some of the things from the tape, the support of your husband—sounds like he's really come through for you, has been supportive, and has been there for you. Maybe it's no one thing, but you've been discovering a variety of things that seem to help. So I congratulate you! Look at the work you've already done—50% of the work for us. [*Connie laughs.*] We only have to help you with the other 50% now.

Until this point, the client seems to have been unaware of the amount of control she has over her thoughts and the extent to which her thoughts have centered around dying. These troubled thoughts were externalized by the clinician. The percentage that is now offered by the client—that she is troubled by these thoughts only 50% of the time—is evidence, we believe, of the impact of the therapeutic conversation. A best guess is that if the client had been asked the same question at the beginning of the session, she would have reported a higher percentage of time that she was troubled by anxiety and thoughts of dying. The conversation has drawn forth a new reality: The problem is not the panic attacks; rather, it is the fear of dying. It is not her behavior that is troublesome but her thoughts and the particular belief that she might die prematurely. The constraining belief—the belief at the heart of the matter—has been distinguished and challenged.

The clinician now takes a break to meet with the clinical team. The discussion with the clinical team centers on what to offer for the "end-of-session intervention." Of course, the phrase "end-of-session intervention" is a misnomer. It inadvertently suggests that the only intervention is the one that is offered at the end of the session. In our clinical practice, the clinician returns to the family and begins with a commendation, followed by offering the opinions or suggestions of the team. Initially, in the intersession discussion, the team discussed ideas to offer the family. As the discussion unfolded, however, so did a split opinion. The dilemma of the team is offered to Connie in the following manner:

LMW: Well, the team had a disagreement, and we're going to ask you to help us out with this. The disagreement was a very positive disagreement. First of all, though, the team wanted me to convey to you how impressed they are with your coping with two serious chronic illnesses. You've got arthritis, and you've been dealing with that and trying to live alongside it. And I'm really impressed with that. I grew up in a home with my grandmother who had arthritis and suffered with it, so I have a real compassion for people who have arthritis. I admire how you've been trying to live alongside your arthritis and deal with that. Then to have another whammy—a coronary at a very young age. You've been trying to master it, trying to prevent having another one and all the things you've been doing with that. But then these anxiety and panic attacks snuck up. [*The distinction is drawn between Connie's chronic illness (arthritis) that she "lives alongside of" and the life-threatening illness (coronary) that she wants to master in order to prevent another.*]

CONNIE: Yes.

LMW: They set you back. You were making all this great progress with managing and maintaining your health and trying to prevent having another coronary at a young age. Like you say, you'd like to live at least until your mother's age . . .

CONNIE: Yes.

LMW: So here's where we, the team members, differ though. The team certainly agrees that you've made wonderful progress. We are all just thrilled to say, "On her own, she went from 100% down to 50% being scared and fearful and anxious and panic attacks related to a fear of dying." However, here's where we differ. Part of the team thinks that maybe it would be better to continue to see you, but that you continue what you've been doing and keep discovering things that work for you. They said, "Listen! she's doing it on her own. She keeps discovering things that are working—reading books helps, talking to her husband helps. She's done it on her own. She doesn't need us to keep giving her more ideas." So this part of the team thinks we could learn from you if you would go out and keep discovering things that help you, and we could learn from you. You could come back and tell us what's helping, what's working, and we could pass it on to other families and learn from that. But the other part of the team says *no!* They think that maybe we could offer some ideas that would be helpful to you. Now we don't know if these ideas will help. Maybe [they'll] only help like the acupuncture. We don't know if [they] will help you go all the way to the 50%; maybe we could help you 10% . . .

CONNIE: Yes.

LMW: . . . or 15%, and then you would do the other 35% or something. So that's where we disagree. So we said, "Why not leave it up to Connie to decide?" Do you want the first option, that you continue to meet with us if you would like to? You would keep trying to discover things that help bring this down from 50% of being so fearful of these troubling thoughts to 40% or 20%. Hopefully this would help you reach your ultimate goal, to be rid of these thoughts. Or do you want to go the other option? I can tell you what ideas the team had and you could try them out and see if they're useful. Or I guess another option is we could save our opinions if you wanted to come back for one or two sessions without hearing our ideas and try more on your own and let us know how it goes. So, whatever you would like. We disagreed whether to give you our ideas or have you keep trying on your own . . .

CONNIE: On the weekend, I felt pretty good, you know and . . .

LMW: Well you did, yes.

CONNIE: So I thought, I'm done with it, you know.

LMW: Yes, so I'm sure coming here sort of stirred things up a bit and . . .

CONNIE: Yes, but you see I feel better now just talking about this, so maybe I should just try on my own a little bit. Yes, give it a try.

The client says that she is better and teaches us once again that the therapeutic conversation is enough! There really is no further need for other ideas to be offered by our clinical team. She is prepared *to take her own advice* and develop her own ideas about how to manage her anxiety attacks.

LMW: Sure, I certainly would be encouraging of you to do that. We're just so impressed with what you've accomplished already.

CONNIE: But what I want to know is like, if I have to take a tranquilizer, am I supposed to feel guilty for taking one?

LMW: I think that depends on what you believe about that. Do you believe . . . ?

CONNIE: I don't know, I just get so worked up . . .

LMW: Yes? What is your belief about taking medication to help you overcome some anxiety?

CONNIE: Well, I certainly wouldn't want to get addicted to them, let's put it that way.

LMW: Yes, and that's what you're scared of?

CONNIE: Yes, I think that's what I'm scared of, so I don't know.

LMW: Well, could I just make a comment? I've only met you for a brief time this afternoon, but you strike me as a woman who is very sensitive about those kinds of things. You've had alcohol and drug abuse problems in your family [she had reported her father was an alcoholic].

CONNIE: Yes.

LMW: You're very sensitive to that, and I think you would use your own intuition and your own instincts to know if that was becoming a problem or that you needed to cut back before it would even become a problem . . .

CONNIE: Yes, that I would know.

LMW: Yes, I think you've got good instincts in that area. You've been sensitized to it because of your family life . . .

CONNIE: Yes.

LMW: I don't have that concern for you. If that's the fear behind taking a tranquilizer, that you might get addicted, I have full confidence in you that that wouldn't happen. So I would suggest just take them as you think is best for you.

CONNIE: Let me try on my own then.

LMW: Okay, would you be willing to come back? I know it's a long drive. I know it's asking a lot for you to come back and tell us what you're learning and how things are going but we would very much like that, if you would want to. But I don't want to impose that on you.

CONNIE: Sure, like how long a time span should I go?

LMW: Whatever you think.

CONNIE: Like what if I go 2 weeks or something, and I'm not getting any better?

LMW: Maybe then we should set an appointment and then you know that you've got that time to come back and report that to us about how things are going. Then we can learn from you about what was better or what didn't go so well. Are you still 50% from your goal, or are you now 45% from your goal? Or maybe it's a miracle— you're only 10% from your goal! So that'll be tremendous!

While the team phones with an appointment date, they offer, "Just tell her that we're impressed that she would think of 2 weeks because, obviously we're even wondering if she's maybe conquered 55% or 60%, because someone at 50% might say a week. I think she's changed 65%, [don't] you?"

LMW: Okay great, thanks. Well guess what the message is from the team? They're saying, "If Connie is saying that she could wait 2 weeks," they think maybe you've mastered [the problem] 55%. They think you're not giving yourself enough credit.

CONNIE: Yes, maybe. I get so down on myself . . .

LMW: They said, "We think she's probably already a little bit further along than she thinks she is right now." So they said, "Listen, would you please pass on to Connie that we think that maybe it's even 55% not 50%!"

CONNIE: Well maybe.

LMW: So they've got even a bit more confidence . . .

CONNIE: I think that maybe if I can think better of myself . . . I'm being hard on myself.

LMW: Well Connie, I've really enjoyed meeting with you and learning from you, and I just want to congratulate you. That is a tremendous accomplishment to be trying to overcome this fear and these thoughts you have. You've done it, you know—50% is a tremendous attempt. You've been trying a variety of things, and the thing that we believe is that each person knows what's best for them. I mean we can offer different ideas, but in the end, you know what works for you. We can say, "Do this, do that, do the other thing." But that's why part of the team said, "Listen! Connie's doing so well. Why don't we just let her go and encourage her to just keep discovering what's working for her and have her come back and report to us, and we can learn from that and pass it on to other families."

Session 1 ends with a crescendo and an effort to solidify the condensed and compressed changes that have evolved within the session. Throughout the session, the clinician not only maintains therapeutic curiosity but continually invites the client to be curious about her situation and possibilities. The session demonstrates what happens when the context for change is cocreated: Multiple distinctions are drawn; therapeutic risk taking allows the clinician to go past the usual or expected; connections between thoughts, feelings, and behavior are drawn forth; and the belief at the heart of the matter is identified and challenged.

## SECOND SESSION

Although Connie suggested at the close of the first session that she would like to schedule the second session in 2 weeks, winter storms prevented her from keeping the appointment. Consequently, the second session with Connie took place 8 weeks after the first session. Once again, she was seen individually. A segment of videotape that is 12 minutes in length was chosen by the clinical research team as the salient change segment for this session. The conversation between the clinician and client centers around the client's being invited to describe the changes that have occurred. The clinician's stance is one of insatiable curiosity—asking questions about the change the client is reporting and showing enthusiasm, delight, and surprise when change is reported. (Refer to chapter 7 for more elaboration on distinguishing change.)

CONNIE: . . . and so I'm just trying to take an attitude.
LMW: How have you done that? What kinds of things have you done? Do you think you are less hard on yourself than when I met you?

CONNIE: Yes.

LMW: Yes?

CONNIE: I've tried to let loose, kind of, you know . . .

LMW: Yes? Terrific . . . so how do you . . .

CONNIE: Actually I feel 100% better than . . .

LMW: Really! Wow! [*Connie's laughing.*] So, I'm dying to ask you all kinds of questions around that, but tell me, I'm still curious about how you sort of loosened up on yourself.

Therapeutic transparency is shown in the sharing of the clinician's dilemma about what question to ask next. It may be a deliberate way of slowing down the exploration of change to ensure that the exploration is thorough and useful. However, it also shows the clinician talking about the therapeutic process in an explicit manner. Notice the implicit message the clinician provides when she shows curiosity about how the client explains the change. The questions are directed toward giving credit for the change to the effort and expertise of the client rather than the expertise of the clinician. Of course, it is both.

CONNIE: Well, I still haven't quit smoking yet. I think about it and I think now, "What are you doing to yourself?" And, "you shouldn't be doing this." But I think, well, I'm not going to. I don't know how to explain it.

LMW: Yes.

CONNIE: I think to myself, well, don't feel so guilty, you know, you're trying . . .

LMW: Yes, that's what I was curious about. What have you been telling yourself to not be so hard on yourself? So one thing you tell yourself is, "Don't be so guilty!"

The clinician focuses on a theme from Session 1: that internal conversations and behavior are linked. The clinician invites the client to describe the internal conversations: what she is saying to herself that enables the change. The client reports a change in behavior, so the clinician goes after an exploration of how the cognition has changed.

CONNIE: Yes. [*pause*]

LMW: This is terrific.

CONNIE: You know, I'm trying to make an effort to do the best I can with the condition I have and . . .

LMW: So that's another thing you tell yourself, "I'm doing the best I can." Let me get that down, okay? This is terrific! "I'm doing the best I can."

Audible note taking, repeating the client's words verbatim, and refocusing are all used to reinforce the client's changes and to keep the conversation focused on distinguishing that change. All of these moves by the clinician are designed to make the change more real and to affirm the change. The client is accorded ownership for the change. The clinician refuses to get sidetracked by problems at this point in time. One may have been tempted to inquire about the description of guilt about smoking: when, where, why? Instead the clinician asks, "What have you been telling yourself to *not* be so hard on yourself?"

CONNIE: Like I know I could probably do better, but I feel like I'm doing pretty good.

LMW: Right! Wow, so you're telling me that since—so now let's get into the details of how things have been going. You're saying, since you saw me last, you said things are 100% better.

CONNIE: Oh yes, it's gone.

LMW: One hundred percent? What is gone?

CONNIE: I don't feel nervous anymore. [*laughing*]

LMW: You don't feel nervous?

CONNIE: Well I do, off and on, but not near like I was.

LMW: So you would say, 100% better?

CONNIE: Oh yes.

LMW: So when I was asking you last time . . . you said last time that you thought you had been able to manage taking your anxiety from 100% anxious to 50%, and so now you're telling me . . .

CONNIE: I'd say 95%.

LMW: So now you're 95% anxiety-free.

CONNIE: Yes.

LMW: So, you're just keeping 5% around . . .

CONNIE: Mmhm . . .

LMW: . . . just for old time's sake.

CONNIE: Yes, really. Yes.

LMW: So 95% anxiety-free! That is incredible.

CONNIE: Yes, I feel pretty good, actually, compared to what I did feel.

LMW: Yes, 'cause anxiety was really ruling you, wasn't it?

CONNIE: Mmhm.

The use of percentages helps describe the change in a concrete manner. The meaning of the remaining 5% is explored through humor, and the clinician embeds volition, such that any amount of anxiety that remains is not to be feared but is being kept "for old time's sake." The clinician shows continued curiosity about the client's expertise in reducing the influence that anxiety had over her. The client's effort, rather than the clinician's effort, is elevated, articulated, and celebrated. The client emerges as creator and chooser of change. The changes become more real, more palpable. There is awe and wonder of change present and the belief that change deserves respect and attention. Throughout the segment, we experience the irony that the tenacity of the clinician, which seems to drag things out, actually speeds up change.

LMW: So can you tell me how you got rid of the other 45%?

CONNIE: Well I think just talking about it here helped a lot.

LMW: Yes.

CONNIE: Like I don't consciously think of it that way, but I think it did, because talking to a stranger that I don't know . . .

LMW: That's really impressive, isn't it . . .

CONNIE: Yes.

LMW: To be able to go in and talk to somebody you don't know—that's hard, I mean to open up about our personal lives. So part of it was talking here.

CONNIE: Yes and I think . . .

LMW: What else?

CONNIE: I try to think now instead of wondering what's going to happen to me, I try and accept things the way they are. I try to do it that way instead of always wondering when and what's going to happen.

LMW: Okay, so accepting things the way they are instead of thinking about the future? Is that right?

CONNIE: Instead of thinking, like, "What's going to happen? Am I going to die?"

The client provides evidence that her belief about dying that was uncovered during the first session was indeed a core belief at the heart of the matter. Notice the way the clinician puts the client in the position of expert about her experience by inviting her opinion about the clinician's ideas.

LMW: Yes, I'm sure that's tough. That's a question I guess that we all would struggle with if we thought about it. However, because of having an illness . . .

CONNIE: Yes.

LMW: . . . those questions come to your mind more than someone like myself, who isn't struggling with an illness. I don't think about those questions as much, but they're there for all of us, aren't they?

CONNIE: Yes.

LMW: You just made me think of something I was going to ask your opinion on. I just wrote a chapter with one of my students about dealing with a life-threatening illness. I was trying to write about one of the hardest things, I think, for people with a life-threatening illness, or what I call a life-shortening illness. In this particular family we wrote about, the mother had cancer. I got this idea working with this family that we should try to make a difference between people worrying about when am I going to die . . .

CONNIE: Mmhm.

LMW: . . . and make a distinction between worrying about when you're going to die and your prognosis.

CONNIE: Yes.

LMW: Because a lot of times you get a diagnosis, like in your case, a coronary, and immediately we associate that with, "Gee, when am I going to die?"

CONNIE: Right.

LMW: And people get so focused on when are they going to die . . .

CONNIE: That's right.

LMW: . . . that they don't live anymore. So one of the things I was suggesting in this paper was that nobody can predict the time of death. Even with this young woman who was given a prognosis that she had a few months to live, nobody can really predict that.

CONNIE: Yes.

LMW: So I was trying to write about that. It's helped me in my thinking a lot, in working with this family. I was wondering, what do you think about that idea? Do you think it's useful?

The client is put in the expert position by virtue of her own experience of coming to grips with death; the clinician is put in the expert position of coming to grips with the knowledge derived from clients' narratives about their struggles with prognosis.

CONNIE: Yes, I do, because it's hard not to think about it all the time, like when am I going to die, it really is. Not to say that I'm going to die, but I could, you know.

LMW: Yes. And it is something that I'm sure can preoccupy you, can't it?

CONNIE: It can. Some days I catch myself thinking about it quite a bit.

LMW: So how do you separate that for yourself? You had an experience with a serious illness, but on the other hand not always focusing on "when am I going to die" because that keeps you from living.

CONNIE: Well, the way I've tried to think of it is I try and do what I can do, like exercise and eat right and stuff like that to prevent another one. Yet I know I probably will, 'cause I think that's the way it goes.

LMW: You probably will?

CONNIE: Have another one. But I've tried to think, I've tried to be calmer about it. You know what I mean?

LMW: Yes, so in the meantime you're trying to focus on living as much as you can . . .

CONNIE: Trying to, yes.

LMW: . . . and living as fully as you can, it sounds like, as well, exercise, eating, and . . .

CONNIE: Yes.

LMW: Well, good for you! Okay. So you think the idea I have about not getting so focused on trying to predict the time of death is a useful idea for families . . .

CONNIE: Yes.

LMW: Okay, not focusing. [*writing*] Okay. Are there other things that you can think of that you've done that have [enabled you] to drop the anxiety 45%?

CONNIE: Not really. If I feel myself getting quite nervous and I start getting short of breath, I try to take deep breaths and concentrate on relaxing. That is what I try to do. That seems to help.

LMW: Terrific, so you've learned ways, relaxation ideas.

CONNIE: Yes.

LMW: Relaxation ideas. . . . Wow! You really haven't let anxiety rule the roost anymore, have you?

CONNIE: Not anymore, no.

The move of repeating and refocusing on what the client has accomplished is central to distinguishing change. The clinician looks for every way to accentuate, embellish, acknowledge, and distinguish the specifics of change. What cognition, affect, or behavior has changed that explains the change and makes it more understandable? The clinician's belief here is that if change can be made more real, more understandable, and more of an outcome because of the client's efforts, it is more likely that the client will be able to sustain the change.

LMW: Do you think it's a good thing to keep 5% around? I mean are you a person who believes you have to get rid of even the 5%?

CONNIE: I think I'll always have it with me. I mean, I'm just that type of person.

LMW: Yes. So you think 5% is just an acceptable part of your nature?

CONNIE: Yes, like I never really thought about it before, you know, my nerves and that, until I had it real bad. And then compared to what I feel like now, I've always felt like this. But I never really thought about it before. I just figure, you know that's just the way you are.

LMW: Yes, so there is 5% of you that's just a natural part of your makeup?

CONNIE: Yes.

LMW: So if you didn't get rid of that 5%, you wouldn't be down on yourself?

CONNIE: No.

The belief that cure must be a 100% reduction in symptoms is challenged. The move that is offered is an attempt to understand the remaining 5% and to offer that perhaps keeping 5% around is good, natural, and even "part of the client's nature." The client's accomplishments are not allowed to be diminished, not even by 5%!

LMW: Oh good, so you would feel good about yourself. You'd still say, "Gee! this is a tremendous accomplishment." Because you know . . . it's terrific what you've accomplished!

Throughout the process of distinguishing change, there has been a focused, purposeful effort by the clinician to reflect, distinguish, and embellish the changes so that they are made more relevant and more important than perhaps the client may have initially viewed the changes. Not only has there been excitement and enthusiasm shown by the clinician, but the change has been amplified and elevated to a level to be marveled at.

CONNIE: Yes. When I came home from here [the FNU], it was a couple of weeks after that I was bad, and I figured, "Oh God! Nothing's going to work." Then it just gradually, every day, it just started getting less and less and less. Well, obviously, it's in my head.

LMW: Has anybody else, I'm wondering, noticed this change in you?

This is a major shift from the exploration of the client's description, attribution, and explanation of her improvement to a focus on what others have noticed. We have called this move "reflecting on another's reflections."

CONNIE: No.

LMW: Nobody's noticed? You were pretty good at masking your anxiety?

CONNIE: Yes.

LMW: So your friends, your husband, your kids wouldn't have picked up on this?

CONNIE: Oh, I think my husband knows. I'm not so crabby all the time, if you could put it that way.

LMW: Ah, so that's one difference. If he was here he would maybe not comment on the anxiety, but he would comment on that difference in you?

CONNIE: Yes.

LMW: Not as crabby? Anything else that your friends or family would notice about you?

CONNIE: No.

LMW: No? They would say, "No, I don't see much difference in you." So it's really . . .

CONNIE: All in the inside.

LMW: . . . inside, um. Do you think you would like to have anybody know about your success story?

The client offers that she doesn't think anyone has noticed the change. Rather than letting that idea diminish the change, the clinician gives the client credit for how skillful she was at masking her anxiety from others.

CONNIE: Not really.

LMW: No?

CONNIE: 'Cause it, I don't know, it's not really, I don't really consider it a success story.

LMW: What kind of a story is it for you?

CONNIE: I don't know.

LMW: The story of . . . could I tell you something? I think of it as a success story.

CONNIE: Oh, is that right?

The client is still not sure her efforts should be called a "success story." The clinician explores what the client thinks they should be called and then offers the idea of "success story" with an authoritative voice, which validates the change. Notice the way the clinician invites the client into her view by punctuating it with an invitation: "Could I tell you something?" There is embellishment of the rationale and the comparison of this client with others. The transparency of the clinician is seen in her explanation of why she uses family stories to be helpful to other families. In so doing, the client story and experience are elevated and connected to those of other families.

LMW: Absolutely. I've worked with a lot of families over the last 15 years, and you're the first woman I've met who . . . you know, I've met other women who've had coronaries, I've worked with other women with coronaries. But you're the first woman I've met, though, that was able to kick out 95% anxiety, down from 50% to 45% to only 5% in just a couple of months.

CONNIE: Oh, is that right?

LMW: Yes, you're the first one that I've met. So to me that is an incredible success story.

CONNIE: Well, I don't know, I can't explain why it went away or anything. You know it's really hard.

LMW: Well, I think some of the explanation is just what you've been
telling me. Accepting things the way they are, relaxation ideas, and
talking about it.

CONNIE: Yes.

LMW: Because, talking about anxiety is one of the things that anxiety
doesn't like . . .

CONNIE: Yes.

LMW: Because if you don't talk about it and you keep it to yourself, then
that's great for anxiety because then it builds up more. But if you
talk about it—anxiety doesn't like it much when you talk about it.

CONNIE: Yes, and I think that's probably what helped, I really do, to be
able to sit here and say what I want to say and not worry about
offending somebody's feelings. I really do, you know.

LMW: Wow, well I think you're an incredible success story. In fact, so
much so, I have a favor to ask you. [*Connie laughs.*] I'm wondering
if you would be willing, that the next time I meet another woman
with a coronary or maybe a man with a coronary, and they're very
anxious like you have been about the future for themselves and
what's going to happen to them and the terrible fear that they
might die soon from it, would you allow me to tell them about
you?

CONNIE: Sure. [*no hesitation*]

LMW: And I could relate your success story?

CONNIE: Sure.

LMW: And what you did?

CONNIE: Oh yes.

LMW: And these ideas?

CONNIE: Sure, it's worth a try.

To give the clinician's rationale for calling the client story a success
even more credibility, the clinician asks if she can share the client story
with others, implying that it is a story that will help others. We have
called this move "publishing success." This move expands the audience
even more dramatically. It puts the client in the observing position:
observing others observing her success. The clinician later expands on
this idea by asking the client for permission to show the videotape of
this client talking about her "success story" in conquering anxiety.

This segment of therapeutic conversation from the second session
with Connie documents incredible changes reported by the client in
relation to her cognition (as evidenced by her internal conversations),
her behavior, and her affect (a dramatic decrease in her symptoms of

anxiety). This segment powerfully illustrates that it is not sufficient simply to acknowledge the change and offer congratulations. Instead, the changes need to be distinguished and languaged until new beliefs and stories have coevolved through the leadership the clinician provides in continually rolling over change in every possible way. The client's efforts, experience, and expertise in the change process are specified, amplified, and celebrated.

In the following segment, the clinician shares another success story about a man who faced cancer and a heart attack at a young age. A sermonette by the clinician invites the client into a reflecting position:

LMW: . . . and he wrote a book about it because after that not only did he have a coronary but then he had testicular cancer . . .

CONNIE: Oh, no!

LMW: . . . so he had these two major blows in a year, one right after the other, and he wrote a book about his experiences with illness. I'd like to get your opinion on one thing he said: "Illness takes away parts of your life, but in doing so it gives you the opportunity to choose the life you will lead" [Frank, 1991, p. 1].

CONNIE: Aha, it does.

LMW: Would you agree with this statement?

CONNIE: Yes.

LMW: "Illness takes away parts of your life, but in doing so it gives you the opportunity to choose the life you will lead."

CONNIE: It does.

LMW: I was just thinking about that as you were talking in the last couple of minutes. When I was asking you about your advice to others, it seems to me like you've chosen to live a life, not to focus on dying but focus on living . . .

CONNIE: Aha.

LMW: . . . and living the best you can even with the thought that perhaps in the future, you may have another coronary, or you may not. I think reading a book like that might help people . . .

This sermonette summarizes this woman's struggle, striving, and success. At the end of the session, Connie was invited to observe with the clinician from behind a one-way mirror while the clinical team reflected on Connie's successes. The culmination of our work with Connie was embodied in the following therapeutic letter that was sent to her:

Dear Connie:

Season's greetings from the Family Nursing Unit! As part of completing our clinical work with families, we send a closing letter as a summary and record of our time spent together. We had the opportunity to meet with you on two occasions.

It was only a short time ago, Connie, that you presented yourself at the Family Nursing Unit as a woman with many questions of herself. During our first session, you related your story of a life-threatening event, specifically a heart attack which had occurred the previous year. You then experienced your mother having triple bypass surgery six months later. This surgery drew forth the similarities in your lives. It was at this time that anxiety entered your life, showing itself as panic attacks. You asked the questions of us that you had been asking of yourself: "Am I going to get through this? Am I normal? Am I going crazy?"

You had a strong belief that if you could change the way you were thinking, the physical feelings of anxiety would go away. You stated the hardest thought to kick out of your mind was the fear of another heart attack. Underneath this fear was the fear of dying and the resultant loss to your family.

Consequently, it was with great admiration and respect that we heard you answering these same questions for yourself, within our first visit together! You stated that anxiety had gone from 100% a day to 50%. You had been able to discover solutions such as: "think positive" [and] "keep busy," and reading about stress helped you to reduce anxiety. We were most impressed that you chose to continue to discover your own solutions to your challenges in life and not hear the solutions that our clinical team had to offer! By following your own instincts, we are convinced that you developed greater confidence in yourself.

It was during our second session that our admiration and respect for you grew ever further. You had not only managed to rid your life of 95% of the anxiety, but you had learned to appreciate yourself. "Don't feel so guilty" and "I'm doing the best I can" are new beliefs that you now tell yourself. These beliefs will serve you well in the future.

Connie, you are truly a woman of great courage, strength and tenacity. You are an example of the words of Arthur Frank (1991) in his book *At the Will of the Body*. He wrote: "Illness takes away parts of your life, but in doing so it gives you the opportunity to choose the life you will lead" (p. 1). You are living these words.

As nurses, we have learned from you that we are truly witnesses to the impact of a life-threatening illness on a woman's life and the miracle of human strength and soul. We have learned that the choice of choosing to focus on living rather than dying is a true celebration. You are your own ship's captain and can choose your course through the stormy and still waters of life with courage. When you believe in yourself, you increase your options.

It was truly a privilege to work with you, Connie. We have sent you a certificate of celebration as a reminder of the seas you have explored and charted. Season's greetings!

> Sincerely,
> Lorraine M. Wright, R.N., Ph.D., and other members of the clinical nursing team

## CONCLUSION

This clinical exemplar offers an inspiring clinical story of the application of our advanced clinical practice approach. It highlights how the beliefs and expertises of both the client and family members can be brought together in poignant and meaningful therapeutic conversations. In the end, both the client and clinician are changed through conversations of affirmation and affection rooted in therapeutic love.

# EPILOGUE

THIS BOOK WAS WRITTEN in the midst of intermittent and persistent illnesses. When we commenced the book, we believed that our personal illness narratives, as offered in the Introduction, would only be retrospectives. However, as the manuscript for this book unfolded, an increase of illness experiences in our own families occurred, and our experiences as family members relating to health care professionals increased also. An irony was that we often could not write about beliefs, families, and illness because we were using our energies and ideas to participate as family members when illness was ebbing and flowing. These deeply affective experiences as family members have intensified our belief in the need for families to be provided with opportunities to talk about their illness experiences and to obtain assistance to decrease their suffering.

Through the writing of this book, our biopsychosocial–spiritual structures have been changed, as have our beliefs about beliefs, families, illness, therapeutic change, and clinicians. Our beliefs about beliefs have been revisited, refined, and sometimes refuted, as have been our beliefs about families, illness, therapeutic change, and clinicians. We believe more passionately concerning some things and less regarding others. Some of the things we believe more passionately include the following:

- We believe that beliefs are the heart of healing.
- We believe illness is a family affair. Everyone in a family experiences the illness; no one family member "has" cancer, MS, chronic pain, or renal failure. From the onset of symptoms, through diagnosis and treatment, other family members are impacted by and reciprocally influence the illness.

288

- We believe illness invites a wake-up call about life, which usually leads one into the spiritual domain as the meaning of life is queried or reviewed.
- We believe there is a distinction between disease and illness and between medical narratives and illness narratives. We believe illness narratives include stories of sickness and suffering as well as stories of survival and strength that need to be told.
- We believe that the control paradigm of illness limits healing. Options for managing illness, such as making a place for illness, living alongside illness, and putting illness in its place, increase possibilities for healing.
- We believe cellular and "soulular" changes occur through conversations. Our network of conversations and our relationships can contribute to illness or wellness.
- We believe a clinician's worldview can open or close opportunities for family members to diminish their suffering from illness. We believe a worldview that facilitates therapeutic conversations is one that acknowledges another person as a legitimate other, even though one may not embrace or agree with the other's opinions.
- We believe one key to therapeutic change is a respectful, curious, nonoppressive, and compassionate relationship between a clinician and family members that facilitates discussion of even the most difficult topics and invites the consideration of alternative or modified beliefs.
- We believe therapeutic change is facilitated when the core belief—the belief at the heart of the matter—is distinguished and challenged or solidified. We believe that the gold nuggets worth panning for, in therapeutic conversations with families, are the core beliefs.
- We believe core constraining beliefs are not impacted through mantras of positive thoughts. The Stewart Smalley (*Saturday Night Live*) approach to life—"I'm smart enough, I'm good enough, and doggone it, people like me"—is not sufficient to alter constraining beliefs.
- We believe therapeutic change involves the synergism between the expertise of family members about the experience of illness and the expertise of the clinician about managing illness.
- We believe that distinguishing therapeutic change sustains and maintains change.
- We believe that changes in beliefs involve changes in the biopsychosocial–spiritual structures of family members and clinicians.

We want to balance the articulation of these stated beliefs with another belief: We believe it is important to review and question continually our own beliefs to uncover those that are no longer useful.

In Canada in the late 1950s, a favorite children's television program was about a delightfully curious young girl, Maggie Muggins, who was always excited about the ever-evolving events of life. At the end of each program, Maggie Muggins would turn to her older neighbor, Mr. McGarity, and say with enthusiasm, "I don't know what will happen tomorrow!" That is also our stance. We do not know what the next conversation with the next family will teach us, what beliefs of our own will be strengthened or challenged, or what new therapeutic move will unfold. We experience this therapeutic uncertainty as energizing. At this time, we find the whole notion of beliefs quite captivating and compelling. We believe that what we believe matters—very much.

# APPENDIX A

# Description of Research Families

XCERPTS OF THERAPEUTIC CONVERSATIONS with families are repeatedly used as examples throughout the book. All families have provided consent for their clinical stories to be used for research and publication. In addition to five research families (designated as Research Families 1 to 5), the clinical stories of other families from our practice have been used to illustrate particular aspects of the therapeutic process. To help the reader distinguish among families, each example has been described either as Research Family 1, 2, 3, 4, or 5 or as a clinical family. The names of families, as well as professionals unrelated to the Family Nursing Unit, University of Calgary, have been changed to protect their identities.

Detailed background information is provided here for each research family. The clinical records and videotapes of the five families were used in our funded, hermeneutic research project. (For a description of the research method, see Appendix B.) These families were chosen as "exemplary families" from a case review of families seen over a 4-year period (1989–1993) at the Family Nursing Unit, University of Calgary. We have defined *exemplary families* as families who showed and reported dramatic, positive therapeutic change during our clinical work with them, that is, cognitive, behavioral, or affective change; symptom reduction; or a combination of these types of change.

## RESEARCH FAMILY 1

Paul (age 63) and Alice (age 62) moved across Canada to care for their only son, Mark (age 34), who had been diagnosed with multiple sclerosis at age 27 (see genogram, figure A1). They had been living in Mark's home and caring for him for 3 years when they referred themselves to the Family Nursing Unit. The presenting problem was the parent's "difficulty in coping with tension in the home" related to the care of Mark. We worked with the family for four sessions over 6 months. Mark and his parents came to Sessions 2 and 3. Only the parents were seen in Sessions 1 and 4.

FIGURE A1

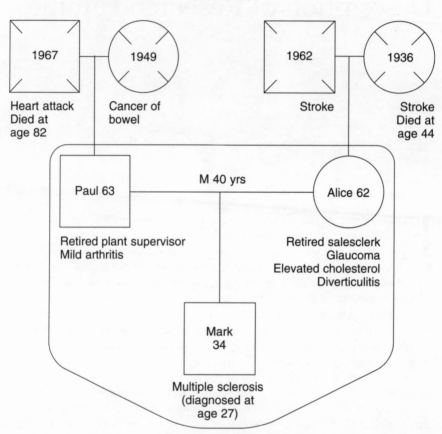

The encirclement indicates those
family members who live together

During the first session, each parent responded differently to the "one question question" (Wright, 1989). Mother: "How can we reduce the tension?" Father: "How can we get a break—both of us together?"

Approximately 1 year after the completion of the clinical sessions, the family participated in a follow-up evaluation interview. They reported being very satisfied with the assistance they had received from the Family Nursing Unit. The father said the family sessions "helped put my mind at ease. We are interested in going places now and don't feel like we are discarding our son." The mother offered that the family sessions "helped me speak freely about what was bothering me. I wasn't able to do that before." Mark reported that he was "now aware of more possibilities to solve problems." When asked who benefited most from the family sessions, both the mother and father agreed that their son had benefited most: "He pursued options and other avenues to go to for assistance. We didn't have to do it all." The son responded by saying, "We were starting to feel trapped. No one got a day off. There is less tension now. We feel freed up."

Alice referred herself to the Family Nursing Unit 6 years later for two sessions. She was grieving the loss of her husband, who had died of amyotrophic lateral sclerosis (ALS) 6 months before. She reported that Mark was hospitalized in an extended care facility and, despite his need for total nursing care, was in "good spirits." Alice's "one question question" at the time of referral was, "How can I cope with this fear?" She was fearful about what would happen to Mark if she died first and what would happen to her if Mark died first.

## RESEARCH FAMILY 2

Connie (age 39) was married and living with her husband of 10 years, their two children, and Connie's 17-year-old son from a previous marriage (see genogram, figure A2). She had experienced a heart attack at age 38 and was taking a number of medications for her heart condition, hypertension, and arthritis. She was also experiencing frequent panic attacks; when asked to rate her anxiety, she said that anxiety ruled each day 100% of the time. She had a strong family history of cardiac illness. Her maternal grandfather had died of heart disease, and her mother, age 69, had experienced four heart attacks and undergone triple bypass surgery 6 months earlier. Connie referred herself to the Family Nursing Unit. We worked with her for two sessions over 8 weeks. She was the only family member who attended the sessions. Her answer to the "one question question" at the first session was, "How can I get over this [anxious thoughts and panic attacks] . . . how can I be totally over it?"

Two years after the clinical sessions were completed, Connie participated in a follow-up evaluation interview. She reported that the panic attacks had been eliminated. When asked what was most helpful about the assistance she had received from the Family Nursing Unit, she responded, "Being able to talk about my problem." She reported that her husband, who had not attended either session, had noticed positive changes in her and that her marriage had improved since she began to "understand my panic attacks." When asked how she accounted for the changes, Connie offered, "My ability to put my feelings and fears into perspective—not to say there are no fears now—just that I deal with them better."

## RESEARCH FAMILY 3

John (age 40) and Nicole (age 40) had two daughters: Alison (age 16) and Sarah (age 13) (see genogram, figure A3). Sarah was a diabetic (diagnosed at age 6)

FIGURE A2

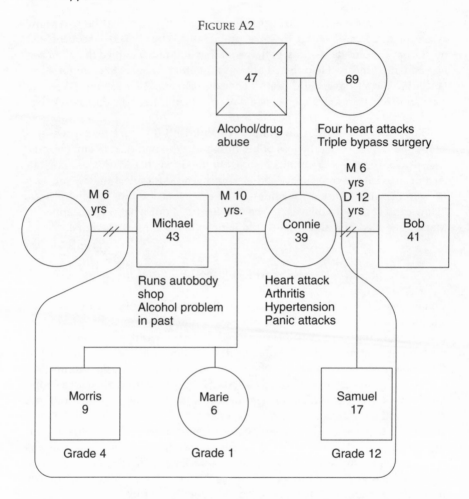

and had been experiencing chronic fatigue syndrome for 4 months. She felt too tired to attend school and was being tutored at home. The mother was on a leave of absence from her work as a health care professional because she was "stressed." She was the family member in charge of Sarah's illness care, responsible for coordinating appointments with numerous health care professionals, monitoring symptoms and medication regimes, and providing daily care to her ill daughter. She initiated the referral to the Family Nursing Unit.

The family was seen for four sessions over 10 weeks. All family members attended each session. Sarah was seen alone during part of the third session. The mother's answer to the "one question question" posed at the first session was, "Can we get through this [illness experience] healthier for the future?"

The family participated in a follow-up evaluation interview approximately 1 year after completion of the clinical sessions. The father related that the original problem that prompted them to seek help was as follows: "Nicole [the mother]

FIGURE A3

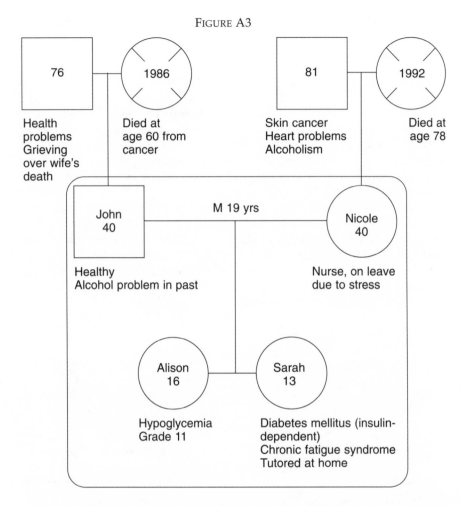

felt everything was on her shoulders. We needed help to cope with the chronic fatigue syndrome as a family." The chronic fatigue syndrome was "better." According to the elder daughter, "It's not there as much. If Sarah is sick or tired we do worry about it, but we handle it better." The mother said, "It's not that we don't think about the chronic fatigue syndrome now, but it's in small letters rather than in big letters." When asked if family members' thinking about the problem had changed, the mother offered, "My understanding of the problem is much broader now; the feelings of helplessness are gone because we all have strengths." Sarah answered, "I didn't know what the time limit of my illness was. We were uncertain, but I got it under control. I could handle it!" When asked what was most helpful about coming to the Family Nursing Unit, the mother responded, "The nonjudgmental, educated people in the field who helped me find my strengths." What changes did the mother notice since the family sessions? She offered that her husband "became more caring. He acknowledges my concerns and feelings. He is more perceptive and less indifferent." She also noticed that Sarah is "much less frustrated with her illness. She is much stronger at handling difficulties."

RESEARCH FAMILY 4

The fourth research family consisted of a single-parent family: a mother and her four children (see genogram, figure A4). Linda (age 36) had been divorced for 2 years when she sought help from the Family Nursing Unit. Her ex-husband, Carl, visited the children in their home every Sunday. The four children consisted of David (age 13), Nicholas (age 9), Susan (age 8), and Timothy (age 6).

Linda suspected that the children may have been abused by their father, who suffered from hydrocephalus and had experienced personality changes. He had taken care of the children while Linda was a full-time student. Linda was worried that the children might be repressing their feelings and wondered if this explained Timothy's temper tantrums or David's withdrawn behavior. Her response to the "one question question" was, "How can we overcome the things that have happened to us, and where do we go from here?"

FIGURE A4

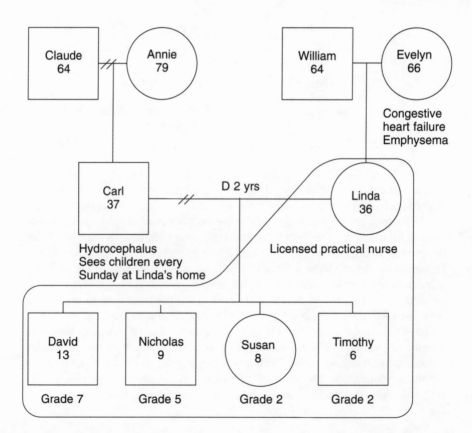

The family was seen for four sessions over 10 weeks. Linda and her four children attended the first and third session. Only Linda and her eldest child, David, were seen in Session 2, and this dyad was joined by the youngest son, Timothy, for Session 4.

A year after the completion of the sessions, follow-up evaluation data were scheduled to be collected from this family. Unfortunately, they had moved and could not be located.

## RESEARCH FAMILY 5

Robert (age 45) and Julie (age 39) had been married 20 years and had two children: a son, Dixon (age 12) and an adopted daughter, Robbie (age 7; see genogram, figure A5). Robert was referred to the Family Nursing Unit by a cardiac research nurse. He had suffered two heart attacks during the previous year and was enrolled in an experimental cardiac drug trial. Julie suffered from

FIGURE A5

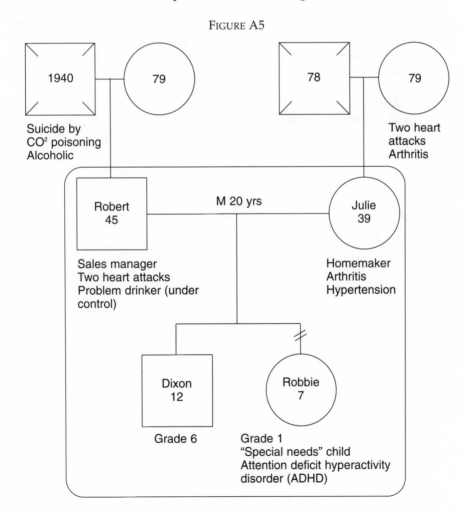

hypertension, arthritis, and neck and back problems. There was a strong history of heart disease in her family of origin.

During the first session, the couple reported that "stress blankets everything." They wanted assistance to lower their experience of stress. Neither was able to answer the "one question question" during the first session; however, when they returned for the second session, they each answered it. Julie: "How do we share more family responsibilities together?" Robert: "How can I make life easier for Julie?" Issues concerning marital conflict and spousal abuse were explored.

The couple was seen together for five sessions over 8 weeks. During Session 3, the husband and wife were seen separately for part of the session.

One year after the completion of the clinical sessions, both Robert and Julie participated in a follow-up evaluation interview. In answer to what was most helpful about the family sessions, Robert said, "It opened up communication." Julie offered that what had been most helpful were "Dr. Wright's advice and information." Robert thought he had benefited most from the family sessions: "I became more aware of things—my wife's feelings, needs, and our relationship. I am more accommodating." The original problem—"a combination of Robert's two heart attacks and our marital problems"—was better. Julie described the changes she noticed since the conclusion of the family sessions in this way: "We try to work with each other instead of against each other. Robert doesn't blame me for things anymore and he controls his anger better. I've made an effort to care for myself better (be more rested), and as a result, I am able to cope with my stressors and everyone is happier."

# Overview of
# the Research Method

OUR CLINICAL MODEL has evolved from more than 20 years of clinical practice with families and 10 years of collaboration as a clinical research team. Our ability to articulate the clinical model in this book is also the result of a funded research project, which allowed us to examine the expert clinical practice of Dr. Lorraine Wright and Dr. Wendy Watson in the Family Nursing Unit, University of Calgary. The research helped us to uncover new understanding about our clinical approach and gave us a language with which to describe the therapeutic process.

This is a story of women's work: women clinicians and researchers examining a clinical practice in a university context with predominantly middle-class, Caucasian families experiencing illness (physical or emotional illness). The clinical teams of faculty and graduate students who worked with these families were primarily female.

The research project, funded by the Alberta Foundation for Nursing Research, was entitled "Exploring the process of therapeutic change in family systems nursing practice: An analysis of five exemplary cases." Our clinical research team comprised Dr. Janice Bell (principal investigator), Dr. Lorraine Wright, Dr. Wendy Watson, and two research assistants: former graduate students Dianne Tapp and Lori Limacher. Consultation concerning the research method was provided by Dr. Catherine Chesla from the University of California, San Francisco. The research question was "How does therapeutic change occur?" Our clinical research team reviewed all the families we had worked with from 1989 to 1993 and chose five exemplary cases. In each of these cases, the family showed dramatic cognitive, affective, or behavioral change during the family interviews, which ranged from two to five sessions. The families also corroborated that change had occurred by reporting improvement in the presenting problem or a reduction in symptoms when they were interviewed 1 year after the completion of the clinical sessions for our Family Nursing Unit outcome study. Four of the families were seen by Dr. Lorraine Wright (with graduate students and faculty viewing from behind a one-way mirror); the clinical work for one family was conducted by Dr. Wendy Watson (again, with a clinical team observing).

Hermeneutic phenomenology was the method of choice in this project. *Hermeneutic phenomenology* is a research method that evolved from the philosophy of Heidegger (1927/1962) as explicated by Dreyfus (1991). Benner (1994) has described in detail the background and possibilities of this method and has demonstrated use of the method in the study of health, illness, and health care practice. One of the basic assumptions of this method is that human beings are "situated in their worlds, constituted by their worlds, engaged in everyday activity and moved by their concerns in day-to-day life" (Chesla, 1995, p. 63). Meaning is not subjectively held but is already present in shared language and everyday practices. By examining the structure of everyday action through the narrative, meaning is uncovered. The word *hermeneutic* refers to the theory and practice of interpretation and understanding (Odman, 1988). When the narrative is examined and interpreted (in this case, the narrative-in-action of the family member and the clinician during a clinical session), specific situations are recounted, temporal relations become visible, natural language is used, and the person of the narrator is evident.

What attracted us to this research method was our wish to examine the clinical knowledge embodied in our practice with families. Research concerning nursing practice (Benner, 1984; Benner, Tanner, & Chesla, 1996; Benner & Wrubel, 1989; Tanner, Benner, Chesla, & Gordon, 1993) and other practice disciplines (Dreyfus & Dreyfus, 1985) has suggested that expert clinicians have implicit knowledge that allows for pattern recognition and intuitive responses. Because the knowledge is implicit and embodied, however, the clinician can describe this knowledge only vaguely. Hermeneutic phenomenology offered a way to uncover this valuable clinical understanding of how to assist families experiencing illness. By reflecting on and systematically studying specific instances of our practice, we hoped to offer a better interpretation of our practice, one that brought to light the ways in which we worked with families to influence change.

Previously videotaped clinical sessions of all five exemplary families constituted the data set for our research project. Every family seen at the Family Nursing Unit provides consent to videotape and is also asked for permission to use the videotapes for research. The research process began by examining the videotaped clinical sessions for each of the five exemplary families in the following manner: We first reviewed the videotape of each session to get an understanding of the whole of the clinical work with the family. (Across the five families, there were 19 sessions, ranging from 60 to 100 minutes in length.) Analysis was done family by family.

Next, each member of the research team (Bell, Wright, and Watson) selected segments of the session she considered salient to the process of therapeutic change for each family session. We called these excerpts *change segments*. We completed the selection by studying each session to see how change unfolded. What happened in the clinical interview (in the therapeutic conversation) that seemed to invite change or was evidence of change? How did the clinician respond to the family, and how did the family respond to the clinician? *Change segments* were defined as portions of the therapeutic conversation that were hypothesized to contribute significantly to the change that was observed. The members of the research team then convened to discuss their choice of change segments for each session and to arrive at a consensus among the team members. The change segments agreed on by the team members were then transcribed into text. Hermeneutic interpretation was done using the text of the change segments. (Across the five exemplary families, 92 change segments were identified and analyzed.) Many of these change segments are included as exemplars in this book. We have previously described our story of using this method of hermeneutic interpretation (Gale, Chenail, Watson, Wright, & Bell, in press).

As we entered the "hermeneutic circle" (Packer & Addison, 1991), we acknowledged that as a clinical research team, we came with a forestructure of understanding about our worlds. We are single (two of us) and married (one) Caucasian women, nurses, academics, family therapists, and are Mormon (two of us) and Seventh Day Adventist (one). We are also family members with first-hand experience with illness. We can list other aspects of our lives that influence our worldviews, namely, we are daughters, mother, aunts, sisters, and friends. We also came with a forestructure of understanding about our clinical work. We acknowledged the influence of Maturana, Bateson, systems theory, cybernetics theory, change theory, communication theory, and narrative theory in our thinking about families. We acknowledged the rich contributions of the Milan team, Michael White, David Epston, and other narrative and constructivist approaches to what we did and said that was helpful to families suffering from illness. In the process of our interpretations, we challenged our forestructure and turned it over by asking the following questions: What is happening here from the clinician's perspective and from the family's perspective? Is this move or intervention unique or is it similar to another? Has it happened before? Do we have a usual name for this move? What else could we call it? This interpretive hermeneutic process has allowed us to uncover the personal, contextual, and cognitive processes that form the clinician's formulation of any given case and has given us a language to describe the moves, or interventions, we use in our clinical model.

The interpretive process is circular and engaged. Paradigm cases were chosen, and the whole of the work for each family was reviewed to get a "feel" of the data. The process moved from wholes to parts and then back to wholes and continued in this circular manner. After the change segments were transcribed to text, there was a careful word-by-word, line-by-line reading of the text to uncover the qualitatively distinct ways that we worked with particular families and the problems and concerns that they brought to treatment. The new understandings were then described and accounted for in the larger understanding of the clinical work done with each family and across the five families. As a research team, we consensually validated our interpretations of each segment by first writing individual interpretations and then working out the interpretation as a group. When there were disagreements, we returned to the text or to the videotapes to work out the "best interpretation." Each interpretive session of the research team was videotaped, creating an audit trail. Describing our practice moved from a distant overview to the detailed, focused account of macromoves and micromoves contained in chapters 4 through 7. Throughout, we tried to remain faithful to the families' and clinicians' concerns, languages, emotions, and behaviors.

We acknowledge that not all interpretations are equal. We understand that our interpretations of our current practice are provisional and incomplete. We have rendered the most systematic, inclusive, and meaningful account that we can offer, given our current access to the practice through our work with these five families. We acknowledge that we have focused on what works rather than points of breakdown in our practice, because, as in our work with families, we believe the most benefit can be gained in that way. We also acknowledge the recursive nature of having two research team members who were also clinicians for one or more of the paradigm cases. This dual role in our clinical and research team brought both strength and limitations. The strength was that the starting point for interpretations was a deep understanding of the practice from years of working together. The limitation was that although we accessed our practice in new ways, from the more distant vantage point of looking at the videotapes and from the transformation of the change portions of the session into text, blind spots about our practice may remain and will require the articulation of others.

It is important to note that the interviews conducted with the families were not phenomenological interviews; that is, families were not interviewed about their experience with illness. Rather, the interviews were the actual clinical sessions conducted in the Family Nursing Unit, University of Calgary, with family members who presented as experiencing difficulties with a health problem. The clinical sessions were conducted to assess and intervene with these families to assist them in their difficulties. Therefore, the hermeneutic inquiry focused not on research interviews but on interpreting the clinical process through the text of the therapeutic conversation as it unfolded in an actual clinical session.

The ideas of Humberto Maturana, a Chilean biologist, have deeply influenced our thinking about clinical practice and research. Maturana and Varela (1992) have offered a biological theory of knowing. They assert that reality is brought forth through language, individuals are structurally determined, and an invitation to a reflection is the ultimate act of knowing. These ideas have invited us to practice in a self-reflective, deeply interpretive manner and acknowledge the open and subjective nature of truth. Our clinical practice with families has closely paralleled the theory that guided the research process and has strengthened our ability to use interpretive hermeneutics as a research method.

We believe that our interpretation of our clinical work and the description of practice contained in this book constitute only a snapshot of our best understanding at this time. Our understanding of families, illness, and the process of therapeutic change will remain the same only until we see the next family!

# Ways to Examine and Measure Beliefs

A LTHOUGH THERE IS NOT an overabundance of measuring instruments, some efforts have been made to examine and measure individual and family beliefs. Following is a brief description of the Core Beliefs Inventory, the Relationship Belief Inventory, and the Health Belief Model. This list is by no means intended to be inclusive of the instruments available but simply to give readers a sampling of instruments that might be useful.

## CORE BELIEFS INVENTORY

The Core Beliefs Inventory (CBI), which contains 100 true and false statements, was developed by Matthew McKay and Patrick Fanning (1991). A respondent's scores are clustered into 10 topics such as control, love, autonomy, and justice. The authors state that these topics are important areas of everyone's life, about which everyone has some sort of belief, whether conscious or not. They state that this inventory is designed to identify an individual's core beliefs and not to pass judgment on them. The authors of this inventory emphasize that individual results are neither good nor bad but indicate how restricted or free one is in making choices in one's life.

## RELATIONSHIP BELIEF INVENTORY

Epstein and Eidelson (1981) developed the Relationship Belief Inventory (RBI) to assess what they refer to as dysfunctional beliefs about intimate relationships. The view that dysfunctional beliefs can harm intimate relationships is consistent with that of cognitive behavior therapists. The RBI is a list of 60 items that describe how a person might feel about a relationship with another person. Each item is evaluated by indicating how strongly one believes that the statement is true or false. For example, there are statements such as "I get very upset if my partner does not recognize how I am feeling and I have to tell him/her" and "I do not expect my partner to sense all my moods." The inventory consists of five subscales with a score derived for each subscale and a total score. The internal consistency of the subscales ranges from .72 to .81.

## HEALTH BELIEF MODEL

The Health Belief Model (HBM), although some 40 years old, still enjoys considerable theoretical and research attention. Evidence for this statement is found in two comprehensive reviews. The first review was published in 1974 in the *Health Education Monographs,* which devoted an entire issue to the HBM. This initial review provided considerable support for the model. In 1984, a second review of numerous HBM-related studies also recommended that consideration of HBM dimensions be a part of health education programming (Janz & Marshall, 1984). The HBM was initially developed in the early 1950s by a group of social psychologists at the United States Public Health Service in an attempt to understand the widespread failure of the use of preventative measures or screening tests for the early detection of asymptomatic disease (Rosenstock, 1974). Later, the model was also applied to patients' responses to symptoms and to compliance with prescribed medical regimens. These reviews provided substantial empirical support for the HBM, with findings from prospective studies at least as favorable as those obtained from retrospective research. In the context of health-related behavior, the studies examined the desire to avoid illness (or if ill, to get well) and the belief that a specific health action will prevent or ameliorate illness.

The HBM consists of the following dimensions: perceived susceptibility, perceived severity, perceived benefits, and perceived barriers. Janz and Marshall (1984) cautioned that although the HBM reveals relevant attitude and belief dimensions, it does not give direction for any particular intervention strategies for altering these beliefs. Another caution is the need to standardize the tools that measure HBM components. One final observation is that some research has demonstrated the importance of variables that may fit conceptually within the HBM framework but were not developed in that context. One example of this is the behavioral model developed by Ajzen and Fishbein (1980), which emphasizes the importance of considering the person's beliefs that specific individuals or groups think he should or should not possess and the resultant behavior.

## COMMENT

Although the CBI and RBI might provide some interesting data about the beliefs of family members encountered in our professional lives, neither gives direction on how to be helpful to any particular family. In particular, how can one intervene concerning beliefs that are constraining or limiting and offer other ways of viewing an illness, a family member's response to an illness, or a way of coping with the exacerbations of an illness? Chapters 4 through 7 offer specific ideas concerning how to intervene in a manner that increases family members' solution options for the difficulties they face.

# REFERENCES

Ajzen, I., & Fishbein, M. (1980). *Understanding attitudes and predicting social behavior*. Englewood Cliffs, NJ: Prentice-Hall.

American Psychiatric Association. (1994). *Diagnostic and statistic manual of mental disorders* (4th ed.). Washington, DC: Author.

Andersen, T. (1987). The reflecting team: Dialogue and meta-dialogue in clinical work. *Family Process, 26,* 415–428.

Andersen, T. (Ed.). (1991a). *The reflecting team: Dialogues and dialogues about the dialogues*. New York: Norton.

Andersen, T. (1991b). Basic concepts and practical considerations. In T. Andersen (Ed.), *The reflecting team. Dialogues and dialogues about the dialogues* (pp. 15–41). New York: Norton.

Anderson, H., Goolishian, H. A., & Winderman, L. (1986). Problem determined systems: Towards transformation in family therapy. *Journal of Systemic and Strategic Therapies, 5*(4), 1–13.

Anderson, H., Goolishian, H. A., Pulliam, A., & Winderman, L. (1986). The Galveston Family Institute: Some personal and historical perspectives. In D. Efron (Ed.), *Journeys: Expansion of the strategic-systemic therapies* (pp. 97–122). New York: Brunner/Mazel.

Anderson, R. (1993). The healing environment. In B. Moyers (Ed.), *Healing and the mind* (pp. 25–45). New York: Doubleday.

Armstrong, D. (1984). The patient's view. *Social Science and Medicine, 18,* 737–744.

Bateson, G. (1972). *Steps to an ecology of mind*. New York: Ballantine Books.

Bateson, G. (1979). *Mind and nature*. New York: Dutton.

Beck, A. T. (1988). *Love is never enough*. New York: Harper & Row.

Benner, P. (1984). *From novice to expert: Power and excellence in clinical nursing practice*. Menlo Park, CA: Addison-Wesley.

Benner, P. (Ed.). (1994). *Interpretive phenomenology, embodiment, caring and ethics in health and illness*. Thousand Oaks, CA: Sage.

Benner, P., & Wrubel, J. (1989). *The primacy of caring: Stress and coping in health and illness*. Menlo Park, CA: Addison-Wesley.

306

Benner, P. E., Tanner, C. A., & Chesla, C. A. (with contributions by H. Dreyfus, S. Dreyfus, & J. Rubin). (1996). *Expertise in nursing practice: Caring, clinical judgement and ethics.* New York: Springer.

Berg, I. K., & de Shazer, S. (1993). Making numbers talk: Language in therapy. In S. Friedman (Ed.), *New language of change* (pp. 5–24). New York: Guilford Press.

Bergin, A. E. (1980). Psychotherapy and religious values. *Journal of Consulting and Clinical Psychology, 48,* 95–105.

Bergin, A. E. (1983). Religiosity and mental health: A critical reevaluation and meta-analysis. *Professional Psychology: Research and Practice, 14,* 170–184.

Bergin, A. E. (1988a). The spiritual perspective is ecumenical and eclectic (rejoinder). *Counseling and Values, 33,* 57–59.

Bergin, A. E. (1988b). Three contributions of a spiritual perspective to counseling, psychotherapy, and behavior change. *Counseling and Values, 33,* 21–31.

Bergin, A. E. (1991). Values and religious issues in psychotherapy and mental health. *American Psychologist, 46,* 394–403.

Bernstein, A. (1994, Summer). Profiles 1993 Diversity Award Honorable Mention Freida Hopkins-Outlaw and Cary Wright. *American Family Therapy Academy Newsletter,* 45–48.

Bordin, E. S. (1979). The generalizability of the psychoanalytic concept of the working alliance. *Psychotherapy, 16,* 252–260.

Borhek, J. T., & Curtis, R. F. (1975). *A sociology of belief.* New York: Wiley.

Boscolo, L., & Bertrando, P. (1993). *The times of time: A new perspective in systemic therapy and consultation.* New York: Norton.

Boscolo, L., & Cecchin, G. (1980, March). *Milan group family therapy workshop* [Audio, Video]. Health Sciences Centre, University of Calgary, Calgary, Alberta, Canada.

Boscolo, L., & Cecchin, G. (1980, October). *The family therapy workshop with the Milan group* [Audio, Video]. Health Sciences Centre, University of Calgary, Calgary, Alberta, Canada.

Bragdon, E. (1994). *A sourcebook for helping people with spiritual problems.* Aptos, CA: Lightening Up Press.

Breulin, D. C., & Cade, B. (1981). Intervening in family systems with observer messages. *Journal of Marital and Family Therapy, 7,* 453–460.

Brother, B. J. (1992). *Spirituality and couples: Heart and soul in the therapy process.* Binghamton, NY: Haworth Press.

Buffington, P. W. (1990, October). Say what you mean, mean what you say. *SKY,* pp. 110–113.

Burman, B., & Margolin, G. (1992). Analysis of the association between marital relationships and health problems: An interactional perspective. *Psychological Bulletin, 112,* 39–63.

Burnard, P. (1987). Spiritual distress and the nursing response: Theoretical considerations and counselling skills. *Journal of Advanced Nursing, 12,* 377–382.

Burton, L. A. (Ed.). (1992). *Religion and the family: When God helps.* Binghamton, NY: Haworth Press.

Byng-Hall, J. (1973). Family myths used as a defence in conjoint family therapy. *British Journal of Medical Psychology, 46,* 239–250.

Byng-Hall, J. (1979). Re-editing family mythology during family therapy. *Journal of Family Therapy, 1*, 103–116.

Byng-Hall, J. (1988). Scripts and legends in families and family therapy. *Family Process, 27*, 167–180.

Cade, B. W., & Cornwell, M. (1985). New realities for old: Some uses of teams and one-way screens in therapy. In D. Campbell & R. Draper (Eds.), *Applications of systemic family therapy: The Milan approach* (pp. 47–57). London: Grune & Stratton.

Campbell, T. (1986). Family's impact on health: A critical review. *Family Systems Medicine, 4*, 135–328.

Carlson, R., & Shield, B. (1989). *Healers and healing.* Los Angeles, CA: Jeremy P. Tarcher.

Carter, S. L. (1993). *The culture of disbelief.* New York: Anchor Books.

Cecchin, G. (1987). Hypothesizing, circularity, and neutrality revisited: An invitation to curiosity. *Family Process, 26*, 405–413.

Cecchin, G., Lane, G., & Ray, W. A. (1994). Influence, effect and emerging systems. *Journal of Systemic Therapies, 13*(4), 13–21.

Chesla, C. A. (1995). Hermeneutic phenomenology: An approach to understanding families. *Journal of Family Nursing, 1*, 63–78.

Colapinto, J. (1985). Maturana and the ideology of conformity. *The Family Therapy Networker, 9*(3), 29–30.

Colapinto, J. A. (1995). Dilution of family process in social services: Implications for treatment of neglectful families. *Family Process, 34*, 59–73.

Connell, G. M., & Connell, L. C. (1995). In-hospital consultation: Systemic interventions during medical crisis. *Family Systems Medicine, 13*, 29–38.

Cousins, N. (1979). *Anatomy of an illness as perceived by the patient.* New York: Bantam Books.

Cousins, N. (1989). *Beliefs become biology* [Videotape]. British Columbia, Canada: University of Victoria.

Covinsky, L. E., Goldman, L., Cook, E. F., Oye, R., Desbiens, N., Reding, D., Fulkerson, W., Connors, A. F., Lynn, J., & Phillips, R. S. (1994). The impact of serious illness on patients' families. *Journal of the American Medical Association, 272*, 1839–1844.

Dallos, R. (1991). *Family belief systems, therapy and change.* Philadelphia: Open University Press.

Deatrick, J. A., Faux, S. A., & Moore, C. M. (1993). The contribution of qualitative research to the study of families' experiences with childhood illness. In S. L. Feetham, S. B. Meister, J. M. Bell, & C. L. Gilliss (Eds.), *The nursing of families: Theory/research/education/practice* (pp. 61–69). Newbury Park, CA: Sage.

DeFrain, J., & Stinnett, N. (1992). Building on the inherent strengths of families: A positive approach for family psychologists and counselors. *Topics in Family Psychology and Counseling, 1*(1), 15–26.

de Shazer, S. (1985). *Keys to solution in brief therapy.* New York: Norton.

de Shazer, S. (1991). *Putting difference to work.* New York: Norton.

de Shazer, S. (1993). Creative misunderstanding: There is no escape from language. In S. Gilligan & R. Price (Eds.), *Therapeutic conversations* (pp. 81–90). New York: Norton.

de Shazer, S., & Berg, I. K. (1988). Constructing solutions. *The Family Therapy Networker, 12*(5), 42–43.

Dewar, A. L., & Morse, J. M. (1995). Unbearable incidents: Failure to endure the experience of illness. *Journal of Advanced Nursing, 22,* 957–964.

Doherty, W. J., & Whitehead, A. (1986). The social dynamics of cigarette smoking: A family systems perspective. *Family Process, 25,* 453–459.

Donoghue, P. J., & Siegel, M. E. (1992). *Sick and tired of feeling sick and tired: Living with invisible chronic illness.* New York: Norton.

Dossey, L. (1993). *Healing words: The power of prayer and the practice of medicine.* San Francisco: HarperSanFrancisco.

Dreyfus, H. L. (1991). *Being-in-the-world: A commentary on Heidegger's Being and Time, Division I.* Cambridge, MA: MIT Press.

Dreyfus, H. L., & Dreyfus, S. E. (1985). *Mind over machine.* New York: Free Press.

Duhamel, F. (1994). A family systems approach: Three families with a hypertensive family member. *Family Systems Medicine, 12,* 391–404.

Duhamel, F., Watson, W. L., & Wright, L. M. (1994). A family systems approach to hypertension. *Canadian Journal of Cardiovascular Nursing, 5*(4), 14–24.

Duncan, B. L., Hubble, M. A., & Rusk, G. (1994). To intervene or not to intervene? That is not the question. *Journal of Systemic Therapies, 13*(4), 22–30.

Efran, J., & Lukens, M. D. (1985). The world according to Humberto Maturana: Epistemology and the magic kingdom. *The Family Therapy Networker, 9*(3), 23–28, 72–75.

Efran, J. S., Lukens, R. J., & Lukens, M. D. (1988). Constructivism. What's in it for you? *The Family Therapy Networker, 12*(5), 27–35.

Ellis, A. (1962). *Reason and emotion in psychotherapy.* Secaucus, NJ: Citadel Press.

Epstein, N., & Eidelson, R. (1981). Unrealistic beliefs of clinical couples: Their relationship to expectations, goals and satisfaction. *American Journal of Family Therapy, 9,* 13–22.

Evans-Pritchard, E. E. (1976). *Witchcraft, oracles and magic among the Azande.* Oxford, England: Clarendon Press.

Felten, D. (1993). The brain and the immune system. In B. Moyers (Ed.), *Healing and the mind* (pp. 213–237). New York: Doubleday.

Ferreira, A. J. (1963). Family myth and homeostasis. *Archives of General Psychiatry, 9,* 457–467.

Fisher, L., Ransom, D. C., & Terry, H. A. (1993). The California Health Project: VII. Summary and integration of findings. *Family Process, 32,* 69–86.

Fleuridas, C., Nelson, T. S., & Rosenthal, D. M. (1986). The evolution of circular questions: Training family therapists. *Journal of Marital and Family Therapy, 12,* 113–127.

Foucault, M. (1978). *The history of sexuality* (Vol. 1). New York: Basic Books.

Frank, A. W. (1991). *At the will of the body: Reflections on illness.* Boston: Houghton Mifflin.

Frank, A. W. (1994). Interrupted stories, interrupted lives. *Second Opinion, 20*(1), 11–18.

Freeman, J. C., & Lobovits, D. (1993). The turtle with wings. In S. Friedman (Ed.), *The new language of change* (pp. 188–225). New York: Guilford Press.

Friedman, S. (Ed.). (1993). *The new language of change: Constructive collaboration in psychotherapy.* New York: Guilford Press.

Friedman, S. (Ed.). (1995). *The reflecting team in action: Collaborative practice in family therapy.* New York: Guilford Press.

Friedman, S., & Fanger, M. T. (1991). *Expanding therapeutic possibilities: Getting results in brief psychotherapy.* New York: Lexington Books/Macmillan.

Furman, B., & Ahola, T. (1992). *Solution talk: Hosting therapeutic conversations.* New York: Norton.

Gale, J., Chenail, R. J., Watson, W. L., Wright, L. M., & Bell, J. M. (in press). Research and practice: A reflexive and recursive relationship. Three narratives and five voices [Special issue: Methods and methodologies of qualitative family research]. *Marriage and Family Review.*

Gergen, K. (1985). The social constructionist movement in modern psychology. *American Psychologist, 40,* 266–275.

Gilligan, S., & Price, R. (Eds.). (1993). *Therapeutic conversations.* New York: Norton.

Gilovich, T. (1991). *How we know what isn't so: The fallibility of human reason in everyday life.* New York: Free Press.

Glenn, M. (1984). *On diagnosis: A systemic approach.* New York: Brunner/Mazel.

Glenn, M. L. (1987). Structurally determined conflicts in health care. *Family Systems Medicine, 5,* 413–427.

Goldberg, J. R. (1994). Spirituality, religion, and secular values: What role in psychotherapy? *Family Therapy News, 9,* 16–17.

Goldner, V., Penn, P., Sheinberg, M., & Walker, G. (1990). Love and violence: Gender paradoxes in volatile attachments. *Family Process, 29,* 343–364.

Gonzalez, S., Steinglass, P., & Reiss, D. (1989). Putting illness in its place: Discussion groups for families with chronic medical illnesses. *Family Process, 28,* 69–88.

Gottman, J. (1991). Predicting the longitudinal course of marriage. *Journal of Marital and Family Therapy, 17,* 3–7.

Gottman, J. (1994a). *What predicts divorce? The relationship between marital processes and marital outcomes.* Hillsdale, NJ: Erlbaum.

Gottman, J. (1994b, March/April). What makes marriages work? *Psychology Today,* pp. 38–43, 68.

Gottman, J. (1994c). Why marriages fail? *The Family Therapy Networker, 18*(3), 40–48.

Gottman, J., & Silver, N. (1994). *Why marriages succeed or fail.* New York: Simon & Schuster.

Griffith, J. L., & Griffith, M. E. (1994). *The body speaks: Therapeutic dialogues for mind-body problems.* New York: Basic Books.

Guardian, T. (1993, November 6). Belief in the stars may prove fatal. *The Gazette,* p. 6.

Harkaway, J. E., & Madsen, W. C. (1989). A systemic approach to medical noncompliance: The case of chronic obesity. *Family Systems Medicine, 7,* 42–65.

Heidegger, M. (1962). *Being and time* (J. Macquarrie & E. Robinson, Trans.). New York: Seabury Press. (Original work published 1927)

Higginson, J. W. (1948). *Epictetus, the enchiridion.* New York: Macmillan.

Hoffman, L. (1985). Beyond power and control: Toward a "second-order" family systems therapy. *Family Systems Medicine, 3,* 381–396.

Hoffman, L. (1990). Constructing realities: An art of lenses. *Family Process, 29,* 1–12.

Hoffman-Hennessy, L., & Davis, J. (1993). Tekka with feathers: Talking about talking (about suicide). In S. Friedman (Ed.), *New language of change* (pp. 345–373). New York: Guilford Press.

Hymers, M. (1995, November). *Truth and objectivity.* University of Calgary, Calgary, Canada.

Ignatieff, M. (1994). *Scar tissue.* Toronto: Penguin Books.

Imber-Black, E. (1988). *Families and larger systems: A family therapist's guide through the labyrinth.* New York: Guilford Press.

Imber-Black, E. (1991). The family-larger-system perspective. *Family Systems Medicine, 9,* 371–396.

Jahn, R., & Dunne, B. (1987). *Margins of reality: The role of consciousness in the physical world.* New York: Harcourt Brace Jovanovich.

Janz, N. K., & Marshall, J. B. (1984). The health belief model: A decade later. *Health Education Quarterly, 11*(1), 1–47.

Jevne, R. (1994). *Voice of hope in the cancer experience.* Calgary, Canada: University of Calgary.

Kabat-Zinn, J. (1993). Meditation. In B. Moyers (Ed.), *Healing and the mind* (pp. 115–143). New York: Doubleday.

Kahoe, R. D. (1987). Toward a radical psychotheology. *Psychologists Interested in Religious Issues Newsletter: Division 36-American Psychological Association, 12*(3), 2–6.

Kelley, G. (1955). *The psychology of personal constructs.* New York: Norton.

Kierkegaard, S. (1939). *The point of view for my work as an author.* (W. Lowrie, Trans.). London: Oxford University Press. (Original work published 1859)

Kleinman, A. (1988). *The illness narratives.* New York: Basic Books.

Koltko, M. E. (1990). How religious beliefs affect psychotherapy: The example of Mormonism. *Psychotherapy, 27*(1), 132–141.

Koop, C. E. (1995). Everett Koop on the ministry of medicine: Making the rounds in health, faith and ethics. *Park Ridge Center, 1*(2), 6–7.

Kung, H. (1981). *Does God exist?* New York: Vintage Books.

Kushner, J. (1981). *When bad things happen to good people.* New York: Schocken Books.

Lamb, E. J. (1979). Does adoption affect subsequent fertility? *American Journal of Obstetrics and Gynecology, 234,* 138–144.

Lazarus, R. S. (1991). *Emotion and adaptation.* New York: Oxford University Press.

Lazarus, R. S., & Folkman, S. (1984). *Stress, appraisal and coping.* New York: Springer.

Levac, A. M., McLean, S., Wright, L. M., & Bell, J. M. (in press). A couple's collaborative work with a nursing team: Reflections on grief and grief therapy. *Journal of Family Nursing.*

Lewis, F. M., Hammon, M. A., & Woods, N. F. (1993). The family's functioning with newly diagnosed breast cancer in the mother: The development of an explanatory model. *Journal of Behavioral Medicine, 16,* 351–370.

Leyland, M. L. (1988). An introduction to some of the ideas of Humberto Maturana. *Journal of Family Therapy, 10,* 357–374.

Loos, F., & Bell, J. M. (1990). Circular questions: A family interviewing strategy. *Dimensions in Critical Care Nursing, 9*(1), 46–53.

Lynam, M. J. (1995). Supporting one another: The nature of family work when a young adult has cancer. *Journal of Advanced Nursing, 22,* 116–125.

Mackinnon, D., Helmeke, K., & Stander, V. (1994, November). *Integrating spirituality and religion into family therapy.* Paper presented at the meeting of the American Association for Marriage and Family Therapy Annual Conference, Chicago, IL.

Marmar, C. R., Horowitz, M. J., Weiss, D. S., & Marziali, E. (1986). The development of the therapeutic alliance rating system. In L. S. Greenberg & W. M. Pinsof (Eds.), *The psychotherapeutic process: A research handbook* (pp. 367–390). New York: Guilford Press.

Mason, M. (1995, Spring). Mountains, metaphors, and safaris of the spirit. *American Family Therapy Academy Newsletter, 59,* 21–23.

Maturana, H. R. (1970). Biology of cognition. *Boston studies on the philosophy of science* (Vol. 100). Boston: Boston University Press.

Maturana, H. R. (1978). Biology of language: The epistemology of reality. In C. A. Miller & E. Lennenberg (Eds.), *Psychology and biology of language and thought: Essays in honor of Eric Lennenberg* (pp. 27–63). New York: Academic Press.

Maturana, H. R. (1988a). *Telephone conversation: The Calgary/Chile coupling* [Telephone transcript]. Calgary, Canada: University of Calgary.

Maturana, H. R. (1988b). Reality: The search for objectivity or the quest for a compelling argument. *Irish Journal of Psychology, 9*(1), 25–83.

Maturana, H. R. (1992, May). *The biological roots of human understanding* [Audiotapes 7]. Calgary, Canada: Vanry & Associates.

Maturana, H. R. (1992, November). *Biology, emotions and culture* [Videotape 6]. Calgary, Canada: Vanry & Associates.

Maturana, H. R., & Varela, F. G. (1980). *Autopoiesis and cognition: The realization of the living.* Boston: Reid.

Maturana, H. R., & Varela, F. (1992). *The tree of knowledge: The biological roots of human understanding* (Rev. ed.). Boston: Shambhala.

McCulloch, W. (1988). *Embodiments of mind.* Cambridge, MA: MIT Press.

McElheran, N. G., & Harper-Jaques, S. R. (1994). Commendations: A resource intervention for clinical practice. *Clinical Nurse Specialist, 8*(1), 7–10.

McGuire, M. B., & Kantor, D. J. (1987). Belief systems and illness experiences: The case of non-medical healing groups. *Research in the Sociology of Health Care* (6th ed., pp. 221–248). Greenwich, CT: JAI Press.

McKay, M., & Fanning, P. (1991). *Prisoners of belief: Exposing and changing beliefs that control your life.* Oakland, CA: New Harbinger.

McLuhan, M., & Fiore, Q. (1967). *The medium is the message.* New York: Random House.

Medalie, J., & Goldbourt, V. (1976). Angina predictors among 10,000 men: II. Psychosocial and other risk factors as evidenced by a multivariate analysis of a five year incidence study. *American Journal of Medicine, 60,* 910–921.

Mendez, C. L., Coddou, F., & Maturana, H. R. (1988). The bringing forth of pathology. *Irish Journal of Psychology, 9*(1), 144–172.

Mince, J. (1992). Discovering meaning with families. In J. D. Atwood (Ed.), *Family therapy: A systemic behavioral approach* (pp. 321–343). Chicago: Nelson-Hall.

Minuchin, S. (1974). *Families and family therapy.* London: Tavistock.

Mittelmeier, C., & Friedman, S. (1993). Toward a mutual understanding: Constructing solutions with families. In S. Friedman (Ed.), *The new language of change* (pp. 158–181). New York: Guilford Press.

Morse, J. M., & Johnson, J. L. (1991). Toward a theory of illness: The Illness-Constellation Model. In J. M. Morse & J. L. Johnson (Eds.), *The illness experience: Dimensions of suffering* (pp. 315–342). Newbury Park, CA: Sage.

Nichols, M. P. (1995). *The lost art of listening.* New York: Guilford Press.

Nunnally, E., de Shazer, S., Lipchik, E., & Berg, I. (1986). A study of change: Therapeutic theory in process. In D. E. Efron (Ed.), *Journeys: Expansion of the strategic-systemic therapies* (pp. 77–96). New York: Brunner/Mazel.

Odman, P. J. (1988). Hermeneutics. In J. P. Keeves (Ed.), *Educational research, methodology and measurement: An international handbook.* Oxford: Pergamon Press.

O'Hanlon, W. H. (1993). Possibility therapy: From iatrogenic injury to iatrogenic healing. In S. Gilligan & R. E. Price (Eds.), *Therapeutic conversations* (pp. 3–17). New York: Norton.

Ornish, D. (1993). Changing life habits. In B. Moyers (Ed.), *Healing and the mind* (pp. 87–113). New York: Doubleday.

Packer, M. J., & Addison, R. B. (Eds.). (1991). *Entering the circle: Hermeneutic investigation in psychology* (pp. 275–292). Albany, NY: SUNY Press.

Papp, P. (1980). The Greek chorus and other techniques of paradoxical therapy. *Family Process, 19,* 45–57.

Papp, P. (1983). *The process of change.* New York: Guilford Press.

Parry, A., & Doan, R. E. (1994). *Story re-visions: Narrative therapy in the postmodern world.* New York: Norton.

Patterson, J. M., & Garwick, A. W. (1994). Levels of meaning in family stress. *Family Process, 33,* 287–304.

Patterson, J. M., & Leonard, B. J. (1994). Caregiving and children. In E. Kahana, D. E. Biegel, & M. Wukle (Eds.), *Family caregiving across the lifespan* (pp. 133–158). Newbury Park, CA: Sage.

Patterson, R. B. (1994, June). Learning from suffering. *Family Therapy News,* pp. 11–12.

Patton, M. L. (1994). *Guide-lines and God-lines for facing cancer.* San Antonio, TX: Langmarc.

Radley, A., & Green, R. (1986). Bearing illness: Study of couples where the husband awaits coronary graft surgery. *Social Sciences and Medicine, 23,* 577–585.

Ransom, D. C., Fisher, L., & Terry, H. E. (1992). The California Family Health Project: II. Family world view and adult health. *Family Process, 31,* 251–267.

Register, C. (1987). *Living with chronic illness: Days of patience and passion.* New York: Free Press.

Reichlin, S. (1993). Neuroendocrine-immune interactions. *New England Journal of Medicine, 329,* 1246–1253.

Reiss, D. (1981). *The family's construction of reality.* Cambridge, MA: Harvard University Press.

Reiss, D. (1982). The working family: A researcher's view of health in the household. *American Journal of Psychiatry, 139,* 1412–1420.

Reiss, D., Gonzalez, S., & Kramer, N. (1986). Family process, chronic illness, and death: On the weakness of strong bonds. *Archives of General Psychiatry, 43,* 795–804.

Remen, R. N. (1993). Wholeness. In B. Moyers (Ed.), *Healing and the mind* (pp. 343–363). New York: Doubleday.

Roberts, J., "Alexandra," & "Julius." (1988). Use of ritual in "redocumenting" psychiatric history. In E. I. Black, J. Roberts, & R. Whiting (Eds.), *Rituals in families and family therapy* (pp. 307–330). New York: Norton.

Robinson, C. A. (1993). Managing life with a chronic condition: The story of normalization. *Qualitative Health Research, 3,* 6–28.

Robinson, C. A. (1994a). *Women, families, chronic illness and nursing interventions: From burden to balance.* Unpublished doctoral dissertation, University of Calgary, Alberta, Canada.

Robinson, C. A. (1994b). Nursing interventions with families: A demand or an invitation to change? *Journal of Advanced Nursing, 19,* 897–904.

Robinson, C. A., Wright, L. M., & Watson, W. L. (1994). A nontraditional approach to family violence. *Archives of Psychiatric Nursing, 8*(1), 30–37.

Rokeach, M. (1969). *Beliefs, attitudes and values: A theory of organization and change.* San Francisco: Jossey-Bass.

Rolland, J. (1984). Toward a psychosocial typology of chronic and life threatening illness. *Family Systems Medicine, 2,* 245–262.

Rolland, J. S. (1987). Chronic illness and the life cycle: A conceptual framework. *Family Process, 26,* 203–221.

Rolland, J. (1994). *Families, illness and disabilities: An integrative treatment model.* New York: Basic Books.

Rosenstock, I. M. (1974). Historical origins of the health belief model. *Health Education Monographs, 2,* 328.

Ross, B., & Cobb, L. (1990). *Family nursing: A nursing process approach.* Redwood, CA: Addison-Wesley.

Ross, C. E., Mirowsky, J., & Goldsteen, K. (1990). Impact of family on health: The decade in review. *Journal of Marriage and the Family, 52,* 1059–1078.

Rossman, M. (1989). *Illness as an opportunity for healing.* In R. Carlson & B. Shield (Eds.), *Healers on healing* (pp. 78–81). Los Angeles, CA: Jeremy P. Tarcher.

Salamon, E., Grevelius, K., & Andersson, M. (1993). Beware the siren's song: The AGS Commission Model. In S. Gilligan & R. E. Price (Eds.), *Therapeutic conversations* (pp. 330–343). New York: Norton.

Schmidt, D. D. (1983). Family determinants of disease: Depressed lymphocyte function following the loss of a spouse. *Family Systems Medicine, 1,* 33–39.

Schultz Hall, J. (1995). A place for spirituality in family therapy. *The Calgary Participator, University of Calgary: A Family Therapy Newsletter, 5*(2), 40–42.

Segal, L. (1986). *The dream of reality: Heinz von Foerster's constructivism.* New York: Norton.

Selekman, M. D. (1993). Solution-oriented brief therapy with difficult adolescents. In S. Friedman (Ed.), *New language of change* (pp. 138–157). New York: Guilford Press.

Sells, S. P., Smith, T. E., Coe, M. J., Yoshioka, M., & Robbins, J. (1994). An ethnography of couple and therapist experiences in reflecting team practice. *Journal of Marital and Family Therapy, 20,* 247–266.

Selvini Palazzoli, M., Boscolo, L., Cecchin, G., & Prata, G. (1978). *Paradox and counterparadox.* New York: Jason Aronson.

Selvini Palazzoli, M., Boscolo, L., Cecchin, G., & Prata, G. (1980a). Hypothesizing, circularity, neutrality: Three guidelines for the conductor of the session. *Family Process, 19,* 3–12.

Selvini Palazzoli, M., Boscolo, L., Cecchin, G., & Prata, G. (1980b). The problem of the referring person. *Journal of Marital and Family Therapy, 6,* 3–9.

Sideleau, B. F. (1987). Irrational beliefs and interventions. *Journal of Psychosocial Nursing, 13*(4), 138–144.

Simon, R. (1985). Structure is destiny: An interview with Humberto Maturana. *The Family Therapy Networker, 9*(3), 32–37.

Smith, R. L., & Stevens, S. P. W. (1992). A critique of healthy family functioning. *Topics in Family Psychology and Counseling, 1*(1), 6–14.

Smith, T. E., Sells, S. P., & Clevenger, T. (1994). Ethnographic content analysis of couple and therapist perceptions in a reflecting team setting. *Journal of Marital and Family Therapy, 20,* 267–286.

Soul Making. (1995, Winter). *The Calgary Participator, University of Calgary: A Family Therapy Newsletter, 5*(2).

Spirituality. (1994, June). *American Association for Marriage & Family Therapy Newsletter.* Family Therapy News.

Spirituality: The path and the leap. (1995, Spring). *American Family Therapy Academy Newsletter, 59.*

Stewart, K., Valentine, L., & Amundson, J. (1991). The battle for definition: The problem with (the problem). *Journal of Strategic and Systemic Therapies, 10*(2), 21–31.

Stratton, P., Preston-Shoot, M., & Hanks, H. (1990). *Family therapy: Training and practice.* Birmingham, AL: Birmingham Venture Press.

Taggart, S. R. (1994). *Living as if: Belief systems in mental health practice.* San Francisco: Jossey-Bass.

Tanner, C. A., Benner, P., Chesla, C. A., & Gordon, D. R. (1993). The phenomenology of knowing the patient. *Image, 25,* 273–280.

Taylor, S. (1989). *Positive illusions: Creative self-deception and the healthy mind.* New York: Basic Books.

Thomas, R. B. (1984). Nursing assessment of childhood chronic conditions. *Issues in Comprehensive Pediatric Nursing, 7,* 165–176.

Thorne, S. E., & Robinson, C. A. (1989). Guarded alliance: Health care relationships in chronic illness. *Image: The Journal of Nursing Scholarship, 21*(3), 153–157.

Tomm, K. (1984a). One perspective on the Milan systemic approach: Part 1. Overview of development, theory and practice. *Journal of Marital and Family Therapy, 10,* 113–125.

Tomm, K. (1984b). One perspective on the Milan systemic approach: Part 2. Description of session format, interviewing style and interventions. *Journal of Marital and Family Therapy, 10,* 253–271.

316    *References*

Tomm, K. (1985). Circular interviewing: A multifaceted clinical tool. In D. Campbell & R. Draper (Eds.), *Applications of systemic family therapy: The Milan approach* (pp. 33–45). London: Grune & Stratton.

Tomm, K. (1987a). Interventive interviewing: Part I. Strategizing as a fourth guideline for the therapist. *Family Process, 26*(1), 3–13.

Tomm, K. (1987b). Interventive interviewing: Part II. Reflexive questioning as a means to enable self-healing. *Family Process, 26*(6), 167–183.

Tomm, K. (1988). Interventive interviewing: Part III. Intending to ask lineal, circular, strategic, or reflexive questions? *Family Process, 27*(1), 1–15.

Tomm, K. (1989). Externalizing the problem and internalizing personal agency. *Journal of Strategic and Systemic Therapies, 8*(1), 54–59.

Tomm, K. (1990, June). *Ethical postures that orient one's clinical decision making.* Paper presented at the meeting of the American Family Therapy Academy, Philadelphia, PA.

Tomm, K. (1993). The courage to protest: A commentary on Michael White's work. In S. Gilligan & R. E. Price (Eds.), *Therapeutic conversations* (pp. 62–80). New York: Norton.

Tomm, W. (1994). Beyond "family models": Family as dialogical process in a cultural house of language. *Journal of Feminist Family Therapy, 6*(2), 1–20.

Tomm, K., & Lannamann, J. (1988). Questions as interventions. *The Family Therapy Networker, 12*(5), 38–41.

Tomm, K., & Wright, L. M. (1979). Training in family therapy: Perceptual, conceptual and executive skills. *Family Process, 18,* 227–250.

Varela, F. (1979). *Principles of biological autonomy.* New York: North-Holland.

von Wright, G., & Abscombe, G. (1979). *Ludwig Wittgenstein: Notebooks 1914–1916* (2nd ed.). Chicago: University of Chicago Press.

Watson, W. L. (Producer). (1988a). *Aging families and Alzheimer's disease* [Videotape]. Calgary, Canada: University of Calgary.

Watson, W. L. (Producer). (1988b). *A family with chronic illness: A "tough" family copes well* [Videotape]. Calgary, Canada: University of Calgary.

Watson, W. L. (Producer). (1988c). *Fundamentals of family systems nursing* [Videotape]. Calgary, Canada: University of Calgary.

Watson, W. L. (Producer). (1989a). *Families and psychosocial problems* [Videotape]. Calgary, Canada: University of Calgary.

Watson, W. L. (Producer). (1989b). *Family systems interventions* [Videotape]. Calgary, Canada: University of Calgary.

Watson, W. L., Bell, J. M., & Wright, L. M. (1992). Osteophytes and marital fights: A single case clinical research report of chronic pain. *Family Systems Medicine, 10,* 423–435.

Watson, W. L., & Lee, D. (1993). Is there life after suicide? The systemic belief approach for "survivors" of suicide. *Archives of Psychiatric Nursing, 7*(1), 37–43.

Watzlawick, P., Weakland, J., & Fisch, R. (1974). *Change: Principles of problem formation and problem resolution.* New York: Norton.

Weakland, J. H., & Fisch, R. (1984). Cases that "don't make sense": Brief strategic treatment in medical practice. *Family Systems Medicine, 2,* 125–136.

White, M. (1984). Pseudo-encopresis: From avalanche to victory, from vicious to virtuous cycles. *Family Systems Medicine, 2,* 150–160.

White, M. (1986). Negative explanation, restraint, and double description: A template for family therapy. *Family Process, 25,* 169–184.

White, M. (1988, Winter). The process of questioning: A therapy of literary merit? *Dulwich Centre Newsletter,* pp. 8–15.

White, M. (1988/1989). Externalizing of the problem and re-authoring of lives and relationships. *Dulwich Centre Newsletter,* pp. 3–21.

White, M. (1995). *Re-authoring lives: Interviews and essays.* Adelaide, South Australia: Dulwich Centre.

White, M., & Epston, D. (1990). *Narrative means to therapeutic ends.* New York: Norton.

Wolin, S., O'Hanlon, B., & Hoffman, L. (1995, November). *Three strength-based therapies* [Audiotape]. A special symposium at the annual meeting of the American Association for Marriage and Family Therapy, Baltimore, MD.

Wolpert, M., & March, P. (1995). Stories we tell each other: A comparison of families' and their therapists' explanation of presenting problems. *Contemporary Family Therapy, 17,* 159–173.

Wolterstorff, N. P. (Ed.). (1984). *Reason within the bounds of religion* (2nd ed.). Grand Rapids, MI: Eerdmans.

Wortman, C., & Schetter, C. D. (1979). Interpersonal relationships and cancer: A theoretical analysis. *Journal of Social Issues, 35,* 120–155.

Wright, L. M. (1989). When clients ask questions: Enriching the therapeutic conversation. *The Family Therapy Networker, 13*(6), 15–16.

Wright, L. M. (1990). Research as a family therapy intervention technique. *Contemporary Family Therapy: An International Journal, 12,* 477–484.

Wright, L. M. (in press). Multiple sclerosis, beliefs and families: Professional and personal stories of suffering and strength. In S. H. McDaniel, J. Hepworth, & W. Doherty (Eds.), *Stories of patients, families, and their therapists: The shared experience of illness.* New York: Basic Books.

Wright, L. M., & Leahey, M. (1987). Families and life-threatening illness: Assumptions, assessment and intervention. In M. Leahey & L. Wright (Eds.), *Families and life-threatening illness* (pp. 45–58). Springhouse, PA: Springhouse.

Wright, L. M., & Leahey, M. (1994a). Calgary Family Intervention Model: One way to think about change. *Journal of Marital and Family Therapy, 20,* 381–395.

Wright, L. M., & Leahey, M. (1994b). *Nurses and families: A guide to family assessment and intervention* (2nd ed.). Philadelphia: F. A. Davis.

Wright, L. M., & Levac, A. M. (1992). The non-existence of non-compliant families: The influence of Humberto Maturana. *Journal of Advanced Nursing, 17,* 913–917.

Wright, L. M., & Nagy, J. (1993). Death: The most troublesome family secret of all. In E. Imber-Black (Ed.), *Secrets in families and family therapy* (pp. 121–137). New York: Norton.

Wright, L. M., & Park Dorsay, J. (1989). A case of Marilynitis or a Marilyn Monroe infection. *Dulwich Centre Newsletter,* pp. 7–9.

Wright, L. M., & Simpson, P. (1991). A systemic belief approach to epileptic seizures: A case of being spellbound. *Contemporary Family Therapy: An International Journal, 13,* 165–180.

Wright, L. M., & Watson, W. L. (1982). What's in a name: Redefining family therapy. In A. Gurman (Ed.), *Questions and answers in the practice of family therapy* (Vol. 2, pp. 27–30). New York: Brunner/Mazel.

Wright, L. M., & Watson, W. L. (1988). Systemic family therapy and family development. In C. J. Falicov (Ed.), *Family transitions: Continuity and change over the life cycle* (pp. 407–430). New York: Guilford Press.

Wright, L. M., Bell, J. M., & Rock, B. L. (1989). Smoking behavior and spouses: A case report. *Family Systems Medicine, 7,* 158–171.

Wright, L. M., Bell, J. M., Watson, W. L., & Tapp, D. (1995). The influence of the beliefs of nurses: A clinical example of a post-myocardial-infarction couple. *Journal of Family Nursing, 1,* 238–256.

Wright, L. M., Watson, W. L., & Bell, J. M. (1990). The Family Nursing Unit: A unique integration of research, education and clinical practice. In J. M. Bell, W. L. Watson, & L. M. Wright (Eds.), *The cutting edge of family nursing* (pp. 95–109). Calgary, Canada: Family Nursing Unit Publications.

Wynne, L. C., Shields, C. G., & Sirkin, M. I. (1992). Illness, family theory, and family therapy: I. Conceptual issues. *Family Process, 31,* 3–18.

Zukav, G. (1979). *The dancing wu li masters: An overview of the new physics.* New York: Morrow.

# INDEX